Ius Gentium: Comparative Perspectives on Law and Justice

Volume 129

Ius Gentium is a book series which discusses the central questions of law and justice from a comparative perspective. The books in this series collect the contrasting and overlapping perspectives of lawyers, judges, philosophers and scholars of law from the world's many different jurisdictions for the purposes of comparison, harmonisation, and the progressive development of law and legal institutions. Each volume makes a new comparative study of an important area of law. This book series continues the work of the well-known journal of the same name and provides the basis for a better understanding of all areas of legal science.

The *Ius Gentium* series provides a valuable resource for lawyers, judges, legislators, scholars, and both graduate students and researchers in globalisation, comparative law, legal theory and legal practice. The series has a special focus on the development of international legal standards and transnational legal cooperation.

Cristina Hermida del Llano
Editor

The Freedom of Expression for Judges in the Sphere of the Judicial Ethics

Springer

Editor
Cristina Hermida del Llano
Department of Public Law
Universidad Rey Juan Carlos
Madrid, Spain

ISSN 1534-6781 ISSN 2214-9902 (electronic)
Ius Gentium: Comparative Perspectives on Law and Justice
ISBN 978-3-032-06503-2 ISBN 978-3-032-06504-9 (eBook)
https://doi.org/10.1007/978-3-032-06504-9

This work was supported by Ministerio de Ciencia, Innovación y Universidades (PID2021-127122NB-I00).

This Springer imprint is published by the registered company Springer Nature Switzerland AG
The registered company address is: Gewerbestrasse 11, 6330 Cham, Switzerland

In memoriam Professor Eugen Chelaru

Contents

Introduction . . . 1
Cristina Hermida del Llano

The Concept of "Tolerance" in John Locke's Liberal System . . . 11
Piero Di Giovanni and Maria Antonia Rancadore

Freedom of Expression for Magistrates in ECHR's Jurisprudence in Cases Versus Romania . . . 27
Andreea Elena Tabacu

Judges Under Pressure: Judicial Reforms in Poland and Their Impact on Judges' Freedom of Expression in the Adjudication Process . . . 43
Anna Rytel-Warzocha

Justice of the Future, a Possible Transformation Through the Digitalization of Justice Procedures Using Artificial Intelligence . . . 57
Manole Decebal Bogdan

Violation of the Principles of Judicial Ethics-Ground for the Disciplinary Responsibility of Judges . . . 81
Andra Puran and Ramona Duminică

Ethics and Integrity for Judges: Comparative Study with Other Public Professions in the Romanian Framework . . . 93
Mihaela Miruna Tudorașcu

Judicial Ethics and Freedom of Expression: An Average or Worst-Case Scenario . . . 103
Agustina Martínez Rubio

Constitutional and Legal Framework of Judicial Ethics in Brazil . . . 121
Renato Braz Mehanna Khamis and Daniel Ferreira Limaverde

Freedom of Expression for Judges or a Witch Hunt? The Case of Poland . . . 131
Andrzej Jackiewicz

Freedom of Expression of Judges and Its Limitations in the Context of the Right to an Impartial Court in the Czech and European Context . . . 149
Pavel Klíma

Harmonizing Rights and Regulations: National Judges and Urban Planning Through the Lens of European Court of Human Rights—Insights from Romania . . . 163
Chelaru Raluca

Judges Under Pressure: A Few Remarks About "Ethical Courage" of Judges in Poland . . . 181
Maciej Serowaniec and Zbigniew Witkowski

Does the Freedom of Expression of Judges Allow Them to Postpone the Trial of Cases, as a Form of Protest Against the Social Policy with Impact on Their Right to a Service Pension? . . . 191
Carmen Constantina Nenu and Daniela Iancu

Does the Wels Declaration of Ethics, Adopted by the Association of Austrian Judges on 8 November 2007, Infringe upon the Freedom of Expression for Judges Within the Framework of Respect for the Principles of Judicial Ethics? . . . 201
Heribert Franz Koeck

The Judge and Justice: Contradictions of Contemporary Justice . . . 253
Marius Andreescu and Andra Puran

The Right to Freedom of Expression of a Judge and Its Limits in the Polish Legal System . . . 269
Agnieszka Malicka

An Ethical Vision of Judicial Secrecy and Judicial Discretion in an Environment of Transparency . . . 283
Cristina Hermida del Llano

The Rule of Law, Civil Law and the Judges' Freedom of Expression . . . 299
Rainer Arnold

Introduction

Cristina Hermida del Llano

This collective book originated from the research project *La libertad de expresión del juez en el marco del respeto a los principios de ética judicial en España* (PID2021-127122NB-I00), financed by MCIN/ AEI /10.13039/501100011033/ and by FEDER *Una manera de hacer Europa*. It brings together papers presented at the International Congress *Freedom of expression for judges within the framework of respect for the principles of judicial ethics. In memoriam Prof. Eugen Chelaru*, which took place on November 16 and 17, 2023 at the Universidad Rey Juan Carlos (Vicálvaro Campus).

As the principal investigator of this project, let me pay tribute to a good man, a great academic, and dear friend Prof. Eugen Chelaru. He was an outstanding academic who, thanks to extraordinary and hard work, was a credit to the Faculty in Pitesti (Romania) and its international image. In this collective book, from an interdisciplinary point of view, collaborators from different countries (Italy, Germany, Austria, Czech Republic, Romania, Poland, Brazil and Spain) and from various disciplines who participated in the research group of the Universidad Rey Juan Carlos addressed the ethical issues surrounding the exercise of the freedom of expression by judges, knowing that, as García Paz has pointed out, a law without ethics is a law without a soul, a monster.

Yet the Rule of Law is under threat itself, as some governments seek to undermine the independence of the judiciary. The protection of the Rule of Law is a growing concern in many European countries and, in fact, in recent years, considerable efforts have been made to stem the deterioration of the Rule of Law and ensure the proper functioning of national judicial systems. At the European Union (EU) level, the Rule of Law 2020 Report forcefully stated that effective judicial systems are

C. H. del Llano (✉)
Department of Public Law, Universidad Rey Juan Carlos, Madrid, Spain
e-mail: cristina.hermida@urjc.es

C. Hermida del Llano (ed.), *The Freedom of Expression for Judges in the Sphere of the Judicial Ethics*, Ius Gentium: Comparative Perspectives on Law and Justice 129, https://doi.org/10.1007/978-3-032-06504-9_1

essential to the Rule of Law: <<Independence, quality and efficiency are the defining parameters of an effective judicial system, regardless of the model of the national legal system and the tradition in which it is embedded. (…) The independence of national courts is crucial to ensure this judicial protection. (…) Despite reform efforts in several Member States to improve judicial independence, developments in some of them are giving cause for concern>>.

Independence, impartiality and integrity are the basis of the Rule of Law in a healthy democracy, which is why numerous international standards have emphasized the importance of ethical conduct in the legal professions. The transformation of the legislative Rule of Law into a constitutional rule of law undergirds judicial ethics. This collective work explores the role of ethics as the hard core of the Rule of Law, examines the normative and ethical limits of the freedom of expression of the judge, considered as a public servant, and suggests solutions that promote and enrich today's democratic society.

For instance, in Spain, the Judicial Ethics Commission, an independent body of the General Council of the Judiciary, has formulated criteria for how judges should exercise their freedom of expression without compromising the integrity and impartiality of the judicial system. In several opinions, among others, the Opinion (Consultation 03/22), dated April 26, 2022, this Commission issued guidelines to ensure both the impartiality and the appearance of impartiality of judges and magistrates in Spain. This opinion made clear that judges, like any other persons, may freely express their thoughts, ideas or opinions, as this is a fundamental right recognized and protected in Article 20.1.a) of the Spanish Constitution. Along the same lines, the Principles of Judicial Ethics, which were adopted by the General Council of the Judiciary, specify in principle 31 in general that "the judge, as a citizen, has the right to freedom of expression…", although it is recognized that this right is subject to certain limitations imposed by the need to "preserve their independence and appearance of impartiality and maintain social confidence in the judicial system and in the courts".

In other words: freedom of expression may be exercised by judges and magistrates, but "with prudence and moderation", which is necessary to preserve their independence and appearance of impartiality, and with respect for political neutrality. The opinion states that "in no case can social network and media manifestations by judges that seriously undermine the rule of law, the constitutional order and democracy itself be protected by the principle of freedom of expression". The principles of judicial ethics imply a commitment to respect and safeguard the image of Justice. The scope of these principles extends to all members of the Administration of Justice.

The first contribution in this collective book is entitled *The concept of "tolerance" in John Locke's liberal system,* by Piero Di Giovanni and María Antonia Ranccadore.. Piero Di Giovanni is a full professor for history of philosophy of the University of Palermo (Italy), distinguished by his scientific production in the field of contemporary thought in comparison with ancient thought. He has written four volumes on the history of Western philosophy, relating the classical, middle, modern and contemporary ages, including significant monographs on Plato, Marx,

Nietzsche and Freud. María Antonia Ranccadore is a Professor of History of Contemporary Philosophy at the University of Palermo (Italy). She collaborates with Piero Di Giovanni in many fields of research and is a member of the research group of the Biblioteca di Studi Filosofici, member of the Società Italiana di Storia della Filosofia (SISF), of the Association des Sociétés de Philosophie de Langue Française (ASPLF) and of the Société d'Études Kantiennes de Langue Française (SEKLF).

In *The concept of "tolerance" in John Locke's liberal system*, the authors highlight the moral and juridical nature of the concepts of "toleration" (relating to the indulgence granted to the citizen) and "tolerance" (relating to freedom of thought and religious belief) in John Locke's liberal system. The notion of "tolerance", in the context of contemporary culture, concerns the right of the citizen (and of the magistrate) to freedom of expression. The primary references to the English phi losopher are, above all, the texts *Two Treatises of Government*, *Essay Concerning Toleration* and the four letters on toleration. Toleration derives from the Latin *tolerantia* and concerns the freedom of expression that judges must also be able to enjoy.

Andreea Tabacu's chapter on *Freedom of expression for magistrates in ECHR's jurisprudence in cases vs. Romania* discusses how United Nations Guidelines show that magistrates are entitled to freedom of expression but must exercise it with due regard to the values and principles set out in the law. Legal professionals also have the duty to raise issues of public concern to improve the legal system. Still, they must show restraint in exercising their freedom of expression in cases where the authority and impartiality of the judiciary are in question. The violation of this obligation, provided that the conditions in ECHR jurisprudence are fulfilled, could lead to them becoming liable. Tabacu has a Ph.D in Law and is Associate Professor at the Faculty of Economic Sciences and Law, UNST "Politehnica" Bucharest and a member of the teaching staff at the University of Pitesti (Romania) since 1997. She was lawyer in Argeş Bar Association (1998–2004) and judge at the Pitesti Local Court, Argeş District Court. Now, since 2004, she is judge at the Pitesti Court of Appeal and author and co-author of over 40 books and over 100 legal articles.

Turning to Poland, Anna Rytel-Warzocha's chapter *Judges under Pressure: Judicial Reforms in Poland and Their Impact on Judges' Freedom of Expression in the Adjudication Process* explores how the constitutional crisis facing Poland since 2015 has undeniably undermined the constitutionally guaranteed principle of judicial independence, and negatively affected judicial ethics and freedom of expression. For example, the judges face the dilemma of whether to apply unconstitutional statutory provisions or apply the constitution directly. Coping with political pressure and facing disciplinary liability constitute new challenges for the judges in common courts. Rytel-Warzocha has a Ph.D. hab and is Associate professor in the Department of Constitutional Law and Political Institutions at the University of Gdansk (Poland). She is an author of more than 120 scientific publications of various types (books, articles, book chapters, entries in encyclopedias) published in Poland and abroad. Her research interests focus mainly on the following areas: direct and participatory democracy, constitutional systems of foreign states, constitutional justice, current political changes, European aspects of constitutional law, local self-government, citizenship and protection of human rights.

Manole Decebal Bogdan analyzes *Justice of the future, a possible transformation through the digitalization of justice procedures using Artificial Intelligence*. According to this author, in the beginning, social groups resolved their disputes through customary law and living, unwritten law. Later, society specialized and created new legal instruments and institutions. But now human activities are being transferred to computer programs, which are self-improving and solve issues quickly and cheaply. These tools of digital technologies do not have reason and emotions, they do not empathize, and yet some people recommend the computer program as a potential substitute for the judge in the administration of justice. Bogdan is a University lecturer at the Faculty of Law and Social Sciences at the "1 Decembrie 1918" University in Alba Iulia (Romania) since 2007. His fields of specialization are legal sociology, digital economy law, commercial insurance law, environmental law, sustainable development and environmental protection.

Andra Puran has written two contributions to this anthology. The first is with Ramona Duminicâ and is entitled *Violation of the principles of judicial ethics-ground for the disciplinary responsibility of judges*. Andra Puran is a Lecturer Ph.D. at the University of Science and Tehnology Politehnica Bucharest and at the Faculty of Economic Sciences and Law, Pitesti University (Romania) She is the author and co-author of more than 20 books and over 100 scientific articles. Ramona Duminicâ is a Lecturer Ph.D. at the University of Science and Tehnology Poliltehnica Bucharest and at the Faculty of Economic Sciences and Law, Pitesti University (Romania). Member of numerous scientific associations, both national and international. She is the author and co-author of 10 books and over 120 scientific articles. Puran and Duminicâ argue that compliance with the principles of professional ethics by judges strengthens public trust in the justice system of a state and allows a better understanding of the role the judge has in society. However, the magistrate's position in society does not exempt him from legal liability in the event of a violation of the law.

Mihaela Miruna Tudoraşcu is a Ph.D. Associate Professor and, since 2016, Dean at the University 1 Decembrie 1918 of Alba Iulia (Romania). She is also a lawyer in Hunedoara Bar. The title of her contribution is *Ethics and integrity for judges – comparative study with other public professions in Romanian framework*. The study underlines what a Romanian judge can or cannot do in his profession, specifically in connection with the liberty of expression, explores whether this right interferes with the ethics and integrity of the profession and compares judges to a number of other public professions, asking whether there are similarities or essential differences.

Agustina Martínez Rubio is a Ph.D. Assistant Professor at the Universidad Complutense de Madrid. She has practiced law for 12 years in the field of Family Law, specializing in Law and Religion, State Ecclesiastical Law, and Private International Law. Her lines of research include Civil Registry and marriage, police and judicial ethics. She has been a member of several competitive research projects. *Judicial ethics and freedom of expression: an average or worst-case scenario* is the title of her contribution. She argues that the principles of judicial ethics should not be considered as a limit to the exercise of the right to freedom of expression. The assimilation and observance of these principles by the judge are a means to avoid situations that undermine the dignity of the judicial function, as well as the impartiality, independence, and integrity of the members of the judiciary. A balance should be struck between the exercise of this fundamental right and the duty of neutrality required of a judge, who occupies an elevated position within one of the branches of government, to reinforce the confidence of citizens in justice.

Renato Braz Mehanna Khamis is a Full Professor at the Master Program of Law of the Santa Cecília University (Brazil) and Daniel Ferreira Limaverde is part of the post-graduate program in Law at Santa Cecilia University, and a lawyer in Brazil. The title of their contribution is *The Code of Ethics of the Brazilian judges and its limitations to the freedom of speech*. They analyze the Code of Ethics for Brazilian judges in regard to the limitations imposed on them, especially those related to their freedom of speech. Starting with the Brazilian Constitution, the article then passes on to the Brazilian Organic Law of Magistracy to finally arrive at the main focus, the Brazilian Code of Ethics, where the article will focus.

Andrzej Jackiewicz is an Associate Professor of Constitutional Law at the Department of Constitutional Law at the University of Bialystok (Poland). He is author of more than 100 scientific publications (monographs, commentaries, articles, chapters and glosses) about his academic interests: constitutional systems of modern states, parliamentary law, sources of law and human rights. The title of his contribution is *Freedom of expression for judges or a witch hunt. The case of Poland.* The number of disciplinary proceedings against judges in Poland has increased dramatically in recent years. The paper analyzes statistical data in this regard and highlights the most interesting cases. Based on the grounds for disciplinary responsibility of judges and the procedural aspects of this responsibility, which have changed thoroughly over the past few years, the paper addresses the question of whether judges in Poland are entitled to freedom of expression.

Pavel Klima is a Ph.D. lecturer at the Metropolitan University Prague, specialized in Law of the European Union and Criminal Law. Since 2011 he has worked as an attorney-at-law. He is also an arbitrator at the Arbitration Court attached to the Economic Chamber of the Czech Republic and Agricultural Chamber of the Czech Republic. He is polyglot and has published professional articles in the domestic and foreign professional press and is co-author of many collective monographs. The title of his contribution is *Freedom of expression of judges and its limitations in the context of the right to an impartial court in the Czech and European context.* The author deals with the complex interconnection between the freedom of expression of judges and the imperative of maintaining an impartial court, both in the Czech legal framework as well as in the broader European context. The author presents the standards of judicial conduct in general terms and examines how the freedom of expression of judges, limited by the nature of their profession, intersects with the right to an impartial court. At the European level, the author points out the fact that the European Convention on Human Rights forms a key background and reflects on the delicate balance between the right of judges to freedom of expression and the need for an impartial judiciary. In addition, the author refers to the case law of the European Court of Human Rights concerning subjective and objective tests of judicial impartiality. The author also examines the Czech legal context, detailing the constitutional and statutory provisions relating to the conduct of judges.

Raluca Chelaru is a Notary Public in the National Union of Notaries Public (Romania) and Ph.D. in Real Estate Law at the Faculty of Law, University of Bucharest (Romania). *Harmonizing Rights and Regulations: National Judges and Urban Planning Through the Lens of European Court of Human Rights—Insights from Romania* is the title of her contribution. The balance between the State's discretion in urban planning and an individual's property rights is a delicate interplay. While the State does possess a broad margin of discretion, it is not a blank check for limitless action. Article 1 of Protocol No. 1 to the Convention on Human Rights lays out the principles of property rights, signifying the inviolability of property, the conditions for deprivation of the same, and the allowance for regulation aligned with the public good. But these latter issues should not infringe on the fundamental principle of undisturbed property enjoyment. After delving into the intricate rulings and nuances of various legal cases, one undeniable truth emerges: the dance between law and individual rights often sways on a tightrope. From the Romanian Constitutional Court's directives to the complex interplay between property rights and environmental protections, these legal tapestries weave a story of balancing societal interests with individual liberties.

Maciej Serowaniec and Zbigniew Witkowski are both professors at the Faculty of Law and Administration, Nicolaus Copernicus University, Toruń (Poland). On the one hand, Dr hab. Maciej Serowaniec is Associate Professor at the Faculty of Law and Administration of the Nicolaus Copernicus University in Toruń; he has participated as investigator in the project RED-SPINEL (Horizon Europe). He is a Laureate of both the European Court of Auditors Postgraduate Research Grant Programme and the Scholarship of the Minister of Science and Higher Education for outstanding young scientists. On the other hand, Prof. dr hab. Zbigniew Witkowski is a Full Professor and Dean of the Faculty of Law and Administration at the Nicolaus Copernicus University in Toruń. Author of over 300 scientific publications. Member of the Advisory Board of the Centro di Ricerca Sulle Amministrazioni Pubbliche "Vittorio Bachelet" in Rome and of the Committee of Legal Sciences of the Polish Academy of Sciences. Both authors have written the contribution entitled *Judges under pressure – a few remarks about "ethical courage" of judges in Poland*. Since 2017, as part of a package of legislative changes to the judiciary, a disciplinary system has been in place in Poland to ensure that judges are subservient to political will. As a result, judges who were against unconstitutional changes to the judiciary were subject to removal at gunpoint. It is noteworthy that a significant number of judges have nevertheless shown remarkable 'ethical courage' in the fight for respect of constitutional standards. This paper presents examples of this "ethical courage".

Carmen Constantina Nenu is an Associate professor, Ph.D. Lecturer at the National University of Science and Technology Politehnica Bucharest (Romania). She is a member of Argeş Bar Association since 2010. Daniela Iancu is Ph.D. at the

National University of Science and Technology Politehnica Bucharest (Romania). Carmen Constantina Nenu and Daniela Iancu are coauthors of the contribution *Does the freedom of expression of judges allow them to postpone the trial of cases, as a form of protest against the social policy with impact on their right to a service pension?* This study analyzes the right of judges to make requests and comments on their status, including social policy regarding service pensions. The analysis considers the freedom of expression of judges in the relationship with the Government and the Parliament in matters of interest to the justice system and their obligation to show restraint in their behavior to avoid compromising their independence and impartiality.

Heribert Franz Koeck is Dr. iur., Dr. h.c. mult., M.C.L. Representative for East and South East Europe, an emeritus Full Professor of Law and also for two decades Dean at the Johannes Kepler University Linz. He has numerous books and other publications. The title of his contribution is *Does the Wels Declaration of Ethics, adopted by the Association of Austrian Judges on 8 November 2007, infringe upon the freedom of expression for judges within the framework of respect for the principles of judicial ethics?* According to the author, the Wels Declaration of Ethics of 2007 considers membership in a political party or activities within such a party to be detrimental to the credibility of independent jurisdiction. Non-observance of this principle is likely to be used as a negative criterion in procedures for admission to, or promotion in, the judicial career. The Wels Declaration is intended to dissuade present or future judges from political activities. It is at variance with rights guaranteed in articles 10 and 11 of the European Convention on Human Rights, with the appreciation of political activities which forms the basis of EU Regulation No. 1141/2014 on European Political Parties and European Political Foundations, and with the Austrian Constitution according to which "the existence and the variety of political parties are essential parts of the democratic order of the Republic of Austria (Art. 1 Federal Constitutional Law, Off. Journal 1/1930)".

The second contribution written by Andra Puran in this collective book is with Marius Andreescu, who is Doctor in Law and member of the teaching staff at the University of Pitesti (Romania) since 1997. He is a judge at the Pitesti Court of Appeal and has been President of the Criminal Section (2002–2019). He has written 14 monographs and held 18 university courses. The title of their contribution is *The Judge and Justice. Contradictions of contemporary Justice.* This essay represents an attempt to highlight, from a philosophical perspective, the most significant contradictions that can affect justice throughout a period of social crisis. The object of the analysis consists of the contradictions between the law and justice; the justice and society and the act to fulfill the justice in what is called "the fall in exteriority" of the justice.

Agnieszka Malicka is a Ph.D. Assistant Professor at the Faculty of Law, Administration and Economics of the University of Wrocław (Poland). She is Head of the Department of Teaching Law in Foreign Languages and Director of the School of German Law. She teaches Polish constitutional law at the School of Polish Law at the Humboldt University in Berlin. She is Vice President of the German-Polish Lawyers Association in Berlin (DPJV e.V. Berlin). Her research interests are Constitutional Law, in particular Human Rights issues. The title of her contribution is *The right to freedom of expression of a judge and its limits in the Polish legal system.* In Polish law, freedom of expression is one of the fundamental rights of an individual guaranteed in the Constitution and in the norms of international law binding on Poland. However, this is not an unlimited right. In the case of judges, the Polish legislator has provided certain restrictions for judges. They result primarily from the special position of judges in the system of authorities and their specific public function. The study is an attempt to find answers to the following questions: Can a judge participate in public debate, express his opinions on current reforms in the judicial system, or comment on political events?

Cristina Hermida del Llano is the editor of this collective book. She is a Full Professor for Philosophy of Law at the Rey Juan Carlos University of Madrid (Spain). She has been president of the Association of Philosophical Hispanism, as well as Director of the Journal *Revista de Hispanismo Filosófico. Historia del pensamiento iberoamericano* from 2017–2023. Director-Coordinator editor-in-chief of the collection *Pensamiento Ibérico e Hispanoamericano* of the Sindéresis publishing house since 2017. Since 2020 she has been a member of the Judicial Ethics Commission at the General Council of the Judiciary in Spain. Member of the Spanish Association of Philosophical Hispanism since 1995 and of the Spanish Association Alexander von Humboldt since 2001. Corresponding member of the Royal Academy of Jurisprudence and Legislation of Madrid since 2006. She is a member of the Bank of Experts of the State Research Agency in Spain since 2022. In 2013 she obtained the title of Jean Monnet Professor, followed by the Jean Monnet Chair—Jean Monnet Professor—by the European Commission in 2017.

She is the author of six books, about one hundred book chapters and more than two hundred articles on Spanish thought in the twentieth century, legal-political philosophy and European Union Law. She is PI of the Research Group on Immigration and Management of Cultural Diversity of the Rey Juan Carlos University (INGESDICUL) considered high performance since 2019. General co-editor of the Encyclopedia of Contemporary Constitutionalism edited by Springer. She is also PI of the Knowledge Generation 2021 project (2022–2026), Non-Oriented Research Type B, Ref. PID2021-127122NB-I00, entitled *The Freedom of Expression of the Judge in the framework of respect for the principles of judicial ethics in Spain*, having led in recent years other research projects at the national and international level.

An ethical vision of judicial secrecy and judicial discretion in an environment of transparency is the contribution written by Cristina Hermida del Llano, as coordinator of this collective work and as PI of the ongoing research project. The text collected here was presented at the International Congress Quale Filosofía ad inicio del XXI secolo?, held in Palazzo Steri - Palermo, in November 2022 and published in *Newsletter of the Academy of Yuste* n° 20, October, 2022. In this text it is emphasized that the sap that feeds the Rule of Law is precisely the civic ethics of the citizens. The translation of ethics to the Rule of Law necessarily involves professional ethics. It is therefore emphasized that the Rule of Law is not an immutable legal structure, but rather depends for its development on the continuous action of citizens. It is emphasized here that the Rule of Law constitutes a field of dialogue, debate and rational confrontation of social projects focused on the reform of existing institutions, where ethics cannot be relegated to the background.

This contribution reviews the three main principles enshrined in judicial ethics (independence, impartiality and integrity) and shows how ethics have become pillars for the Rule of Law (legality, separation of powers, and protection of fundamental rights and freedoms). Within the professional ethics of judicial power, a distinction is made between the ethic virtues of an impartial, independent and upright judge or magistrate, which are related to the principles of judicial ethics, and the professional skills exercised by the judge or magistrate in his or her specific professional activity (diligence, listening skills, empathy, circumspection, caution, etc.). The task of judging is proper to a "craftsman of the law". The author reflects on the ethical duty of judicial secrecy, and how judicial secrecy and judicial discretion in an environment of transparency implies that every judgment must be "pronounced according to the right reason of prudence".

Dr. Dr.h.c.mult. Rainer Arnold received his nomination to become Full Professor at the University of Regensburg in 1978, named Chair of Public Law (Dean 1982/3), and was previously a professor at the University of Konstanz. He held the Jean Monnet Chair of EU Law (1999), of the Jean Monnet Chair ad personam "Legal Relations of the EU with Central, Eastern and South-Eastern Europe" (2008) and hostujíci professor at the Charles University Prague (2000). Corresponding Member of the Academy of Sciences of Bologna, Membre titulaire de l'Académie international de droit comparé, Fellow of the European Law Institute. Since 2003 individual member of the IACL. Former Fernand Braudel Fellow and various times Visiting Fellow in many universities. Member of numerous Constitutional Law Associations and editorial/scientific journal boards. Over 500 publications. Organization of twenty-three International Congresses on European and Comparative Constitutional Law (in Regensburg, co-organized in Kishinau, Gdansk, Vilnius, Madrid, New York).

In his contribution, entitled *The Rule of Law, Civil Law and the Judges' Freedom of Expression*, Rainer Arnold explains that the Rule of Law is the basis and essential element of a constitutional order. Law is not only the formal instrument of order, but also conveys the fundamental values of the state community. This is not only important for the vertical relationship between the state and the individual, but also has a manifold effect on the horizontal relationship between private individuals, i.e. in Civil Law. An independent, functioning judiciary is essential for the Rule of Law. This is also linked to the specific question of the extent to which a judge may express his opinion and the extent to which he must exercise restraint.

The aim of this collective book, by bringing together different approaches and themes, is to create a space for debate and serene reflection concerning how judges should exercise the right to freedom of expression in the light of judicial ethics to ensure public confidence in the administration of justice. When the exercise of professional activity demands excellence, then mere compliance with legal norms is insufficient. In other words: if we were to deprive the law of ethics, then we turn it into an inert normative framework without a heart.

The Concept of "Tolerance" in John Locke's Liberal System

Piero Di Giovanni and Maria Antonia Rancadore

Abstract In John Locke's liberal system, it is necessary to highlight the moral and juridical nature of the concepts of "toleration" (relating to the indulgence granted to the citizen) and "tolerance" (relating to freedom of thought and religious belief). The notion of "tolerance", in the context of contemporary culture, concerns the right of the citizen (and of the magistrate) to freedom of expression.

In this sense, the reference texts of the English philosopher are above all *Two Treatises of Government*, *Essay Concerning Toleration* and the four letters on toleration. Toleration derives from the Latin tolerantia and also concerns the freedom of expression which judges must also be able to enjoy.

1 The History of Seventeenth-Century Britain

The proposed theme, on "freedom of expression for judges", suggests we reflect on the history of modern thought, with particular reference to the second half of the eighteenth century. This theme cannot ignore the development and affirmation of the principle of freedom of thought, as defined above all in Great Britain with the establishment of the constitutional monarchy in 1689 by William III of Orange-Nassau. The ideologist of this historical phase in Great Britain, but we can say throughout Europe, appears to have been John Locke, to be remembered not only as a theorist of empiricism, but also as the author of a series of texts centered on the

---

The first part of this chapter (1. *The History of seventeenth-Century Britain*) is written by Piero Di Giovanni. The second part of this chapter (2. *The principles of freedom and expression in John Locke*) is written by Maria Antonia Rancadore.

P. Di Giovanni (✉) · M. A. Rancadore
University of Palermo, Palermo, Italy
e-mail: pietro.digiovanni@unipa.it; mariaantonia.rancadore@unipa.it

C. Hermida del Llano (ed.), *The Freedom of Expression for Judges in the Sphere of the Judicial Ethics*, Ius Gentium: Comparative Perspectives on Law and Justice 129, https://doi.org/10.1007/978-3-032-06504-9_2

principle of tolerance and therefore of freedom of thought. In this sense, it must be underlined that, if today we can discuss the right to freedom of expression by judges, this is due to the fact that, in the context of modern western culture and history, we have acquired the right to freedom of thought for each citizen. Therefore, it is appropriate to focus preliminarily on John Locke's vast and complex production.

According to this perspective, first of all, regarding John Locke, it is necessary to remember the publication in 1690 of *Two Treatises of Government*[1] and *An Essay concerning human Understanding*.[2] Secondly, we need to remember *An Essay concerning Toleration*[3] written in 1667 but not published until 1876; followed by the writing in Holland, at the end of the year 1685, of *Epistola de tolerantia*,[4] published in May 1689 in Latin by Philipp van Limborch and, in October of the same year, in English with the title *A Letter concerning Toleration*[5] edited by William Popple; in 1690 the publication of *A second Letter concerning Toleration*[6] and in 1692 of *A third Letter for Toleration*[7]; finally, in 1704, there came the writing of *A fourth Letter for Toleration*,[8] published posthumously in 1706. The "letters on tolerance" (but also Locke's *Essay concerning Toleration*, written in 1667) denote the intense debate that took place in Great Britain during the second half of the eighteenth century, even before reaching the phase of the French Enlightenment with the appearance (in 1686) of the text *De la tolérance. Commentaire philosophique* by Pierre Bayle and in 1763 of the *Traité sur la tolérance* di François-Marie Arouet (aka Voltaire). The dates indicated testify that the so-called "Siècle des Lumières" finds its original source in the seventeenth century, which we prefer to define as the "Siècle d'or" for the results also achieved on the scientific level, which from its appearance in 1541 of the work of Nicolaus Copernicus *De revolutionibus orbium coelestium* leads to the appearance in 1687 of Isaac Newton's work *Philosophiae naturalis principia mathematica*.

Having said this, throughout the history of modern western culture, the right to freedom of thought and expression takes on a particular meaning for both the common citizen and the magistrate. In this second case, however, we must emphasize that, if we focus on the judge's right freely to express his personal opinions, we must underline the delicacy of the role played in his professional activity. If the judge is recognized as having the right to participate in public or private discussions on the various themes that characterize history or news, it is necessary to reiterate the delicacy of the work carried out by the judge; freedom of expression cannot compromise the rigor of his activity, which among other things falls within the three

[1] See Locke (1997e).

[2] See Locke (1997a).

[3] See Locke (2006).

[4] See Locke (1689).

[5] See Locke (1997f).

[6] See Locke (1997g).

[7] See Locke (1997h).

[8] See Locke (1997i).

constitutional powers of the liberal state. The fact is that no one can be denied the right to freedom of thought; in the case of the judge, freedom of expression coincides precisely with the freedom of thought guaranteed to him as a citizen. Among other things, we must note that judges are organized in "trade union" associations to protect their members, considered as "workers" to be protected. However, if the autonomy of the judiciary is invoked, the union organizations of judges could be understood as a weakening of the institutions of the liberal state. Invoking the respect and autonomy of the judiciary entails respect for and autonomy of the other two powers of the liberal state (government and parliament), so that criticism of the government and parliament by the judiciary (albeit through its trade unions) sometimes finds no justification. The principle of the autonomy of the judiciary is based on the general principle of the autonomy of each of the three powers of the liberal state, where (as is stated by John Locke), among the three powers, the one to be most safeguarded is the legislative one, as descending directly from the sovereign people.

The debate, which took place also and above all in Italy in the twentieth and twenty-first centuries, highlighted the fact that sometimes in a liberal state a political crisis arises, which involves the legislative power of parliament itself; this historical circumstance, however, cannot lead to the judiciary considering replacing the legislative power of parliament; in this case we would have a degeneration of the constitutional system of the liberal state. Let us say that we must "resign ourselves" to the crisis, which can be generated within a state in certain phases of its history; therefore the effort to be made is by individual citizens committing themselves to "reviving" the conditions of their highest institution (i.e. that of the state). Over the course of recent Italian history, the criticism expressed by the various (trade union) components of the judiciary has been aimed at the political system, which however represents the popular will. We know that, in a liberal state, the power of the government, while enjoying constitutional autonomy, is closely linked to the power of parliament. Government and parliament, despite being two distinct and separate powers, constitute the complex system of politics; the judiciary appears to represent a power which guarantees autonomy with respect to every other component of politics, while respecting both the government and parliament. Having clarified that the judiciary cannot confuse its autonomy with criticism, not only of the other components of civil society, but also of the other institutions of the liberal state, we can focus on the right to freedom of expression to be safeguarded by the judge (as a citizen). In this sense, the judge does not enjoy a double privilege compared to the common citizen; indeed, compared to the common citizen, he finds himself in a delicate position, carrying out work of particular importance. In essence, the citizen-judge, when he decides to resort to freedom of expression, must not overlook the peculiarity of his role. It is never the judge who speaks, but the citizen who can never forget that he is a judge.

The right to freedom of expression, for the judge and for every single citizen, represents an achievement of a non-negligible social and historical dimension, as can be seen from the production of John Locke and the various representatives of "freethinking". The cultural context of Great Britain allows us carefully to consider the principle of freedom of thought and expression, as an objective achieved during the second half of the seventeenth century at the foundation of European and international culture. Among the "freethinkers", we include above all John Toland, Anthony Collins and Matthew Tindal, all of whom were inspired by *De veritate* by Edward Herbert of Cherbury, which appeared in 1624. But, among the philosophers (or men of culture) of the time, we must especially keep in mind John Locke, for his texts dedicated to the principle of tolerance. We must immediately highlight Locke's character, as well as moral and legal, in relation to the key words "toleration" (relating to the indulgence granted to the citizen by the established power) and "tolerance" (relating to freedom of thought and religious belief, which every single citizen in a liberal state must be able to have). If we look at this from this angle, it is necessary to mention the two authors who are behind John Locke: first of all, Baruch Spinoza, as well as for *Tractatus theologico-politicus* (published anonymously in 1670) and for *Tractatus politicus* (begun in 1676, but left unfinished), for *Ethica ordine geometrico demonstrata* (completed in 1675, but published posthumously); secondly, Pierre Bayle, as well as for *Pensées diverses sur la comète* (published in 1682), for the essay *De la tolérance. Commentaire philosophique* (1686) and for *Dictionnaire historique et critique* (1697). Therefore Spinoza and Bayle represent the evolution of political thought, which from 1651, the year of publication of *Leviathan* by Thomas Hobbes, leads to 1690, the year of publication of John Locke's *Two Treatises of Government.*

The critical comparison between Spinoza, Bayle and Locke allows us to deduce the evolution of the concept of tolerance, which during the eighteenth century we will find in Voltaire's *Traité sur la tolérance*, published in 1763. In this way we arrive at *The unanimous Declaration of the thirteen united states of America* (or *Declaration of Independence*) promulgated on 4 July 1776 by the thirteen English colonies that held a congress in Philadelphia; furthermore we come to the *Déclaration des droits de l'homme et du citoyen*, promulgated in Versailles on 26 August 1789. For the sake of completeness, it is necessary to mention the *Universal Declaration of Human Rights*, adopted by the United Nations General Assembly at the session of 10 December 1948 held in Paris. The path which from John Locke leads to the declaration of human rights of the United Nations Organization, is indeed multifaceted and complex. In this journey, we should not overlook the seventeenth century, which saw Great Britain devastated by revolutions and civil wars led by Oliver Cromwell. Great Britain, and in particular England, during the seventeenth century was characterized by political and cultural events of considerable importance, so it can and must be reiterated that the origins of the Enlightenment can be found in Great Britain, even before France. The *Siècle des Lumières* found its origins in the Great Island at the end of the seventeenth century and moved to the European continent in the eighteenth century. During the seventeenth century, Great Britain transitioned from the Tudor and Stuart dynasties to the Orange-Nassau one; with this dynasty, coming from the Netherlands, Great Britain moved from absolute monarchy to constitutional monarchy, but above all to the foundation of the modern liberal state, centered on the distinction of the three powers, namely legislative (of parliament), executive (of the government) and judicial (of the judiciary).

Let us now try to summarize the salient events in the history of Great Britain during the seventeenth century. In 1603, upon the death of Elizabeth, as there were no heirs of the Tudor dynasty, James I of the Stuart dynasty, King of Scotland, was called to the throne of England, being the son of Mary Stuart (a Catholic), but brought up as a Calvinist by Elizabeth; thus James I became king of England, Scotland and Ireland. Upon the death of James I, in 1625, the throne went to his son Charles I, who was executed in 1649. The years between 1625 and 1649 were difficult ones, characterized by the clash between the supporters of royal absolutism, on the one side, and parliamentarians, on the other. In 1649 Charles I was even tried and beheaded following the political and social conflict arising from the republican system represented by Oliver Cromwell. In 1653, Cromwell took the title of Lord Protector, and the expression "Commonwealth of England" was coined, full of formal and concrete meaning. The new parliamentary form of government was maintained by Oliver Cromwell from 1653 to 1658 and by his son Richard from 1658 to 1659. The key word "Commonwealth" literally stands for "common wealth"; therefore it was coined to represent the parliamentary system as opposed to the absolutist regime of the old monarchy; it also refers to the Latin word "res publica". Hence it is not strange that "Commonwealth", albeit with a broader meaning, was taken to mean the "Commonwealth of Nations", founded during the twentieth century by the United Kingdom, on the plane of peaceful coexistence with the former colonies of the old empire. During the seventeenth and eighteenth centuries, it should be underlined that the civil wars found their definitive epilogue with the "Act of Union" passed in 1707, when the parliaments of the kingdoms of England and Scotland approved the constitution of the kingdom of Great Britain, ruled over by Anne Stuart, who sat on the throne of England from 1702 to 1714. Therefore it should be noted that, with the "Act of Union" passed on 1 August 1800, the United Kingdom of Great Britain and Ireland was established; thus England (with Wales), Scotland and Ireland were united.

Reflecting on the history of Great Britain in the seventeenth century, it should be underlined that the Stuarts, after James I and Charles I, also reigned with Charles II from 1660 to 1685 and with his son James II from 1685 to 1688. At the end of the second revolution, in 1689, on the throne of Great Britain (including England, Scotland and Ireland), there sat William III of Orange-Nassau. The throne of Great Britain went to William III of Orange-Nassau due to the fact that he was the husband of Mary II Stuart (eldest daughter of James II). However, it should be remembered that William III was "stadtholder" of the Republic of the Netherlands from 1672; and that in 1677 he had married Mary II Stuart, daughter of James II, who on his death had left no male heirs. Therefore a foreigner, coming from the Low Countries, i.e. from the republic of the Seven United Provinces (Holland, Zeeland, Utrecht, Guelders, Overijssel, Friesland and Groningen) headed by the respective capital cities (including The Hague, Utrecht), was called to sit on the throne of Great Britain. The Netherlands, a Calvinist country, and Great Britain, with a Church that had broken away from Rome, stood out in the Europe of the time, projected in the direction of the Siècle des Lumières with the affirmation of the principle of tolerance and freedom of thought.

With the arrival of William III of Orange-Nassau in Great Britain, an important provision was the passing of the "Bill of Rights" by parliament in 1689, with which there began the constitutional monarchy much praised by John Locke in his *Two Treatises of Government* published in 1690. The "Bill of Rights", also called "Declaration of Rights", anticipates the first ten amendments to the Constitution of the United States of America approved in 1791, founded on the principle of freedom of each individual citizen and on the autonomy of each of the three fundamental powers of the state (legislative, governmental and judicial). Therefore, we cannot overlook the fact that the "Siècle des Lumières" was thus defined in France; instead in England it was called "Enlightenment", in Germany "Aufklärung", in Italy "Illuminismo" and in Spain "Ilustración". In England, the "Siècle des Lumières", as well as "Enlightenment", was called the "Age of Enlightenment", or "the Century of Lights". The "Siècle des Lumières" was also called the "Age of Reason", confirming the primacy of reason over faith; therefore reason is taken as the foundation of the new culture in the dual humanistic and scientific version.

2 The Principles of Freedom and Expression in John Locke

In the cultural and social context of seventeenth-century Great Britain, a leading role was played by John Locke, who owed his mature education to his stays in France, Italy and above all Holland. In 1684, a year after his stay in Amsterdam, Locke met the liberal theologian Philipp van Limborch, from whom he acquired the ideological and philosophical principles transferred to his works. It is no coincidence that the Latin drafting of the text *Epistola de tolerantia*[9] dates back to 1685. It was dedicated precisely to his friend van Limborch; it was published anonymously in Gouda in May 1689 in Latin by van Limborch himself and in October of the same year in the English version (*A Letter concerning Toleration*[10]) edited by William Popple. In 1690, one year after the appearance of *Epistola de tolerantia*, there came the publication of *Two Treatises of Government*[11] and *An Essay concerning Human Understanding.*[12] Then in 1690 Locke published *A second Letter concerning Toleration*[13] polemicizing with Jonas Proast, who, with *The Argument of the Letter concerning Toleration, Briefly Consider'd and Answer'd*,[14] had criticized Locke's liberal ideas. So we cannot be surprised at Locke's "insistence" on the theme of tolerance in the other two letters, i.e. the third one, dated 1692 (*A third*

[9] See Locke (1689).

[10] See Locke (1997f).

[11] See Locke (1997e).

[12] See Locke (1997a).

[13] See Locke (1997g).

[14] See Proast (1690).

Letter for Toleration[15]) and the fourth one (*A fourth Letter for Toleration*[16]) published in 1704. It could therefore be asserted that John Locke opens the floodgate to the "Siècle des Lumières", marking a radical turning point in the direction of the new culture; the principle of freedom, recognized to belong to the individual citizen, is the basis of the topic proposed here on freedom of expression for judges.

If we look at it from this angle, it should be stressed that, in 1691, Locke had retired to Oates (in Essex), as a guest of Sir Francis Masham, the husband of Damaris Cudworth, a friend and admirer of his. In the home of the Masham-Cudworth couple, as early as 1691, Locke published *Some Considerations of the Consequences of the Lowering of Interest, and Raising the Value of Money*;[17] the following year, there came *A third Letter for Toleration* (mentioned just above), demonstrating an interest in economic themes. In 1693 he completed *Some Thoughts concerning Education*[18] and in 1694 did the second edition of *An Essay concerning Human Understanding*. In 1695 he wrote the essays *The Reasonableness of Christianity*[19] and *An Examination of P. Malebranche's Opinion of seeing all Things in God*;[20] the latter appeared posthumously in 1706. In 1697 the controversies over Christian doctrine continued, both with John Edwards (a theologian) and with Edward Stillingfleet (bishop of Worcester). *Of the Conduct of the Understanding*[21] is the title of an essay composed in 1697 to supplement *An Essay concerning Human Understanding* (1690). 1700 is the year in which Locke dedicated himself to commenting on some letters of Paul of Tarsus (to the Galatians, Corinthians, Romans, Ephesians), with *A Paraphrase and Notes on the Epistles of St. Paul*,[22] which appeared posthumously. In 1706 he published *A Discourse of Miracles*[23] and *Some Thoughts concerning Reading and Study for a Gentleman*.[24] Therefore philosophy is combined with theology and ideology with morality, on the basis of a peculiar concept of *paideia*.

During the second half of the seventeenth century, the theme of freedom of thought and religious tolerance was deeply felt throughout Europe. In this regard, it should be remembered that in 1685, in France, Louis XIV issued the Edict of Fontainebleau to revoke the Edict of Nantes issued in 1598 by Henri IV; hence freedom of worship (but also the recognition of political, military and territorial rights), granted at the end of the sixteenth century to the Huguenots (the French Protestants who harked back to Hugh Capet), was lost, with the consequence that the Protestants

[15] See Locke (1997h).
[16] See Locke (1997i).
[17] See Locke (1997d).
[18] See Locke (1997l).
[19] See Locke (1997j)
[20] See Locke (1997m).
[21] See Locke (1997b).
[22] See Locke (1997k).
[23] See Locke (1997n).
[24] See Locke (1997c).

had to take refuge in Holland. Therefore the French philosopher Pierre Bayle, like the English philosopher John Locke, was forced to move to Holland (to Rotterdam), to avoid incurring persecutions by the absolutist king Louis XIV. Not surprisingly, in 1686, Bayle completed the pamphlet *De la tolérance. Commentaire philosophique*,[25] with the aim of underlining the value of freedom of conscience against all forms of religious and political repression. Bayle's *Commentaire philosophique* (*De la tolérance*), dated 1686, is placed at the center of the philosophical debate of the time, as can be seen from the years of the appearance of *Pensées diverses sur la comète*[26] (1682) and of *Dictionnaire historique et critique*[27] (1697), but also of the foundation in 1684 of the journal *Nouvelles de la République des Lettres*, written in French but published in Amsterdam.

Bayle's works suggest backdating the analysis of the concept of tolerance, mentioning the production of Baruch Spinoza, the author in 1670 of *Tractatus theologico-politicus*[28] dominated by the principle of freedom and expression. *Tractatus theologico-politicus* implies a relationship between theology and philosophy, claiming the autonomy of reason from faith and every form of religion. Therefore to *Tractatus theologico-politicus* we have to relate both *Tractatus politicus*[29] and *Ethica ordine geometrico demonstrata*,[30] works in which Spinoza expresses his aversion for the restrictions of religious and political power. In this cultural context of Europe, Locke plays a leading role, following Spinoza and Bayle only in chronological terms. The liberal ideology of the English philosopher can be found above all in *Two Treatises of Government*, presented as follows by Locke himself: "In the former, the false principles and foundation of Sir Robert Filmer, and his followers, are detected and overthrown;"[31] "the latter is an essay concerning the true original, extent, and end of civil government."[32] Robert Filmer, who died in 1653, was the author of the essay *Patriarcha; or The Natural Power of Kings*,[33] published posthumously in 1680, with which he supported the divine origin of the monarchy and its absolute power. In the wake of James Tyrrell (the author of *Patriarcha non Monarcha*,[34] published in 1681) and Algernon Sidney (the author of *Discourses*

---

[25] See Bayle (2014).

[26] See Bayle (2007).

[27] See Bayle (2015).

[28] See Spinoza (1670). It is the *Tractatus theologico-politicus*, originally published anonymously, because of Spinoza's fear of coming up against the rigors of censorship, as happened in 1674 with the Dutch Courts.

[29] See Spinoza (1677b). It is the *Tractatus politicus*, contained in the collection *Opera Posthuma* with other works: *Ethica ordine geometrico demonstrata*, *Tractatus de intellectus emendatione*, *Epistolae*, *Compendium grammatices linguae Hebraeae*.

[30] See Spinoza (1677a).

[31] Locke (1997e), p. 207.

[32] Locke (1997e), p. 207.

[33] See Filmer (2008).

[34] See Tyrrell (1681).

concerning Government,[35] published posthumously in 1698), John Locke instead supported the constitutional and liberal character of the monarchy established in Great Britain in 1689 by William III of Orange-Nassau.

In the first chapter of the first book of *Two Treatises of Government*, Locke writes: "Slavery is so vile and miserable an estate of man, and so directly opposite to the generous temper and courage of our nation, that it is hardly to be conceived, that an Englishman, much less a gentleman, should plead for it."[36] Hence *Two Treatises of Government* (published in 1690) are to be related to *Some Thoughts concerning Education* (published in 1693); in 1703 Locke was to publish *Some Thoughts concerning Reading and Study for a Gentleman*, highlighting his peculiar concept of "gentleman", or "free man", to be considered in the cultural and social context of the time. With *Two Treatises of Government*, the English philosopher fits fully into the debate that also developed in England with the appearance in 1643 of the monograph by Philip Hunton, *A Treatise of Monarchy*,[37] with which the author highlights a form of mediation between the powers of the king and parliament. At this point, it should be stressed that, from the year of publication (1651) of Hobbes' *Leviathan*[38] to that of Locke's *Two Treatises of Government* (1690), only 39 years passed, during which and following which there was a radical change in the cultural model centered on the principle of freedom, reprised during the nineteenth century by John Stuart Mill with the essay *On liberty*[39] (1859). The text of Locke's *Two Treatises of Government* constitutes the basis of liberal ideology, centered on the distinction of the three institutional and constitutional powers of the modern state. Therefore it should be underlined that the English philosopher highlights the primacy of the legislative power compared to the other two, as the legislative power of parliament emanates directly from the people. On this point he remarks: "The legislative power is that, which has a right to direct how the force of the commonwealth shall be employed for preserving the community and the members of it."[40]

The principle of liberty, expounded in *Two Treatises of Government*, must be related to the principle of toleration expounded in *An Essay concerning Toleration* and in the four letters dedicated specifically to this key word. We have already emphasized that *An Essay concerning Toleration* dates back to 1667, a difficult and controversial year in the history of England, if we only consider that, at the end of Richard Cromwell's protectorate (in 1659), the conditions were created for the return of Charles II, proclaimed king of England, Scotland and Ireland on 23 April 1661. Over time, Charles II Stuart abolished parliament (in 1679), ruling as an absolute sovereign until the year of his death (1685). In 1667 Locke had become a collaborator of Anthony Ashley Cooper, chancellor of the kingdom of England and 1st

[35] See Sidney (1996).

[36] Locke (1997e), p. 77.

[37] See Hunton (2017).

[38] See Hobbes (2017).

[39] See Mill (2001).

[40] Locke (1997e), p. 424.

Earl of Shaftesbury, who even welcomed him into his home in Exeter House near London. Following Anthony Ashley Cooper's fall from grace, Locke was forced to leave England and take refuge on the continent (France, Italy and Holland); in 1683 he settled in Amsterdam, where he met the "remonstrant theologian" Philipp van Limborch, whose liberal and non-conformist ideas allowed him to develop his own ideas, transferred to the writings of his mature years.

It is no coincidence that the drafting of the *Epistola de tolerantia* dates back to 1685; dedicated to his friend van Limborch, it was to be published in 1689. Its content, however, is to be correlated with *An Essay concerning Toleration* (1667), given that already in 1667 Locke had underlined the duty on the part of the established power to recognize the fundamental principle of the freedom of the individual. Questioning the divine origins of the monarchy, Locke refers to the content of *Magna Carta Libertatum* (promulgated in England in 1215 by John Lackland under pressure from the barons). Therefore, he recognizes the right to exercise and freely express one's opinions, especially on the religious side in a country that, with Henry VIII, in 1534, with the passing of the Act of Succession and the Act of Supremacy, had aimed to separate and make the Anglican Church independent of the Roman Church. 1685 was a difficult year in the history of England and in the life of John Locke; upon the death of Charles II, his brother James II succeeded to the throne of England, Scotland and Ireland. Although he was in Holland, Locke was suspected of being part of the "Monmouth Rebellion" group that, led by James Scott, 1st Duke of Monmouth, wanted to depose the Catholic King James II. Locke preferred to remain in Holland, after having left England (in 1675) following the fall from grace of his protector Anthony Ashley Cooper. 1685 is a difficult year in the history of Europe due to the fact that it marks the accession of the Catholic King James II to the throne of England, Scotland and Ireland, but also, as underlined above, due to the revocation, in the same year 1685, of the Edict of Nantes (promulgated by Henry IV in 1598), by Louis XIV, King of France, with the issuing of the Edict of Fontainebleau, with which it was possible to resume the persecutions of Huguenots by Catholics. Therefore *Epistola de tolerantia*, written in 1685, takes on a peculiar and important meaning. The theme expounded by Locke denotes both a moral and juridical character, for which our author writes: "The toleration of those that differ from others in matters of religion, is so agreeable to the gospel of Jesus Christ, and to genuine reason of mankind, that it seems monstrous for men to be so blind, as not to perceive the necessity and advantage of it, in so clear a light."[41] In this way, Locke sees freedom as a moral virtue against all forms of religious fanaticism, to be fought against peacefully with the force of reason.

It may seem strange that in 1690, just a year after the publication of *Epistola de tolerantia*, Locke felt the need to write *A second Letter concerning Toleration*. Immediately after the publication of *Epistola de tolerantia*, Locke was criticized by conservative circles; for example, as well as by the already mentioned Jonas Proast (with *The Argument of the Letter concerning Toleration, Briefly Consider'd and*

[41] Locke (1997f), p. 9.

Answer'd), by Thomas Long (with *The letter for toleration decipher'd and the absurdity and impiety of an absolute toleration demonstrated*[42]). Hence in *A second Letter concerning Toleration* Locke writes: "Sir, you will pardon me if I take the same liberty with you, that you have done with the author of the Letter concerning Toleration; to consider your arguments, and endeavour to show you the mistakes of them."[43] Specifically, *A second Letter concerning Toleration* turns out to be a response to the objections raised against Locke by Proast, in a political and cultural context that changed in 1689 with the accession to the throne in Great Britain of William III of Orange-Nassau. Therefore the English philosopher can support the fundamental reasons of the principle of tolerance, as we read in the same essay of 1667 (*An Essay concerning Toleration*), where he asserts "That the whole trust power & authority of the magistrate is vested in him for no other purpose, but to be made use of for the good, preservation, & peace of men in that society over which he is set."[44] Placing himself in stark contrast to Hobbes' political conception, Locke considers that the "magistrate" (a term by which he means the representative of the legislative power of parliament, directly related to the supreme will of the people) must himself respect the laws. The consensus of the people is therefore the basis of political power, in whatever form it is exercised.

Following the chronicles of the time, we must note that Locke, after the first and second letters, was almost forced to write a third and fourth letter, with which he intended to respond to the controversy raised by Proast with his rather critical writings. Not by chance, in *A third Letter for Toleration*, written in answer to Proast's *The Argument of the Letter concerning Toleration*, Locke addresses his interlocutor in these terms: "you take occasion all along to lay a load on me for charging you with the absurdities of a power in the magistrates to punish men, to bring them to their religion."[45] Evidently the problem posed by Locke is not only of a religious order, but also of a political, social and cultural order. Therefore, within *A fourth Letter for Toleration*, Locke reiterates his position, which is completely distant from Proast's, for whom the use of force by the magistrate is justified to induce individuals to respect the law and religion itself. Through the pages of this letter, Locke defends himself against the criticisms leveled against him by Proast, analyzing and refuting them one by one. Finally, he addresses his interlocutor in these terms: "what is it but to erect yourself into a state of infallibility above all other men of different persuasions from yours, which yet they have as good as a title to as yourself?"[46] This concept is found in other writings, including the aforementioned *Some Thoughts concerning Education*, which appeared in 1693, the essay on *The Reasonableness of Christianity*, published in 1695, and *An Examination of*

[42] See Long (1689).

[43] Locke (1997g), p. 61.

[44] Locke (2006), p. 269.

[45] Locke (1997h), p. 142.

[46] Locke (1997i), p. 569.

P. Malebranche's Opinion of seeing all Things in God, which was written in 1695 but appeared posthumously in 1706.

With these works, Locke addresses all humanity, believing it to be his duty to consider freedom the right of every citizen. Therefore the English philosopher closes a historical era in the direction of the *Siècle des Lumières*, looking forward to themes developed and expounded by Kant, especially in *Kritik der reinen Vernunft* with the postulate on the freedom of the ego. Taking into consideration *Some Thoughts concerning Education*, it can be noted that the author continues on his thematic segment by referring to the classics. It does not appear strange that reference is made to Juvenal's *Satires*, for the expression "mens sana in corpore sano", mentioned precisely at the opening of *Some Thoughts concerning Education*, with the aim of reiterating the close relationship between philosophy and *paideia*. In the wake of the Latin poet and rhetorician (who lived between the first and second centuries), Locke hopes that: "a man is able to deny himself his own desires, cross his own inclinations, and purely follow what reason direct as best, though the appetite lean the other way."[47]

In this regard, further reflection is necessary on the content of the first of *Two Treatises of Government*, where the author highlights the principle of justice, which leads from Plato to Hume himself. Specifically, Locke refers to the state of nature, during which men lived in complete freedom without any restrictions. On this point he observes that the state of nature does not guarantee civil coexistence between men, which instead must be found in the liberal state. Therefore, at the basis of civil coexistence, he places respect for the laws, that is, for positive law and established sovereignty, represented by the common judge. To the three powers of the liberal state, Locke adds the federal one, which is responsible for "the power of war and peace, leagues and alliances, and all transactions, with all persons and communities without the commonwealth; and may be called federative."[48] Reading *Two Treatises of Government*, it is clear that the executive and federative power is the competence of the government, which is recognized to have "the management of the security and interest of the public without, with all those that it may receive benefit or damage from."[49] From this assumption derives the modern principle of "federation" (from the key word "*foedus*"), to be understood precisely as the possibility of stipulating a pact between those who have at heart the maintenance of justice in the context of civil society. Therefore political theory, developed by Locke, has an undisputed ethical value to be correlated to the modern principles of justice and fairness.

Scrolling through the index of the history of modern thought in the eighteenth century, we reach the contemporary age, having however to underline that the eighteenth century is closely linked to the nineteenth century, not only on a chronological level, but also on a theoretical level. The theme which links the two centuries is

[47] Locke (1997l), p. 27.

[48] Locke (1997e), p. 425.

[49] Locke (1997e), p. 425.

that of tolerance and freedom of thought, supported in the context of the revolutions in America (1776) and France (1789). As far as the history of ideas is concerned, from Locke's *An Essay concerning Toleration* (1667) we come down to Voltaire's *Traité sur la tolérance* (1763), to codify the general principle of social justice extolled by John Rawls in 1971 (with *A Theory of Justice*). The American political philosopher is proof that we often deal with themes that have been developed in the past and which we sometimes discuss without taking the past into account, if not even ignoring its historical substratum. Even before passing through Locke's *An Essay concerning Toleration* to Voltaire's *Traité sur la tolérance*, it is appropriate to remember that the principles of freedom of conscience and tolerance were upheld by Thomas More in his text on *Utopia*, published as early as 1516. Voltaire's *Traité sur la tolérance* is enriched by the contents of the works of other authors (from More to Locke), who preceded him on this theme during the modern age. However, one need only think about the *Encyclopédie, ou Dictionnaire raisonné des sciences, des arts et des métiers, par une société de gens de lettres*, set going in 1751 mainly on the initiative of Denis Diderot and Jean-Baptiste Le Rond d'Alembert. Among other things, in 1745 Diderot translated *An inquiry concerning virtue, or merit*[50] by Anthony Ashley Cooper, 3rd Earl of Shaftesbury, who was born in London in 1671 and died in Naples in 1713, who recognized the autonomy of morality with respect to logic.

Upstream of Locke's production, we must focus on the current of "freethinking", represented by John Toland, Anthony Collins and Matthew Tindal, in the wake of the work of Edward Herbert of Cherbury *De veritate*, published in 1624. Thus, Voltaire's *Traité sur la tolérance* appears in all its maturity and problematic nature, however without this meaning it represents an absolute novelty for modern thought compared with contemporary thought. The dates are indicative: in 1763 Voltaire published *Traité sur la tolérance*, while in 1764 there came the first edition of the *Dictionnaire philosophique*, published several times in an expanded form. The year of Voltaire's death (1778) is also significant, even for Friedrich Nietzsche, author of the first volume of *Menschliches, Allzumenschliches*, written a hundred years after Voltaire's death, not by chance *Dem Andenken Voltaire's gewaiht zur Gedächtniss-Feier seines Todestages, des 30. Mai 1778.*[51] So *Menschliches, Allzumenschliches*, in the subtitle, was conceived as *Ein Buch für freie Geister*, which leads precisely from the Preplatonists to Voltaire. If we look at it from this perspective, Voltaire is to be compared with Bayle, if only we remember the titles of *Dictionnaire philosophique* (by Voltaire) and *Dictionnaire historique et critique* (by Bayle), that is, the two pamphlets that characterized European culture between the end of the seventeenth century and during the eighteenth century. The primacy of reason is the basis of the new culture of the Siècle des Lumières; if we read the entry "egalité" in *Voltaire's Dictionnaire philosophique*, we find the central theme that has always been addressed throughout the history of culture: "Tous les hommes," writes the

[50] Ashley Cooper (1977).

[51] Nietzsche (1967).

French philosopher, "seraient donc nécessairement égaux s'ils étaient sans besoins. La misère attachée à notre espèce subordonne un homme à un autre homme; ce n'est pas l'inegalité qui est un malheur réel, c'est la dépendence."[52] Therefore he believes that "Il est impossible, dans notre malheureux globe, que les homme vivant en société se soient pas divisés en deux classes, l'une d'oppresseurs, l'autre d'opprimés; et ces deux se subdivisent en mille, et ces mille ont encore des nuances différentes."[53]

Continuing to read the *Dictionnaire philosophique*, we could be prompted to reflect on the entries "tolérance" and "vertu", with the consequence of once again highlighting the theme of tolerance and virtue, based on the key words of good and evil. Tolerance is understood as man's willingness to understand the weaknesses of mankind, and virtue as the willingness to act in favor of one's fellow man. In fact, on this point, Voltaire remarks that "la vertu entre les hommes est un commerce de bien-faits",[54] to be placed in relation with the *Traité sur la tolérance*, published in 1763, a year before the appearance of *Dictionnaire philosophique*. To be sure, *Traité sur la tolérance* denotes the distinction between the sphere of natural law and that of positive law. In it we read: "Ne fait pas ce que tu ne voudrais pas qu'on te fit"[55]; "Crois ce que je crois, et ce que tu ne peux croire, ou tu périras."[56]

From these statements we can denote the elaboration of fundamental notions in the context of modern culture, projected into the context of contemporary culture. From natural law to positive law, the underlying theme of the new culture remains that of freedom of thought and expression, taken as an achievement of the individual and of civil society. For this reason, ethics and law are closely linked, due to the full affirmation of the principle of tolerance and freedom of thought. So, once again, John Locke's production is central to what concerns freedom of expression for every single man, whatever the type of his work, from the common man to the magistrate.

References

Ashley Cooper A (1977) *An inquiry concerning virtue, or merit*. Manchester University Press, Manchester

Bayle P (2007) *Pensées diverses sur la comète*. Flammarion, Paris

Bayle P (2014) *De la tolérance. Commentaire philosophique*. Honoré Champion, Paris

Bayle P (2015) *Dictionnaire historique et critique*. Le Belles Lettres, Paris

Filmer R (2008) *Patriarcha; or the natural power of kings*. Dodo Press, UK

Hobbes T (2017) *Leviathan*. Penguin Books, Harmondsworth

[52] Voltaire (1934), p. 167.

[53] Voltaire (1934), p. 167.

[54] Ivi, p. 330.

[55] Voltaire (2023), p. 55.

[56] Voltaire (2023), pp. 55–56.

Hunton P (2017) *A treatise of monarchy: containing two parts. I. Concerning monarchy in general. II. Concerning this particular monarchy, also a vindication of the said treatise*. Hansebooks, Norderstedt
Locke J (1689) *Epistola de Tolerantia*. Goudae, Apud Justum ab Hoeve
Locke J (1997a) *An Essay concerning human understanding*. In: *The works of John Locke*, reprint of the 1794 edn, Vol. I, pp 1–510; Vol. II, pp 1–298
Locke J (1997b) *Of the conduct of the understanding*. In: *The works of John Locke*, reprint of the 1794 edn, Vol. II, pp 321–401
Locke J (1997c) *Some Thoughts concerning Reading and Study for a Gentleman*. In: *The works of John Locke*, reprint of the 1794 edn, Vol. II, pp 403–412
Locke J (1997d) *Some considerations of the consequences of the lowering the interest, and raising the value of money. In a Letter sent to a Member of Parliament*. In: *The works of John Locke*, reprint of the 1794 edn, Vol. IV, pp 1–206
Locke J (1997e) *Two treatises of government*. In: *The works of John Locke*, reprint of the 1794 edn, Vol. IV, Routledge/Thoemmes Press, London, reprint of the 1794 edn, pp 207–485
Locke J (1997f) *A letter concerning Toleration*. In: *The works of John Locke*, reprint of the 1794 edn, Vol. V. Routledge/Thoemmes Press, London, pp 5–58
Locke J (1997g) *A second letter concerning toleration*. In: *The works of John Locke*, reprint of the 1794 edn, Vol. V, pp 61–136
Locke J (1997h) *A third letter for toleration*. In: *The works of John Locke*, reprint of the 1794 edn, vol. V, pp 141–546
Locke J (1997i) *A fourth letter for toleration*. In: *The works of John Locke*, reprint of the 1794 edn, vol. V, pp 549–574
Locke J (1997j) *The reasonableness of Christianity, as delivered in the scripture*. In: *The works of John Locke*, reprint of the 1794 edn, Vol. VI, pp 1–158
Locke J (1997k) *A paraphrase and notes on the epistles of St. Paul to the Galatians, Corinthians, Romans, Ephesians*. In: *The works of John Locke*, reprint of the 1794 edn. Vol. VII, pp 1–449
Locke J (1997l) *Some Thoughts Concerning Education*. In: *The works of John Locke*, reprint of the 1794 edn, Vol. VIII, pp 1–205
Locke J (1997m) *An examination of P. Malebranche's opinion of seeing all things in God*. In: *The works of John Locke*, reprint of the 1794 edn, Vol. VIII, pp. 211–255
Locke J (1997n) *A discourse of miracles*. In: *The works of John Locke*, reprint of the 1794 edn, Vol. VIII, pp 256–265
Locke J (2006) *An essay concerning toleration: and other writings on law and politics, 1667–1683*, Edited with an Introduction and Notes by J.R. Milton and Philip Milton. Clarendon Press, Oxford, pp 267–302
Long T (1689) *The letter for toleration decipher'd and the absurdity and impiety of an absolute toleration demonstrated by the judgment of Presbyterians, Independents, and by Mr. Calvin, Mr. Baxter, and the Parliament*, 1662, Printed by Freeman Collins and are to be sold by R. Baldwin, London
Mill JS (2001) *On liberty*. Batoche Books, Kitchener
Nietzsche F (1967) *Menschliches, Allzumenschliches*. In: *Werke*. Kritische Gesamtausgabe, IV, 2, Walter De Gruyter & Co., Berlin, pp 5–375
Proast J (1690) *The Argument of the Letter concerning Toleration, Briefly Consider'd and Answer'd*, Printed at the Theatre, for George West, and Henry Clements, Oxford
Sidney A (1996) *Discourses concerning government*. Liberty Fund, Indianapolis
Spinoza B (1670) *Tractatus theologico-politicus*. Apud Henricum Künrath, Hamburgi
Spinoza B (1677a) *Ethica ordine geometrico demonstrata*. In: *Opera Posthuma*, Quorum series post Praefationem exhibetur, pp 1–264
Spinoza B (1677b) *Tractatus politicus*. In: *Opera Posthuma*, Quorum series post Praefationem exhibetur, pp 265–354

Tyrrell J (1681) *Patriarcha non Monarcha. The Patriarch unmonarch'd: being observations on a late treatise and divers other miscellanies, published under the name of Sir Robert Filmer, Baronet*. Printed for Richard Janeway in Queens-head-Alley in Pater-Noster-Row, London
Voltaire (1934) *Dictionnaire philosophique*. Flammarion, Paris
Voltaire (2023) *Traité sur la tolérance, à l'occasion de la mort de Jean Calas*. La République des Lettres, Paris

Freedom of Expression for Magistrates in ECHR's Jurisprudence in Cases Versus Romania

Andreea Elena Tabacu

Abstract United Nations Guidelines show that the magistrates are entitled to freedom of expression but must exercise it with due regard to the values and principles set out in the law.

Legal professionals also must raise issues of public concern to improve the legal system. Still, they must show restraint in exercising their freedom of expression in cases where the authority and impartiality of the judiciary are in question. The violation of this obligation can lead to their liability so is important to verify the criteria revealed in the ECHR's jurisprudence regarding the restriction of freedom of expression.

The paper presents rulings retained by the Court of Strasbourg in the analyzed field to reveal in summary the procedural and substantive aspects that are essential for magistrates in guiding their conduct when exercising their freedom of expression.

1 Presentation

The freedom of expression for the professional exercising public authority must be assessed in relation to the purpose of the function he exercises, the court frequently carries out an analysis of the relationship (fair balance) between the person's right to free expression and the need for a democratic society to be achieved the purposes set out in Article 10 paragraph 2 by the hand of the respective authority.[1]

[1] Bîrsan (2010), p. 776.

A. E. Tabacu (✉)
National University of Science and Technology POLITEHNICA Bucharest, University Centre Pitești, Faculty of Economic Sciences and Law, Department of Law and Public Administration, Pitești, Romania

C. Hermida del Llano (ed.), *The Freedom of Expression for Judges in the Sphere of the Judicial Ethics*, Ius Gentium: Comparative Perspectives on Law and Justice 129, https://doi.org/10.1007/978-3-032-06504-9_3

Like any other person, the magistrate benefits from freedom of expression, but international and domestic regulations provide for certain limitations to ensure the effectiveness of the principles that characterize the judicial system, especially the independence of these legal professionals.[2]

Thus, Article 10 of the European Convention on Human Rights recognizes freedom of expression, but shows that in the exercise of public authority, the holder may be subject to certain limitations to achieve the purposes for which that authority is established according to the law, for example, to ensure national security, the integrity territorial or public safety, order and crime prevention, protection of health or morals, protection of reputation or rights of others.

Regarding those who exercise judicial authority,[3] a certain reserve must be shown,[4] on the one hand, to ensure the authority of the judicial power, which must be characterized, among other things, by sobriety and a high moral level and, on the other hand, to the respective public function is not affected, in particular by the loss of independence and impartiality, as essential values for a European judicial system.[5]

The Strasbourg Court has set out in an orderly manner in its jurisprudence the conditions under which a legitimate restriction of a person's freedom of expression can be considered, having to solve several cases also regarding the exercise of freedom of expression by magistrates.[6]

2 The Freedom of Expression and Its Restriction. Overview

Freedom of expression is an essential condition for a functioning democracy,[7] the cases involving this freedom receiving special attention, the control of the Strasbourg Court is initially oriented towards aspects related to admissibility and which aim at the importance of the damage suffered by the plaintiff, if there are elements such as the contribution to a debate of general interest and whether the case involves the press or other news media.[8]

The Strasbourg Court analyses the cases in which article 10 of the Convention is invoked through the criteria of the results of its jurisprudence, at the center of which is the idea of interference, which, in order not to be considered an impairment of the right to free expression, must pass the test of legality, the legitimate aim pursued and its necessity in a democratic society.

---

[2] Chiriță (2008), pp. 54–55.

[3] Puran and Drăghici (2016), p. 269.

[4] Bîrsan (2010), p. 797.

[5] See Art.10 European Convention on Human Rights where it is shown that the exercise of these freedoms may be subject to such formalities, conditions and restrictions.

[6] Baka v. Hungary (2016); Morice v. France (2015); Anbayrak v. Turkey (2008); Wille v. Liechtenstein (1997); Di Giovanni v. Italy (2013); Slavov and others v. Bulgary (2015) etc.

[7] Appleby and others v. UK, nr. 44306/98, para 39.

[8] Sylka v. Poland (2014), para 28.

The interference can be represented by: sanctions applied by a court decision (criminal sentenced to prison,[9] even with the suspension of the execution of the sentence, fine or, the obligation to pay some compensation,[10] detention or custody,[11] closure, confiscation[12] of a publication, application of a disciplinary sanction,[13] withdrawal of an accreditation[14] etc.

The interference must be provided for by law, in the sense that it must be based on a clear and precise norm, to such an extent that simply reading it or even calling on the advice of experts allows the person to adapt his behaviour, thus being able to foresee, in a reasonable manner in the circumstances of the case, the consequences he would bear in the event of a violation of the norm.

The interference must also pursue a legitimate purpose, such legitimacy being recognized by law for the situations mentioned in Art. 10 para. 2 of the Convention.

The interference must be necessary in a democratic society, in the jurisprudence of the Strasbourg Court, a vast analysis has been carried out detailing the criteria for ensuring the proportionality of the measure or interference with the intended purpose.

The restriction must be necessary to ensure one of the purposes listed in Art. 10 para. 2 of the Convention regarding national security, public order, protection of health, morals, reputation, or rights of others, etc.

Regarding the necessity of interference, the court has developed a theory that it applies in its judgments in which it starts from the imperative nature of that necessity, somewhere between indispensable and reasonable, assesses the gravity and nature of the sanctions applied[15], and verifies the analysis at the national level of the relevant reasons for the justification of the interference.

3 The Freedom of Expression and Its Restriction. Magistrates

The independence of the judiciary and the proper functioning of the system are important requirements for a democratic legal system, the role of judges in maintaining the rule of law being essential as they ensure compliance with the law and restore the violated legal order.

Under these conditions, the freedom of expression of the magistrates falls, first of all, in the criteria provided by the convention and developed in the jurisprudence

[9] Cumpănă and Mazăre v. România (2004).

[10] Morice v. France (2015); Petro Carbo Chem v. România (2020).

[11] Açık and others v. Turkey (2009).

[12] Handyside v. UK (1976).

[13] Kozan v. Turkey (2022), Kövesi v. România (2020).

[14] Gafiuc v. România (2021).

[15] Women On Waves and others v. Portugal (2009), Bayev and others v. Russia (2017).

of the court, for the freedom of expression of civil servants or those who exercise functions of public authority, for them being imposed an obligation of reserve and being recognized to the states a wider margin of appreciation regarding the limitations they can impose on those who exercise public authority.

In particular, the representatives of the judiciary, in relation to the position they have in society, must be reserved when expressing their opinions, since, on the one hand, the magistrate must objectively analyze any situation in all cases,[16] unlike other persons, and on the other hand, when he speaks he engages the image of the entire judicial system and must preserve his independence.

Whether it is about cases before the courts or topics of general interest related to the functioning of the judiciary,[17] magistrates must show reserve in expressing their opinions in order not to affect the independence of the judiciary.

The state can limit their freedom of expression, however, when the interference aims to apply a disciplinary sanction to the magistrate, being practically in the presence of labor disputes for judges,[18] their independence and the principle of separation of powers in the state must be taken into account, in order not to allow the legislative or executive power to adopt measures that would eliminate free access to justice for magistrates in these situations.

The independence of judges is also ensured depending on the guarantees they benefit from in disputes regarding their removal from office or the working conditions of judges[19]since the hypothesis that they would not have access to a court in such situations, justified by the possibility of the state to the limit for public positions, the independence of magistrates would be affected as they will be at the disposal of the state without the possibility of defending themselves.[20]

In the cases before the courts, that concern magistrates (as plaintiffs), it must first be analyzed whether the respective measure taken against the magistrate represents an interference with his freedom of expression, in all cases the Court of Strasbourg refers to the concrete factual situation and the relevant legislation in the respective state,[21] analyzing the position of the respective magistrate within the system, the content of the statement and the conditions in which it was made.

---

[16] Ciobanu (1996), pp. 70–71.

[17] The state and each judge are responsible for promoting and protecting judicial independence - point 3 Independence of judges from the Magna Carta of judges.

Also the Opinion no. 3 (2002) of the CCJE on the principles and rules regarding professional imperatives applicable to judges—Impartiality and extrajudicial conduct of judges, para 34, provides that "judges should be allowed to participate in certain debates concerning national judicial policy. They should be able to be consulted and play an active part in the preparation of legislation concerning their statute and, more generally, the functioning of the judicial system".

[18] Gârbuleţ (2016), p. 56.

[19] Alexe (2008), pp. 213–215.

[20] Baka v. Hungary, para 98–99.

[21] Baka v. Hungary, para 140 and 166, Kudeshkina v. Russia application no.29492/05 judgment from 26 February 2009, para 79.

In assessing the possibility of the state limiting the freedom of expression of magistrates, the dissuasive effect of such prohibitions must also be taken into account, as other magistrates, seeing themselves threatened by the measures taken against a colleague, could be discouraged from participating in any public debate on issues of interest to justice or the judicial system, which is likely to affect society as a whole and affect democracy.[22]

Concerning the freedom of expression exercised against magistrates, it is noted the need for them to bear criticism at a higher level than other people, however, the exercise of the right to free expression by other people cannot affect the principle of judicial independence, influencing or tending to cause pressures on the system in a particular case.

4 Relevant Procedural Aspects in Cases Against Romania

In a case against Romania, the applicant was appointed by the country's president as chief prosecutor of the National Anti-Corruption Directorate, further reffered as DNA[23] for a three-year term, until May 16, 2016. At the beginning of 2016, the Minister of Justice submitted a proposal for the reinstatement of the applicant to the Superior Council of Magistracy, further reffered as CSM, for approval in the position of chief prosecutor of the DNA for a new three-year term, citing that she organized the institution that she led with the greatest efficiency and that she addressed the issue of corruption at the highest level, the CSM issued a favourable opinion to the proposal retaining the applicant's merits (remarkable activity), and the President of Romania reinstated the applicant in the position of chief prosecutor of the DNA for a new three-year term (until May 16, 2019).

After the December 2016 parliamentary elections, the newly formed government adopted an emergency ordinance amending certain provisions of the Criminal Code and the Criminal Procedure Code (Government Emergency Ordinance No. 13 from 2017[24]), which drew the population to the streets, in protest.

In this context, DNA, through the applicant, issued press releases informing the public that a complaint had been submitted regarding how certain normative acts had been adopted and that checks had been carried out in this regard, but no facts had been identified of corruption. However, it was decided to send the file to the Prosecutor's Office attached to the High Court of Cassation and Justice, the competent authority to continue the investigation of possible crimes that consist in the intentional presentation of misleading data to the Parliament or the president

[22] Baka v. Hungary, para 167.

[23] A structure of the Prosecutor's Office attached to the High Court of Cassation and Justice specialized in the investigation of medium and high-level corruption offenses.

[24] Art. I from the Ordinance provided the decriminalization of abuse of office committed on the approval or adoption of all types of legislation when it causes material damage higher than 200,000 lei, a lower penalty for that crime when the damage was higher than the 200,000 lei.

regarding the activity of the Government or a ministry to conceal the commission of acts against the interests of the state, the theft or destruction of documents, the theft or destruction of evidence and forgery.

A few months later, at the request of the Minister of Justice, the CSM ordered an inspection at DNA to establish the managerial efficiency of the applicant, concluding that she met all the requirements of her position and could continue her activity.

In the meantime, the Minister of Justice announced that an in-depth reform of the judicial system is planned (about the laws on the status of judges and prosecutors, on the judicial organization and the organization and operation of the CSM, which attracted criticism in Romania and internationally, he received two negative opinions from the CSM, with memoranda signed by over 4000 judges and prosecutors, with their and civil society's protests taking place, proceedings at the Constitutional Court and international institutions, including the Venice Commission.

At the beginning of 2018, the Minister of Justice formulated a proposal to remove the applicant from her position, criticizing her managerial efficiency and the way she fulfilled her obligations, claiming that in a single year, three complaints were submitted to the Constitutional Court regarding alleged violations of the Constitution by the DNA,[25] in two of which violations of the Constitution were found.[26] It was also claimed that the applicant was personally involved in the investigations carried out by the prosecutors under her supervision and that she made a series of statements, through which she challenged the general binding nature of the decisions of the Constitutional Court, arguing as a legislator and as the Court Constitutional as well.

The CSM approved the proposal of the Minister of Justice for removal from office, but the President of Romania refused to comply with the proposal to remove the applicant from office submitted by the Minister of Justice. As a result, the Prime Minister submitted to the Constitutional Court a request for the resolution of a legal conflict of a constitutional nature between the Minister of Justice and the President of Romania, and between the Government of Romania and the President of Romania, determined by the President's refusal to comply with the request for the removal from office of the chief prosecutor of the DNA. The request stated that, in the

[25] In the first case it was alleged that that the plaintiff arrogated the competence to carry out a criminal investigation in a field that exceeds the legal framework, considering herself competent to verify the appropriateness, compliance with the legislative procedure and, implicitly, the legality of the adoption of the Government's emergency ordinance, which can lead to an institutional deadlock - Constitutional Court decision no. 68 of 27 February 2017 para 25–27.

In the second it was alleged that the plaintiff refused to appear before the Special Commission of Inquiry set up by the Romanian Parliament to verify the aspects related to the organization of the 2009 elections and the results of the presidential election - Constitutional Court decision no. 611 of 3 October 2017, para 5.

The third case regarded the opening of an investigation by the DNA against several public officials, including a member of the Government, for corruption in connection with the adoption of a Government decision—Constitutional Court decision no 757 of 23 November 2017.

[26] Constitutional Court decision no. 68 of 27 February 2017 and Constitutional Court decision no. 611 of 3 October 2017 cited above.

procedure for appointing and dismissing the chief prosecutors, the main role belongs to the minister of justice, while the president, who does not have a veto right to the proposal, is forced to follow through on the proposal.

The Constitutional Court, by decision published in the Official Gazette,[27] confirmed the existence of a legal conflict of a constitutional nature and ordered that the president should sign the decree revoking the applicant from the position of chief prosecutor of the DNA. The Constitutional Court held that it is neither the role of the President of Romania nor that of the Constitutional Court to carry out control of the reasons cited by the Minister of Justice in his proposal to remove the Chief Prosecutor of the DNA, as provided for in the Constitution.[28]

Therefore, in July 2018, the President of Romania dismissed the applicant from her position by Presidential Decree, published in the Official Gazette.

---

[27] Constitutional Court decision no 358 of 30 May 2018 para 69, 72, 73, 78:

> 69. The fact that the President's decree is an administrative act does not mean that all the relations he has with the other public authorities, who lead to the issuance of the decree, are relations of administrative law [...]
>
> 72. It follows from the above that, in a first phase, constitutional law relations are established between the Minister of Justice and the President of Romania, and the act issued by the President of Romania or the refusal to issue it gives rise to an administrative law report only within the limits of verification the legality of the conduct of the revocation procedure from the management position. That is why, in the first phase, the competence of the Constitutional Court is engaged, and in the second, that of the administrative court.

73. The legal issue with which the Constitutional Court was referred is that of determining the scope and content of the phrase "under the authority of the Minister of Justice" contained in art. 132 para 1 of the Constitution, by reference to art. 94 lit. c) from the Constitution, an aspect that is subject to a report of pure constitutional law. Depending on the interpretation given by the [Constitutional] Court to this phrase, the scope of the competence of the Minister of Justice, respectively of the President of Romania, is also objectified. Therefore, the two authorities will apply the decision of the Constitutional Court, and the control of the application and compliance of the decision by them will not fall to the administrative court, but to the constitutional court.

Thus, the administrative litigation court will retain only the control competence stricto sensu of the legality of the decree/refusal to issue it, respectively: issuer, legal basis, the existence of the proposal of the Minister of Justice to revoke the prosecutor from the management position and its communication in order to issue the opinion by the Superior Council of the Magistracy - Section for prosecutors, the signature and, as the case may be, the publication in the Official Gazette of Romania, while the constitutional court has the competence to resolve conflicts of competence between the two authorities resulting from different interpretations given by to them of the incidental constitutional texts, as in the present case. [...]

78. [...] Also, considering the scope, importance and extent of the constitutional law report found, the administrative law report is reduced only to the legal aspects referred to in paragraph 73 of this decision.

[28] In the same decision the Court retained in the para 117: [...] Thus, the President of Romania, openly, arrogated to himself a discretionary power of his own, non-existent according to the Constitution, which annihilated, by way of consequence, the minimal discretionary competence of the Minister of Justice, which represents eo ipso a violation of the provisions of art. 132 para. (1) of the Constitution.

In this context it is relevant that the plaintiff did not file any complaint against the Activity Evaluation Report, Constitutional Court Decision no. 358/2018, or the presidential decree, the competent court showing that it had no other previous cases with similar situations.

The CSM mentioned that the Section for Prosecutors had previously dismissed as unfounded two disciplinary actions taken against the applicant upon referral to the Directorate of Judicial Inspection and that there were two other pending disciplinary actions against the applicant on its paper, which were subsequently rejected by the Section for Prosecutors.

The Strasbourg Court, unanimously, decided that Article 10 of the Convention was violated, since the removal of the applicant from the position of Chief Prosecutor of the DNA did not pursue any of the legitimate goals listed in Article 10 § 2 and was not a measure "necessary in a democratic society" within the meaning of this provision,[29] the premature removal of the applicant from the office being in contradiction with the maintaining the independence of the judiciary and discourage other magistrates from expressing opinions about the independence the judicial system.

An interesting aspect, of a procedural nature, which arose in the case, concerned the submission of the inadmissibility of the request to refer the court because the applicant did not follow the internal procedures or the submission of inadmissibility determined by the non-exhaustion of the internal appeals and the non-compliance with the 6-month deadline, since the administrative litigation court was not notified against the act considered harmful by the applicant.

The Court rejected the submission, holding that: the report of the Minister of Justice could not produce independent effects, being a preliminary act that led to the adoption of the presidential decree and the jurisprudence revealed that in such cases the petitioners were not successful; the decision of the CSM of February 27, 2018, was favorable to the applicant; although the removal decree issued by the president can be challenged before the administrative courts, in the present case the Constitutional Court considered that such control was limited to the stricto sensu legality of the decree, respectively, the issuer, the legal basis, the existence of the minister's proposal the justice of revocation from office and the communication of this proposal in order to issue the opinion by the CSM, the signature and, as the case may be, the publication in the Official Gazette of Romania (formal control).[30] However, the essence of the plaintiff's complaint was given by the fact that her removal was based on the fact that she publicly expressed her views on legislative reforms, an aspect that would have required an examination of the substance and internal legality of the presidential decree.

The cases in which the Court establishes the possibility of directly referring an act of an administrative nature that affects a certain person, without following the internal procedures expressly provided by law and allowed against that act and without there being a court decision there are not frequent.

[29] Kovesi v. Romania, para 211.

[30] Kovesi v. Romania, para 149–150, 153.

The particularity of the present situation was given by the fact that in the decision of the Constitutional Court, published in the Official Gazette, it was mentioned that the act issued by the president of the country could only be deferred to a judge from a formal perspective, so that, even if a procedural step had been followed against it, the substance of the act could not have been censured by the courts, which are compelled to respect the decisions of the Constitutional Court.

Moreover, in the analysis carried out on the documents issued by the administrative authorities, considering the course of events, the court established, in the absence of an internal court decision, that Article 10 was violated, as there were no incidents regulated in paragraph 2 of the text that would be justified interference with the applicant's right to free expression.

In its analysis, the Court found that most of the reasons cited by the minister in the report containing the proposal to remove the applicant referred to the opinions expressed by her in a professional capacity on various occasions, including regarding the legislative reforms proposed by the Government and the criminal investigations related to these reforms and substantive arguments regarding its managerial activity and conduct were examined by the CSM, which found that the accusations are not real.

Although it does not carry out a substantive analysis of the merits of these accusations, the court observes that since they could not be verified before the domestic courts, they founded the administrative act of removal, respectively the interference with the applicant's right to free expression, although she had the opportunity to express her opinions regarding justice reform, in her capacity as head of the prosecutor's office, respectively as a prosecutor could issue professional opinions in the documents prepared and issue press releases regarding ongoing investigations, within certain limits.

It is also interesting that, in this situation, the court, after noting that the interference is provided for by law but that it does not satisfy a legitimate purpose, in which case, as a rule, it would have stopped by finding a violation of Article 10 of the Convention, chooses to continue to analyse and see whether that interference was necessary for a democratic society.

The Court insisted on the fact that in the given hypothesis the position that the applicant had within the system is essential, being the head of the DNA prosecutor's office at the national level, a position in which she expressed a critical point of view regarding the legislative reform aimed at justice, without attacking other people or criticizing the leaders of the other powers, on the contrary, acting professionally.

In relation to the position of the applicant, the court held that higher-than-normal protection of freedom of expression is necessary since the analysed issue was one of general interest of particular importance, and the applicant's position not only allowed but also required her to present a point in view, precisely for the defence of the independence of the judicial system.

The "chilling effect"[31] was also taken into account by the court, in the context in which the removal of the applicant from such an important position, for the reason of expressing criticism of the reform proposed by the executive for the judicial system, could cause fear in on all other professionals of the system to express their point of view and exercise their freedom of expression regarding the reform.

A similar situation but of lesser impact, in a case against Romania,[32] this time concerned the exercise of the right to free expression for the communication to the public of some information regarding an ongoing investigation.

The public has the right to know the existence of files that concern aspects of general interest, the prosecutor's offices, and the courts, through the representative appointed for this purpose, are required to inform the public about the existence of such cases.[33]

In that case, the prosecutor held a press conference in which he informed the public that a case had been established for corruption (influence peddling), with an inmate handing over a sum of money to the trafficker to be forwarded to the parole committee members and judges who ordered on this measure.

Aspects declared by the parties heard in the file were revealed, which in the opinion of some people could have determined the identification of the judge who would have been the recipient of the sums, in this sense a series of speculations were made in the press, including in a televised news show.

As such, a complaint was filed against the prosecutor, who was subject to a disciplinary investigation and to whom a sanction was applied for how he understood to communicate information to the public regarding an ongoing case, being also revoked from the position of the first prosecutor of the prosecutor's office.

The Court, after finding that the interference is provided for by law, the offense is clearly expressed in the statute of the magistrate, notes that it pursued a legitimate purpose, namely, until the completion of the criminal trial, the presumption of innocence of the prosecuted person must be respected, being also relevant the necessity protecting the way magistrates formed their opinion in that case, which could be affected if the public knew the facts of the case and began to speculate about guilt.

However, as regards the necessity of interference in a democratic society, it was found that this requirement is not accomplished since nothing in the applicant's statements allowed the internal authorities to accuse him of violating the right to a protected public image of any of his fellow magistrates.[34]

The Court analysed two aspects: on the one hand, the impact that the press release given by the applicant had on the confidentiality of the information in the criminal file, and the other hand, on the consequences it produced on the reputation of another colleague (the judge identified to be the recipient of the amount of the crime of influence peddling).

---

[31] Nikula v. Finland (2002), para. 54; Elci and others v. Turkey (203) para 714.

[32] Brisc v. Romania (2019).

[33] Morice v. France (2015) para 152 and Brisc v. Romania (2019) para 107.

[34] Brisc v. Romania, para 125.

In the case, it was held that the applicant proceeded with caution, refraining from identifying any of the persons involved by name until the completion of the judicial investigation, and did not first take any position as to the guilt of any of the persons involved, but only briefly described the case.

Secondly, the Strasbourg court analysed the relationship between Article 10 and Article 8 of the Convention, in a consistent jurisprudence holding that to establish a violation of the latter text, the attack on a person's reputation must reach a certain level of seriousness and affect a person's exercise of the right to respect for his private life.

In this point, the court found that the national authorities did not strike a fair balance between the interest of the respective judge's reputation to be protected and the applicant's right to communicate information on topics of general interest, given that he did not nominate any person in the press release or the televised interview, the respective conclusions being drawn by third parties and the statement was the result of the statements made by the defendant during the investigations, without representing the personal opinion of the spokesperson (complainant) or the respective prosecutor's office.

The court carried out a substantive analysis regarding the exercise of freedom of expression by a person who has duties in communicating to the public some matters of general interest, finding that the national authorities, both administrative and judicial, do not apply the Court's jurisprudence in the matter of exercising the right to free expression.

The court's decision is binding for the member states and for the domestic courts that apply rules in the analysed matter, however, it can be observed that in the present case, the court did not understand how to define the ambit (to decide if something falls within the ambit of an article) or reclassify the requests made by the party that invoked Article 10 of the Convention in relative to the content of the motivation. A claim or the basis of a claim is not necessarily accepted by the court referred to, in the context in which it observes that the claim must be framed in another text or that it does not comply with the normative provision invoked by the interested person.

The applicant invoked Article 10 of the Convention and the Court analysed as such the violation of the freedom of expression of the prosecutor who issued the press release as the spokesperson of the prosecutor's office, although, as follows from the dissenting opinion,[35] rather the situation presented would be within the scope of Article 8 of the Convention, the private life of the applicant being in question.

Indeed, the applicant invoked freedom of expression before the domestic courts, and this normative provision was taken as such during the entire procedure, being also invoked before the Strasbourg Court. But, in its essence, the request did not concern the violation of the prosecutor's freedom of expression because it was not about the communication of ideas freely, with the respective prosecutor's own opinion, but about the transmission of information of general interest regarding a

[35] Brisc v. Romania (2019), dissenting opinion, para 24 and 27.

criminal investigation, in his capacity as spokesperson for the prosecutor's office. In other words, the prosecutor was in the exercise of his position and exercising his professional obligations when he issued the respective press release, which was later interpreted and speculated in the written and televised media.

If it is not about the communication of information, data, or ideas, freely, but only about taking over some aspects that emerge from the respective file, to generically describe its situation to bring it to the public's attention, it cannot be about the exercise of freedom of expression but about the exercise of an obligation under the profession carried out, the respective prosecutor endowed with power and authority, additionally having the authority to communicate information of general interest to the public.[36] If he had made this communication on his initiative, manifesting his freedom, and expressing personal ideas outside of his duties, his freedom of expression could have been in question, but here the court, in the majority opinion, chose an extensive approach, broadening the scope of Article 10 very much.

Therefore, the relationship between Articles 10 and 8 of the Convention does not in all cases concern the limits of freedom of expression when it affects the private life of another person but can be analysed even with a view to the correct qualification of the situation deduced from the Court's analysis.

In another case also against Romania,[37] the court found that Article 10 of the convention had not been violated, given that the national authorities had established that the reserve obligation of a magistrate, which requires moderation and restraint in the presentation of his opinions, was violated, by the publication of an article, which affected the moral and professional probity of a fellow judge.

The applicant wrote an article about the president of the High Court of Cassation and Justice, which was printed in a widely circulated newspaper and posted on a legal website. The judicial inspection was notified ex officio, carrying out a preliminary investigation against the applicant because the article published by her referred to the professional career of the head of the supreme court, the limits of the right to freedom of expression being violated, and it was proposed to start disciplinary proceedings against the applicant.

The Section for judges of the Superior Council of Magistracy was notified, which decided that the plaintiff violated the provisions of art. 18 para. (2) of the Code of Ethics of Judges and Prosecutors. The appeal filed before the plenary session of the CSM was rejected and the appeal before the High Court of Cassation and Justice against the plenary decision was also rejected.

After 2 years, the plaintiff requested the CSM to remove from her professional file the decision of the section for judges of October 16, 2012, the decision of the Plenary of the CSM of January 23, 2013, the decision of the supreme court of November 1, 2013, and any other information regarding the violation of the Code of Ethics. As the CSM rejected the request, the plaintiff referred the court, which, in

[36] Bărbulescu v. Romania (2017), Denisov v. Ukraine (2018).

[37] Panioglu v. Romania (2021).

turn, rejected the request to remove the mentioned documents from the professional file.

Subsequently, the applicant submitted her nomination to occupy a position as a judge at the High Court of Cassation and Justice for which she was declared eligible, but the Judicial Inspection initiated a procedure to verify the applicant's professional probity, which resulted in the finding of the applicant's inability to occupy such a position.

Although the applicant claimed that the legal basis that served to establish her impossibility to get such a position is not clear and precise, her request was rejected.

More than 2 years later, at the request of another judge, the High Court of Cassation and Justice found the nullity of the respective normative act, the decision of the Superior Council of the Magistracy regarding the adoption of the code of ethics of the magistrates.

The plaintiff notified the ECHR and criticized the measure (an obstacle to her participation in exams that would have led to her professional advancement), invoking Art. 10 of the Convention, also supporting the unpredictability of art. 18 para. (2) of the Code of Ethics, insofar as it did not define the concept of an opinion expressed regarding the moral and professional probity of a colleague, and which represented a violation of his freedom of expression.

In this case, analysing by Article 10 of the Convention the referral made, the Court retained an aspect of inadmissibility, starting from the essential condition of the violation, which must be of a certain minimum gravity,[38] in relation to the freedom of expression of the respective judge.

Thus, compared to its previous jurisprudence, the court recalled that the seriousness of the violation must be analysed both against the subjective perceptions of the plaintiff and against the objective stake of a given case, the lack of importance of the damage can be given by the financial impact of the matter in dispute or the importance of the case for the plaintiff, without being automatically related to a patrimonial damage. However, a subjective impression of the plaintiff is not sufficient to establish that the person in question has suffered significant damage, as it is necessary for the plaintiff's perception to be justified by objective reasons.

In this analysis, the court held that the plaintiff suffered significant damage because of the Code of Ethics procedure initiated against her, even if no pecuniary consequences were produced.

The fact that freedom of expression was exercised in "important matters of principle" such as reform of the justice system as well as the fact that the sanction imposed was permanently recorded in the professional file and could be considered

[38] "The severity of a violation should be assessed considering both the applicant's subjective perceptions and what is objectively at stake in a particular case. In other words, the absence of any "significant disadvantage" can be based on criteria such as the financial impact of the matter in dispute or the importance of the case for the applicant. However, the applicant's subjective perception cannot alone suffice to conclude that he or she has suffered a significant disadvantage"—Panioglu v. Romania (2021) para 73.

in the event of a promotion procedure at the High Court of Cassation and Justice, led the court to remembers the importance of the damage suffered.[39]

On the merits, however, the court considered that although it is an interference with the petitioner's freedom of expression, it is provided for by a clear law[40] and should have been considered foreseeable for the applicant, who was in a position to understand what it means to express opinions about to the moral and professional probity of a colleague and if he had doubts about the exact scope of the contested provision, he could have refrained from publishing the article,[41] which he did not.

This dismissal was given in the context where, before the court's decision, but several years after the completion of the disciplinary procedure, the internal supreme court had annulled the provision of the Code of Ethics that served as the basis for the investigation of the applicant, because the notion of a colleague was not clear.[42]

Regarding the justified character of the interference in a democratic society, it was held that given the lack of a sufficiently accurate factual basis for the applicant's accusations, the arguments of the domestic authorities are correct, and the applicant should have been aware and careful about the risks of publishing the article and to the impact it could have had on the professional life of Judge L.D.S., as well as on the judicial authority.

The requirement of the proportionality of the interference was considered fulfilled because even if the decision from the deontological procedure could have a certain "dissuasive effect" on the exercise of the applicant's freedom of expression, this decision was not excessive in the circumstances of the case,[43] since the applicant was not effectively prevented by the sanction from registering to participate and participating in the promotion contests by deciding to withdraw from the contest.

5 Conclusions

In the court's jurisprudence in the field of freedom of expression exercised by magistrates, interesting aspects of a procedural nature were noted, since, starting from the particular importance of this freedom which determines a careful analysis by the court in cases of this kind, the court was tempted to reject exceptions of inadmissibility that even seemed well founded at the time of their invocation or to refrain from qualification of the request regarding the effective inclusion in the provisions of article 10 to have the opportunity to resolve in this area.

---

[39] Panioglu v. România, para 75.

[40] Art. 18 para. (2) of the Code of Ethics (2005) provided that judges cannot express their opinion on the professional and moral probity of their colleagues.

[41] Panioglu v. România, para 106.

[42] The question arose whether by "colleague" is meant exclusively one from the same court, or one who worked in any other court.

[43] Antonescu v. România (2012), para. 33.

Equally, the court went beyond procedural aspects when it analysed the freedom of expression of a magistrate outside the concrete exercise of the profession, to verify whether the obligation of reserve that each national system must recognize about its magistrates when exercising their freedom of expression was respected.

Jurisprudence

Açık and others v. Turkey, application no. 31451/03, judgement from 13 January 2009
Antonescu v. România, application nr. 31029/05, judgment from 21 February 2012
Appleby and others v. UK, nr. 44306/98
Anbayrak v. Turkey, application no. 38406/97, judgment from 31 January 2008 final on 7 July 2008
Baka v. Hungary, application no.20261/12, judgment from 23 June 2016
Bayev and others v. Russia 67667/09, judgment from 20 June 2017, final 17 November 2017
Bărbulescu v. Romania, application no. 61496/06, judgment from 5 May 2017
Brisc v. România, application no. 26238/10, judgment from 11 December 2018, final on 11 March 2019
Cumpănă and Mazăre v. România, application no. 33348/96, judgement from 17 December 2004
Denisov v. Ukraine [(MC), nr. 76.639/11, 25 September 2018
Di Giovanni v. Italy, application no. 51160/06, judgment from 9 July 2013
Elci and others vs. Turkey, application no. 23145/93 and 25091/94, 13 November 2003
Gafiuc vs. România, application no. 59174/13, judgment from 13 October 2020, final on 13 January 2021
Handyside v. UK, Application no. 5493/72, judgment from 7 December 1976
Kozan v. Turkey, application no. 16695/19, judgment from 1 March 2022
Kövesi v. România no.3594/19, judgment from 5 May 2020, final 5 August 2020
Morice v. France, application no.29369/12, judgment 23 April 2015
Nikula v. Finland, application no. 31611/96, judgment 21 March 2002, final 21 June 2002
Panioglu v. Romania, application no. 33794/14, judgment from 8 December 2020 final on 19 April 2021
Petro Carbo Chem v. România, 21768/12, judgment from 30 June 2020, final on 30 September 2020
Slavov and others v. Bulgary, application no.58500/10, judgment from 10 November 2015
Sylka v. Poland, application no. 19219/07, judgment from 3 June 2014
Wille v. Liechtenstein, application no. 28396/95, judgment from 27 May 1997
Women On Waves and others v. Portugal, application no 31276/05, judgment from 3 February 2009
Constitutional Court of Romania decision no 68 of 27 February 2017, published in Official Gazette of Romania no 181 of 14 March 2017.

Constitutional Court of Romania decision no 611 of 3 October 2017, published in Official Gazette of Romania no 877 of 7 November 2017
Constitutional Court of Romania decision no 757 of 23 November 2017, published in Official Gazette of Romania no 33 of 15 January 2018
Constitutional Court of Romania decision no 358 of 30 May 2018, published in Official Gazette of Romania no 473 of 7 June 2018

Regulations

Magna Carta of Judges - (Fundamental Principles) Consultative Council of European Judges, https://rm.coe.int/16807482c6
Opinion no. 3 of the Consultative Council of European Judges (CCJE) to the attention of the Committee of Ministers of the Council of Europe on the principles and rules governing judges' professional conduct, in particular ethics, incompatible behaviour and impartiality, https://rm.coe.int/168070098d
Government Emergency Ordinance No. 13 from 2017, published in Official Gazette of Romania no 92 from 1st February 2017
Code of Ethics for Judges and Prosecutors published in Official Gazette of Romania no 815 din 8 September 2005

References

Literature

Alexe CE (2008) The judge in the civil process, between active and arbitrary role, vol I. C.H.Beck Publishing House, Bucharest
Bîrsan C (2010) The European convention on human rights, commentary on the articles, 2nd edn. CH Beck Publishing House, Bucharest
Chiriţă R (2008) The right to a fair trial. Universul Juridic Publishing House, Bucharest
Ciobanu VM (1996) Theoretical and practical treaty on civil procedure, volume I, general theory. National Publishing House, Bucharest
Gârbuleţ I (2016) Disciplinary misbehaviour of magistrates. Universul Juridic Publishing House, Bucharest
Puran AN, Drăghici A (2016) Specifics of the misbehaviours of magistrates, in: supplement of Valahia university law study, 2016. Bibliotheca Publishing House, Târgovişte

Judges Under Pressure: Judicial Reforms in Poland and Their Impact on Judges' Freedom of Expression in the Adjudication Process

Anna Rytel-Warzocha

Abstract This article examines the impact of judicial reforms in Poland, implemented since 2015, on judges' freedom of expression, particularly within the framework of dispersed constitutional review. The analysis focuses on how these reforms have undermined judicial independence and created an environment where judges face increasing political pressure and disciplinary actions. The article argues that while dispersed constitutional review offers a crucial mechanism for safeguarding constitutional supremacy, its effectiveness hinges on the ability of judges to freely express their constitutional concerns without fear of reprisal. The reforms targeting the Constitutional Tribunal, combined with the expansion of disciplinary proceedings and the establishment of controversial bodies like the Disciplinary Chamber, have created a chilling effect on judges, discouraging them from engaging in robust constitutional scrutiny and fostering self-censorship. Through selected case studies, this article demonstrates how disciplinary actions are used to suppress judicial independence, often targeting judges who dare to challenge governmental actions. Despite these pressures, many Polish judges continue to exercise their right to conduct dispersed constitutional review, showcasing their commitment to the rule of law. However, the article concludes that the current system is unsustainable and threatens the very foundations of a democratic society. Protecting and strengthening judicial independence and the freedom of expression of the judiciary is essential to ensure the effective operation of dispersed constitutional review and to safeguard against arbitrary government action. Therefore, the article calls for a re-evaluation of the measures eroding judicial independence in Poland and the adoption of con-

Publication has been prepared as part of a research project funded by the National Science Centre in Poland (competition OPUS 18, decision no. 2019/35/B/HS5/03215).

A. Rytel-Warzocha (✉)
University of Gdansk, Department of Constitutional Law and Political Institutions, Gdańsk, Poland
e-mail: anna.rytel@prawo.ug.edu.pl

C. Hermida del Llano (ed.), *The Freedom of Expression for Judges in the Sphere of the Judicial Ethics*, Ius Gentium: Comparative Perspectives on Law and Justice 129, https://doi.org/10.1007/978-3-032-06504-9_4

crete steps to reinforce the separation of powers, protect judicial autonomy and the freedom of expression of the judiciary.

1 Introduction

Since 2015, the judicial system in Poland has undergone significant reforms that have fundamentally altered its structure and functioning. These changes have particularly affected the independence of judges, with a notable impact on the freedom of their expression in the adjudication process. The imposition of stringent disciplinary actions for judges whose opinions diverge from the ruling political power has created an atmosphere of fear and repression, undermining the role of judges as impartial interpreters of the law. This chapter analyzes the restrictions on judges' freedom of expression in Poland, with a particular focus on their significance for the control of constitutionality of law within the dispersed system of constitutional review.

A central premise of dispersed review, a key element of the Polish legal order, is the right and obligation of every judge to assess the compliance of applied regulations with the Constitution. This, in turn, requires independent thinking and freedom of judges to express their legal interpretations, particularly in constitutional matters. The effectiveness of dispersed review thus depends on the possibility of judges openly articulating constitutional doubts. Without an adequate level of freedom of expression, judges may feel discouraged from questioning the constitutionality of provisions, which weakens the entire mechanism of dispersed review. The principle of judicial independence plays a crucial role here, guaranteeing judges the freedom to express their legal position, including constitutional issues. Restricting this freedom can lead to self-censorship and avoidance of difficult legal matters. It should be emphasized that the freedom of expression of judges is not absolute and must be exercised within the bounds of professional ethics and with respect for the dignity of the office. However, overly extensive restrictions on this freedom can negatively affect the effectiveness of dispersed review of the constitutionality of law.

The primary aim of this study is to examine the impact of recent legal reforms on judicial independence and on the ability of Polish judges to carry out an effective constitutional review within a dispersed system. Specifically, the chapter aims to assess the extent to which these reforms restrict the freedom of judges to challenge unconstitutional regulations and how this, in turn, affects the functioning of the entire judiciary. The central research question is: To what extent have recent legal and institutional changes in Poland restricted the freedom of judges to express their views on the constitutionality of laws, and what impact does this have on the functioning of the judicial system and constitutional review?

This chapter hypothesizes that the recent legal reforms in Poland, including the introduction of disciplinary measures and changes in the process of appointing judges, have created a restrictive environment for judges, which significantly undermines their ability to conduct constitutional review and apply the law independently.

This hypothesis stems from the conviction that judicial independence is the foundation of the rule of law, and any compromise on this issue constitutes a serious threat to democratic governance and the protection of constitutional rights. The choice of this topic is justified by the increasing attention that Poland attracts in international legal and political debates, particularly regarding the erosion of judicial independence. The reforms introduced by the Law and Justice government have raised concern not only in Poland but also in the European Union, the Council of Europe, and other international bodies monitoring the rule of law. Analyzing these reforms is crucial for understanding the evolution of the judiciary's role in Poland, and the broader implications for democratic governance in post-communist Europe.

Methodologically, the paper uses a qualitative approach, combining dogmatic legal analysis with an analysis of jurisprudence and legal practice. Key legal documents, including amendments to disciplinary procedures, are critically examined. Additionally, case studies of judges subjected to disciplinary proceedings for decisions deemed politically controversial are analyzed to highlight the practical implications of these reforms. Existing scholarship on judicial independence in Poland is extensive, but much of it focuses on general trends in judicial reform and political influence. Scholars are alarmed by the gradual erosion of judicial independence, and some suggest that the judicial system has become increasingly politicized and subjected to executive control. However, the specific issue of restricting judges' freedom of expression, especially in the context of the adjudication process and constitutional review, remains insufficiently explored. This chapter aims to fill this gap through a detailed analysis of how the reforms have affected judges' ability to engage in adjudication in constitutional matters, which is crucial for maintaining the rule of law.

2 Undermining Judicial Independence: The 2015 Reforms and Their Implications for Constitutional Review

The period from 2015 to 2023 has been a tumultuous one for Poland, marked by a constitutional crisis that began following the parliamentary elections in the autumn of 2015. This marked the first instance in Poland's political history where a single political party secured an absolute majority in both chambers of parliament—the Sejm and the Senate. Coupled with the victory of the same party's candidate in the presidential elections just six months earlier, this gave the ruling party near-complete freedom to govern. Most notably, it provided them with the power to legislate without significant opposition, setting the stage for a series of actions that would ultimately lead to a constitutional crisis.[1] This concentration of power, combined with the government's agenda, laid the groundwork for a weakening of the system of

[1] See Sadurski (2019).

checks and balances, which would later directly impact the judiciary and its ability to act as an effective check on governmental authority.

The initial systemic reforms pursued by the ruling party focused on the judiciary, beginning with the Constitutional Tribunal, followed by the Supreme Court, the ordinary courts, and the National Council of the Judiciary.[2] In December 2015, the Polish parliament enacted the first of what would be termed the "recovery laws," amending the 2015 Act on the Constitutional Tribunal. Among the changes introduced, the most significant concerned the procedural rules governing the Tribunal. The ruling party argued that these new rules should apply immediately upon their publication, bypassing any legislative delay (*vacatio legis*). While the reforms were sweeping in nature, the most consequential effect was their potential to paralyze the Constitutional Tribunal, rendering it incapable of fulfilling its core function of constitutional review. Subsequent amendments in 2016 further altered the Tribunal's functioning, the status of constitutional judges, and the procedural framework. These changes resulted in the Constitutional Court's effective inability to perform its constitutional review duties, and, following changes in personnel, it became politically subordinated to the government. This weakening of the Constitutional Tribunal not only undermined the system of checks and balances at the highest level but also had significant implications for the effectiveness of the dispersed constitutional review system, by depriving lower courts of a strong, independent judicial voice at the apex of the judicial system. Furthermore, this atmosphere of weakened constitutional oversight could potentially create an environment where judges in ordinary courts might fear openly expressing their doubts about the constitutionality of laws, especially given the potential for disciplinary repercussions. By significantly curtailing the independence of the Constitutional Tribunal, the government undermined the overall mechanisms for the protection of constitutional rights and set the stage for further reforms aimed at limiting judicial independence.

3 Empowering Judges or Endangering Independence? The Dynamics of Dispersed Constitutional Review

This situation prompted widespread debate about alternative mechanisms to safeguard the supremacy of the Constitution within the Polish legal framework. One key point of contention was whether the power of constitutional review could be vested in ordinary courts. The 1997 Constitution of Poland does not provide a clear answer. While it is undisputed that the model of constitutional review established in 1982 and subsequently followed in 1997 is based on the Kelsenian principle of centralized constitutional review by a specialized constitutional court, the Constitution does not explicitly preclude the ordinary courts from examining the constitutionality of legal norms in the course of their application. It is important to emphasize that

[2] See Chmielarz-Grochala and Sułkowski (2018), p. 91and next; Rytel-Warzocha (2020), pp. 90–105; Kovács and Scheppele (2018); Duncan and Macy (2020-2021); Ziółkowski (2020).

such an arrangement would not replace the Constitutional Tribunal but rather complement its functions, potentially creating a hybrid system of constitutional review that combines elements of both centralized and decentralized review. This raises the critical question of whether ordinary judges, empowered with the ability to assess constitutionality, can truly act as an effective check on unconstitutional legislation, especially in a political climate where judicial independence is under pressure.

The debate surrounding the right of ordinary judges to assess the constitutionality of laws applicable to specific cases, and consequently, to refrain from applying laws deemed unconstitutional, is grounded in several constitutional provisions. On one hand, the Constitution of Poland meticulously outlines the competencies of the Constitutional Tribunal (Articles 188–197). At the same time, it does not explicitly confer upon ordinary courts the authority to conduct constitutional review independently. However, Article 193 does stipulate that "Any court may submit a legal question to the Constitutional Tribunal regarding the compliance of a normative act with the Constitution, ratified international agreements, or a statute, if the answer to the legal question determines the outcome of the case pending before the court". On the other hand, Article 8 declares that "1. The Constitution is the supreme law of the Republic of Poland. 2. The provisions of the Constitution shall be applied directly, unless the Constitution provides otherwise". When considered alongside Article 178, paragraph 1, which asserts that "judges are independent and subject only to the Constitution and the laws," it is evident that, in adjudicating a case, a judge is generally required to apply both constitutional and statutory norms. However, in instances where a conflict arises between the two, the constitutional norm must take precedence and be applied. This inherent tension between the hierarchy of norms and the principle of judicial independence is at the core of the debate surrounding dispersed constitutional review and emphasizes the importance of a judge's freedom of interpretation and expression.

In situations of doubt, the judge has a choice: either to refrain from applying a provision deemed unconstitutional, or to suspend the proceedings and refer a legal question to the Constitutional Tribunal regarding the constitutionality of the challenged provision. The decision to take one course of action over the other lies with the individual judge, who must weigh various considerations, including their sense of competence in evaluating the constitutionality of a provision, as well as the procedural dynamics of the case. Given that some cases require swift resolution, it is often impractical to delay proceedings awaiting the Constitutional Tribunal's answer to the legal question posed by the court. For example, in the context of auction proceedings—specifically those related to statutory changes governing the sale of agricultural land—it has been argued that, in cases where doubts arise over the constitutionality of a provision restricting bidders, it would be unreasonable to expect the judge to suspend the proceedings pending a ruling from the Constitutional Tribunal.[3] However, the decision of a judge to not apply a law due to its perceived unconstitutionality requires not only theoretical knowledge, but also the courage to openly express that opinion.

[3] See Rytel-Warzocha (2022), pp. 25–37.

It is important to note that doctrinal discussions on the admissibility of dispersed constitutional review in Poland began as early as the late 1990s, shortly after the adoption of the 1997 Constitution. At that time, the majority of constitutional law scholars held that the intent of the constitutional framers was to establish an exclusively centralized system of constitutional review, with courts being granted only the competence to submit legal questions to the Constitutional Tribunal. This view was based on the argument that any competence granted by the Constitution must be explicitly stated, rather than inferred from other provisions. The Constitutional Tribunal itself maintained this position, affirming that the proper procedure for resolving doubts about the constitutionality of a statutory provision applicable to a case was to refer a legal question to the Tribunal.[4] Initially, some courts adopted an opposing view, arguing that judges should have the right to refrain from applying a law when its unconstitutionality is self-evident and its application would lead to an unjust outcome.[5] However, these courts eventually aligned with the stance of the Constitutional Tribunal and the prevailing opinion within constitutional law doctrine.[6]

In the wake of the constitutional crisis in Poland following 2015, views within the legal doctrine regarding dispersed constitutional review have evolved significantly. There is now near-universal consensus that courts possess the right to refrain from applying laws they deem unconstitutional. This position is framed as complementary to, rather than contradictory of, the centralized model of constitutional review. The court's decision to disregard an unconstitutional provision applies only to the specific case at hand and does not affect the binding force of the law in general. Proponents argue that the admissibility of dispersed constitutional review is justified by the doctrine of necessity, particularly given that the Constitutional Tribunal is unable to effectively fulfill its constitutional review function.[7] This situation, it is contended, reflects a form of constitutional self-defense (Bień-Kacała and Jackiewicz 2017, pp. 25–41). Notably, despite the political pressures and the risk of disciplinary actions, Polish judges have increasingly utilized this mechanism, demonstrating their commitment to upholding the Constitution and their willingness to challenge legislation that they deem incompatible with it. This increase in the practical application of dispersed constitutional review reflects a growing awareness among the judiciary of their role as guardians of the rule of law and the necessity to counteract legislative overreach, especially in light of the Constitutional Tribunal's diminished effectiveness. However, the effectiveness of this 'constitutional self-defense' mechanism depends heavily on the ability of individual judges to freely exercise their interpretive autonomy and to openly voice their constitutional concerns without fear of reprisal.

---

[4] See: Judgment of the Constitutional Tribunal of 7 April 1998 (I PKN 90/98), resolution of the Constitutional Tribunal of 4 July 2001 (III ZP 12/01), Judgment of the Constitutional Tribunal of 4.10.2000 (P 8/00).

[5] F. ex. The judgment of the Supreme Court of 18 November 1994 (II URN 44/94).

[6] The judgment of the Supreme Court of 16 April 2004 (I CK 291/03), The resolution of the Civil Chamber of the Supreme Court of 24 November 2015 (II CSK 517/14).

[7] Mikuli (2018), p. 635 and next; Mikuli (2002), p. 185 and next.

Nonetheless, the issue of dispersed constitutional review is undeniably complex. On one hand, it presents a theoretical challenge regarding the interpretation of the Constitution, while on the other, it raises practical concerns related to the jurisprudential practice of judges. Constitutional review undoubtedly poses a significant challenge for ordinary judges, who may face numerous practical difficulties in its application. The first question that arises is whether the typical judge in Poland possesses the requisite competence to conduct constitutional review. As noted by M. Granat, judges in the centralized model of constitutional review, or judges performing judicial review in the United States, are equipped with specific attributes that allow them to carry out such a task effectively. In contrast, civil and criminal judges in Europe often lack the political experience and "political sensitivity" necessary to conduct constitutional review.[8] This argument, while valid, should also be balanced by the observation that the current climate of political pressure and disciplinary actions against judges may be more of a barrier to active constitutional review than a lack of experience. The fear of negative consequences can still lead to a degree of self-censorship, yet the increased application of dispersed review shows that many judges are not deterred by such risks. This highlights the tension between potential self-censorship and the growing courage to openly challenge unconstitutional norms through the application of dispersed review.

However, this view is difficult to fully endorse. It is important to note that, after 26 years of operation, the Polish Constitution has been subject to extensive theoretical interpretation and is complemented by a rich body of jurisprudence from the Constitutional Tribunal. Moreover, courts in Poland have long been tasked with assessing the legality of regulations, including their compliance with both statutory law and the Constitution, as part of the law application process. Judges already have various interpretive tools at their disposal, such as advanced and comprehensive methods of legal interpretation, which can assist in conducting constitutional review. Judges themselves have also emphasized that introducing a complementary system for judicial review of the constitutionality of laws could be beneficial in judicial practice, improving their ability to navigate these complex issues. Thus, it is not merely a matter of formal competence, but of creating a safe space for judges to express their interpretations and to act as an independent force in upholding the constitution.

4 Beyond Accountability: Disciplinary Actions as a Threat to Judicial Independence and Dispersed Review

A much more pressing concern, however, arises from the lack of adequate guarantees for judicial independence. Until the parliamentary elections held on 15th October 2023, Polish judges operated in an environment where the constitutional principles of judicial independence and the independence of judges were consistently undermined. Deprived of essential legal and constitutional safeguards, judges

[8] Granat (2024).

who engaged in the aforementioned constitutional review often faced accusations of "politicizing" their adjudication or "violating the rule of law." Such accusations frequently led to disciplinary proceedings or arbitrary dismissal from judicial duties. It is also noteworthy that statutory changes affecting common courts and the National Council of the Judiciary have made it easier to exert influence over judges in ordinary courts, compared to judges serving on the Constitutional Tribunal. For example, the heads of courts were often appointed based on political affiliations, making it easier to reprimand or remove judges who "misinterpreted" the Constitution. The fear of disciplinary liability became a powerful tool to ensure judges applied all legally binding laws without questioning their compliance with the Constitution. This fear of disciplinary liability has had a chilling effect on judges, discouraging them from actively engaging in dispersed constitutional review and from openly expressing doubts about the constitutionality of laws. However, it is crucial to note that despite these pressures, many Polish judges have not been deterred and continue to utilize dispersed constitutional review, showcasing their commitment to safeguarding the rule of law.

In the draft parliamentary bill on amendments to the Law on the System of Common Courts, the Law on the Supreme Court, and certain other laws, presented to the Polish parliament on 12 December 2019, a proposal was included that sought to classify the refusal to apply a law on the grounds of its unconstitutionality (if not previously ruled by the Constitutional Tribunal) as a clear and flagrant violation of the law, qualifying as a disciplinary offense for the judge. While this provision was not enacted in its original form, the new regulations created an environment in which such a refusal could lead to disciplinary consequences. This threat alone served to further limit the scope of judicial interpretation and encourage self-censorship among judges, particularly in cases involving politically sensitive legislation. Nevertheless, the ongoing utilization of dispersed constitutional review by many judges stands as a testament to their resilience and determination to fulfill their role as guardians of the constitution, despite the risks.

The issue of disciplinary liability for judges of common courts, including district, circuit, and appellate courts, as well as the system of disciplinary jurisdiction, is primarily regulated by the Law of 2001 on the System of Common Courts. Significant amendments to the rules governing disciplinary liability were introduced in 2017, 2020, and 2022.[9] Prior to these amendments, the scope of disciplinary liability for judges was defined by two categories of offenses. The first category concerned manifest and flagrant misconduct, typically involving a judge's violation of specific provisions of the law, especially in the adjudicatory sphere. These violations were usually considered to involve procedural law, rather than substantive law, such as issuing judgments without legal basis, depriving a party of the right to defend themselves, or unjustly depriving a person of their liberty. The second category of misconduct involved violations against the dignity of the office, such as breaches of the judicial oath, failure to maintain irreproachable character, or actions

---

[9] See Gajda-Roszczynialska and Markiewicz (2020), pp. 456–466.

undermining the dignity of the judicial position or casting doubt on a judge's impartiality.

In February 2020, an amendment to the Act on Common Courts came into force, expanding the catalogue of disciplinary offenses by adding three new types of acts. Due to its repressive nature, this amendment became widely known as the "muzzle law." It was perceived by many as an attempt to instill a chilling effect among judges who were involved in defending the rule of law in Poland—particularly those who refused to collaborate with judges appointed by the newly established National Council of the Judiciary, referred preliminary questions to the Court of Justice of the European Union, or made public statements that criticized the government. The law introduced several new types of disciplinary offenses. As a result, under the current wording of Article 107 § 1 of the Act on Common Courts, a judge of a common court may be held liable for the following disciplinary offenses: manifest and flagrant violation of the law (point 1), refusal to administer justice (point 1a), acts or omissions that prevent or significantly impede the functioning of the judiciary (point 2), actions challenging the legitimacy of a judge's official relationship or the validity of a judicial appointment (point 3), public activities incompatible with the principles of judicial independence (point 4), and misconduct contrary to the dignity of the office (point 5). These broadly defined categories of disciplinary offences gave the authorities a wide range of options to discipline judges who were considered critical of the government or its policies, further restricting their freedom of expression, yet the ongoing practice of dispersed review demonstrates that judges have not completely abandoned their role as constitutional gatekeepers.

These changes were also reflected in the catalogue of disciplinary penalties, which traditionally ranged from the mildest to the most severe: admonition, reprimand, removal from office, reassignment to another post, and dismissal from the judiciary. In April 2018, the penalty catalogue was expanded to include the possibility of reducing a judge's basic salary by 5% to 50% for a period ranging from six months to two years. The "muzzle law" introduced an even more severe sanction: a fine equivalent to one month's salary and allowances for judges.

Furthermore, the procedure for disciplinary proceedings against common court judges was modified by the introduction of the new Act on the Supreme Court, which came into force on April 3, 2018. A significant provision in this reform was the creation of a new Disciplinary Chamber of the Supreme Court, which was tasked with considering disciplinary cases of judges and other legal professionals. In principle, this chamber was designed to serve as the second instance for disciplinary cases (with the courts of appeal remaining the first instance), although in some cases it acted as a first instance court. The chamber's controversial nature stemmed from the fact that all its members were appointed by the National Council of the Judiciary, a body whose composition was itself a point of contention, and included non-professional judges. Critics pointed out that the Chamber functioned as an exceptional court, which, under the Constitution, was to be abolished as of July 2022. Nevertheless, the practical significance of these changes should not be overstated, as a new Chamber of Professional Responsibility with a similar mandate was established instead. The establishment of the Disciplinary Chamber, particularly given its disputed composition, raised concerns about the impartiality and fairness of disciplinary proceedings, further increasing the chilling effect on judges' willingness to challenge the government's policies. This, combined with rulings from the Court of Justice of the European Union, which questioned its legitimacy, made the Disciplinary Chamber a significant factor in undermining judicial independence and freedom of expression in Poland, but not a deterrent strong enough to completely extinguish the practice of dispersed constitutional review.

Since 2018, disciplinary proceedings have become one of the forms of pressure exerted on judges of common courts in Poland. Judges have faced disciplinary actions for a variety of reasons, including cases directly linked to their judicial activity. These cases, often stemming from the judges' application of dispersed constitutional review or expressing views contrary to the government's agenda, highlight the direct link between disciplinary measures and the suppression of judicial independence and the freedom of expression. However, it is crucial to recognize that even amidst this repression, the courageous actions of many judges, continuing to apply dispersed constitutional review, underscore the ongoing importance of this mechanism as a safeguard of constitutional supremacy.

5 The Price of Constitutional Scrutiny: Disciplinary Cases and the Suppression of Judicial Expression

One of the most emblematic examples of disciplinary proceedings involving judicial decisions is the case of Judge Paweł Juszczyszyn, a judge of the District Court in Olsztyn. On November 20, 2019, Judge Juszczyszyn issued a ruling regarding an appeal in a case involving a judge appointed by the current National Council of the Judiciary. Referring to a ruling from the Court of Justice of the European Union (CJEU), which outlined criteria for assessing the independence of the National Council, Judge Juszczyszyn ordered the head of the Chancellery of the Sejm to present certain documents concerning the appointment of judges to the National Council (including the lists of citizens and lists of judges supporting candidates to the National Council of the Judiciary and declarations of citizens or judges withdrawing such support) under penalty of a fine. This action, which sought to verify the independence of the National Council of the Judiciary, was perceived by the ruling authorities as a direct challenge to the legitimacy of their judicial appointments. A week later, the Disciplinary Spokesperson for Judges of Common Courts initiated disciplinary proceedings against Judge Juszczyszyn, accusing him of exceeding his powers by assessing the legality of judicial appointments, which was deemed to be a violation of judicial dignity. Subsequently, the Minister of Justice dismissed Judge Juszczyszyn from his position at the district court and reassigned him to the regional court, while suspending him from his duties for one month. In February 2020, the Disciplinary Chamber of the Supreme Court extended the suspension indefinitely, as well as reduced his salary by 40%. Judge Juszczyszyn remained suspended for over two years, only returning to his duties in May 2022 after the Disciplinary Chamber revoked the suspension. He was reassigned to a different department of the court.[10] This case serves as a stark example of how disciplinary measures can be used to punish judges who dare to question the actions of the government and uphold the rule of law through dispersed constitutional review.

Another example of disciplinary proceedings linked to judicial decisions involves Judge Alina Czubieniak. In this case, Judge Czubieniak revoked a provisional arrest order for a man suspected of a sexual offense, arguing that the suspect, who had an intellectual disability and could not read, had not been provided with a lawyer, despite being entitled to one under the law. Disciplinary proceedings were initiated at the request of the Minister of Justice, who argued that Judge Czubieniak had committed an obvious and flagrant violation of the law. This case, while seemingly about procedural issues, demonstrates the willingness of the authorities to use disciplinary proceedings even in cases of judicial interpretation intended to protect human rights. While the disciplinary court of first instance acquitted Judge Czubieniak in January 2018, the Minister of Justice appealed the decision, and in the Disciplinary Chamber of the Supreme Court, Judge Czubieniak was issued a formal reprimand.[11]

Other notable cases of disciplinary action against judges involved Judges Ewa Maciejewska and Igor Tuleya, who, in September 2018, referred questions for a preliminary ruling to the Court of Justice of the European Union. The Disciplinary Ombudsman for Judges of Common Courts argued that these actions infringed on the proper course of proceedings and thus violated judicial dignity. By referring questions to the CJEU, Judges Maciejewska and Tuleya sought to uphold European legal standards and the rule of law. However, this act of seeking clarity from the EU's highest court was interpreted as an affront to national sovereignty and judicial dignity by the disciplinary authorities. In November 2020, the Disciplinary Chamber of the Supreme Court ruled to lift Judge Tuleya's judicial immunity, suspended him from office, and reduced his salary by 25%.[12]

The changes in the legal framework governing disciplinary liability for judges, alongside the increasingly frequent use of disciplinary proceedings in recent years, underscore a critical point: any move to empower common court judges with the competence to review the constitutionality of laws must first address the question of judicial independence. Without robust guarantees for judicial independence, the introduction of dispersed constitutional review risks remaining purely theoretical. In a legal environment where judges may face disciplinary action for the substance of their rulings, the fear of professional and financial consequences could deter judges from exercising their constitutional review powers, leaving them reluctant to challenge the legality of laws on constitutional grounds. These cases serve as a powerful illustration of how the threat of disciplinary sanctions, even when

[10] See Kalisz an Szuleka (2022).

[11] See Zechenter (2019).

[12] See Nowicki (2023).

ultimately overturned, can act as a significant deterrent to judicial independence and freedom of expression. They highlight the real risk of self-censorship among judges, ultimately undermining the effective implementation of dispersed constitutional review and the very foundations of a democratic legal system.

6 Conclusions and Final Remarks

This chapter has explored the complex interplay between judicial reforms in Poland and their impact on judges' freedom of expression in the adjudication process, with a particular focus on the mechanism of dispersed constitutional review. We have demonstrated that the legal and institutional changes implemented since 2015 have significantly undermined judicial independence, creating an environment where judges are increasingly susceptible to political pressure and disciplinary actions. These actions, ostensibly aimed at ensuring accountability, have instead become a tool to restrict judicial autonomy and suppress dissenting opinions, thereby eroding the very foundations of the rule of law.

The initial reforms targeting the Constitutional Tribunal (as discussed in Sect. 2) weakened its capacity to act as an independent check on legislative power. This, in turn, created a void in the system of constitutional review, placing an increased responsibility on ordinary courts to safeguard the supremacy of the constitution. However, as shown in Sect. 3, the theoretical framework for dispersed constitutional review, while present in the Polish Constitution, can only be effectively implemented when judges have the freedom to express their constitutional concerns without fear of reprisal. The current environment, characterized by the expansion of disciplinary proceedings and the creation of controversial bodies such as the Disciplinary Chamber (analyzed in Sect. 4), has actively discouraged judges from engaging in robust constitutional scrutiny.

The selected case studies presented in subchapter—of judges such as Juszczyszyn, Czubieniak, Maciejewska and Tuleya—serve as stark reminders of the real consequences faced by judges who dare to challenge governmental actions and engage in dispersed constitutional review. These cases demonstrate that the threat of disciplinary action is not merely a theoretical concern, but a tangible and frequently utilized tool to suppress judicial expression. Furthermore, these cases highlight that it is not just about formal competences of judges, but more so about the need for a safe space where judges can express their interpretation without the threat of sanctions and that they can act as an independent force in upholding the Constitution.

Despite these constraints, it is crucial to acknowledge that many Polish judges have not been deterred and continue to exercise their right to conduct dispersed constitutional review, demonstrating their unwavering commitment to upholding the rule of law. Their courage in the face of adversity is a testament to the importance of independent judicial systems in protecting fundamental rights and ensuring that legislative power remains within constitutional boundaries. However, it is clear that the current system is not sustainable. The chilling effect of disciplinary actions on judges creates an atmosphere of self-censorship, which ultimately undermines the effectiveness of dispersed constitutional review and the capacity of the judiciary to protect fundamental rights.

In conclusion, while dispersed constitutional review offers a valuable mechanism for safeguarding constitutional supremacy, its effectiveness is contingent upon the existence of a truly independent judiciary, where judges are free to exercise their interpretative autonomy and to openly voice their constitutional concerns without fear of reprisal. The reforms implemented in Poland since 2015 have severely hampered this system, turning the dispersed constitutional review into a mere theoretical exercise and creating a climate of fear, which undermines judges' freedom of expression. Protecting and strengthening judicial independence and the freedom of expression of the judiciary is not only a matter of upholding constitutional principles; it is also essential to ensure that the judiciary can effectively fulfill its role as a bulwark against arbitrary government action. Further analysis should focus on detailed comparative studies of other countries and what measures can be implemented to safeguard judicial independence. Furthermore, further research should explore how to shield judges and the judiciary from unwarranted disciplinary proceedings.

Therefore, it is imperative to re-evaluate the measures that have eroded judicial independence in Poland and to adopt concrete steps that will reinforce the principles of separation of powers, protect judicial autonomy and freedom of expression, and thus ensure the effectiveness of dispersed constitutional review as an essential component of the rule of law. Without such measures, the very foundation of a democratic society is at risk.

Case Law

Judgment of the Constitutional Tribunal of 7 April 1998, I PKN 90/98.
Resolution of the Constitutional Tribunal of 4 July 2001, III ZP 12/01.
Judgment of the Constitutional Tribunal of 4 October 2000, P 8/00.
Judgment of the Supreme Court of 18 November 1994, II URN 44/94.
Judgment of the Supreme Court of 16 April 2004, I CK 291/03.
Resolution of the Civil Chamber of the Supreme Court of 24 November 2015, II CSK 517/14.

References

Literature

Bień-Kacała A, Jackiewicz A (2017) Militant democracy – demokracja, która sama się broni (?). Państwo i Prawo 2017(8):25–41

Chmielarz-Grochala A, Sułkowski J (2018) Wybór sędziów Trybunału Konstytucyjnego w 2015 r. jako początek głębokiego kryzysu ustrojowego w Polsce. Przegląd Konstytucyjny 2018(2):91–108

Duncan A, Macy J (2020–2021) The collapse of judicial independence in Poland: a cautionary tale. Judicature 104(3):41–50

Gajda-Roszczynialska K, Markiewicz K (2020) Disciplinary proceedings as an instrument for breaking the rule of law in Poland. Hague J Rule Law 2020(12):451–483

Granat M (2024) Turbulent times in the constitutionalism of Central and Eastern European countries. In: Granat M (ed) Constitutionality of law without a constitutional court. A view from Europe. Routledge

Kalisz M, Szuleka M (2022) Postępowania dyscyplinarne przeciwko sędziom sądów powszechnych w Polsce. Raport z monitoringu w 2022 r. Helsińska Fundacja Praw Człowieka

Kovács K, Scheppele KL (2018) The fragility of an independent judiciary: lessons from Hungary and Poland—and the European Union. Communist Post-Communist Stud 51(3):189–200

Mikuli P (2002) W sprawie ewentualnej możliwości kontroli konstytucyjności ustaw przez sądy. In: Grzybowski M (ed) Szkice o zasadach i instytucjach ustrojowych II i III Rzeczypospolitej. Wydawnictwo ABC, Kraków, pp 185–210

Mikuli P (2018) Doktryna konieczności jako uzasadnienie dla rozproszonej kontroli konstytucyjności ustaw w Polsce. Gdańskie Studia Prawnicze, 2018 (XI)

Nowicki MA (2023) Środki dyscyplinarne wobes sędziego za publiczną krytykę reformy sądownictwa. Tuleya przeciwko Polsce [wyrok z 6.07.2023 r., Izba (Sekcja I), skarga nr 21181/19 i 51751/20]. Palestra 2023(9):121–132

Rytel-Warzocha A (2020) Contemporary problems of the judicial power in Poland. Gdańskie Studia Prawnicze, 2020(4) (48):90–105

Rytel-Warzocha A (2022) Jak nie Trybunał Konstytucyjny to co? O rozproszonej kontroli konstytucyjności prawa w Polsce. Przegląd Prawa Konstytucyjnego 2022(3) (67):25–37

Sadurski W (2019) Poland's constitutional breakdown. Oxford University Press

Zechenter E (2019) ABA CHR Report: The Case of Judge Alina Czubieniak: Threats to Judicial Independence in Poland through the Use of Judicial Disciplinary Procedures. Available at SSRN: https://ssrn.com/abstract=3525993 or https://doi.org/10.2139/ssrn.3525993

Ziółkowski M (2020) Two faces of the Polish Supreme Court After "Reforms" of the judiciary system in Poland: the question of judicial independence and appointments. Eur Pap 2020(1):347–362

Justice of the Future, a Possible Transformation Through the Digitalization of Justice Procedures Using Artificial Intelligence

Manole Decebal Bogdan

Abstract Conflict resolution accompanies and adapts to the evolution of society. In the beginning, social groups resolved their disputes through customary and unwritten laws. Over time, societies specialized their mechanisms for justice, creating legal instruments and judicial institutions. Today, we face new challenges, including the advent of artificial intelligence (AI) in legal decision-making, which raises profound questions about reason, empathy, and the human role in administering justice. This paper examines the historical development of the judicial institution, the implications of digital technologies, and the philosophical considerations of delegating justice to AI. While these tools promise efficiency and cost savings, they lack key human traits such as empathy and moral reasoning.

Can a machine truly replace the judge? The answer may define the next milestone in this enduring institution.

1 Introduction

The rapid evolution of artificial intelligence (AI) is reshaping professions across the globe, and the legal field is no exception. From predictive analytics in case outcomes to automated document review, AI offers a tantalizing vision of efficiency and precision. Yet, for a profession deeply rooted in the principles of fairness, equity, and universality, the wholesale adoption of AI poses unique challenges that demand cautious deliberation. The question is not whether AI should be integrated into legal practice, but how it can be integrated in a manner that preserves and enhances the core values of justice?

Historically, the legal profession has encountered significant technological and philosophical shifts, each met with initial skepticism and eventual adaptation. The

M. D. Bogdan (✉)
"1 Decembrie 1918" University of Alba - Iulia, Alba Iulia, Romania
e-mail: decebal.bogdan@uab.ro

C. Hermida del Llano (ed.), *The Freedom of Expression for Judges in the Sphere of the Judicial Ethics*, Ius Gentium: Comparative Perspectives on Law and Justice 129, https://doi.org/10.1007/978-3-032-06504-9_5

printing press revolutionized the accessibility of legal texts, democratizing knowledge that was once confined to an elite few. The codification movements of the nineteenth century sought to bring order and universality to disparate legal systems, though not without intense debate over the merits of tradition versus innovation. More recently, the advent of computerized legal research tools like LexisNexis transformed how legal professionals accessed and analyzed information, enhancing efficiency without compromising the profession's human-centric ethos. These historical parallels underscore the importance of measured adaptation, ensuring that technological advancements align with the fundamental mission of the legal system: delivering justice.

The integration of AI into legal practice brings immense promise but also profound risks. On the one hand, AI can enhance efficiency, reduce costs, and democratize access to legal services for underserved populations. On the other hand, the opaque nature of AI algorithms and their potential to perpetuate systemic biases present significant ethical dilemmas. The risk of dehumanizing the practice of law—reducing it to algorithmic calculations devoid of empathy and moral reasoning—looms large. These concerns are not merely technical or procedural; they strike at the heart of the moral fabric of the legal profession.

This paper argues for a slow and deliberate integration of AI into legal practice, grounded in ethical considerations and historical lessons. By examining past instances where technological or philosophical changes transformed the legal profession, we can identify strategies to harness AI's potential while safeguarding the principles of fairness and universality. The goal is not merely to adapt to technological change but to ensure that such adaptation serves the broader mission of achieving universal and fair justice. Through a measured approach, we can strike a balance between innovation and ethical integrity, ensuring that the law remains a human-centric institution in an increasingly automated world.

2 Historical Precedents of Transformative Change in Legal Practice

2.1 The Evolution of Legal Research

The transition from physical law libraries to digital databases marks a pivotal transformation in legal research. Before the advent of digital tools, legal practitioners relied heavily on extensive physical collections of casebooks, statutes, and secondary sources. This traditional approach, while thorough, often demanded significant time and resources, creating barriers to efficient legal reasoning and accessibility of precedents. For example, studies have shown that manual research could take up to 60% longer than its digital counterpart due to the need to physically locate and cross-reference materials.[1]

[1] Smith and Taylor (2017), pp. 145–167.

The introduction of computerized legal research platforms like Westlaw and LexisNexis revolutionized the field. These platforms not only streamlined the search for relevant case law and statutes but also democratized access to legal information. For instance, practitioners in smaller firms and underserved regions gained the ability to conduct comprehensive legal research, leveling the playing field in a profession often dominated by resource-rich institutions. However, the integration of these tools was not without challenges. Early adopters faced skepticism from peers who questioned the reliability of digital databases and the implications for traditional legal research skills. Critics also raised concerns about over-reliance on algorithmically ranked search results, which could potentially overlook critical but less prominent cases.[2] Over time, the profession adapted, and these tools became indispensable, offering lessons in balancing technological innovation with professional values.

2.2 *Procedural Justice Reforms*

The pursuit of procedural justice has long driven innovations in legal practice. The introduction of court reporters and standardized transcription systems marked a significant leap in ensuring accurate and reliable records of courtroom proceedings. These systems reduced discrepancies arising from human memory or biased recounting, thereby strengthening the evidentiary foundation of trials. For example, research indicates that the accuracy of court records improved by nearly 35% with the adoption of professional transcription services.[3] This shift from reliance on oral traditions to standardized written records enhanced accountability and transparency within the justice system.

Similarly, the evolution from oral to written arguments transformed appellate procedures. In earlier eras, oral advocacy dominated legal practice, with limited documentation of arguments and judicial reasoning. This often resulted in less structured deliberations and left significant room for subjective interpretations. The gradual emphasis on written submissions allowed for more thorough preparation, detailed reasoning, and a clearer record for future reference. Studies have highlighted that written briefs enable appellate judges to review arguments more systematically, leading to better-considered decisions.[4] These reforms underscore the importance of procedural innovations in enhancing fairness and accessibility while maintaining the integrity of the legal process.

These historical precedents highlight the legal profession's capacity to adapt to transformative changes while safeguarding its foundational principles. They

[2] Johnson (2019), pp. 234–256.

[3] Brown (2020), pp. 87–104.

[4] Miller (2018), pp. 45–63.

provide a roadmap for approaching the integration of AI into legal practice, emphasizing the need for caution, deliberation, and alignment with the profession's core mission of delivering justice.

3 Is AI Even Compatible with the Theory of Law?

3.1 Legal Positivism and Technological Change

Legal positivism, as articulated by H.L.A. Hart, offers a valuable framework for understanding the integration of new technologies into the legal system. Hart's concept of law emphasizes the importance of a clear and systematic structure of rules, which can adapt to incorporate modern tools. The advent of AI, much like earlier technological innovations, requires an extension of Hart's framework to address the evolving nature of legal systems. For instance, while AI can efficiently identify and apply legal rules, it cannot replicate the nuanced human judgment essential for legal reasoning.[5]

The strength of Hart's framework lies in its ability to evolve alongside societal changes, ensuring that legal norms remain relevant and effective. However, this adaptability is contingent upon the continued involvement of human agents in interpreting and applying the law. Human judgment serves as a necessary counterbalance to the rigidity of algorithmic logic, ensuring that legal outcomes reflect the complex interplay of societal values, cultural contexts, and ethical considerations. Critics of over-reliance on AI highlight the risk of undermining this dynamic interplay, reducing the law to a mere mechanical application of rules divorced from their social underpinnings.[6]

The "rule of recognition," a core aspect of Hart's theory, underscores the role of societal acceptance in legitimizing legal norms. As AI becomes a tool for interpreting and applying these norms, maintaining human oversight ensures that the social thesis—the connection between law and societal values—remains intact. Without this oversight, the risk arises that AI's algorithmic logic could diverge from the human values underpinning the legal system. The gradual adaptation of AI into legal practice allows for the preservation of this balance, ensuring that technological advancements enhance rather than undermine the legitimacy of legal reasoning.[7]

Yet, legal positivism's limitations also come into sharp focus when addressing the ethical dilemmas posed by AI. Hart's framework prioritizes the structure and

[5] Hart (1994).

[6] Fuller (1978), pp. 345–367.

[7] Perry (2006), pp. 311–346.

[8] Rawls (1971).

operation of the law over its substantive moral content. While this approach offers clarity in adapting legal rules to technological innovations, it risks neglecting deeper questions about justice and equity. For instance, how should the law address cases where AI-generated outcomes perpetuate systemic biases or inequalities? These challenges highlight the need for a complementary philosophical approach that emphasizes fairness and social justice.

3.2 Rawlsian Justice and Technological Access

John Rawls's theory of justice, particularly his concept of the "original position" and the "veil of ignorance," provides an ethical framework for evaluating the integration of AI into legal practice. By imagining a scenario where decision-makers are unaware of their own societal status, Rawls advocates for principles that ensure fairness and equality. Applying this framework to AI adoption, we must ask: How can this technology be deployed to benefit all members of society, particularly the most disadvantaged?[8]

Rawls's framework is particularly relevant in addressing the distributive implications of AI in legal practice. The introduction of AI-powered tools has the potential to widen existing disparities between well-resourced legal institutions and smaller firms or underfunded legal aid organizations. To align with Rawlsian principles, efforts must be made to ensure equitable access to these technologies. For example, public funding or subsidies could be allocated to provide smaller firms with access to advanced AI tools, thereby democratizing the benefits of technological innovation.[9]

The "veil of ignorance" further underscores the importance of designing AI systems that are transparent and unbiased. Transparency ensures that the reasoning behind AI-generated decisions can be scrutinized and understood, fostering trust and accountability. Bias mitigation strategies, such as diverse training datasets and ongoing algorithmic audits, are critical in preventing the perpetuation of systemic inequalities. However, achieving these objectives requires deliberate policy interventions and regulatory oversight, as market-driven incentives alone may not suffice to prioritize fairness over profitability.[10]

Despite its strengths, Rawlsian justice also encounters challenges when applied to the complexities of AI integration. Critics argue that the abstract nature of Rawls's

---

[9] Susskind (2017).

[10] Binns (2018), pp. 149–160.

[11] Gasser and Almeida (2017), pp. 58–62.

[12] Barocas et al. (2019).

principles makes them difficult to operationalize in concrete policy decisions. For instance, determining what constitutes a "fair distribution" of AI resources may involve trade-offs between competing values, such as efficiency and equity. Moreover, the focus on distributive justice may overlook other ethical considerations, such as the potential impact of AI on individual autonomy and agency. These critiques highlight the need for a multi-dimensional approach that combines Rawlsian insights with other ethical frameworks to address the full spectrum of challenges posed by AI in legal practice.

4 Understanding Non-Human Systems

4.1 Understanding the Current AI Landscape

To address the ethical implications of a non-human justice system, it is essential first to establish a clear understanding of what contemporary AI systems are—and what they are not. Most legal AI systems today rely on large language models (LLMs), a subset of artificial intelligence. An LLM, like OpenAI's GPT, is trained on vast amounts of text data to generate coherent and contextually relevant responses to prompts. These systems are adept at recognizing patterns, summarizing information, and even mimicking the tone and structure of human writing. However, their capabilities are limited to processing and synthesizing information that exists in their training data—they cannot independently "understand" or "create" in the same way humans do.

A related but distinct concept is Artificial General Intelligence (AGI). Unlike current systems, AGI refers to a hypothetical AI capable of performing any intellectual task a human can do, including abstract reasoning, creativity, and ethical judgment. However, AGI remains a theoretical construct, far removed from the machine learning systems in use today. For our purposes, we focus on specialized AI systems—those designed to perform specific tasks like legal document review, case prediction, or contract analysis.

While specialized machine learning systems excel at tasks involving data analysis, they lack key human abilities such as creativity, contextual awareness, and moral reasoning. For example:

- Creativity: AI systems cannot generate genuinely original ideas. They can simulate creativity by recombining existing information in novel ways but cannot conceptualize something entirely new or resolve unprecedented legal disputes innovatively.
- Context: While LLMs can understand linguistic context to a degree, they struggle with nuanced, implicit meanings that depend on cultural, historical, or personal factors. For example, a legal case involving social norms or ethical gray areas might confound an AI.

- Ethical Inference: AI cannot independently evaluate moral dilemmas. While it can apply rules it has been trained on, it cannot weigh competing ethical values or resolve questions requiring empathy, intent analysis, or social judgment.

Understanding these limitations is crucial in assessing whether AI systems can (or should) participate in or replace human roles within the justice system.

4.2 Capabilities and Limits of a Non-Human Justice System

Current AI systems already demonstrate remarkable potential in certain areas of legal practice. For example:

- Efficiency in Routine Tasks: AI excels at automating time-intensive tasks such as contract analysis, e-discovery, and summarization of legal opinions. This efficiency can reduce costs and improve access to justice for underserved populations.
- Predictive Analytics: Machine learning algorithms can analyze large datasets of past cases to predict outcomes with a degree of accuracy. Such tools can help lawyers advise clients and assess litigation risks.
- Decision Support: AI can serve as an assistant to judges and lawyers, offering case precedents, relevant statutes, or risk assessments that would otherwise require exhaustive research.

Despite these strengths, the notion of delegating higher-order legal decision-making to a non-human system encounters significant obstacles:

1. Contextual Understanding

Law is deeply contextual, requiring an understanding of societal norms, historical developments, and specific circumstances. AI, trained on static datasets, cannot account for dynamic or evolving societal values. For instance, interpreting a freedom of speech case in light of emerging social media norms would require judgment beyond an AI's capabilities.

2. Moral and Ethical Judgment

The justice system often deals with ethical dilemmas, such as balancing individual rights against public safety. These situations demand moral reasoning informed by empathy, cultural understanding, and ethical theory—qualities AI does not possess. For example, a sentencing decision might weigh not just legal precedent but also the defendant's intent, remorse, and potential for rehabilitation, none of which can be assessed solely through data.

3. Unpredictability of Human Behavior

The law governs human conduct, which is inherently unpredictable and influenced by a multitude of factors such as emotion, irrationality, and cultural values. AI, limited to probabilistic reasoning, cannot account for the intricacies of human behavior that often define legal disputes.

4. Risk of Bias and Discrimination

Machine learning systems are only as unbiased as the data they are trained on. If historical data reflects systemic biases, AI will perpetuate those biases. For example, studies have shown that AI systems used in criminal justice risk assessments disproportionately label minority groups as high-risk due to biased historical data.

5. Opacity and Accountability

AI systems, particularly those using deep learning techniques, are often described as "black boxes," meaning their decision-making processes are not fully transparent or explainable. This lack of transparency undermines accountability and raises significant concerns about fairness in judicial outcomes.

4.3 The Ethical Dilemmas of Delegation

4.3.1 The Human Role in Justice

The legal system is fundamentally a social construct, designed to reflect the collective values and moral judgments of a society. As such, it relies on human agents—judges, lawyers, jurors—to interpret and apply the law in ways that account for the subtleties of individual cases. Delegating this responsibility to AI challenges the moral legitimacy of legal decisions. For instance, a defendant sentenced by an AI may question the fairness and validity of the outcome if the reasoning behind the decision cannot be adequately explained. This erosion of trust risks alienating individuals from the legal system, undermining its primary function as a mechanism for resolving disputes and promoting social cohesion.

Moreover, the legal process often involves considerations that go beyond the strict application of rules. Sentencing decisions, for example, are informed by factors such as remorse, intent, and the potential for rehabilitation—all of which require empathy and moral judgment. AI lacks the capacity to assess these qualitative dimensions of human behavior, making it ill-suited for decisions that hinge on such factors.[11] Studies on existing AI applications in criminal justice have shown that algorithmic systems often fail to account for social and cultural contexts, leading to outcomes that may be procedurally correct but substantively unjust.[12]

[13] Angwin et al. (2016).

[14] Richardson et al. (2019), pp. 192–211.

4.3.2 Balancing Efficiency with Humanity

The drive for efficiency and cost reduction in the legal system is understandable, particularly given the high costs and delays often associated with traditional legal processes. However, efficiency must not come at the expense of the justice system's human-centric values. The law is not merely a set of rules but a dynamic institution that evolves in response to societal values and human experiences. Removing the human element from legal decision-making risks reducing the law to a mechanical process devoid of the flexibility and empathy required to address complex moral dilemmas.

Consider the example of criminal sentencing. Research has shown that while AI systems can identify patterns in sentencing data, they often replicate existing biases rather than correcting them.[13] For instance, predictive policing algorithms have been criticized for disproportionately targeting minority communities due to biased training data.[14] Such outcomes highlight the limitations of AI in addressing systemic inequalities—a critical function of the justice system.

4.3.3 Accountability and Oversight

Accountability is a cornerstone of justice. When human judges make errors or display bias, their decisions can be scrutinized, challenged, and overturned through established mechanisms of appeal and review. AI systems, by contrast, often operate as "black boxes," making decisions through processes that are not fully transparent or explainable.[15] This lack of transparency raises significant ethical and legal concerns. If a defendant cannot understand or challenge the reasoning behind an AI-generated decision, their right to a fair trial is effectively compromised.

To mitigate these risks, rigorous oversight mechanisms must be established. These include:

Algorithmic Auditing: Regular audits to ensure AI systems operate in compliance with legal and ethical standards.
Bias Mitigation: Developing and implementing strategies to identify and address biases in training data and algorithms.
Transparency Requirements: Mandating that AI systems provide clear and understandable explanations for their decisions.

---

[15] Mittelstadt et al. (2016), pp. 851–874.

[16] Wachter et al. (2017), pp. 76–99.

[17] https://www.astonbond.co.uk/british-judge-used-chat-gpd-for-case-ruling/.

However, oversight alone is insufficient without robust accountability frameworks. Who is responsible when an AI system makes an error? The programmer, the vendor, or the human operator? Resolving these questions requires a comprehensive regulatory framework that addresses the unique challenges posed by AI.[16]

5 Elements of Judicial Practice Using Digitalization and Artificial Intelligence

The evolution of contemporary society surprises even the people who actively participate in social development. The implication in daily life of the "binary" language, which underpins the evolution of the computer, 40 years ago, has become a necessity today with a professional or social media addiction of people to digitized information technology.

In the beginning, the computer was mainly used for technical editing and script records of databases. In the field of justice, digital technologies bring an evolution in the activity of the judge. In the beginning, an information base composed of printed official journals, legal treatises, and printed books in the field of procedures and law itself was used. Digital technologies make available to "judges" from the courts electronic books that update legal information in real time, called: "Benchbook". An electronic volume of the *Benchbook* type provides an overview of the legal procedure for a "judge" and is used during the hearing of cases as a guide in their resolution. The *Benchbook* is not a source of substantive law, but can be a procedural guide, being used in conjunction with the Codes of Civil or Criminal Procedure. A *Benchbook* contains documents related to the case and the relevant legal authority.

In our research, we found that some states have introduced online Benchbooks. In Vietnam, for example, the Supreme People's Court has such an online guide that updates in real time since 2006. The printed version is updated as laws change, or certain parts of the law text need to be amended or improved. These guidelines are used in several justice systems around the world. The United States Department of Justice has a criminal justice standards procedure for Special Court judges. The advantage of the artificial intelligence used lies in the fact that the procedures are updated in real time and the search criteria save time for the judge.

Now, the situation is evolving exponentially and there are states where electronic "justice" is being tested. In certain cases, litigations of lesser complexity, computer programs compile texts from electronic archives and relate them to cases like the one under trial, elaborating a verdict. The verdict is, however, subject to a preventive

[18] https://www.judges.org/news-and-info/most-judges-havent-tried-chatgpt-and-they-arent-impressed/.

control, made by a judge. We have mentioned in the daily news and the situation of a judge of the Court of Appeal of the United Kingdom,[17] Lord Justice, Colin Birss, who stated that the judgment was given based on the statement made by the ChatGPT software, an AI chatbot in essence. The judge stated that the AI tool is useful, but it is very important to rely on AI if you are not familiar with the subject. The cases are as diverse as they are controversial or contested around the world. A July 2023 study/survey by *The National Judicial College*[18] shows:

1. 75% of the 332 judges surveyed have never tried using ChatGPT;
2. 7% of the 332 judges surveyed have tried using ChatGPT and do not like it;
3. 17% of the 332 judges surveyed have used ChatGPT and like it;

The study expands on the survey results and presents the differing views of the judges, including: *J. Jeremiah Mahoney, chief administrative law judge for the US Department of Housing and Urban Development, said he is now notifying new litigants that they are required to disclose to the Court* "any use of generative AI in all filings and … certify the corroboration of assertions of fact and law in such filings by identified human attorneys or paralegals"; *This was catchy, compared to another unnamed judge who accused AI of* "degrading our society/social connections"*;* "At the rate we're going," *the judge wrote,* "chatbots will replace judges and decisions will be made solely on the basis of algorithms." When people's lives hang in the balance, it's beyond scary to think that the human factor can be eliminated!" *Limiting AI to just* "research and other legal tasks," *as stated in the survey question,* "is only the beginning of a disastrous end," the judge predicted.

J. Jeremiah Mahoney, chief administrative law judge for the U.S. Department of Housing and Urban Development, said he now notifies new litigants that they are required to disclose to the Court "any use of generative AI in all filings and … certify corroboration of assertions of fact and law in such filings by identified human attorneys or paralegals."

"At the rate we're going," the judge wrote, "'chatbots' will replace judges and decisions will be made solely on algorithms. When people's lives hang in the balance, it is beyond scary to think that the human factor may be removed entirely!" Limiting AI to merely "research and other legal tasks," as mentioned in the poll question, "is only the beginning to a disastrous end," the judge predicted.

Now, 30 years ago, the computer with artificial intelligence tools is shyly entering the legal professional societies. Nowadays, professional activities are overwhelmed by computer dependence and digitized information technology. Some professions are more dependent on artificial intelligence that they use in a more advanced form, and other professional activities are less dependent. Activities in the field of legal sciences have a lower dependence on the computerized society based on artificial intelligence. At a first analysis, we are tempted to say that "artificial intelligence" cannot replace the *legal professional*, but reality and the evolution of society contradict this statement. The evolution of artificial intelligence has reached the point where the "output" is beyond any human intelligence. In practical terms, artificial intelligence compiles not only texts and ideas, but also legal arguments, having at its disposal a huge database on which humanity itself has transferred classical texts into digital texts. We can say that *artificial intelligence* has access to the *collective memory of humanity* with the possibility of multi-criteria search. Also, the court based on digitalization has available online open sources and in conjunction with the social control software "a priori" and "a posteriori" exercised by the authorities through digitalization provide elements to support the decision/judgment in more detail and with more arguments. Of course, a technical sentence based on evidence collected from the Internet of Things can be a profound miscarriage of justice. Digital technology allows everything, including tampering with evidence by creating videos of false actions where the subject of law was not at the scene of the crime, also the performance of voice synthesizers allows texts to be attributed to subjects of law who never said what was heard in the digital file. Likewise, texts, communications, documents that overturn reality and the burden of proof can be substituted and replaced.

Recently, the software that compiles and composes value judgments, ChatGPT, is revolutionizing the whole society. The software uses *collective memory* information from virtual space and issues its own value judgments that humans take as truth value. This "truth" leads us to a social non-value, extremely dangerous for legal truth. Based on the elements presented above, we believe that the justice of the future will face many more problems than now. If right now the key to justice is to answer the situation: "guilty" or "innocent", "true" or "false", the future will be uncertain.

Artificial intelligence can overturn facts and evidence, creating new realities with asserted truth value. AI can easily manipulate evidence and mislead the judge, especially if witness evidence and forensic expertise are eliminated or undervalued. At this point, we assert that forensic science and the institution of forensic expertise need to update their procedures on new challenges.

In our argument we will state: *How to trust an electronic judge*?

Let's imagine what it would be like to plead in front of artificial intelligence, i.e. a computer, and dismantle the accusations of opposing parties in defense of your client's interests? The accusations will be based in the indictment on the basis of systematized evidence from sources coming from the artificial intelligence database, as follows: (a) telephone conversations and audio/video/text messages sent by the parties through the parties' social media; (b) images from ubiquitous surveillance cameras with facial and retina recognition; (c) exact and real-time routes processed by the location application software; (d) biological, alcohol/narcotics and DNA samples taken and processed in real time and with increased accuracy.

If we ask ourselves:

> What will it be like to be investigated and sent to court to be tried by work units with prosecutor and judge duties whose decisions are based on artificial intelligence?

At this moment, we have one certainty: The space of "Artificial Intelligence" is introduced into everyday life and society has moved from "tolerance" to "trust" in artificial intelligence. We trust, consciously or not, in computer programs for different social and economic segments: Medicine, Transport, Military Activities, Logistics, etc. The question arises: How will trust be manifested when the software decides for us and for our relatives or loved ones without considering the context and the social reality on the ground?

With specific reference to the professions in the field of *Legal Sciences* and *Legal Sociology* with all their ramifications and interdependencies, we must consider in the challenge of the future: integration in the progress and evolution of society the extraordinary ability of software to learn continuously and adapt through self-learning. Basically, the performance of artificial intelligence cannot be measured in our classical system of understanding things and phenomena. The decision developed through digitized processes is based on a vast database of information to which is added a speed of processing, analysis, synthesis, and elaboration of the response that is amazing for humans. Within seconds, we turn to internet search and get selective answers. The reaction speed seems normal, as we have a rhythm to search for information on the Internet. At no point do we analyze what is behind it? How many texts and situations or video files has the software used identified and researched so that we can receive the respective results in a few seconds. Thus, we can have an overview of the processing power of digital technology through ordinary computers, which are based on a language built in bits. There are also supercomputers that use qbits, or quantum bits, which have exponential processing power.[19]

Our work does not have the role of providing solutions through formulated conclusions, but we consider it to be a point of reference and starting point for new research horizons in the science of law. This research must start from the realities of the moment, the influences of digitized processes in society and justice, as well as the opportunities in relation to the systemic risks of the influence of artificial intelligence.

We are discussing potential artificial intelligence applications that can be used in the future for judicial procedures!

5.1 The Judge and Artificial Intelligence

In the future, the institution of law will have two judgment coordinates. The first coordinate is the judge as a human factor, helped in the judgment decision by artificial intelligence, which will act as a judge's assistant. The multitude of information in the virtual space will be of real use for a fair judgment, since the act itself will refer to the legal texts, to similar cases and existing circumstances, on which the wisdom of the human judge will allow a good decision. The second coordinate is the decision given by the software (computer program), which is based exclusively on search algorithms, on the digitized collective memory, defined as Big Data. For a correct correlative report: *Human judgment vs. technical judgment generated by the big database* (BIG DATA) we will define in our material the future IT judge "judging data unit". The evolution of the institution of the Judge. Over time, the

[19] https://ro.wikipedia.org/wiki/Calculator_quantic.

institution of the judge went through a series of phrases that transformed the attribute from the FATHER OF THE FAMILY (pater familias)—THE VILLAGE OLDMAN (THE COUNCIL OF THE ELDERLY)—JUDGE. The first sentences applied were based on a "LIVING LAW" with unwritten collective norms, transmitted by word of mouth to contemporaries and future generations. These unwritten rules were constituted in human information stores at the level of the brain and were stored with age. The elder in the social group of the community was the bearer of essential information and gained the respect of the community who accepted his judgment. With the passage of time, we witness the transfer of human knowledge about the world on written support through symbols then texts written in stone or wood and then on paper. The wisdom accumulated from the accuracy of information transmitted and preserved on written sports becomes exponential as "many" contributed to a "common database" in volumes of written books (incunabula) or printed on paper, stored in libraries. Trust in the act of justice has become more acceptable through the memory of humanity stored in libraries.

The act of justice is brought to perfection through specific legal RULES, correlated with the needs and developments of society and elaborated within reasonable terms for the correction of social acts and facts. However, serious judicial errors are sometimes made. We observe specific situations in which some people involved in the act of justice (judges, prosecutors, lawyers) have a low morality and nevertheless carry out the act of justice. Sometimes we also observe a deficient, inconsistent act of justice.

Let's give an example: The same cause of litigation in the same Court, the legal subjects receive diametrically opposite solutions through Court Sentences. Judicial practice is often non-unitary. Litigants, however, trust and accept the solution of "justice" received through court decisions.

Let's discuss these elements by introducing the future judge into the scheme, which we will define as "judging data unit". The basis of the judgment will be the algorithm created by the human mind (the computer scientist with the help of the legal specialist) and the fundamental legal norms introduced in the program (software). The immensity of information and cases constitutes a basis for analysis that will allow a more correctly substantiated Decision, from a technical point of view, than in the classic system. The obvious disadvantage is that it cannot be applied in all cases, the disappearance of the emotional factor can influence the sentence to be more discussed and not accepted in all cases.

[20] IBM - International Business Machines, is an American corporation producing advanced technology. The company is headquartered in Armonk, New York (www.ibm.com).

[21] Watson is a computer system with artificial intelligence, capable of answering questions posed in natural language. It was developed through the DeepQA - IBM project by a research team led by David Ferrucci. Watson was named after IBM's first president, Thomas J. Watson.

There is a program (software) created by IBM,[20] called WATSON.[21] This general culture software has achieved the feat of answering any question generated by intellect. Watson understands natural language, human-style communication, and can understand both the intent of the person asking and the context in which the question was asked.[22] His answer is based on the relevance and rationale of the facts pleaded. Let's imagine the litigation resolved by the "data unit that judges" which responds correlatively to the pleas generated by "parties through lawyers' representations". In the analysis of the case, the judging unit has behind it a huge database with access to open information sources, from other databases stored on the server or Blockchain.[23] Meanwhile, software such as Chat GPT provides legal arguments for judgments and court sentences with generally valid texts, which do not consider the particularities of the case, that is, of the matter under trial.

What Is Blockchain?
A Blockchain is an immutable serial record of data that is distributed and managed by a group of computers.

By allowing digital information to be shared but not copied, Blockchain technology has created the backbone of a new kind of internet. Originally designed for the digital currency, Bitcoin, the tech community has found other potential uses for this technology.

The judgment of the future in the act of justice carried out on artificial intelligence, which is based on the res judicata "cases", will probably be sustainable and more easily assimilated by the legal system in Great Britain. The English system can more easily assimilate the reasoning of such sentences delivered by artificial intelligence technologies with greater accuracy because it is based on cases and precedent. The judged case will refer to the evolution of the facts and cases in history, the similarity of the case, previous decisions on similar cases, in which the supremacy of the law will have greater accuracy through the analyzed database.

If we refer to the modern legal systems based on the Constitution, the diversity is quite large and different. This aspect reduces the application of a common denominator of database work. The constitutions of the states being diverse under the local political spectrum, in change, the guarantees of the state are different from state to state. We have legal norms under the political spectrum of frequent change with correlative implications in the application of coercive sanctions for compliance with

[22] https://www.contributors.ro/era-sistemelor-cognitive-inteligen%C8%9Ba-artificiala-big-data/#_edn2.

[23] https://blockgeeks.com.

the law! The "judgment" carried out by Artificial Intelligence will not be able to respond to the factors that are always changing due to the causes of social evolution, human evolution, economic evolution. Legal truth will be increasingly individualized from social truth.

Let's imagine an AI unit trial for a case based on *heresy*[24] or a case against the idea of civil partnership!!! Artificial intelligence based on historical data would give a verdict contrary to accepted political developments in certain areas of the world.

At this moment "human justice" intervenes, adding to the letter and spirit of the law benchmarks of the reason to "be" and "not to be" in a certain space and time.

The institution of the "Prosecutor" as an artificial intelligence unit of the future.

The function of the Prosecutor, guarantor of the observance of the law and the protection of the fundamental rights of the individual against the aggression of third parties, cannot be reduced to passive actions, only of interpreting the facts through theoretical documentation from the database. Artificial intelligence reduces the legal experiment to an "a posteriori" interpretation of facts based on documentation and less on causality and motivation of the perpetrator. Lacking reason, the Softs cannot integrate emotion and discernment alongside history and precedent. The information in: record creates the profile of the individual, but it is not enough.

The prosecutor, although he sometimes has human weaknesses and relative morality, can sometimes show a lack of interest and training, but he cannot be replaced by artificial intelligence, because he "accuses"! One cannot imagine a prosecution system based on the record of artificial information. Let's not forget that the system is based on open sources, and everyone writes what they want, sometimes unverified, or maliciously directed at their peers. The artificial intelligence system cannot discern information from misinformation. The classic, current, system of control of the act of justice allows a censorship of deviations. An inhumane system based on technological justice puts the legitimate interest, the interest of MAN, on the back burner.

5.2 The "Notary" Institution

The job of NOTARY derives from the activity of the official of NOTA (lat. Notarius). The notary is the public official charged with authenticating legal documents, legalizing signatures, issuing legalized copies, certificates, etc.

The present, based on artificial intelligence technologies, presents systems based on trust and not on the guarantee of states that people turn to for the preservation of values. We have parallel banking systems guaranteed by the state by issuing crypto currency that the population trusts. Chains of trust are created through cyber security. In these chains of trust given by the encryption of information, the state does not intervene, but the citizen has the certainty of authenticity.

Security of authenticated documents. The electronic system is based on issuing two encryption keys, one public and one private. Extrapolating: a document encrypted by a person with the private key that keeps it secret can be read with another public decryption encryption key. The public key can be transmitted by the person who encrypts, but it cannot be modified or re-encrypted. The electronic signature applied by the issuer/owner absolutely confirms and guarantees the authenticity of the document. The document cannot be changed or forged by anyone. It is an absolute guarantee.

In the logic of using artificial intelligence for notary activities, the following questions arise:

1. *How do we sign a sales purchase agreement?*

Both the seller and the buyer sign with private keys. Everyone's public key can be shared with anyone interested in viewing the parties' will. Decryption is practically impossible, technologically.

> The document computer generates a number consisting of 100 digits. These digits are encrypted by mathematical algorithm generated by the private key. The document will have an associated Hash identifier that gives it an IRREVOCABLE characteristic. A transaction hash usually looks like a random set of letters and numbers.

2. *Where are the documents stored?*

They can be stored at the state level, but also in private archiving systems. The technology of spreading information through Blockchain, encrypted, described above, makes it impossible to falsify and modify the agreed and signed document. Safety is universal and almost total.

3. *What are the disadvantages and risks*?

The disadvantages are given by the existence of the computer, the power supply. The risks boil down to the loss of the numbers that form the encryption "private key".

[24] Heresies (Gr. hairesis and Lat. haeresis <=>option, choice) are a historical-religious and theological term that designates a system of thought or beliefs contrary to a dominant system (www.wikipedia.org).

5.3 *The "Lawyer" Institution in the Digital Environment*

Digitized database, unconditional access to information helps the legal profession in building pleadings. There is a current of opinion that claims that computer systems can generate: subpoenas, written conclusions, notes, only based on the parameters entered the program by the litigious parties. It is an assumption regarding the legal profession that is based on simplifying their obligations. Although it seems simple, the lawyer profession at first glance may undergo transformations, but we believe that it is the last one to disappear from the judicial architecture.

We believe that the justice act can be modernized. The judiciary may undergo profound transformations. A first transformation will occur by translating the act of justice from the judiciary to alternative mediation and arbitration systems. A second transformation of the future of justice will probably be achieved through the creation of IT platforms with complex databases! These "electronic justice units" that the lawyers of the parties will plead with arguments, and the artificial intelligence system answers according to the Watson software system that currently has problems answering questions that have short clues and contain only a few words. The software, Watson, has access, without an INTERNET connection, to over 200 million pages of structured and unstructured content totaling over 4 Terabytes of disk storage, including the full text of the Wikipedia website.

6 Conclusion: Augmentation, Not Replacement

The transition from a classic society to a digital society cannot be disputed. It is an administrative solution desired and accepted by society.

The influence of artificial intelligence from a "social and professional partner" operational support manifests itself in many sectors of professional activity, but also in the lives of private individuals (see the ALEXA system).

Many professions use artificial intelligence that robots the activities, until recently, exclusively dedicated to humans. In a relatively short time horizon, artificial intelligence can take over absolutely all human activities. At the high-level meeting held at Bletchley Park in north London, where policy makers and entrepreneurs from the leading digital technology companies met and recognized that without concerted action to temper the development of artificial intelligence, this becomes a real danger for humanity. The danger lies in the social control over people and the fact that they lose their social definition, professional skills, desires, and aspirations to be someone and do something. The G7 agreed on a code of conduct for artificial intelligence (AI) developers. The leaders called on the European Union to speed up legislation, but pointed out that over-regulation can be harmful, especially in the face of competition from China and the United States. In the United Kingdom, political and business leaders gathered at the first global summit on AI safety, pledging to work together.[25]

In the legal field, the professions are assisted by artificial intelligence with a predilection for the support activities for the administration of justice (operational records, case records, facial recognition, lie detector, alcohol, and toxic breath tests, tracking through the global positioning system, expertise, evidence DNA, etc.). The act of justice carried out by the human factor, for the moment, cannot be replaced exclusively by "artificial intelligence" even if there are viable premises for some types of cases.

The act of justice will translate with a large weight towards amicable settlement systems: arbitration or mediation. Virtual platforms with large software and databases hosted on the BLOCKCHAIN system will ensure good historical documentation and increased security regarding content protection.

The fear of change also comes from the vulnerabilities of the system that can generate judicial errors in the absence of intellectual thinking, but also man in his decision generates errors with consequences, even if he later assumes them.

The Electronic Lawyer, the electronic Notary, the electronic Clerk, the Mediator, and the Arbitrator are professions to which Artificial Intelligence will be imposed, in time, but the electronic Prosecutor and Judge will have a harder time replacing the Man who contributes to the act of justice.

The integration of artificial intelligence into legal practice represents a pivotal moment in legal evolution that demands careful consideration and measured implementation. Our analysis demonstrates that transformative changes in legal practice succeed most when implemented gradually and with careful attention to both practical and ethical consideration as mentioned by our past legal scholars both to see if AI might fit in our current function of the judiciary and then to see how compatible and synergistic the two fields are.

Holmes's seminal work provides a foundational argument for our approach. In "The Path of the Law" (1897),[26] he argues: "The life of the law has not been logic; it has been experience." This observation directly supports our thesis for measured AI integration, as it emphasizes the importance of practical experience over theoretical possibilities. Holmes continues: "The law embodies the story of a nation's development through many centuries, and it cannot be dealt with as if it contained only the axioms and corollaries of a book of mathematics." This precisely aligns with our argument that AI integration must respect the experiential and human elements of legal practice.

However, when examining this argument against Pound's perspective in "The Spirit of the Common Law" (1921),[27] we find additional nuance. Pound asserts: "Law must be stable and yet it cannot stand still." *He elaborates that legal systems must* "respond intelligently to the needs of life in a changing society while

[25] https://www.hotnews.ro/stiri-international-26656807-viitorul-inteligentei-artificiale-liderii-mondiali-discuta-despre-riscuri-reglementare-colaborare.htm.

[26] Holmes (1897), pp. 457–478.

preserving the essential elements of the legal order." This dual requirement of stability and adaptability strengthens our framework for measured integration, though it somewhat challenges Holmes's more conservative approach.

Dworkin's concept of law as integrity, presented in "Law's Empire" (1986), offers crucial support for our position. He argues: "Law as integrity denies that statements of law are either backward-looking factual reports of conventionalism or forward-looking instrumental programs of legal pragmatism. It insists that legal claims are interpretive judgments and therefore combine backward- and forward-looking elements."[28] This integrated view perfectly supports our argument for gradual AI adoption while maintaining essential human oversight.

Reviewing these arguments against Susskind's more recent work in "Online Courts and the Future of Justice" (2019),[29] we find both validation and challenge. Susskind argues: "The time has come to think more imaginatively about ways of delivering justice." However, his enthusiasm for technological adoption needs to be tempered with Pasquale's warnings in "New Laws of Robotics" (2020): "Rather than asking what tasks currently performed by professionals can be automated by robots and AI, we should ask what tasks performed by machines should be complemented or replaced by human professionals."[30]

After reviewing these scholarly perspectives, I find our conclusion needs strengthening in two areas:

1. The emphasis on human oversight should be more explicitly tied to Dworkin's concept of interpretive judgment. This strengthens our argument for maintaining human involvement in legal decision-making while adopting AI tools.
2. We should incorporate Pound's dual requirement of stability and adaptability more explicitly in our framework for measured integration.

The path forward requires a careful balance between innovation and tradition, as articulated by our greatest legal minds. Following Dworkin's framework of law as an interpretive practice, we must ensure that AI integration enhances rather than replaces human legal judgment. This aligns with Pound's vision of legal evolution that maintains stability while adapting to social needs. The success of this integration will be measured not merely by efficiency gains, but by its contribution to what Rhode terms in "Access to Justice" (2004) as "effective access to legal services"—a system that is both technically advanced and fundamentally just.[31]

This revised conclusion more effectively ties our sources to our thesis while maintaining the argument for measured integration. The scholarly support is more

[27] Pound (1921).

[28] Dworkin (1986).

[29] Sunstein (2008).

[30] Pasquale (2020).

directly linked to specific aspects of our framework, strengthening the overall argument.

Fuller's perspective in "The Morality of Law" (1964)[32] provides a crucial foundation for our argument about measured AI integration. He states: "Law is the enterprise of subjecting human conduct to the governance of rules." His emphasis on the purposive nature of law supports our position that technological integration must serve legal principles rather than merely efficiency. Fuller's eight principles of legality, particularly the requirements that laws must be publicly promulgated and intelligible, raise important considerations about AI transparency and interpretability.

Calabresi's work "A Common Law for the Age of Statutes" (1982)[33] offers another valuable perspective. He argues: "The role of courts is not merely to interpret legislation but to maintain the consistency and contemporary relevance of the entire legal framework." This supports our argument for maintaining human oversight while suggesting a framework for how AI could assist in identifying legal obsolescence and inconsistencies.

Hart's distinction between primary and secondary rules in "The Concept of Law" (1961)[34] provides additional theoretical support. He notes: "The union of primary and secondary rules is at the center of a legal system." This framework suggests that while AI might effectively handle primary rules, secondary rules—those about how to recognize, change, and adjudicate laws—require human judgment and interpretation.

Unger's "The Critical Legal Studies Movement" (1986)[35] offers a challenging perspective that strengthens our argument by highlighting potential risks. He argues: "The fetishism of institutional arrangements and legal doctrine has repeatedly prevented the legal system from adapting to social needs." This warning about institutional rigidity supports our call for measured but definitive technological integration.

Integrating these perspectives with our earlier analysis, we can strengthen our conclusion with the following insights:

1. Fuller's emphasis on law's purposive nature suggests that AI integration must be evaluated not just on efficiency but on how well it serves fundamental legal principles.
2. Calabresi's framework for legal obsolescence provides a potential model for how AI could assist human judgment without replacing it.
3. Hart's distinction between primary and secondary rules offers a natural boundary for AI integration—suggesting areas where automation might be more or less appropriate.
4. Unger's critique reminds us that resistance to change can be as dangerous as hasty adoption.

[31] Rhode (2004).

[32] Fuller (1964).

These additional perspectives support our central thesis while providing more nuanced guidance for implementation. As MacCormick argues in "Rhetoric and the Rule of Law" (2005)[36]: "The rule of law requires that we maintain human judgment in legal decision-making while embracing tools that enhance our capacity for reasoned judgment."

This expanded scholarly foundation suggests that successful AI integration must:

1. Preserve the purposive nature of law (Fuller)
2. Maintain systematic coherence (Calabresi)
3. Respect the distinction between different types of legal rules (Hart)
4. Avoid both technological fetishism and institutional rigidity (Unger)
5. Enhance rather than replace human legal reasoning (MacCormick)

Website Source

http://www.asianlii.org/vn/other/benchbk/336-en.html (The first version of the Benchbook was from June 2006)
https://www.astonbond.co.uk/british-judge-used-chat-gpd-for-case-ruling/,
https://www.judges.org/news-and-info/most-judges-havent-tried-chatgpt-and-they-arent-impressed/
https://ro.wikipedia.org/wiki/Calculator_quantic
www.ibm.com
https://www.contributors.ro/era-sistemelor-cognitive-inteligen%C8%9Ba-artificiala-big-data/#_edn2
https://blockgeeks.com
www.wikipedia.org
https://www.hotnews.ro/stiri-international-26656807-viitorul-inteligentei-artificiale-liderii-mondiali-discuta-despre-riscuri-reglementare-colaborare.htm

[33] Calabresi (1982).
[34] Hart (1961).
[35] Unger (1986).
[36] MacCormick (2005).

References

Literature

Angwin J, Larson J, Mattu S, Kirchner L (2016) Machine Bias. ProPublica
Barocas S, Hardt M, Narayanan A (2019) Fairness and machine learning. MIT Press
Binns R (2018) Fairness in machine learning: lessons from political philosophy. In: Proceedings of the 2021 ACM Conference on Fairness, Accountability, and Transparency, 5(1)
Brown L (2020) Accuracy in legal transcriptions: a historical analysis. Proced Just Quart 12(2)
Calabresi G (1982) A common law for the age of statutes. Harvard University Press
Dworkin R (1986) Law's empire. Harvard University Press
Fuller L (1978) Human interaction and the law. J Leg Stud 7(3)
Fuller LL (1964) The morality of law. Yale University Press
Gasser U, Almeida V (2017) A layered model for AI governance. IEEE Internet Comput 21(6)
Hart HLA (1961) The concept of law. Oxford University Press
Hart HLA (1994) The concept of law, 2nd edn. Oxford University Press
Holmes OW (1897) The path of the law. Harv Law Rev 10(8)
Johnson P (2019) Algorithmic bias in legal databases. Int J Law Technol 21(4)
MacCormick N (2005) Rhetoric and the rule of law. Oxford University Press
Miller H (2018) The impact of written advocacy on appellate decisions. Appellate Law Rev 8(1)
Mittelstadt B, Allo P, Taddeo M, Wachter S, Floridi L (2016) The ethics of algorithms. Sci Eng Ethics
Pasquale F (2020) New laws of robotics: defending human expertise in the age of AI. Harvard University Press
Perry S (2006) Hart's methodological positivism. Legal Theory 12(4)
Pound R (1921) The Spirit of the common law. Marshall Jones Company
Rawls J (1971) A theory of justice. Harvard University Press, Cambridge
Rhode DL (2004) Access to justice. Oxford University Press
Richardson R, Schultz J, Crawford K (2019) Dirty data, bad predictions. Northwest J Technol Intellect Prop 16(3)
Smith J, Taylor R (2017) The efficiency gains of digital legal research. J Legal Technol Stud 15(3)
Sunstein CR (2008) Laws of fear: beyond the precautionary principle. Cambridge University Press
Susskind R (2017) Tomorrow's lawyers: an introduction to your future, 2nd edn. Oxford University Press
Unger RM (1986) The critical legal studies movement. Harvard University Press
Wachter S, Mittelstadt B, Floridi L (2017) Why a right to explanation of automated decision-making does not exist in the general data protection regulation. In: International Data Privacy Law, ACM Conference on Fairness, Accountability, and Transparency, 5(1)

Violation of the Principles of Judicial Ethics-Ground for the Disciplinary Responsibility of Judges

Andra Puran and Ramona Duminică

Abstract Compliance with the principles of professional ethics by judges strengthens public trust in the justice system of a state and allows a better understanding of the role the judge has in society. However, the magistrate's position in society does not exempt him from any form of legal liability in the event of a violation of the law.

1 Introduction

The role of the magistrate in a state of law is extremely important, given that judges and prosecutors have powers that no other constitutional or public authority has.

In order to achieve these competences, but also to gain public trust, magistrates must be guided in their activity by the norms of ethics and morals, norms that reflect the attitude, character or fundamental values specific to the profession, but also the norms of conduct and natural coexistence, generally accepted in a certain society, that establishes the standards of fairness, honesty, valid for any human being, regardless of profession.

The provisions regarding the ethical conduct of magistrates, both at the national and international level, are general and have a wide scope, as they derive from the principles of the state of law (related to the right to a fair trial), from the ethical principles (the pursuit of the good) and from the principles of the administration of justice in a democratic society (responsibility).[1] Thus, the magistrate must act in accordance with a code of conduct that includes the principles of judicial ethics—minimum standards of professional conduct.

[1] Copoeru (coordinator) et al. (2017), p. 6.

A. Puran (✉) · R. Duminică
The National University of Science and Technology POLITEHNICA Bucharest, Pitești University Centre, Faculty of Economic Sciences and Law, Bucharest, Romania

C. Hermida del Llano (ed.), *The Freedom of Expression for Judges in the Sphere of the Judicial Ethics*, Ius Gentium: Comparative Perspectives on Law and Justice 129, https://doi.org/10.1007/978-3-032-06504-9_6

For the proper functioning of a society governed by the principles of the state of law, magistrates must be independent and impartial,[2] taking into account also Article 6 of the European Convention on Human Rights, which states that "Every person has the right to a fair trial, in a public manner and within a reasonable time, by an independent and impartial court established by law (...)".

Also, the UN Basic Principles regarding the Independence of Justice stipulate that: "the independence of justice must be guaranteed by the state and enshrined by the Constitution or national laws. It is the duty of all governments and other institutions to respect the independence of justice."

In the European Charter on the Statute of Judges, Article 1, General Principles, it is stipulated that: "The Statute of Judges seeks to ensure the competence, independence and impartiality that every person legitimately expects from the courts and from every judge to whom it is entrusted the defense of his rights (...)."

At the level of national legislation, Article 3 of the Code of Ethics of Judges and Prosecutors[3] provides that: "Judges and prosecutors are obliged to defend the independence of justice"[4] and that: "Judges and prosecutors must exercise their function with objectivity and impartiality, having as the sole basis the law, without giving in to pressures and influences of any kind."[5]

The independence of magistrates defines the relationship that justice has with the other powers or institutions of the state, based on the principle of separation and balance of power in the state, not being a privilege but a responsibility that the magistrate has, a responsibility that allows him to resolve disputes without external influences.

Impartiality is an attitude that belongs to the magistrate's conscience and is closely related to independence.

However, the magistrate's position in society does not exempt him from any form of legal liability in the event of violation of the law. Among all forms of legal liability (civil, disciplinary, contraventional and criminal), we will stop our attention only on the disciplinary liability of judges, a matter of interest for the present paper.

2 The Facts That Constitute Disciplinary Misconduct Committed by Romanian Judges

The specificity of the disciplinary liability of judges emerges from the express regulation of the facts that constitute disciplinary misconducts, from the specific rules for triggering and executing the disciplinary procedure, from the competent

---

[2] For developments see Mitrofan (2023), pp. 242–249.

[3] *Code of Ethics for judges and prosecutors from 2005*, issued by the Superior Council of the Magistracy in Romania.

[4] Para. 1 of art. 3 of *The Code of Ethics of Judges and Prosecutors*.

[5] Para. 2 of art. 3 of *The Code of Ethics of Judges and Prosecutors*.

authority to order and carry out the disciplinary investigation as well as from the sanctions expressly provided for by the special law.

The legal liability of judges can be engaged based on the specific statute of this profession regulated by Law no. 303/2022.[6]

Unlike the old law in this domain,[7] which offered a more detailed regulation of disciplinary misconduct[8], providing that: "judges (...) are disciplinary responsible for deviations from official duties, as well as for facts that affect the prestige of justice", the current regulation[9] only provides that: "judges (...) are disciplinary responsible for committing, with guilt, the disciplinary misconducts provided by law".

In the framework of classic labor relations, arising from individual labor contracts, disciplinary misconduct is defined as "a deed related to work and which consists of an action or inaction committed culpably by the employee, through which he violated the legal norms, the internal regulation, the individual employment contract or the applicable collective employment contract, the orders and legal provisions of the hierarchical leaders".[10] However, this definition does not apply to the specific work relationships of judges, not being able to speak of the violation of contractual norms, since they do not conclude an employment contract.

From the current regulations regarding the disciplinary liability of judges, it appears that this form of liability is incident only in the case of committing disciplinary misconducts provided by law. Thus, in the absence of a legal definition, the disciplinary misconduct of magistrates was defined in the doctrine[11] as "his act of culpably violating the legal and regulatory norms that govern the magistrate's status and the activity of carrying out the act of justice".

The only ground for disciplinary liability is disciplinary misconduct, for the existence of which its constituent elements must be cumulatively met, namely: the object, the objective side, the subject and the subjective side. The causal link between the disciplinary misconduct and the harmful result produced by committing it must also be determined.

So, to be in the presence of disciplinary deviation, the action committed by the judge must sums up its building elements. If these elements are not met, the judge's disciplinary responsibility cannot operate. But there are also situations in which, although all the elements are met, the judge's actions are not considered deviations, resulting in the fact that he cannot be held responsible, missing the condition that the deed was committed with guilt, as the law regulates.[12]

---

[6] Law no. 303 of November 15, 2022 regarding the status of judges and prosecutors, published in the Official Gazette of Romania no. 1102 of November 16, 2022.

[7] Art. 98 para. 1 of Law 303/2004 repealed by Law 303/2022.

[8] See Puran and Drăghici (2016), pp. 269–273.

[9] Art. 270 para. 1 of Law 303/2022.

[10] Art. 247 para. 2 of the Labor Code - Law 53/2003 republished in the Official Gazette of Romania no. 345/18 May 2011.

[11] Popa (2007), p. 368.

[12] For development see Puran and Tolbaru (2017), pp. 39–42.

The object of disciplinary misconduct in the case of judges will be a specific one, consisting of service duties and social relations regarding the prestige of justice. Also, the subject is a qualified one, namely the judge.

As we have shown, the current regulation is limited only to listing the facts that constitute disciplinary misconducts for both judges and prosecutors[13]:

(a) violation of legal provisions regarding incompatibilities and prohibitions;
    Incompatibilities and prohibitions are provided by articles 227 to 234 of Law no. 303/2022.
(b) unworthy attitudes during work towards colleagues, other staff of the court or prosecutor's office where they work, judicial inspectors, lawyers, experts, witnesses, litigants or representatives of other institutions;

This disciplinary misconduct presupposes, from the objective side, the existence of an unworthy attitude towards one of the passive subjects expressly listed by the law, an attitude manifested during the exercise of service duties, and, from the subjective side, it presupposes that the respective attitudes are assumed by the judge consciously and willingly or accepted.[14]

Also, the disciplinary court (Superior Council of the Magistracy) stated that "undignified attitude" implies behavioral manifestations contrary to the standards of conduct established by laws and regulations in charge of magistrates. In this sense, the obligations imposed on magistrates to have relationships based on respect and good faith, to show decent and civilized behavior, to show calmness, patience and politeness in work relationships, as they resulted from the provisions of art. 4 para. (1) and art. 90 para. (2) from Law no. 303/2004 (maintained also in the current regulation in art. 4 par. (3) and art. 223 par. (2) of Law 303/2022), art. 5 para. (2) lit. b), lit. d) and letter e) from the Regulation of the courts.

(c) carrying out political activities or expressing political beliefs in public or during work;
(d) the unjustified refusal to receive the requests, conclusions, memoranda or documents submitted by the parties in the process;
(e) unjustified refusal to perform a service duty;
(f) non-compliance by the prosecutor with the orders of the hierarchically superior prosecutor, given in writing and in accordance with the law;
(g) failure to comply repeatedly and for imputable reasons with the legal provisions regarding the resolution of cases with celerity or repeated delay in carrying out the works, for imputable reasons;

From the objective point of view, it was stated that this disciplinary misconduct involves either a repeated action or an inaction that extends over a certain period of time, imputable to the magistrate and having as a consequence the failure to comply

[13] Art. 271 of Law 303/2022.

[14] Decision 21/2021 of February 1, 2021 of the High Court of Cassation and Justice, point 53, www.scj.ro.

with the professional duty to resolve cases with celerity, within the term provided by law or within a reasonable period of time, so that, in order to engage in disciplinary liability, it is necessary to prove both the existence of the culpable conduct and the imputable character of this conduct.[15]

In a case,[16] The High Court stated that in the analysis of disciplinary liability, the appellant's assertions regarding the existence of some objective and subjective causes to remove the imputable nature of the delays in drafting cannot receive the exclusive relevance granted by the defendant, as it is necessary for them to be examined by reporting to the purpose of the judicial act and from the perspective of respecting the legitimate rights of the parties to any litigation, namely to know within the legal term or, in the last instance, within a reasonable term, the considerations that substantiate the solution pronounced in the case in order to be able to decide regarding the exercise of appeals, as well as from the perspective of the presumed legitimate interest in the resolution with celerity of disputes submitted to the courts to be solved.

(h) non-compliance with the duty to abstain when the judge or prosecutor knows that exist one of the causes provided by law for his abstention, as well as the formulation of repeated and unjustified requests for abstention;

In the jurisprudence of the High Court,[17] it was stated that the existence of a disciplinary notice or a criminal complaint does not *eo ipso* represent a cause of incompatibility, since such a hypothesis presents the risk of turning into a way by which the parties could determine the removal of the magistrate to whom it is allocated the cause.

(i) failure to respect the secrecy of the deliberations or the confidentiality of works of this nature, as well as other information of the same nature that he became aware of in the exercise of his duties, except for those of public interest, under the law;

Through Decision 171 of 10 May 2021 of the High Court,[18] it was stated that the violation of this obligation is achieved by bringing to the knowledge of persons who are not qualified or to the public knowledge of data or information contained in confidential works, with the consequences of deterioration of public opinion's trust and respect for the position of magistrate, resulting in damage to the image and prestige of justice as a whole.

(j) unmotivated absences from work, repeatedly or which directly affect the activity of the court or the prosecutor's office;
(k) interference in the activity of another judge or prosecutor;

[15] Decision 139 of May 23, 2022 of the High Court of Cassation and Justice, www.scj.ro.

[16] Decision 184 of September, 26, 2022, www.scj.ro.

[17] Decision no. 23/2021, www.scj.ro.

[18] www.scj.ro.

(l) unjustified non-compliance with provisions or decisions of an administrative nature, ordered in accordance with the law by the head of the court or the prosecutor's office or other obligations of an administrative nature provided for by law or regulations;
(m) using the position held to obtain favorable treatment from the authorities or interventions for the settlement of requests, claiming or accepting the settlement of personal interests or those of family members or other persons, otherwise than within the limits of the legally regulated framework for all citizens;
(n) non-compliance with the provisions regarding the random distribution of cases;
(o) obstructing the activity of judicial inspectors, by any means;
(p) participating directly or through intermediaries in pyramid-type games, games of chance or investment systems for which the transparency of the funds is not ensured;
(q) failure to draft or sign court decisions or judicial acts of the prosecutor, for imputable reasons, within the terms provided by law;

It was stated in the practice of the High Court[19] that from the objective point of view, the violation consists in not fulfilling the obligation to draft court decisions within the terms provided by law, and from the subjective point of view, these facts must be imputable to the magistrate, excluding any case that exonerates him of disciplinary responsibility. At the same time, from the perspective of the subjective side, the High Court found, in agreement with the disciplinary court, that, from the way in which the appellant understood to manage her entire activity and to apply the legal provisions that were required for the drafting of the pronounced decisions, the mental attitude of her was that of predicting the results of his deeds, the production of which, even if she did not follow it, she accepted it.

(r) the use of inappropriate expressions in court decisions or the prosecutor's judicial acts, the total lack of motivation or the motivation clearly contrary to legal reasoning, likely to affect the prestige of justice or the dignity of the position of judge or prosecutor;
(s) exercising the function in bad faith or gross negligence.

Law 303/2022 explains in article 272 when bad faith and gross negligence are considered to exist, not leaving these concepts to be subjectively interpreted by the bodies that carry out the disciplinary investigation.[20]

Thus, there is bad faith when the judge or prosecutor knowingly violates the rules of material or procedural law, pursuing or accepting the injury of a person. Also, there is gross negligence when the judge or prosecutor disregards out of fault, in a serious, undoubted and inexcusable way, the norms of material or procedural law.

---

[19] Decision no. 230 of October, 24, 2022, www.scj.ro.

[20] For the analysis of the disciplinary procedure and the bodies competent to carry out the disciplinary investigation, see Puran and Pîrvu (2018), pp. 197–207.

Regarding the disciplinary misconduct consisting in "exercising the function with gross negligence", in the jurisprudence[21] in the matter of disciplinary liability of judges and prosecutors, it was stated that this misconduct presupposes the cumulative fulfillment of the following conditions:

- in the exercise of the function, the magistrate violates material or procedural law norms;
- violation of the rules to be caused by fault. Fault is defined uniformly by the Romanian legislator in both civil (art. 16 para. (3) Civil Code) and criminal matters (art. 16 para. (4) Penal Code), as the attitude of the author of the deed, which is foresees the result of his deed, but does not accept it, considering without grounds that it will not occur, or does not foresee the result of the deed, although he should have foreseen it. For the disciplinary offense in question, the form of fault imposed by law is gross negligence (culpa lata), in the sense that even the least informed person, with a minimum of diligence, would have foreseen the result of his deed;
- the violation of legal norms may generate serious consequences;
- the violation must be obvious, unquestionable, without justification, in clear contradiction with the legal norm. In order to maintain the existence of gross negligence, it is necessary that the violation concerns an imperative rule of law or resides in the adoption of a decision outside of any rules of law or based on a macroscopic error, for which a reasonable observer (person informed and in good faith) cannot find a justification.

3 Disciplinary Sanctions Applicable to Romanian Judges

According to art. 273 para. 1 of Law 303/2022, the disciplinary sanctions that can be applied to judges and prosecutors, proportional to the seriousness of the misconducts, are:

(a) the warning;
(b) reduction of the gross monthly allowance by up to 25% for a period of up to one year;
(c) disciplinary transfer for an effective period of one to three years to another court or to another prosecutor's office, even of an immediately lower level;
(d) relegation in professional rank;
(e) suspension from the position for a period of up to 6 months;
(f) exclusion from the magistracy.

[21] High Court of Cassation and Justice: Decision no. 48 of February 27, 2017, Decision no. 130 of April 24, 2017, Decision no. 173 of October 5, 2020, Decision no. 21/2021, www.scj.ro.

Through the new regulation of Law 303/2022, the legislator enlarged disciplinary sanctions both in terms of the periods for which they can be ordered and the amount of income reductions, also introducing the sanction of demotion in professional rank.

We note that there are some similarities between these specific sanctions and common law sanctions, such as the warning sanction, the sanction of reducing the gross monthly employment allowance and the most serious sanction, exclusion from the magistracy. As in common law, also in the case of judges, the principle of the uniqueness of the sanction is applied, not being able to order more than one sanction for the same deed that constitutes a disciplinary misconduct.

When applying disciplinary sanctions, the fundamental principle of proportionality must be respected, taking into account several aspects: the seriousness of the disciplinary misconduct committed and its consequences, the causes that determined its commission, the concrete circumstances in which the misconduct was committed, the degree of guilt, the personal circumstances of the investigated person, the general behavior during the service and the existence in the antecedents of the investigated person of other disciplinary sanctions for which the deletion did not take place.[22]

The warning is a sanction with a predominantly moral character, which does not directly imply a material consequence that the judge bears. Unlike the common law where it is specified that the warning must be given in writing, in the case of this sanction provided by Law no. 303/2022 does not provide for this aspect. We assume in this case that the warning can take either a written form or a verbal one. We consider, for logical reasons, that it would be preferable for the warning to take a written form as in the common law. Also, if in labor law the warning can be applied without carrying out the mandatory preliminary investigation, in the case of magistrates, the legislator did not provide for this aspect, as the preliminary investigation is mandatory for all sanctions.

The reduction of the gross monthly allowance by up to 25% for a period of up to one year has a predominantly material character, primarily affecting the judge's income. Regarding the limits of the application of this sanction, as in common law, the legal norms establish both the amount of the reduction and the period for which the disciplinary measure can be ordered. Unlike common law, where in the case of a reduction of the basic salary, the Labor Code establishes both lower and upper limits for the amount of the reduction and for the period during which the reduction can be ordered, Law no. 303/2022 only sets the maximum limits for the two coordinates. Thus, the authority ordering the measure can opt for the reduction of the gross monthly allowance by any percentage, but without exceeding the maximum imposed by law of 25%. Also, the period for which this measure can be ordered can be of any length, without exceeding 1 year. Therefore, the Superior Council of Magistracy has more freedom in establishing this measure than the employer has under common law.

The sanction of disciplinary transfer for a period of one to three years to another court for judges or to another prosecutor's office can be ordered either at a court of

[22] Art. 278, paragraph, 1, letter c) from Law 303/2022.

the same level or at a court of an immediately lower level. In the case of judges from the High Court of Cassation and Justice, this sanction can only be ordered at an immediately lower court.

In the case of this disciplinary sanction, the legislator has established both the minimum and the maximum period for which the measure can be imposed, leaving it up to the Superior Council of Magistracy to determine the specific period, considering the circumstances of the offense.

Judges can obtain a professional degree following promotion competitions. Thus, as a disciplinary sanction, the judge who committed a disciplinary misconduct may be demoted in professional rank.

Another sanction that can be applied is the sanction of suspension from position for a period of up to 6 months. This sanction affects the judge both morally and materially, considering that for a maximum period of 6 months the employment relationships will be suspended. After the end of the period for which the disciplinary measure of suspension was disposed, the judge will automatically return to the position held.

The most serious measure that can be disposed in the event that the judge commits one or more disciplinary misconducts is exclusion from the magistracy. This disciplinary measure is the only one of its kind that is disposed for an indefinite period, not being a temporary nature of the measure as in the case of those stated previously. This sanction can be applied for committing a serious misconduct, such as to make it "impossible and intolerable" to remain in the position of magistrate.[23]

The High Court of Cassation and Justice[24] stated that the disciplinary sanctioning of magistrates has a double purpose, on the one hand, to determine the correction of the magistrate who committed a disciplinary act and, on the other hand, to constitute a mean of prevention, both for the sanctioned magistrate, as well as for all magistrates.

The new regulation introduces the deletion of disciplinary sanctions within 3 years from the date of enforcement, if a new disciplinary sanction is not applied to the judge in this regard. It was absurd for this institution not to find its applicability also within the special employment relationships of judges, considering that it was introduced within the classic employment relationships, being provided for by the Labor Code. Thus, the old regulation from art. 100 of Law 303/2004 was criticized as unconstitutional. The Constitutional Court of Romania admitted the exception of unconstitutionality,[25] noting that the provisions of art. 100 of Law no. 303/2004 on the status of judges and prosecutors were constitutional only to the extent that the disciplinary sanction of exclusion from the magistracy did not have a permanent effect.

---

[23] Diaconu (2007), p. 247.

[24] Decision no. 83 of April 12, 2022, www.scj.ro.

[25] Decision of the Constitutional Court no. 363 of June 8, 2022, published in the Official Gazette of Romania no. 731 of July 20, 2022.

The author of the exception claimed the unconstitutionality of the old regulation in the matter considering the non-existence in the content of Law no. 303/2004 of some provisions that establish certain deadlines after which the disciplinary sanctions applied to judges and prosecutors can be removed, with reference to the sanction of exclusion from the magistracy. The author of the exception claimed, in essence, that the absence of such provisions leads to the impossibility of accessing the profession of lawyer, considering that art. 14 lit. b) second thesis of Law no. 51/1995 on the organization and exercise of the profession of lawyer,[26] states that "it is unworthy to be a lawyer the one who (...) has committed serious disciplinary misconducts, sanctioned with the measure of exclusion from the profession, as a disciplinary sanction."

Through the mentioned Decision, the Court stated that "the perpetuity of this sanction serves a legitimate purpose, that of giving perpetuity to the prestige of the profession and the image of justice, the definitive effects of the sanction of exclusion from the magistracy strengthening the trust of the entire society in the independence, impartiality and effectiveness of justice. At the same time, the permanent effect of the mentioned sanction is appropriate to the purpose it proposes, being, in principle, an appropriate legal option, able to fulfill the legitimate goal pursued."

The Court also stated that the lack of regulation of a term in which the effects of this sanction shall cease constitutes an absolute and perpetual impediment in terms of the fundamental right to work and to freely choose a profession, established by art. 41 para. (1) of the Romanian Constitution.

Although the issue of a legislative omission was raised in the case, which would have brought into question the Constitutional Court's quality as a negative legislator, however, by virtue of its role as guarantor of the supremacy of the Constitution, the Court could not ignore the unconstitutionality flaw created precisely by this omission which generated the violation of the Constitution, through the lack of regulation, within the content of Law no. 303/2004, of a legal mechanism similar to erasure, existing in other normative acts that regulate the status of other professions, so the Constitutional Court emphasized the need to complete the criticized regulation and asked the legislator to consecrate the institution of deletion, after a certain period, of the disciplinary sanction of exclusion from the magistracy. Thus, the new regulation in the matter states the delition of disciplinary sanctions applicable to magistrates.

4 Conclusions

In a democratic society, governed by the principles of the state of law, judges play a very important role, exercising one of the three prerogatives of state power, more precisely the judicial power.

[26] Republished in the Official Monitor of Romania, Part I, no. 440 of May 24, 2018.

In exercising their profession, judges are required to comply with both legal norms and ethical and moral principles in order to ensure the independence and impartiality of justice, as well as its prestige.

In Romania, the status of judges acquired a new regulation through Law no. 303/2022. This normative act regulates the disciplinary liability of judges in all its aspects: facts that constitute disciplinary misconducts, specific rules for triggering and executing the disciplinary procedure, the competent authority to order and carry out the disciplinary investigation as well as the sanctions that can be applied.

The present study aimed to provide a perspective of the disciplinary misconducts that can be committed by judges and the sanctions that can be applied as a result of the culpable commission of these acts, also referring to aspects of jurisprudence in the field, but without caliming to have exhausted this subject.

References

Copoeru I (coordinator), Bert Maan, Iver Huitfeldt, Tron Gundersen (2017) Ghid practic de etică profesională pentru judecători şi procurori (Practical guide to professional ethics for judges and prosecutors). Bucharest

Diaconu C (2007) Management judiciar (Judicial Management). C.H. Beck, Bucharest

Mitrofan F (2023) Reflecting the principles of judicial independence and impartiality in doctrine and jurisprudence. In: Proceedings of the International Scientific Conference History, Culture, Citizenship in the European Union. In Memoriam Prof. Eugen Chelaru, 15th Edition, 26 May 2023, C.H. Beck, pp 242–249

Popa I (2007) Tratat privind profesia de magistrat în România (Treaty regarding the profession of magistrate in Romania). Universul Juridic, Bucharest

Puran A, Drăghici A (2016) Specifics of the misbehaviors of magistrates. Supplement of Valahia University Law Study, 269–273

Puran A, Pîrvu A (2018) Procedural aspects concerning the disciplinary investigation of judges and prosecutors. Supplement of Valahia University Law Study, 197–207

Puran A, Tolbaru C (2017) A short analysis of causes for disciplinary irresponsibility of the employees. J Law Public Adm III(5):39–42

Ethics and Integrity for Judges: Comparative Study with Other Public Professions in the Romanian Framework

Mihaela Miruna Tudorașcu

Abstract The present study will try to underline what a Romanian judge can or cannot do in his profession, especially in connection with the liberty of expression, how can this right interfere with the ethics and integrity of the profession and will follow a few other public professions to see if there are similarities or essential differences. This scientific paper will combine the legal aspects and the practical ones, also to answer some research questions, that will be asked in the introduction of the paper.

1 Introduction

Within the framework of the proposed theme there are a few questions that are raised in our minds, questions that we will try somehow to get answers to, during our research, even if during the time, there were rivers of words regarding this issue. Do the Romanian judges have the liberty of expression in the context of the professional frame? Are there limitations in connection with this right? What kind of liability are we talking about when this right is exceeded?

The content of the scientific paper will make a transition through conceptual aspects, and then through some actual practical issues to see the dynamic of this institution (the liberty of expression for the Romanian judges).

We will also make a comparative analysis with a few other professions to highlight the pluses and the minuses that exist in this fields regarding the magistrates.

M. M. Tudorașcu (✉)
The National University of Political Studies and Public Administration (SNSPA), Bucharest, Romania

University „1 Decemebrie 1918" of Alba Iulia, Alba Iulia, Romania

C. Hermida del Llano (ed.), *The Freedom of Expression for Judges in the Sphere of the Judicial Ethics*, Ius Gentium: Comparative Perspectives on Law and Justice 129, https://doi.org/10.1007/978-3-032-06504-9_7

2 Conceptual Aspects

Article 30 from the Romanian Constitution defines the liberty of expression:

> (1) Freedom of expression of thoughts, opinions, or beliefs, and freedom of any creation, by words, in writing, in pictures, by sounds or other means of communication in public are inviolable. (2) Any censorship shall be prohibited. (3) Freedom of the press also involves the free setting up of publications. (4) No publication shall be suppressed. (5) The law may impose upon the mass media the obligation to make public their financing source. (6) Freedom of expression shall not be prejudicial to the dignity, honour, privacy of a person, and to the right to one's own image.
>
> (7) Any defamation of the country and the nation, any instigation to a war of aggression, to national, racial, class or religious hatred, any incitement to discrimination, territorial separatism, or public violence, as well as any obscene conduct contrary to morality shall be prohibited by law. (8) Civil liability for any information or creation made public falls upon the publisher or producer, the author, the producer of the artistic performance, the owner of the copying facilities, radio, or television station, under the terms laid down by law. Indictable offences of the press shall be established by law.

The European Convention on Human Rights, in art. 10 precises that the right to freedom of expression belongs to all people. This right encompasses the freedom to have opinions and the freedom to receive and disseminate information or ideas across boundaries and without interference from the government. States may still impose licensing requirements on their societies of broadcasting, cinematographic, or television broadcasting businesses in accordance with this article. In a democratic society, certain formalities, conditions, restrictions, or penalties may apply to the exercise of certain freedoms that involve duties and responsibilities. These measures are necessary to protect national security, territorial integrity, or public safety, to protect public order and prevent crime, to protect one's own health or morals, to protect one's reputation or the rights of others, to prevent the disclosure of confidential information, or to ensure the authority and impartiality of the judiciary.

Art. 232 from the Law No 303 of 15 November 2022—on the status of judges and prosecutors[1] settles that it is prohibited for judges, prosecutors, assistant judges, and the legal staff that supports them to be members of political parties or organizations or to take part in or initiate political activity. While doing their duties, they are required to abstain from expressing or making any public display of their political ideas.

On the other hand, the Deontological Code for the Romanian magistrates,[2] settles that it is forbidden for judges and prosecutors to declare or make visible their political beliefs through the actions they take while carrying out their official duties, and that is prohibited for judges and prosecutors to attend to public political gatherings.[3] If they have been the target of defamatory remarks in print media or

[1] Romanian Official Monitor No. 1102 of 16 November 2022.

[2] Judges and prosecutors.

[3] Art. 5—Deontological Code for the Romanian magistrates.

audiovisual content, judges and prosecutors are entitled to publicly voice their opinions regarding the use of their right of reply.[4]

In accordance with the Law No 303 of 15 November 2022—on the status of judges and prosecutors, art. 270 defines what disciplinary liability means in this field:

> (1) Judges, prosecutors, assistant judges and legal staff assimilated to them shall be liable to disciplinary action for committing, with fault, the disciplinary offences provided for by law. (2) Disciplinary liability shall not preclude criminal or misdemeanor liability for the act committed, to the extent that the act violated the duties of office. The disciplinary procedure for the same act and the same person shall be suspended during the criminal proceedings.

Article 271 settles which are the disciplinary misconducts, and for the purpose of our study we enumerate few of these in the mentioned context:

- breach of the laws regarding bans and incompatibility.
- participating in political activities or voicing political opinions in public or while on the job.
- failing to uphold the confidentiality of such work or discussions, as well as any other similar information that he learned while carrying out his duties—apart from information that is legally required to be disclosed to the public—and other similar information.
- the prosecutor's or judge's use of improper language in their rulings or other judicial acts, as well as any lack of logic or logic that is obviously at odds with the law and could damage the reputation of justice or the dignity of their positions as judges or prosecutors.
- acting negligently or in bad faith when performing the function.

According to the same law, the disciplinary sanction proportionally with the grade of the misconduct, are: warning; a maximum 25% reduction in the gross monthly wage allotment for a maximum of one year; disciplinary transfer to a different court or prosecutor's office, even if it is of a lower grade, for an effective term of one to three years; a drop in professional status; expulsion from the judiciary; a maximum 6-month period of suspension from office.

In fact, magistrates have a restricted degree of freedom of expression, which they must use with extreme discretion. This restriction is meant to protect the litigants' regard for and confidence in the magistrates' work. People's esteem and confidence rise when magistrates draw attention to legislative measures that could jeopardize fundamental freedoms and rights. This helps citizens acquire the civic mindset that is essential in a democracy and raises their awareness of the risks they face. In this way, they demonstrate the genuine understanding of citizens' problems and get closer to them in a balanced approach that is constrained by the duty of reserve.[5]

---

[4] Art. 19—Deontological Code for the Romanian magistrates.

[5] See Bodnar (2020), p. 323.

The recommendations of the Romanian Judges' Forum were largely adopted in Opinion No. 934 of July 13, 2018, CDL-PI(2018)007, which was released by the European Commission for Democracy through Law (the Venice Commission) of the Council of Europe.

The Venice Commission recommended that Romania "re-consider the system for the appointment/dismissal of high-ranking prosecutors, including by revising related provisions of the Constitution, with a view to providing conditions for a neutral and objective appointment/dismissal process by maintaining the role of the institutions, such as the President and the Superior Council of Magistracy (SCM), able to balance the influence of the Minister of Justice; remove or better define the provisions enabling the superior prosecutors to invalidate prosecutors' solution for groundlessness; remove the proposed restriction on judges and prosecutors freedom of expression; supplement the provisions on magistrates' material liability by explicitly stating that, in the absence of bad faith and/or gross negligence, magistrates are not liable for a solution which could be disputed by another court; amend the mechanism for recovery action in such a way as to ensure that the action for recovery only takes place once and if liability of the magistrate has been established through the disciplinary procedure; reconsider the proposed establishment of a separate prosecutor's office structure for the investigation of offences committed by judges and prosecutors (the recourse to specialized prosecutors, coupled with effective procedural safeguards appears as a suitable alternative in this respect); re-examine, with a view to better specifying them, the grounds for the revocation of SCM members; remove the possibility to dismiss elected members of the SCM through the no-confidence vote of the general meetings of courts or prosecutors' offices; identify solutions enabling more effective participation, in the work of the SCM, of SCM members who are outside of the judiciary; abandon the proposed early retirement scheme unless it can be ascertained that it will have no adverse impact on the functioning of the system; ensure that the proposed "screening" measures of magistrates are based on clearly specified criteria and coupled with adequate procedural guarantees and a right of appeal to a court of law, and identify ways to strengthen oversight mechanisms of the intelligence services[6]".

The Venice Commission experts' perspective, according to the Romanian Judges' Forum, is instructive in many ways regarding how to uphold Romania's standards for the rule of law considering recent changes to the country's justice laws. One idea that was reiterated was that the Venice Commission's recommendations are helpful to the legislator during the parliamentary process of creating or amending the legislative framework. They are also helpful to the Constitutional Court when evaluating whether a normative adopted by Parliament complies with the Fundamental Law,

[6] The interim Venice Commission opinion on the justice legislation was released in Romanian on September 12, 2018, by the Romanian Judges' Forum Association. The Venice Commission had given its opinion on July 13, 2018. Because the state officials neglected to address the issue, it is the sole translation that has been done up to this point—Cited by: Călin (2020), pp. 19–20.

considering the provisions of Romania's Constitution, art. 11 parag. (1), and the case-law of the constitutional litigation court.[7]

An interesting issue regarding the liberty of expression for the judges that we want to refer to is ***using of social media by judges***.

3 Using of Social Media by Judges

Now, in the modern days, the importance of the social media it cannot be denied anymore. The question is: may the judges use freely these social networks or not? If the answer is yes, which are the limitation. For answering to our question, we will refer to:

a. Practical guide to professional ethics for judges and prosecutors.[8]
b. Recommendations for the use of social media by judges.[9]
c. The contribution of the Venice Commission to the Guidance on judges' use of social media, developed by UNODC[10] Global Judicial Integrity Network.[11]

There are principles of ethics and moral norms that are applicable to each profession, with specifics characteristics in connection with the professional domain. But the deontology of the magistrate's profession is quite different from the rest.

When we are talking about impartiality, proportionality, equity etc. on one hand, these are very articulate principles for the activity of the judges, if we are talking about the liberty of expression, the political affinities etc. we must underline that the status of the magistrates imposes some limitations.

In the following phrases we will try to make an objective framework for the possibility of the judges to make their opinions public through the social media, a modern instrument, very present in our lives.

According to the 'Practical guide to professional ethics for judges and prosecutors', that is interpreting the Deontological Code of the Romanian Magistrates, we

[7] *Idem.*

[8] The guide is the result of the project "Strengthening the capacity of the the Romanian judicial system to respond to the challenges of new changes and institutional changes", implemented by the Superior Council of the Romanian Judiciary (SCM) within the framework of the RO 24 Programme - Strengthening Institutional Capacity and Cooperation, funded by Norwegian Financial Mechanism 2009–2014, with the support of partners donors—the Norwegian Courts Administration (NCA) and the Council of Europe (CoE) – Romania, Bucharest (2017).

[9] United Nations Office on Drugs And Crime, Recommendations for the use of social media by judges, produced by the Global Judicial Integrity Network Viena, (2019).

[10] In November 2018, the UNODC, the United Nations Office on Drugs and Crime, organized an Expert Group Meeting. A preliminary proposal for a set of rules governing judges' use of social media and online platforms was developed during this meeting by judicial and legal experts from various regions. The proposal was based on regional and national standards and experiences, such as the Bangalore Principles of Judicial Conduct and their Commentaries.

[11] Strasbourg, april (2019).

find out that a special focus should be on social media. The magistrate needs to exercise extra caution while sharing anything on social media or on social media platforms. If they wish to have a Facebook, Twitter, or similar account, they should restrict themselves to sharing events, information, and remarks unrelated to his judicial job (including everything unrelated to the magistrate's case files, legislation and justice) or private information, including broad details on the legal industry.

We see that is not forbidden to have such an account, but there is limitation for the content. A special barrier is in connection with the political ideologies that a judge is not allowed to express publicly, so also on these platforms. It should be noted that while judges and prosecutors are free to voice their opinions on issues pertaining to working conditions, it is desirable for a judges' group to bring up these concerns without in any way politicizing the public discourse. Generally, a judge can speak out—even in public and on social media—about concerns such as poor court administration management or other related ones without facing any repercussions. Once more, use of this right must be done so cautiously and, in a way, appropriate to the significance of the information disclosed or discussed.

If we corroborate the second and the third documents that we mentioned in the beginning of this section (3), we can make an introspection at international level. The general conclusion is that the restrictions that are applied on freedom of the expression for the judges, is also appliable for their interactions on social media.

In Table 1, we will make a comparative look over the European Rules[12]:

The conclusion that we manage to underline is that while judges have the same rights as any other citizen to free speech, association, assembly, and belief, they should always act in a way that upholds the dignity of their position and the independence and impartiality of the legal system. The public's opinion of all judges and their level of trust in the legal system may be influenced by the social media usage of a single judge.

4 Practical Aspects in the Romanian System

There was a notorious case in Romania, that had as a main 'actor' the judge Cristi Danilet from the Tribunal Cluj, case that became famous also at international level. The press at that time wrote: "Judge Cristi Danileț, from the Cluj Tribunal, has been excluded from the judiciary by the SCM[13] for two posts made on Tik Tok—one in which he cut the green fence of his house and one in which he cleaned a swimming pool—on charges of "conduct that harms the image of justice".[14]

[12] Table - based on The Contribution of the Venice Commission to the Guidance on judges' use of social media, developed by UNODC Global Judicial Integrity Network.

[13] Superior Council of Magistracy.

[14] Online document, Vulcan (2021) https://romania.europalibera.org/a/judec%C4%83torul-cristi-danile%C8%9B-exclus-din-magistratur%C4%83-de-csm-pentru-post%C4%83rile-de-pe-tik-tok/31607329.html.

Table 1 Comparative look over the European Rules (own processing)

Country	Rules
Austria, Azerbaijan, Bosnia Herzegovina, Croatia, Hungary, Republic of Moldova, Norway, Russia, Serbia, Slovacia, Slovenia	The usage of social networking sites is not subject to any laws.
Belgium	The fundamental rule in the organic law that the dignity of the office must not be compromised is the only particular instruction that the Belgian Constitutional Court has provided regarding the use of social media space.
Czech Republic	There are currently no rules or directives from the Czech Republic's Constitutional Court regarding judges' usage of social media or other online platforms. On the other hand, its press officer often uses internet and social media channels.
Germany	Not specific rules, but there is a provision that settles: "in all matters, both formal and informal, Federal Constitutional Court Judges conduct themselves in a manner that does not compromise the reputation of the Court, the dignity of their office or confidence in their independence, impartiality, neutrality and integrity".
Greece	They do not have specific rules, just references to the Guide (recommendations) for the use of social media by judges.[a]
Irland	No specific rules, but, generally speaking, the judges from Ireland do not appear in public social media.
Switzerland	The Swiss Federal Supreme Court's judges made the decision to document the rules (customs) they adhere to. The guidelines address judges' involvement in social media and clarify that while social media use is a matter of personal preference, it must be handled carefully to avoid casting doubt on the independence, objectivity, and integrity of federal judges as well as the standing of the court.
United Kingdom	There are provisions—a guide that contains recommendations on using social media space/platforms for judges, such as: prudence with the information about family, leaving home for holidays, personal opinions etc.

[a]*Discussion Guide for the Expert Group Meeting*, which was developed at the Global Judicial Integrity Network in Vienna on 5-7 November (2018)

By a majority, admits the disciplinary action brought by the Judicial Inspection against Mr Danileț Cristi Vasilică - Judge at the Cluj Tribunal for the act consisting of the defendant's manifestations on social networks. By a majority, based on Article 100(e) of Law 303/2004 on the status of judges and prosecutors, republished, as subsequently amended and supplemented, imposes on Mr Danileț Cristi Vasilică - judge at the Cluj District Court - the disciplinary sanction of 'exclusion from the judiciary' for committing the disciplinary offence referred to in Article 99(a) of the same law. With right of appeal within 15 days of notification to the five-judge panel of the High Court of Cassation and Justice.[15]

[15] Section for Judges of the Superior Council of Magistracy (SCM).

Manifestations prejudicial to professional honour or probity or to the prestige of justice committed in the exercise or outside the exercise of official duties are implicated in the article cited by the SCM.

From our point of view, for two positions, magistrate Cristi Danileţ was implicated; yet, there is no doubt about his sincerity, independence, or honesty, because subjects pertaining to personal and family matters are not subject to disciplinary action and as an exception, they could result in the magistrate's disciplinary liability only if they have become public knowledge and have been of a nature that calls into question the magistrate's independence, impartiality, or integrity, thereby jeopardizing the dignity, credibility, and standing of the legal system, which was not the case.

Of course, that there were different opinions also, that sustained an easier penalty for the judge, but at that point the majority decided. The judge contested the Decision, and so, on December 2022, a panel of five judges from the High Court of Cassation and Justice reversed the December 2021 Decision made by the SCM, so after one-year distance. The High Court of Cassation and Justice ruled that Danileț should simply get a "warning", the lightest disciplinary sanction. "Admits the appeal brought by Judge Danileț Vasilică-Cristi against the Decision No 28J of 13 December 2021, delivered by the Disciplinary Section of the SCM in case No 25/J/2021. Annuls in part Decision No 28J of 13 December 2021, delivered by the Disciplinary Division of the SCM in case No 25/J/2021", the court decision stated.

Anyway, beginning with December 2022, the law has been changed, and for facts like in this presented case there will not be penalties anymore.

5 Comparative Analysis with Other Professions. Public Officials and Social Media

The article 412 from the Romanian Administrative Code (RAC) settles that: "The right of opinion of civil servants is guaranteed." The question that we must rise in our minds is: the public official (servant) has or has not limitation regarding this right? May he express freely his opinions on social media, in the new technology era (digitalization), that can assure the transparency of the public service and a modern administration.

Article 432 RAC provides:

> (1) Civil servants have the right to freedom of expression under the law. (2) In exercising the right to free expression, public officials shall be under an obligation not to harm the dignity, image and intimate, family and private life of any person. (3) In the performance of their duties, civil servants shall respect the dignity of their public office, linking freedom of dialogue with the promotion of the interests of the authority or public institution in which they work. (4) In their work, public officials shall respect freedom of opinion and shall not be influenced by personal considerations or popularity. In expressing their opinions, civil servants must be conciliatory and avoid generating conflicts through the exchange of opinions.

So, under this provision, correlated also with art. 10 from the European Convention on Human Rights, the Romanian public clerk has the right to have an opinion (publicly), and the liberty of expression, but with some sort of limitations. Here we can say that is a similarity with the liberty of expression of the judges.

Within the workforce of the public sector, civil servants make up a unique category. They are subject to various restrictions in their ability to exercise their fundamental civil rights because of their reserve commitment. The public and private interests can both be used as justifications for restricting the freedom of communication. The public interest primarily pertains to the public authority's or institution's reputation, as well as the reputation of all civil servants collectively. The right to privacy, image, and dignity for those interacting with public servants is considered a private interest. The special law's restrictions must be in line with the requirements of the Constitution and the international agreements that Romania has ratified. These restrictions need to be controlled. They must be justified by upholding principles that are more significant than the right to free speech; they must be required in a democratic society, appropriate considering the circumstances that gave rise to the fence, and not detrimental to the fundamental foundation of the legal system.[16]

So, these reservations are applicable also in the social media for the public clerk, but no so restrictively as in the case of the magistrates.

As a practical case for Romania, a public servant was dismissed because he posted during the work hours jokes on the social media; the decision was no made for the content, but for the fact that these actions took place during the working programme.

Is we are talking about the public institution itself, in the recent years, a public authority's social media presence has not only become standard procedure but also a representation of open and honest communication. Social media presents new avenues for reaching out to populations that are not reached by TV and print media, hence fostering more interaction between public service providers and recipients. Social media platforms offer a promising avenue for enhancing public administration's image and reputation.[17] Public authorities can utilize their social media to their own social networks in order to advertise the services offered, draw in new beneficiaries, and keep hold of current ones, given that beneficiaries use social networks for communication and information.

Instantaneous feedback on the actions of public authorities and the calibre of public services rendered can be obtained through social networks. Additionally, public administrations can greatly benefit from the public viewing the official profile or subscribing to news on that profile, which can assist to promote a positive image and effectively and free of charge advertise public services. However, for this method to be effective, regulations governing the "conduct" of individuals and the

---

[16] See Mocanu (2020), pp. 26–41.

[17] Online document, see Cernega (2014), https://ibn.idsi.md/sites/default/files/imag_file/159-161_1.pdf.

"behaviour" of public officials on social media platforms must exist. Additionally, information placed directly on a user's profile must be presented in a clever, user-friendly, and appealing manner.

6 Conclusion

Undoubtedly, the primary factor in selecting a judge is their integrity. Without a doubt, the most important quality for a candidate to have for a judgeship is integrity, and lacking it completely disqualifies them. Because of this, it's critical to define the notion of integrity and derive from it the methods for evaluating it, making the identification of a person's lack of integrity a crucial component of the selection, advancement, and removal processes for judges. So, if the judge integrity is a question mark in connection with the social media, there is the need of limitation in this way. We will se the trend regarding this subject, specially the digitalisation and the social media is more and more present in our lives.

References

Bodnar A (2020) Young Magistrates' Viewpoint on the Justice System. In: "900 Days of Uninterrupted Siege upon the Romanian Magistracy. A Survival Guide". C.H. Beck Publishing House, Bucharest, p 323

Călin D (2020) Changes Brought to the "Justice Laws" during the 2017-2019 Interval. In: "900 Days of Uninterrupted Siege upon the Romanian Magistracy. A Survival Guide". C.H. Beck Publishing House, Bucharest, pp 19–20

Cernega C (2014) Rețelele de socializare – un nou mijloc de realizare a transparenței și de promovare a imaginii administrației publice, online document. https://ibn.idsi.md/sites/default/files/imag_file/159-161_1.pdf.

Mocanu SM (2020) The Right to Free Expression of Civil Servants in the Context of art. 10 of the European Convention on Human Rights, Acta Universitatis Lucian Blaga. Iurisprudentia, No. 1/2020, Sibiu, pp 26–41

Vulcan D (2021) Judecătorul Cristi Danileț, exclus din magistratură de CSM pentru postările de pe Tik Tok, online document. https://romania.europalibera.org/a/judec%C4%83torul-cristi-danile%C8%9B-exclus-din-magistratur%C4%83-de-csm-pentru-post%C4%83rile-de-pe-tik-tok/31607329.html

Judicial Ethics and Freedom of Expression: An Average or Worst-Case Scenario

Agustina Martínez Rubio

Abstract This study examines the impact of judicial ethics principles on judges' conduct, highlighting the importance of their voluntary adoption. It explores how these principles, functioning as basic guidelines, establish a pattern of behavior that strengthens the impartiality, independence, and integrity of the judicial role without imposing a strict legal obligation. The focus is on the Judicial Ethics Commission's opinions, which interpret and clarify these principles, suggesting that their application relies on each judge's individual conscience. The distinction between judicial ethics and discipline is emphasized: the former encourages excellence through self-regulation, while the latter is based on mandatory rules. Judges are advised to act with prudence and fairness, maintaining a balance between their right to freedom of expression and their duty of institutional neutrality. Furthermore, caution is advised against inappropriate conduct that may undermine public trust in the judicial system. This analysis aims to promote a broader understanding of professional ethics in the judicial field through a cultural and ethical perspective.

A. M. Rubio (✉)
Universidad Complutense de Madrid, Madrid, Spain
e-mail: agustima@ucm.es

C. Hermida del Llano (ed.), *The Freedom of Expression for Judges in the Sphere of the Judicial Ethics*, Ius Gentium: Comparative Perspectives on Law and Justice 129, https://doi.org/10.1007/978-3-032-06504-9_8

1 Introduction

The work presented here analyzes a specific professional sector, judges,[1] whose intervention in public sphere gives rise to different opinions and considerations, under the prism of the principles of judicial ethics[2] and the possible impact on the exercise of their right to freedom of expression.

The treatment that has been carried out on the subject, although it may be subject to criticism, does not have a strictly legal basis, since this field of study goes beyond positive law itself. Thus, some references have been taken from the cultural sphere, such as cinema and literature. The reason for this is due to the need to provide a broader approach or perspective and to offer certain reflections throughout the development of this exposition. Similarly, no study has been made of the fundamental right to freedom of expression, without prejudice to the necessary references, since, as will be seen below, this is beyond the scope of this paper.

In addition, a title has been chosen that suggests the similarity, not equating, that may exist between the functioning of computer algorithms[3] and the principles of judicial ethics. More specifically, and as is clear from the exposition given in the text (without prejudice to the reader's own criteria), these principles seem to resemble an algorithm that functions as an average, since they are not established to provide a solution to each specific case, but rather their basis and effectiveness depends on those who must apply them: the judges.

From this perspective, social networks are one of the forms of communication between people that are becoming increasingly influential in different sectors or areas, transcending borders and allowing information to be exchanged in real time. According to the Constitutional Court "users have gone from a stage in which they were considered mere consumers of content created by third parties, to another -the current one- in which content is produced by themselves. (…) users (because they legally hold such status) have become collaborative subjects, citizens who interact and share in trusted networks what they have, what they know or what they do, and

[1] The terms "judge" or "judges" will be used throughout the text without distinction of gender to achieve a smoother reading. Own translation into English.

[2] Text adopted by the General Council of the Judiciary on December 20, 2016. (cfr. https://www.poderjudicial.es/cgpj/es/Poder-Judicial/En-Portada/El-Pleno-del-CGPJ-asume-el-documento-de-principios-de-etica-judicial.

The text of these principles can be found in: https://www.poderjudicial.es/cgpj/es/Temas/Transparencia/Buen-Gobierno%2D%2DEtica-Judicial-y-Comision-de-Etica-Judicial/Principios-de-Etica-Judicial/.

[3] These algorithms are classified into two groups: algorithms that work in the worst possible cases and algorithms that work on average. The former are prepared to work in all possible use cases, even in the most abstruse or nonsensical ones. This allows the algorithm to work always; however, it consumes a lot of resources, and its design and execution is costly in time and execution; dragging on endlessly. The latter work in most of the possible cases, but not in all of them. They consume few design and execution resources and are fast when applied and executed; however, only in some cases, a few, they have to be corrected, as they were not initially foreseen, but nobody is perfect.

who share with a more or less numerous group of recipients -also users of social networks on the Internet- all kinds of images, information, data and opinions, whether their own or those of others".[4]

Although the advantages cannot be ignored, the interaction between users on the network does raise certain questions about the purpose, scope and limits of the contents that are incorporated into it.

In the first place, and due to the environment in which this interaction takes place, any person accessing the network should reflect on the opinions that are issued or made, as they may have different or diverse intentions. Hence, the most sensible thing to do would be to analyze, consider, contain, or measure, with prudence, both what is read and what is written. This would avoid incurring in unethical actions that generate criticism, censure, reproaches, misunderstandings, misrepresentations, or stumbling into pious sympathy.[5]

Thus, the common thread for the development of this topic is found in the decisions adopted, through its opinions and reports,[6] by the Judicial Ethics Commission (hereinafter, the Commission).[7] This Commission carries out an important work of interpretation of the principles of judicial ethics, "expresses its opinion, and warns about those situations that may affect the principles of ethics in order to clarify any doubts that may arise"[8] among members of the Spanish judiciary.

---

[4] Ruling of the Constitutional Court, 27/2020, of February 24, FJ III. Own translation into English.

[5] Two scenes from the film Viridiana, directed by Luis Buñuel in 1961, are illustrative of this compassion. In the first, the character of Jorge (played by Francisco Rabal) watches as a cart passes by with a dog tied to it. The cart stops and two civil guards get out. Jorge approaches and urges the owner to release the dog and the following dialogue takes place: Jorge: "Oiga, este animal no puede con su alma. Ahora que va vacía la tartana por qué no lo mete dentro". El dueño: "A dentro es sólo para las personas". Jorge: "Pues desátelo, hombre, que él lo seguirá". El dueño: "Y si me lo coge un coche, ¡qué!". Jorge: acaricia al perro y le dice "le compro el perro". El dueño: "Éste es muy bueno para lo conejos. Ya lo sabe bien, cuando vamos al campo si no caza, no come". Jorge: "¿Cuánto quiere?". El dueño: "No pensaba venderlo, pero si le ha gustado deme lo que tenga voluntad". Jorge: "Ande, suéltelo". El dueño toma el dinero y dice: "gracias y a la de Dios. ¡Arrea tú! Y ya lo sabe: cuanto menos coma, más cazador". Jorge: "¿Cómo se llama? El dueño: "¡Canelo!". (Jorge: "Hey, this animal can't handle his soul. Now that the wagon is empty, why don't you put it inside". The owner: "Inside is only for people". Jorge: "Well, untie him, man, he will follow you". The owner: "And what if a car runs over him!" Jorge: "I'll buy you the dog". The owner: "This one is very good for rabbits. You know what I mean, when we go to the country, no hunting, no eating for him". Jorge: "How much do you want?" The owner: "I wasn't thinking of selling it, but if you liked it, give me whatever you want". Jorge: "Go on, let him go". The owner takes the money and says: "Thank you and God bless you. Go ahead! And you know: the less he eats, better hunter". Jorge: "What's his name?" The owner: "Canelo!" -"aka foolish"-). Jorge leaves with the dog. In the next scene, another tartan appears, with another dog in the saddle. Vid. https://www.youtube.com/watch?v=y2kab6WnSPw.

[6] All the opinions and reports cited in this work can be consulted in: https://www.poderjudicial.es/cgpj/es/Temas/Etica-Judicial/Comision-de-Etica-Judicial/Dictamenes/.

[7] For more information on the Commission, its constitution and functions, vid.: https://www.poderjudicial.es/cgpj/es/Temas/Etica-Judicial/Comision-de-Etica-Judicial/Que-es/.

[8] Opinion (Consultation 10/2018) of February 25, 2019, III, 4. Own translation into English.

It should be noted that this Commission does not have, among its functions, to establish or impose sanctions; hence, regardless of the disciplinary liability that a judge may incur,[9] "the ethical assessment to be made of any eventuality and the action to be taken in accordance with such assessment is the responsibility of each judge personally".[10]

Therefore, "the disciplinary regime has nothing to do with judicial ethics. The latter is only conceivable in terms of strict voluntariness and absence of legal responsibility, as opposed to discipline, which is a set of mandatory rules whose violation entails legal consequences. Judicial ethics operates as a positive stimulus insofar as it is aimed at excellence, while discipline operates on the basis of a negative stimulus, which is the sanction. Therefore, the effectiveness of these «Principles of Judicial Ethics» will come from the degree to which each judge assumes them as his or her own and translates them into models of conduct".[11]

This assimilation and voluntary assumption of the principles by members of the judiciary is the subject of study by the Commission in the Opinion (Consultation 10/2018) of 25 February 2019 and will serve to carry out the development of the present work; without prejudice to the references that will be made to other Opinions.

This Opinion includes three specific areas of analysis of judges' access to social networks, which are developed below: firstly, the way in which they access these networks; secondly, the scope and impact of their interventions on these networks; and thirdly, the interaction they have with other users.

---

[9] On this matter, see, among others, Articles 122 of the Spanish Constitution and 414 to 427 of Organic Law 6/1985 of the Judiciary.

[10] Opinion (Consultation 10/2018), cit., III, 4. Own translation into English.

[11] Preamble to the Principles of Judicial Ethics, cit. (Own translation into English). In this sense, Sancho Gargallo states that: "Judicial ethics circumscribes its interest to the acts or behaviors of the judge, in the exercise of his or her function or on the occasion of it. It answers the question of how a judge should behave and goes beyond his or her organic statute or the criminal laws that punish prevarication or any other crime that a judge may commit on the occasion of his or her office, although it includes them, which highlights the connection that exists between public order and morality. He is interested in the model of conduct to which a judge must conform, knowing that this is very broad. That is, judicial ethics requires a paradigm of "Good Judge", which serves to identify the principles that support it, the ethical norms that are deduced from them and explain in greater detail how to «act well» (standards of conduct), with a dual purpose: to encourage these behaviors and, in some cases, to recriminate those that contravene that model of conduct". Sancho Gargallo (2007), p. 119. Own translation into English.

2 Access to Social Networks

The Commission does not object to the use of social networks by judges, either by accessing them under their name and position or through a pseudonym.[12] However, this does not preclude that their interventions may conflict with the observance of certain principles of judicial ethics and with the exercise of the right to freedom of expression.

Judges perform an important function as members of the Judiciary, which conditions their personal performance in public spheres, and specifically in social networks. Therefore, the risks involved in accessing such networks must be assessed, since, as the Commission points out, "the duty of every judge to be aware of the requirement to behave in accordance with the dignity of the judicial function (principle No. 29) and the exercise of freedom of expression with the prudence and moderation necessary to preserve their independence[13] and appearance of impartiality,[14] and to maintain society's confidence in the administration of justice (principle No. 31), constitute ethical obligations that extend to all aspects of life, both personal and professional".[15]

[12] Regarding intervention in social networks under a pseudonym, the Consultative Council of European Judges, in Opinion 25 (2022), on the freedom of expression of judges, states that, "75. The duty of judicial restraint applies to communication on social networks, whether or not judges disclose their identity. There is no basis for preventing judges from using pseudonyms, although the use of pseudonyms is not a license for unethical behavior. Moreover, not mentioning the judicial office or using a pseudonym does not guarantee that the true judicial name or status will not be made public. The inclusion of a disclaimer on social media profiles stating that all content or opinions are expressed in a personal capacity does not exempt judges from exercising moderation". https://www.poderjudicial.es/cgpj/es/Temas/Relaciones-internacionales/Relaciones-internacionales-institucionales/Europa/Consejo-Consultivo-de-Jueces-Europeos/. Own translation into English.

[13] Principle number 1 of judicial ethics: "Judicial independence is a right of every citizen, the protection and defense of which is an unavoidable part of the professional duties of the judge, and not a personal privilege of his or her status". Own translation into English.

Principle number 9 of judicial ethics: "The judge must behave and exercise his or her rights in any activity in which he or she is recognized as such in a way that does not compromise or harm the perception that, in a democratic state governed by the rule of law, society has of the independence of the Judiciary". Own translation into English.

[14] Principle number 10 of judicial ethics: "Judicial impartiality is the detachment of the judge from the parties, to whom they must keep an equal distance, and from the subject matter of the proceedings, in relation to which they must have no interest whatsoever". Own translation into English.

Principle number 16 of judicial ethics: "Impartiality also imposes the duty to avoid conduct that, inside or outside the process, may call it into question and undermine public confidence in justice".

Principle number 21 of judicial ethics: "When democracy, the rule of law and fundamental freedoms are at risk, the obligation of reserve yields in favor of the duty to denounce". Own translation into English.

[15] Judicial Ethics Commission. Opinion (Consultation 10/2018), cit., III, 5.

I think it is illustrative to comment on the words quoted by the Commission by briefly narrating a part of the film entitled *Judge Priest.*[16] Through its protagonist, it shows (to a greater or lesser degree) not only some of the specific features of the judicial function, but also all the principles of judicial ethics that have been mentioned.

Actor Will Rogers gives life to a character, Judge Priest, who, as Torres-Dulce points out, "defines what a judge is".[17] If one takes into consideration that "a good professional is much more than a good technician",[18] in this film Priest could be considered as a prototype of coherence and consistency. In this film, Priest could be seen as a prototype of consistency and rectitude, with a touch of humor, not only as a legal operator, but also on a personal level.

In one scene of the film, Priest enters the barbershop and listens as the barber makes some ill-advised remarks about his own girlfriend. Most of the men in the barbershop laugh, except for the judge and a man sitting next to him, who gets up, punches the barber, and then leaves the barbershop. Priest, maintaining an unbiased and intelligent stance, replies to the barber and the rest of the men: "Wow, that guy is not going to be very popular around here". To which the rest of the men and the barber nod: "Yeah, he's right". And the judge replies: "if there are about 2,000 male citizens here, they're going to be really mad at him, when they find out he took a good punch at him before they did". Priest picks up the shaving bowl and the brush that had his name on it, as a sign that he will not be returning to the barbershop, and before opening the door he says: "yeah, he's going to be very popular around here that man".

Let us transfer this scene to a social network (with a virtual "punch"). Unlike what happens in the social network, where there is a specific cast of characters, in the social network the number of people who can intervene is unknown, which means that there can be an endless number of "threads", an endless number of comments on what happened. If we add to this the fact that there could be "a judge Priest", the most logical consequence is that the rest or part of the participants in the network would ask him to take a position. At this point, the problem arises as to how he should act. Bearing in mind that the network is not the barbershop in the movie, a specific space with a defined and determined number of people, the action of the network would require some reflection and prudence, since the consequences that could arise are unknown.

In the words of the Commission: "The ethical assessment of how to access social networks cannot ignore the difference between access to closed groups formed only by members of the Judiciary, access to closed groups involving people outside the judicial career, and access to open social networks where anyone can access the contents of the publications and the reactions posted by the judge who holds the

[16] Directed by John Ford. Year 1934. The film can be seen in: https://www.youtube.com/watch?v=lIi-1uLSSOo

[17] Torres-Dulce et al. (1998).

[18] Sancho Gargallo (2007), p. 118. Own translation into English.

social network account in question. Clearly, the identification of the judge as such will require a much more thorough ethical assessment in the latter case than in the former".[19]

From this perspective, it should be considered that the intervention of members of the judiciary in social networks does not entail a passive attitude in them, but their actions must be framed within a framework of equanimity and prudence,[20] since judicial ethics, in principle, relies on the behaviors performed by a judge, which entails some basic schemes of action that should be assimilated by the latter.

However, the considerations given by the Commission are left to the discretion and assessment of each judge. Thus, some members of the judiciary are known not only in the networks, but also through the news published in digital newspapers.[21] This situation is causing conflicting opinions regarding the intervention of members of the judiciary in this field. There is a debate within the public opinion, and among judges and other legal operators, about the importance and effectiveness of the principles of judicial ethics and how they affect the exercise of their freedom of expression.

In other words, the principles of judicial ethics establish criteria of conduct that are not binding. Hence, failure to comply with them, *per se,* does not entail a sanction; however, this does not preclude the possibility of incurring disciplinary liability, or a cause for abstention or recusal.[22] However, the question arises as to whether these principles may constitute a limit to the exercise of the right to freedom of expression.

In this context, a position contrary to the idea that those principles could restrict the exercise of the fundamental right is that of Portillo Rodrigo, when he states that: "Let it be clear that we are talking about ethical duties, not legal ones. We are talking about good practice guidelines that only oblige us judges to the extent that each one, individually, wants to feel obliged. Consequently, and beyond the opportunity to conduct oneself in accordance with them (ethics defines right versus wrong, good versus bad, moral versus immoral), it is wrong to present them as limits to our freedom of expression, a fundamental right that we have in the same conditions as other citizens, both outside and inside the RRSS, except for the behaviors that constitute disciplinary offenses".[23]

However, it should be considered that the underlying problem in this matter may not be found in the possible or apparent limitation that the aforementioned

---

[19] Opinion (Consultation 10/2018), cit., III, 7. In similar terms, vid. The same Consultation, III, 10, *in fine*. Own translation into English.

[20] In this sense, Reartes points out that: "The idea of mute judges and totally neutral behavior is unreal". Reartes Diani (2016), p. 39. Own translation into English.

[21] Vid. https://www.larazon.es/espana/20220115/lgnuapwl25chtoutzn5dp52pgu.html; https://www.elconfidencialdigital.com/articulo/el_chivato/jueces-twitteros-esconden-nombre/20201202223958192526.html; https://www.elplural.com/autonomias/andalucia/jueces-tuiteros-ve-plumero_246690102.

[22] Vid. Article 219 of Organic Law 6/1985, of July 1, 1985, of the Judiciary.

[23] Portillo Rodrigo (2019). Own translation into English.

principles exert on this fundamental right (without prejudice to their existence from a normative point of view, as will be mentioned below), but rather in how these principles are assimilated by the judge. In such a way that if there is an observance of them, the participation of the judge in a social network would not provoke claudicating situations, since the judge will be "aware that his behavior or even his criticisms are attributed by the citizens not only to the judge as another citizen but also to the judicial institution, to the power of the State of which he is a part".[24] This would strike "a balance between the fundamental right of an individual judge to freedom of expression and the legitimate interest of a democratic society in preserving public confidence in the judiciary".[25]

In this line, a more accurate criterion could be that of Roca Trías when he states that "the principles of independence and impartiality of judges constitute an indispensable element of the rule of law. Judges' ownership of their right to freedom of expression cannot be eliminated by their status as such. It makes no difference what means they use to exercise their right, but they must abide by the consequences of its exercise, because they can destroy the presumption of impartiality and then they will enter the circle of the causes of recusal and abstention, because only in this way are the principles of the rule of law complied with".[26]

At this point, one of the Bangalore principles,[27] that of propriety, should be highlighted: «Propriety and the appearance of propriety are essential to the performance of all of a judge's activities».[28] The transcendence and incidence of this principle in the exercise of a judge's right to freedom of expression is specified in section 4.5 of the Bangalore principles, which establishes that any member of the judiciary "shall always behave in a manner that preserves the dignity of the judicial functions and the impartiality and independence of the judiciary".[29] Thus, although there is no diminution or limitation in the exercise of that fundamental right, the position held by a judge in a State governed by the rule of law calls for self-demand by the judge.[30]

---

[24] Ordóñez Solís (2016), p. 12. Own translation into English.

[25] Consultative Council of European Judges, Opinion 25 (2022), paragraph 31, cit. Own translation into English.

[26] Roca Trías (2021), p. 44. Own translation into English.

[27] A consultation on these principles and commentary can be found in: https://www.poderjudicial.es/cgpj/gl/Temas/Etica-Xudicial/Principios-de-Etica-Xudicial/Documentos-de-interese/Outros-documentos/Principios-de-Bangalore-sobre-la-conducta-judicial.

[28] Bangalore Principle 4 on Judicial Conduct, cit. Own translation into English.

[29] Ibidem.

[30] In this regard, the Opinion (Consultation 17/2019) of 23 October 2019, III, 9, of the Commission states that: "The central question is not, therefore, whether the judge or magistrate can provide information. The fundamental question and at the same time the most complex and delicate one consist in elucidating in which cases, how and to what extent it is advisable to do so. And here the principles of Judicial Ethics generally introduce several cautions and appeals to self-restraint, which have already been announced: principle 31 speaks of prudence and moderation in the exercise of free expression; principle 19 again appeals to prudence so that their appearance of impartiality is not affected by their public statements". Own translation into English.

This principle of correctness requires "moderation to maintain public confidence in the impartiality and independence of the judiciary".[31] Perhaps, this restraint or care can be concretized, paraphrasing an expression attributed to Pedro Escartín,[32] in the following: "The best referee is the one who goes unnoticed". Therefore, if a judge's participation in a social network can "foreseeably undermine confidence in his or her impartiality"[33] or may expose him or her "to public attacks or be incompatible with the dignity of judicial functions",[34] he or she should refrain from participating in a social network.[35]

In short, it can be concluded that "the precautions and restrictions on participation in (the) social networks can become very demanding in terms of respect for the neutrality of judges in political life, the need for the judge to be jealous of his independence and, finally, the inexcusable impartiality in the knowledge of the judicial processes in which the judge intervenes".[36]

3 Scope and Impact of Interventions in Social Networks

The Commission points out that "social networks constitute a means of communication whose scope and relevance are ever greater in the so-called "information society" in which we live. In this sense, the access of judges identified as such in social networks can favor the fulfillment of ethical duties such as the one expressed in principle no. 20 on the valuable pedagogical role that judges can play in the

[31] Commentary on the Bangalore Principles of Judicial Conduct, cit., p. 88. Own translation into English.

[32] Pedro Escartín was an important figure in Spanish soccer, who stood out for his work as a national and international referee. About him can be seen, for example, in: https://www.libertaddigital.com/deportes/futbol/2014-08-08/pedro-escartin-el-hombre-que-lo-fue-todo-en-el-futbol-espanol-1276525291/. Own translation into English.

[33] Commentary on the Bangalore Principles of Judicial Conduct, cit., p. 88. Own translation into English.

[34] Ibidem.

[35] Although this point of view may be subject to criticism. Thus, Portillo Rodrigo states that "based on this need to safeguard the appearance of impartiality of judges and maintain the confidence of citizens in their Justice, from time to time voices are raised which, based on some of the overreaching statements we have seen, argue that judges should really be limited in their freedom of expression. They conclude that, because we are judges, we should have fewer freedoms than the rest of the citizens: we put on the robe and some of the fundamental rights recognized in the Constitution fall away". Portillo Rodrigo (2019). Own translation into English.

[36] Ordóñez Solís (2016), p. 12. In this regard, it is worth bearing in mind the principle of judicial ethics number 31: "The judge, as a citizen, has the right to freedom of expression which he/she shall exercise with prudence and moderation in order to preserve his/her independence and appearance of impartiality and to maintain social trust in the judicial system and in the jurisdictional bodies". Vid. Opinion (Consultation 6/2020) of February 24, 2021. Own translation into English.

explanation of the law and fundamental rights in the process".[37] This didactic, educational, or formative function is positively highlighted in some media.[38]

However, the pedagogical work mentioned by the Commission[39] does not seem to be what some users are looking for in a social network. An example of this may be what was expressed by Urias, in an article he published in a digital newspaper in September 2018,[40] regarding the intervention of members of the Spanish judiciary in the social network X (Twitter): "It has many positive aspects. On the one hand, it is an open window into the mindset of our judiciary. One can discover that there is a variety of tastes, hobbies and opinions among the people who have the task of passing down justice. There is the judge who collects robots, the magistrate who writes poetry, others who are hooked on television series or classical ballet. This diversity helps to humanize people who are usually only seen with the solemnity of their robes and absolute power in the courtroom. From a legal point of view, the possibility of debating in person on questions of law with those who usually have the last word in its application is interesting. Twitter is making it possible to extend the boundaries of legal discussion through conversations that often also involve professors, lawyers, prosecutors and other legal operators. When they reach a certain depth and take place in a healthy framework of discussion they are undoubtedly enriching for all parties".[41]

In principle, there is nothing to prevent a judge's tastes or hobbies from being publicly known; however, this is not justified by a supposed "humanization" of the members of the judiciary. As far as we are concerned here, the performance and exercise of judicial work is not linked to whether the head of the judicial body is more or less human; for what is decisive and characteristic is that this person, who holds a qualified position, carries out a concrete and specific job, which is subject to certain ethical principles. Moreover, as the Consultative Council of European Judges points out, "judges must ensure that they maintain the authority, integrity, decorum, and dignity of their judicial office. They should be aware that language, dress, photographs, and the disclosure of other personal details can damage the reputation of the judiciary. Allowing judges to share private details, such as their

[37] Opinion (Consultation 10/2018), cit., III, 8. Own translation into English.

[38] Vid. https://www.elespanol.com/social/20180913/quieres-entender-noticias-debes-seguir-jueces-twitter/337716972_0.html.

[39] In this sense, the Commission establishes guidelines on the dissemination work in the media and social networks by indicating that there is "maximum amplitude for what is pure pedagogy, information or dissemination of procedural rules and the requirements of fundamental rights or legal norms: explaining what remedies are available, what the procedural steps are, how matters are deliberated, what solutions can be adopted. And maximum restriction in what are critical opinions or judgments (laudatory or unfavorable). Clarify, explain, translate, divulge, yes; but do not censure, disavow, or enter into controversy with the judicial decision. Even less, to insinuate what should be done or what should not have been done according to one's own opinion, which, let us not forget, is offered by the one who has been called upon to give it precisely because he is a judge". Opinion (Consultation 5/2020) of December 3, 2020, III, 8. Own translation into English.

[40] Urías (2018).

[41] Ibidem. Own translation into English.

lifestyle or family, carries some risks in this regard. Whether an expression potentially compromises the reputation of the judge, or the judiciary must be assessed in the light of the circumstances of the case".[42] From this perspective, the Commission advises prudence and caution in the use of social networks in order not to compromise certain principles of judicial ethics. Thus, "the publication of personal opinions, whether they deal with non-legal matters, and certain reactions to publications by third parties may compromise not only the appearance of impartiality referred to in principle no. 17, but also, in some circumstances, impartiality itself, independence and integrity. This is alluded to, on the one hand, by principle no. 16 when it imposes on the judge the duty to avoid conduct that may call into question his impartiality and damage public confidence in justice and, on the other hand, by principle no. 9 which requires the judge to behave in a manner in the exercise of his rights that does not compromise or damage the perception that society has of the independence of the Judiciary. It should also be recalled that Principle no. 22, referring to integrity, requires the judge to observe in all facets in which he or she is recognizable as a judge a conduct that reaffirms public confidence in the administration of justice".[43]

Moreover, as already noted, one of the principles of judicial ethics is impartiality, which, as Roca Trías points out, "is linked to freedom of expression".[44] While it is true that "all citizens are entitled to the right to freedom of expression, and, as citizens, so are judges, since there is no restriction whatsoever in any constitutional text. True as it is that there is no provision that directly recognizes judges the ownership of their right to express themselves freely, however, the opposite does exist, insofar as art. 10.2 in fine ECHR includes among the limits to the exercise of freedom of expression in general the "guarantee of the authority and impartiality of the judiciary", and would also be implicitly included in art. 20.4 EC".[45]

This entails an exquisite vigilance with respect to the public statements that may be made by a judge, hence it is unwise to externalize personal or legal opinions in a social network, which may lead to an impairment, a loss, a prejudice, in the appearance of impartiality. In short, "the decisive role played by the judge in a democratic rule of law, in which the confidence of citizens in Justice is essential, has led to raise the level of ethical requirements of judges, with respect to other citizens, and that these ethical requirements do not end at the level of «being», but reach the level of "seeming"".[46]

However, Urias seems to support apparent intermediate, or underhandedly opposed, lines that favor a "self-serving" dialogue with members of the judiciary, to the detriment of the judge's impartiality, stating that: "Most judges on Twitter have

---

[42] Consultative Council of European Judges, Opinion 25 (2022), paragraph 72, cit. Own translation into English.

[43] Opinion (Consultation 10/2018), cit., III, 9. Own translation into English.

[44] Roca Trías (2021), p. 16. Own translation into English.

[45] Ibidem, p. 17.

[46] Sancho Gargallo (2007)es, p. 120. Own translation into English.

chosen to hide their identity under pseudonyms. I do not think they do this to avoid sanctions from the CGPJ but to avoid recusals and maintain an appearance of impartiality when they are in their courts. It is a reasonable solution only halfway. Healthy public debate requires a situation of mutual responsibility and equality of arms that does not exist when one debates against someone who takes refuge in the irresponsible freedom that a pseudonym gives him or her. On the other hand, those who present themselves publicly with their name and even their photo must always move in the difficult limit between sincerity and partiality. Surely, the supreme court judge I mentioned at the beginning of this article should not have pronounced sharply on the legal qualification of facts that may reach his own jurisdiction. However, the disappearance of the judicial presence in the network would be a loss for everyone. Despite the fact that some sometimes fall into political prejudice, or intellectual arrogance or corporatism, all this simply shows that judges are people. Getting to know them and dialoguing with them is one of the great contributions of Twitter to the world of law".[47]

Possibly, these statements ignore what Pármeno advised Calisto in Fernando de Rojas play, *La Celestina*, whose context we reproduce for a better understanding: "Pármeno. Digo, señor, que yrían mejor empleadas tus franquezas en presentes y servicios a Melibea, que no dar dinero a aquella que yo conozco, y lo que es peor, hazerte su cautivo. Calisto. ¿Cómo, loco, su cautivo? Pármeno. Porque a quien dizes el secreto, das tu libertad" ("Pármeno. I say, sir, that your kindness would be better spent in gifts and services to Melibea, than not giving money to the one I know, and what is worse, making you her captive. Calisto. How, madman, her captive? Pármeno. Because to whom you tell the secret, you give your freedom").[48]

[47] Urías (2018) (Own translation into English). However, this author seems to show another opinion, after years, when he expressed, in 2020, that: "International justice has repeatedly condemned Spain because of judges who refuse to investigate allegations of police torture if the person who alleges them is a pro-independence person. Twitter shows the ideological bias that could be behind this tendency to give more credibility to some than others. It is not enough to recuse a particular judge, but it seriously damages the credibility of the system. Personally, I was happier when judges did not show in public either their ideology or their serious shortcomings in fundamental rights. I trusted in the functioning of justice and blamed mistakes on overwork or occasional absent-mindedness. Now, with Twitter, they are showing their colors. The only consolation is to know that the majority of good judges in our country, with a high level of preparation and a democratic sense of their function, do not flaunt on Twitter that they are judges. They participate, if at all, as citizens. They achieve less notoriety, but they transmit the confidence that an independent and professional justice requires". Urías (2020). Own translation into English.

[48] De Rojas (1987), p. 134. In this sense, we can also remember the words that Miss Lunatic said to Sara:"A quien dices un secreto, das tu libertad, nunca lo olvides Sara" ("To whom you tell a secret, you give your freedom, never forget it Sara"). Martín Gaite (1999), p. 151. Own translation into English.

4 Interaction Between Members of a Social Network

A guideline of what, in principle, could be the object of social networks was pointed out by Benedict XVI, when he stated that: "although we are astonished by the speed with which the new technologies have evolved in terms of their reliability and efficiency, we should not be surprised by their popularity among users, since this responds to the fundamental desire of people to enter into relationships with one another. This yearning for communication and friendship is rooted in our own human nature and cannot be adequately understood as a response to technological innovations alone (…).

The desire to be in contact and the instinct to communicate, which seem to be taken for granted in contemporary culture, are at bottom modern manifestations of the fundamental and constant tendency of human beings to go beyond themselves to enter into relationship with others. When we open ourselves to others, we realize one of our deepest aspirations and become more fully human. Indeed, to love is what we have been conceived for by the Creator".[49]

Apart from the considerations that may give rise to reflection from a confessional perspective, certainly this "desire to be in contact and the instinct to communicate" specify, in principle, the leitmotiv of those who access these networks and interact with others. However, the use of these networks requires delimiting the terms, scope and consequences of their use, in order to avoid any contradictions or inappropriate behavior.

For this reason, it is convenient to establish criteria or lines of action, which allow to delimit a moral and/or ethical behavior. In this sense, the words of Joseph Ratzinger, which are transcribed below, are very clarifying, since they establish some parameters of action that should not be ignored: "The new technologies have also opened avenues for dialogue between people from different countries, cultures, and religions. The new digital space, called cyberspace, makes it possible to meet and learn about the values and traditions of others. However, for these encounters to bear fruit, honest and correct forms of expression are required, as well as attentive and respectful listening. Dialogue must be based on a sincere and reciprocal search for truth, to foster the development of understanding and tolerance. Life is not a simple succession of facts and experiences; it is rather the search for truth, goodness, and beauty. Our decisions and the exercise of our freedom are directed to these ends, and in them -truth, goodness, and beauty—we find happiness and joy. We must not be deceived by those who are only looking for consumers in a market of undifferentiated possibilities, where choice itself is presented as the good, novelty is confused with beauty and subjective experience supplants truth".[50]

[49] Message of His Holiness Benedict XVI for the XLIII World Communications Day. "New technologies, new relationships. Promote a culture of respect, dialogue, friendship". May 24, 2009. https://www.vatican.va/content/benedict-xvi/es/messages/communications/documents/hf_ben-xvi_mes_20090124_43rd-world-communications-day.pdf. Own translation into English.

[50] Ibidem.

Hence, the risks underlying the use of networks should not be underestimated. As far as we are concerned, the need to search in these public spaces to criticize institutions, individuals, judicial decisions or acts of a political nature, may entail a certain desire for prominence or an inappropriate way of showing disagreement that should be subject to criticism. It should be noted that such publications, revelations, statements, or testimonies have a social and ethical transcendence, since, as the Commission points out, "the actions of the judge in social networks must take into account the provisions of principle no. 3, which commits the judge to promoting in society an attitude of respect and trust in the Judiciary".[51]

It is even possible to incur, without spurious intention, the risk of being misinterpreted, which requires greater aptitude, skill, ability, and restraint in the use of networks. In short, any person who makes a comment in this field must be very aware of the exposure to which he is subjecting himself and, allow us to recall what Miss Lunatic, in the book *Caperucita en Manhattan*, said to Sara: "Mira, Sara -le contestó la anciana en voz baja- cuando se desea mucho una cosa, no hay que decirlo tanto. Disimula" ("Look, Sara -the old lady answered her in a low voice- when you want something very much, you should not say it so much. Just pretend").[52]

From this perspective, the Commission points out that "the characteristics of some social networks encourage haste in the issuance of comments and leave little room for nuances, which hinders reflection, proper of prudence, and facilitates that on occasion the reaction to other people's opinions is unkind, disproportionate, or disrespectful. For this reason, members of the judiciary should be especially prudent in the use of these media. It is always advisable to reread opinions and reactions before publishing them".[53]

The media report news in which supposed members of the judiciary appear, apparently using pseudonyms, in which, for example, they give their opinion on the

[51] Opinion (Consultation 10/2018), cit., III, 11. Principle number 3 of judicial ethics: "Members of the Judiciary must assume an active commitment to the proper functioning of the judicial system, as well as promote in society an attitude of respect and trust in the Judiciary and exercise the jurisdictional function in a prudent, moderate and respectful manner with the other branches of government". Own translation into English.

[52] Martín Gaite (1999), p. 130 (Own translation into English). In this regard, the Commission states that "there is no ethical duty per se to limit the contacts of judges on social networks. Nor does the plurality of contacts eliminate the risk that the judge's participation in social networks may be misinterpreted by third parties and that the appearance of impartiality or independence may be affected. It will be the elementary prudence that must preside over the exercise of the judge's freedom of expression that determines the prior assessment of his participation in social networks and the way it is carried out". Opinion (Consultation 10/2018), cit., III, 14. Own translation into English.

[53] Opinion (Consultation 10/2018), cit., III, 12. Own translation into English.

language policy in the Autonomous Community of Catalonia;[54] or on the political actions of political parties that defend independence in that Community.[55]

On this matter, the Commission had the opportunity to pronounce itself in the Opinion (Consultation 3/22) of April 26, 2022.[56] A consultation is made in which the transcendence is questioned, from the perspective of judicial ethics, the appreciation by citizens on Justice and the appearance of impartiality, the fact that a judge makes, through social networks, statements, and comments in support of convicted politicians belonging to Catalan pro-independence parties, and also declares his opposition to state rules, encouraging their breach.

The Commission points out that, in this context, such manifestations may affect "the confidence of citizens in the right to be judged according to legal parameters".[57]

In addition, the actions of every judge must be framed in the field of political neutrality, since the opinions on social networks about political events involve a violation of the ethical principles of independence, impartiality and integrity,[58] which places "the judge who gives these opinions in an ideological position that may lead the society receiving them to believe that justice is politicized, thus contributing to a lack of confidence of citizens in justice, in the judicial system and in the jurisdictional bodies that comprise it, with the consequent institutional discredit".[59]

The judge's right to freedom of expression must be exercised with prudence and moderation, in line with the principle of integrity. The statements made in favor of certain politicians or incitement to the non-observance of our rules, "can in no way be covered by the freedom of expression of those who hold the status of members of a State power, and therefore subject with greater rigor to the duties of the office they swore or promised at the time, when they acceded to the Judicial Career",[60] and which are specified in the submission to the Constitution and our legal system.

Such statements may "constitute a risk to the rule of law, the constitutional order and democracy itself"[61] and violate the principle of impartiality insofar as, as expressed in principle 21 of judicial ethics, "when democracy, the rule of law and

[54] Vid. https://www.elnacional.cat/es/politica/juez-camuflado-twitter-contra-inmersion-catalan-escuela-randy-watson_674915_102.html.

[55] Vid. https://www.heraldo.es/noticias/sociedad/2019/01/19/la-ultima-victima-ira-independentista-los-jueces-con-seudonimo-twitter-1288004-310.html.

[56] On the political neutrality of members of the judiciary, vid. Opinion (Consultation 4/20) of January 14, 2021.

[57] Opinion (Consultation 3/2022) of April 26, 2022, II, 1. Own translation into English.

[58] Principle number 22 of judicial ethics: «Integrity requires that the judge observe a conduct that reaffirms the confidence of citizens in the Administration of Justice not only in the exercise of jurisdiction, but in all those facets in which he or she is recognizable as a judge or invokes his or her status as such». Own translation into English.

[59] Opinion (Consultation 3/2022), cit., III, 6. Own translation into English.

[60] Ibidem, III, 7.

[61] Ibidem, III, 10.

fundamental freedoms are at risk, the obligation of reserve yields in favor of the duty to denounce".[62]

On the other hand, there are news in which, supposedly, members of the judiciary express their critical opinion on resolutions issued by the courts of justice.[63] In this sense, the Commission made it clear that any legal disclosure can serve to promote the pedagogical work of judges "as long as it is framed within the limits of sound criticism which, in no case, protects attacks on judicial decisions for the simple fact of dissenting from the opinion issued".[64]

However, the networks are being used by some judges to criticize decisions made by their hierarchical superiors[65]; or the governing bodies of the judiciary[66]; or corruption.[67]

However, these actions should not be taken as a generality, since there are other members of the judiciary, who are also in the networks, and criticize such statements and behaviors.[68] This attitude reminds us of another scene from the John Ford film quoted above. The courtroom is full of people, almost the whole town is present, bustle, some talking to others. Judge Priest enters the courtroom and takes a seat. At that moment, the prosecutor, who is anxious to take his seat, challenges the judge, alleging that he has collaborated with the defendant in an assault on the plaintiff. The entire courtroom falls silent. It was a challenge with no factual or legal basis. The courtroom remains silent. Judge Priest, pensive, confused, and overwhelmed, demonstrates the rectitude, dignity and integrity of a judge: he leaves the courtroom and declares before everyone his impartial attitude: "I believe that I have always respected the spirit of the law". In short, an example and a defense of the impartiality of a judge "when it comes to defending the values in which he believes",[69] after 25 years of practice. Even though the prosecutor's cause for recusal is false, Priest prefers to set an example for the entire courtroom.

---

[62] The fifth recommendation of the Consultative Council of European Judges, Opinion 25 (2022), expresses itself in similar terms: "As a general principle, judges should avoid involvement in public controversies. Even in cases where their membership of a political party or participation in public debates is permitted, it is necessary that they refrain from any political activity that might compromise their independence or impartiality, or the reputation of the judiciary". Cit.

[63] Vid. https://cincodias.elpais.com/cincodias/2018/11/12/legal/1542008711_198402.html.

[64] Opinion (Consultation 21/2019) of February 10, 2020, III, 6.

[65] Vid. https://www.cyltv.es/videoSH/5b665772-8d44-4c5d-9bd9-c82fa30a5444/Un-juez-utiliza-las-RRSS-para-denunciar-que-el-presidente-del-TSJ-le-ha-aconsejado-cogerse-una-baja-para-sacar-adelante-sentencias-.

[66] https://www.larazon.es/espana/20220115/lgnuapwl25chtoutzn5dp52pgu.html.

[67] Vid. https://www.publico.es/tremending/2022/04/17/han-pasado-a-proclamar-que-saquean-el-dinero-publico-por-nuestro-bien-el-juez-joaquim-bosch-triunfa-en-twitter-con-este-contundente-mensaje-sobre-la-corrupcion/.

[68] https://cincodias.elpais.com/cincodias/2018/11/12/legal/1542008711_198402.html, *in fine*.

[69] Torres-Dulce et al. (1998).

5 Conclusions

The Commission, in the Opinion of 25 February 2019, addresses the participation of judges in social networks. The contributions and/or interventions of members of the judiciary in them have given rise to an examination and an assessment, from the perspective of judicial ethics, on the form and conditions of access by members of the judiciary, the terms that must be considered regarding the content of the publications and opinions poured by them, and the consequences that may arise when interacting with other users in those networks.

The criteria established by the Commission in these areas show the scope, impact and, ultimately, the virtuality of the principles of judicial ethics and how they do not hinder the exercise of the fundamental right to freedom of expression of judges in social networks; in addition, it highlights the undoubted and necessary role that judges can carry out in social networks by developing a pedagogical work, in line with the provisions of the principle of judicial ethics number 20, in order to explain "the law and the way in which fundamental rights operate within the process", should be highlighted in a very positive way.

For this reason, some conclusions that have been drawn are set out below and synthesized in itemized form.

First: The non-observance of the principles of judicial ethics does not entail legal liability, but this does not prevent them from being appreciated and considered by the members of the judiciary. These principles are based on the behavior of a judge, establishing basic guidelines or schemes of action that should be assimilated by the judge.

Second: The participation of judges in social networks must be governed by an assessment and weighing of the principles of judicial ethics. The observance of these principles implies a self-demand on the part of the judge, to avoid situations that undermine the dignity of the judicial function, and the impartiality, independence and integrity of the members of the judiciary. It will also help to strengthen the confidence of citizens in the justice system.

Third: The use of pseudonyms by the judge in social networks does not exempt him/her from showing due diligence, in order to preserve the principles of independence, impartiality and integrity.

Fourth: Regardless of the legal limits that may exist, the principles of judicial ethics should not be considered as a limit to the exercise of the right to freedom of expression. The assimilation of these principles, their observance, can serve to avoid situations of claudicating. This would strike a balance between the exercise of this fundamental right and the duty of neutrality that is demanded of a judge, holding a qualified position within one of the branches of government.

Fifth: Social networks should not serve as a vehicle for judges to criticize institutions, individuals, judicial decisions, or acts of a political nature, as this may be covered by a possible desire for prominence, or be an inappropriate way to show disagreement. Such conduct is detrimental to the building of trust and respect in the Judiciary.

References

Benedicto XVI (2009) Nuevas tecnologías, nuevas relaciones. Promover una cultura de respeto, de diálogo, de amistad. https://www.vatican.va/content/benedict-xvi/es/messages/communications/documents/hf_ben-xvi_mes_20090124_43rd-world-communications-day.pdf

De Rojas F (1987) La Celestina. Cátedra, Madrid

Martín Gaite C (1999) Caperucita en Manhattan. Siruela, Madrid

Ordóñez Solís D (2016) ¡¡¡Pero bueno, los jueces también están en las redes sociales!!! Diario La Ley 8762:1–15

Portillo Rodrigo F (2019) Jueces y redes sociales. https://elderecho.com/wp-content/uploads/2021/02/Jueces-y-RRSS.pdf

Reartes Diani N (2016) Los límites al Derecho a la ideología de los jueces desde el caso del juez Cebull (EE.UU) y el juez Zaffaroni (Argentina). Cuaderno de Derecho Público 5:29–54

Roca Trías E (2021) Libertad de expresión, independencia, imparcialidad: los jueces en las redes sociales. Un estudio de las decisiones del TEDH. Revista Española de Derecho Constitucional 122:13–45. https://doi.org/10.18042/cepc/redc.122.01

Sancho Gargallo I (2007) Ética judicial: el paradigma del buen Juez. Revista cuatrimestral de las Facultades de Derecho y Ciencias Económicas y Empresariales 72:117–138. https://revistas.comillas.edu/index.php/revistaicade/article/view/410/330

Torres-Dulce E et al (1998) Qué grande es el cine: El juez Priest. https://www.rtve.es/play/videos/que-grande-es-el-cine/grande-cine-juez-

Urías J (2018) Jueces en Twitter. https://www.eldiario.es/opinion/tribuna-abierta/jueces-twitter_129_1946963.html

Urías J (2020) Jueces tuiteros, se les ve el plumero. Disponible en: https://www.elplural.com/autonomias/andalucia/jueces-tuiteros-ve-plumero_246690102

Constitutional and Legal Framework of Judicial Ethics in Brazil

Renato Braz Mehanna Khamis and Daniel Ferreira Limaverde

Abstract This paper presents a review of the framework of judicial ethics in Brazil. To achieve this objective was used an exploratory approach of research, which was done by the analysis of the Brazilian Constitution, laws and regulations created by the Parliament and by the National Council of Justice. In the end were briefly presented some cases regarding to judge's manifestations that could give rise to application of the norms presented in the paper.

1 Introduction

This paper aims to offer the readers an overview through the framework of judicial ethics in Brazil. The proposal of writing it appeared after an invitation to participate in the International Conference "Freedom of expression for judges within the framework of respect for the principles of judicial ethics", that took place in Madrid, Spain.

To achieve its objectives the authors have chosen an exploratory approach of research, which was done by analyzing the Brazilian Constitution, laws and regulations created by the Parliament and by the National Council of Justice. In the final part was offered a brief exemplification of some cases in which the rules analyzed are theoretically applicable.

So, at first will be presented the constitutional norms related to judicial ethics and the freedom of speech. Secondly will be analyzed the organic law of the judicature and, after it, the Judicature Code of Ethics. To end the legal analyzes will be shown the Resolution 305 of the National Council of Justice. To finish the paper will be presented some cases were the legislation presented could be applied.

R. B. M. Khamis (✉) · D. F. Limaverde
Santa Cecilia University, Santos, Brazil
e-mail: renato@mehanna.adv.br; daniel@mehanna.adv.br

C. Hermida del Llano (ed.), *The Freedom of Expression for Judges in the Sphere of the Judicial Ethics*, Ius Gentium: Comparative Perspectives on Law and Justice 129, https://doi.org/10.1007/978-3-032-06504-9_9

2 Brazilian constitution

Regarding the freedom of expression of judges, the Federal Constitution of 1988, also called the Citizen Constitution due to its democratic bias in contrast to the previous regime, outlined on its article 95 three guarantees for judges: life-tenure office, non-removability and irreducibility of compensation:

Article 95. Judges Enjoy the Following Guarantees:

I life-tenure office, which, at first instance, shall only be acquired after two years in office, loss of office being dependent, during this period, on deliberation of the court to which the judge is subject, and, in other cases, on a final and unappealable judicial decision;

II non-removability, except for reason of public interest, under the terms of Article 93, item VIII;

III irreducibility of compensation, except for the provisions of Articles 37, items X and XI, 39, paragraph 4, 150, item II, 153, item III, and 153, paragraph 2, item I.

In turn, the sole paragraph of the same article established five forbidden conducts to the judges, highlighting the prohibition of carrying out political or party activity.

Article 95 (...)

Sole paragraph. Judges are forbidden to:

I hold, even when on paid availability, another office or position, except for a teaching position;

II receive, on any account or for any reason, court costs or participation in a lawsuit;

III engage in political or party activities;

IV receive, on any account or for any reason, financial aid or contribution from individuals, and from public or private institutions, except for the exceptions set forth in law;

V practice law in the court on which they served as judges, for a period of three years following their retirement or discharge.

However, other linked guarantees were sparsely regulated by the constitutional text. In the title II, which regulates the Fundamental Rights and Guarantees, the chapter I, called Individual and Collective Rights and Duties, enshrined, for example, the non-exclusion of jurisdiction, the inadmissibility of court *ad hoc* and, implicitly, the impartiality. It can be found in article 5th, items XXXV, XXXVII and LIII:

Article 5th.
All people are equal before the law, without any distinction whatsoever. Brazilians and foreigners residing in the country are ensured the inviolability of their right to life, liberty, equality, security, and property, under the following terms:

XXXV—the law shall not exclude any injury or threat to a right from review by the judiciary;

XXXVII—there shall be no trial or court *ad hoc*;

LIII—no one will be prosecuted or sentenced except by the competent authority;

The principle of independence, despite not being expressly provided for in the chapters relating to the Judiciary or fundamental rights, was enshrined for all Powers in art. 2nd, in title I – Fundamental Principles. Judicial independence, notably, is an inseparable element of the democratic rule of law.

Article 2nd
The powers of the Union are vested in the legislative, the executive, and the judicial branch, which are independent and harmonious with each other.

It is also pertinent to highlight the principle of impersonality which, although provided for in title III, called State Organization, in its chapter VII, that regulates Public Administration. After all article 37, caput, is a norm that is recognized as being extendable to all State Powers, that is, it is also mandatory to be observed within the scope of the Judiciary in the exercise of its typical and atypical functions. Says the mentioned article:

Article 37
The government bodies and its associated entities in any of the branches of the Union, States, Federal District and Municipalities shall obey the principles of legality,

On the other hand, when it comes specifically to freedom of expression, items IV and IX of article 5th guarantee anyone the right to express their thoughts and the prohibition of censorship.

Article 5th (…)
IV—expression of thought is free and anonymity is forbidden;

IX—the expression of intellectual, artistic, scientific, and communication activity is free, irrespective of censorship or license;

This set of norms constitutes the basic constitutional framework for resolving controversies involving the limits of judge's freedom of expression in Brazil. In this way, it is necessary to weigh, on the one hand, the independence and impartiality of the Judiciary, and on the other, the fundamental right of any individual to freedom of expression as an essential element in the development of human dignity and the formation of a pluralistic society.

However, the issue does not end constitutionally, once the article 93 of the Constitution determines a legal regulation through the statute of the judicature.

3 Organic Law of the Judicature

Despite the Federal Constitution of 1988 providing for the creation of a statute of the judicature, the Complementary Law number 35 of 1979, known as the Organic Law of the Judicature, continues to be applied in Brazil.

Regarding the topic under discussion, this law does not add much to the constitutionally foreseen standards. It included in article 25 the same guarantees of life-tenure office, non-removability and irreducibility of compensation[1] and in article 26 kept the prohibition to the exercise of political or party activity, under penalty of loss of office.[2]

Furthermore, article 35 listed a series of duties for judges, including maintaining irreproachable conduct in public and private life, as a way of reinforcing the trust of citizens in the Judiciary:

> **Article 35. Are Duties of Judges:**
> (...)
>
> VIII—maintain irreproachable conduct in public and private life.

However, going beyond the constitutional predictions, the article 41 brought the authorization for punishing judges for the excessive language or opinions expressed.

> **Article 41**
> Except in cases of impropriety or excessive language, the judge cannot be punished or harmed for the opinions he expresses or the content of the decisions he makes.

These were the norms that supported the control of the abusive exercise by judges of freedom of expression until the creation of the National Council of Justice, whose competence includes, among others, the inspection and monitorization of judges through disciplinary proceedings, being assured the right to full defense.

---

[1] Article 25. Except for the restrictions expressed in the Constitution, the judges enjoy the guarantee of life-tenure office, non-removability and irreducibility of compensation.

[2] Article 26. The judge with life-tenure office will only loose his office: I. in criminal persecution for common or responsibility crime; II. in administrative procedure for loss of office in the following hypothesis: (a) exercise, even if in availability, of any other function, except one higher teaching position, in public or private institution; (b) receipt, in any capacity and under any pretext, of percentages or costs in the processes subject to its order and judgment; (c) exercise of political-partisan activity.

4 Judicature Code of Ethics

Inspired by the Ibero-American Code of Judicial Ethics and also by the Bangalore Principles on Judicial Conduct, the National Council of Justice published in 2008 the Judicature Code of Ethics aiming to increase society's trust in the Judiciary, strengthening its legitimacy and cultivating ethical principles.

Its article 1st. includes several principles, among them independence, impartiality, transparency, dignity, honor and decorum:

> **Article 1st**
> The exercise of the judiciary requires conduct compatible with the precepts of this Code and the Statute of the Judicature, guided by the principles of independence, impartiality, knowledge and training, courtesy, transparency, professional secrecy, prudence, diligence, professional and personal integrity, dignity, honor and decorum.

Nonetheless, the Resolution number 305 of 2019 was the one that brought a real innovation, especially in the use of social media by judges, as can be seen.

5 Resolution 305 of the National Council of Justice

In order to deepen the judges free of expression legal standards, the National Council of Justice edited the mentioned Resolution 305, seeking to normatively discipline the new means of social communication, under the justification of making the judges fundamental right of freedom of expression compatible with the citizens guarantee of being judged by an independent, impartial and honest judge.

This is because the increasingly use of social networks, even outside the scope of judicial activity, can compromise society's trust in the Judiciary. With this resolution the National Council of Justice aims to combat the discredit of the judicial system and, consequently, preserve the legitimacy of the legal order.

It is important to notice that the Resolution 305 adopted a broad concept of social networks, once it was not restricted to public interaction, including the concept of social interaction. Therefore, there is a question about the legality of the restriction applied for judges in private contexts, such as conversations on applications as *WhatsApp* and *Telegram*. That is what statues the article 2nd, sole paragraph:

> **Article 2nd. (…)**
> Sole paragraph. Social networks are considered to be all websites, digital platforms and computer applications or mobile electronic devices aimed at public and social interaction, which enable communication, creation or sharing of messages, files or information of any nature.

The article 3rd recommended to judges several behaviors on social networks, which are divided into three groups. Section I established the rules for judges presence on social networks. It statutes that they must be careful selecting which social networks to join and which to leave out, avoiding exposure that refers to the institution. Furthermore, not even the use of anonymity authorizes the judge to exceed the limits of good ethical conduct.

> **Article 3rd. The Actions of Judges on Social Media Must Comply with the Following Recommendations:**
> I—Regarding presence on social networks:
>
> (a) adopt a selective and judicious approach to joining social networks, as well as identifying in each one of them;
> (b) observe that moderation, decorum and respectful conduct must guide all forms of action on social networks;
> (c) be aware that the use of pseudonyms does not exempt compliance with ethical limits of conduct and does not exclude the application of current regulations;
> (d) refrain from using the institution's brand or logo as a form of personal identification on social networks.

In the other hand, section II took care of the content of judge's statements, to avoid harm to the respectability of the Judiciary or excessive exposure. It suggested the search for institutional support in cases where the judge himself is a victim of offenses on social media, as long as it is due to the exercise of his position. Furthermore, it advised against sharing suspicious content or information, potentially *fake news:*

> II—Regarding the content of the statements, regardless of the use of the real name or pseudonym:
>
> (a) avoid expressing opinions or sharing information that could harm society's concept of the independence, impartiality, integrity and suitability of the judge or that could affect public trust in the Judiciary;
> (b) avoid demonstrations that seek self-promotion or overexposure;
> (c) avoid demonstrations whose content, due to inappropriate, could have a negative impact or go against administrative morality, always observing the prudence of language;
> (d) seek institutional support if you are a victim of offenses or abuse (cyberbullying, trolls and haters), due to your position;
> (e) avoid expressing opinions or advice on concrete or abstract legal topics that, even occasionally, may fall within their attribution or jurisdiction, except for expressions in technical works or in the exercise of teaching;
> (f) refrain from sharing content or expressing support for it without personal conviction about the veracity of the information, avoiding the spread of fake news.

Finally, section III dealt with the privacy and security of the judge and family, as careless access to social networks facilitates tracking and attacks by criminals or enemies. In this sense, one should be extra careful when following people or entities on social media.

III—Relating to privacy and security:

(a) pay attention to the fact that the use of social networks, without due precautions, and the exposure of information and data related to professional and private life may pose a risk to the personal safety and privacy of the judge and their family members;
(b) know the policies, rules and security and privacy settings of the social networks you use, reviewing them periodically;
(c) avoid following people and entities on social networks without due care regarding their safety.

On the other hand, the sole paragraph of article 3rd encouraged the use of social networks when educational or informative content is presented, highlighting social initiatives to promote citizenship, fundamental human rights and access to justice:

Sole paragraph. The educational and instructive use of social networks by judges is encouraged, for the purpose of disseminating scientific publications, content of doctrinal articles, theoretical knowledge, technical studies, social initiatives for the promotion of citizenship, fundamental human rights and initiatives for access to justice.

By it's turn, article 4th listed prohibitions for judges on social media, such as speaking about pending cases, their own or those of their colleagues, self-promotion, including commercial ones, and opinions that constitute discrimination or hate speech.

Article 4th. The Following Are Prohibited Conduct for Judges on Social Media:

I express an opinion on a case pending judgment, whether yours or someone else's, or a derogatory judgment on orders, votes or sentences from judicial bodies, with the exception of criticism in the records and in technical works or in the exercise of teaching;
II issue an opinion that demonstrates performance in party political activity or express public support or criticism of a candidate, political leaders or political parties;
III issue or share an opinion that characterizes discriminatory or hateful speech, especially those that reveal racism, LGBT-phobia, misogyny, anti-semitism, religious or ideological intolerance, among other manifestations of prejudice concerning sexual orientation, physical condition, age, gender, origin, social or cultural;
IV sponsor posts for the purpose of self-promotion or commercial purposes;
V receive sponsorship to express an opinion, publicize or promote commercial services or products;
VI associate your personal or professional image with company brand or commercial product.

However, call attention the content of the article 4th, item II, which prohibited judges from expressing public support or criticism of candidates, political leaders or political parties.

Specifically, regarding this prohibition, it is important to pay attention to the fact that paragraph 1 states that the prohibition of political-party activity does not cover manifestations on issues of public interest or of interest to the Judiciary:

> §1 For the purposes of section II of this article, the prohibition of political-partisan activity does not cover demonstrations, public or private, about government projects and programs, legislative processes or other issues of public interest, interest of the Judiciary or the career of the judiciary, as long as the dignity of the Judiciary is respected.

It is important to say that two constitutional procedures were installed at Brazilian Supreme Court by judge's associations against the Resolution 305 of the National Council of Justice. They were the Direct Actions of Unconstitutionality numbers 6.293 and 6.310. Here follows the main arguments presented against the mentioned norm:

1. The Federal Constitution prohibits prior censorship, especially of a general nature, as it obstructs the free circulation of ideas and information - an essential condition for any democratic regime -, so abuses must be faced after they occur;
2. Judges, like any citizen, have the right to freedom of thought and expression, which can only be relativized in exceptional situations, as long as rationally justified, in accordance with the hermeneutical postulates of maximum effectiveness of fundamental rights and proportionality;
3. The simple dissemination of an opinion by judges, even in matters of political bias, does not compromise the constitutional guarantees of the independence and impartiality of the Judiciary, with rare exceptions (e.g. judge who performs electoral functions), thus preserving its reliability before the society;
4. The principle of equality prevents the inferiority of the right of expression of judges in comparison to other public servants;
5. The prohibition of dedication to political-party activities does not cover public opinion on political issues;
6. The control of judge's conversations in private applications implies, to some extent, a violation of the fundamental rights to privacy and to the secrecy of communications.

Despite the arguments presented, the resolution is still valid and none of the procedures were judged until the day this article was written.

6 A Brief Reflection on Some Public Statements of Judges That Could Fit Into the Legal Framework of Judicial Ethics

Two recent cases stand out with considerable repercussion in national media, even though the consequences were not the same. One of them involves former judge Ludmila Lins Grilo, punished with compulsory retirement by the Court of Justice of Minas Gerais, after prior removal by the National Council of Justice, for violating the Organic Law of the Judicature and the Resolution 305.

The main reason for her punishment was that in one occasion she harshly criticized Justice Alexandre de Moraes, from the Supreme Court, for conducting the famous "Fake News" criminal investigation (Inquiry 4.781) in which himself appears as a victim.

Endorsing the criticisms of part of the doctrine, regarding the lack of impartiality in presiding an investigation where the justice figures as a victim, the former judge expressed the following in one of her speeches:

> An authoritarian act is a judge opening an investigation and acting as a victim, investigator and judge at the same time.

Does the criticism manifested by the former judge really violates the legal framework of judicial ethics? Or the punishment violates her freedom of speech?

Another case involves Justice Luís Roberto Barroso, from the Supreme Court, who, months after an extremely close and divided electoral dispute between former president Jair Messias Bolsonaro and the current president Luiz Inácio Lula da Silva, attended to the conference of the National Union of Students, where, alongside members from the political-party of the recent elected president, pronounced in his speech the following words: "We defeated the bolsonarism."

Faced with the negative repercussion in the next day the justice rectified his comments, through his *Twitter* account, saying the following:

> Yesterday, at the congress of the Nation Union of Students, I used the expression 'We defeated Bolsonarism', but in fact I meant to say the coup and violent extremism that manifested itself on January 8th and which corresponds to a minority.

No administrative procedure was opened against Justice Barroso and, consequently, there was no formal analysis of his words according to the legal framework of judicial ethics.

His words violate the legal framework of judicial ethics? Or are they covered by his right to the freedom of speech?

It is not the objective of this paper analyze these two situations. It will be made in another study with this specifically finality. For now, the idea is just to exemplify how the judicial ethics framework could be applied on real cases.

7 Conclusion

As could be seen, Brazil presents an intense regulation over judicial ethics.

However, most of it, especially the norms most related to the freedom of speech of judges, are above the level of law, once they are concentrated in administrative regulation provided by the National Council of Justice.

Another interesting point that comes straight from this first identification is that the biggest part to the limitation of judge's freedom of speech is an innovation that does not find parameters in the constitution nor in law.

Despite of those conclusions, the examples presented show that there are cases happening in Brazil that provokes the discussion over the limits of judge's freedom of speech in light of judicial ethics.

References

Brazil (1979) Complementary Law 35. https://www.planalto.gov.br/ccivil_03/leis/lcp/lcp35.htm
Brazil (1988) Constitution of the Federative Republic of Brazil. https://www.stf.jus.br/arquivo/cms/legislacaoConstituicao/anexo/brazil_federal_constitution.pdf
Brazil (2008) National Council of Justice: Judicature Code of Ethics. https://www.cnj.jus.br/codigo-de-etica-da-magistratura/
Brazil (2019) National Council of Justice: Resolution 305. https://atos.cnj.jus.br/atos/detalhar/3124#:~:text=Consideram%2Dse%20rede%20social%20todos,de%20informa%C3%A7%C3%B5es%20de%20qualquer%20natureza

Freedom of Expression for Judges or a Witch Hunt? The Case of Poland

Andrzej Jackiewicz

Abstract This article will analyse the legal situation regarding the disciplinary responsibility of judges and provide examples of such proceedings. Based on the procedural aspects of this responsibility and the general situation of the judiciary, which has undergone fundamental changes over the last few years, the question of whether judges in Poland have a right to freedom of expression will be answered.

1 Introduction

In 2015, with the parliamentary elections, a period of intensive systemic change, described as the erosion of the democratic system, began in Poland. Poland's constitutional crisis started with the political hijacking of the Constitutional Tribunal. While the crackdown began with the illegal actions of the outgoing parliament, the most serious problem was the refusal of the President of Poland to swear in properly elected Tribunal judges, followed by the illegal annulment by the Sejm of the resolutions under which they were appointed and then the appointment of new judges in their place, the so-called 'double judges'. In the following years, the Sejm majority filled successive judicial positions in the Tribunal with its nominees, leading to the assumption of total political control over that organ.[1] While the changes affected many institutions of a democratic state, this paper will address problems related to the functioning of the judiciary in terms of judges' freedom of expression and related disciplinary responsibility. In the first part of the article, an outline of normative changes concerning the analysed problem will be presented, with particular

[1] Sadurski (2019), p. 58, Mazur and Żurek (2017) pp. 5–18, Sadurski (2018), p. 63, Pech et al. (2021), pp. 6–8, Gersdorf and Pilich (2020), pp. 354–356 and Bień-Kacała (2020).

A. Jackiewicz (✉)
University of Bialystok, Bialystok, Poland
e-mail: jackiewicz@uwb.edu.pl

C. Hermida del Llano (ed.), *The Freedom of Expression for Judges in the Sphere of the Judicial Ethics*, Ius Gentium: Comparative Perspectives on Law and Justice 129, https://doi.org/10.1007/978-3-032-06504-9_10

emphasis on the National Council of the Judiciary, the Supreme Court and the model of disciplinary responsibility of judges. The second part outlines the specifics of disciplinary proceedings against judges in Poland and provides examples of proceedings in which allegations against judges play a key role. The next section will present examples of such cases, followed by the ECHR's perspective on the freedom of expression of judges stated in relation to Poland.

2 Method of Election of Members of the National Council of the Judiciary

Since 2016, the Polish Parliament has enacted more than 100 amendments to laws concerning the system and functioning of the judiciary in Poland—the Constitutional Tribunal, the Supreme Court, common courts, military courts and administrative courts, as well as the National Council of the Judiciary. For example, only the Law on the System of Common Courts was amended as many as 46 times between 2016 and 2023, and the Law on the Supreme Court, passed on 8 December 2017, was amended 17 times. A significant part of these amendments concerned the legal status of judges, including the system of disciplinary responsibility of judges.[2]

However, one of the most important, if not the most important change with an in-depth systemic impact on the entire justice system in Poland concerned the manner of election of members of the National Council of the Judiciary, the body which, under Article 186 of the Polish Constitution, safeguards the independence of the courts and judges.[3] The Polish Constitution is not remarkably elaborate about this organ. Indeed, the Basic Law defines only the task of this body (Article 186(1)), its composition and term of office (Article 187(1)) and two, potentially very important competencies—the presentation of candidates for judges to the President (Article 179) and the possibility to submit a motion to the Constitutional Tribunal regarding the compliance of normative acts with the Constitution insofar as they concern the independence of the courts and judges (Article 186(2)). With regard to the structure, scope of activities and working procedures of the National Council of the Judiciary, but importantly also about the manner of appointment of its members, the Constitution refers to the law, which is the Law of 12 May 2011 on the National Council of the Judiciary.[4]

The most fundamental issue turned out to be the composition of the National Council of the Judiciary and precisely the appointment of its members. The

[2] The genesis of these changes, and the first reforms, as well as the reaction to them on a Polish and international scale are presented by Hoffmann (2021), pp. 1153–1190. On the public protests and the involvement of various NGO's in Poland against these changes see Matthes (2021), pp. 263–281.

[3] Śledzińska-Simon (2018), pp. 1847–1851.

[4] Consolidated text Journal of Laws of 2021, item 269.

Constitution in Article 187(1) provides that the National Council of the Judiciary shall be composed as follows:

(1) the First President of the Supreme Court, the Minister of Justice, the President of the Supreme Administrative Court and an individual appointed by the President of the Republic;
(2) 15 judges chosen from amongst the judges of the Supreme Court, common courts, administrative courts and military courts;
(3) 4 members chosen by the Sejm from amongst its Deputies and 2 members chosen by the Senate from amongst its Senators.

So while there is little doubt regarding the first and third categories of members, the Constitution is silent regarding the manner of appointment of the 15 judges' representatives, indicating only that they are to be judges of the Supreme Court, common courts, administrative courts and military courts, referring, regarding the manner of their election, to the provisions of the relevant law. While until 2018 the selection was made by the judicial community, i.e. the judges of the different types of courts elected representatives from among themselves, since the amendment of the Act on the National Council of the Judiciary of 8 December 2017 (entered into force on 17 January 2018),[5] it is the Sejm that autonomously selects 15 judges as members of the National Council of the Judiciary, "as far as possible, taking into account the need for representation in the Council of judges of the different types and levels of courts (Art. 9a. para. 2 of the Act on the National Council of the Judiciary). The amending act, by allowing the immediate appointment of judges—members of the Council by the Sejm, terminated, along with their appointment, the membership of the National Council of the Judiciary of judges who had previously served as members of the Council.[6] Such a formation of the National Council of the Judiciary raised fundamental objections from the point of view of compliance with the Polish Basic Law, but also with EU law and international standards, from the moment of the amendment.[7] As Marcin Matczak writes, shaping the NCJ in this way allowed it to take total control over the appointment of Supreme Court judges,[8] but it also had a much broader dimension, affecting the entire judiciary.[9]

Despite continuing doubts in this regard,[10] the NCJ (sometimes referred to as the neo-NCJ) began functioning in its new composition by submitting some 2500 candidates for judges and assessors to the President over a period of 5 years.[11] Among these judges were persons appointed to the Supreme Court, to common courts at all

[5] Journal of Laws 2018, item 3.

[6] Pech et al. (2021) p. 11.

[7] Łukowiak (2019), pp. 101–112, Śledzińska-Simon (2018) pp. 1854–1855 and Grajewski (2018) pp. 19–20.

[8] Matczak (2017).

[9] Pech et al. (2021), p. 12.

[10] The amendment was challenged before the Constitutional Court, which did not share the applicants' doubts. See Jabłońska (2020), pp. 345–351.

[11] Krajowa Rada Sądownictwa (2023).

levels, to administrative courts (including the Supreme Administrative Court) and military courts. Crucially from the point of view of the subject of this study, the NCJ, so appointed, participated, inter alia, in the procedure for the appointment of all judges sitting in the Disciplinary Chamber of the Supreme Court, and is currently participating in this procedure concerning the judges of the Professional Responsibility Chamber, which replaced the infamous Disciplinary Chamber.[12]

3 Changes in the Model of Disciplinary Responsibility of Judges

The second fundamental change in the law from the point of view of the research subject concerned the model of disciplinary responsibility of judges. As a rule, the Polish formula for disciplinary proceedings against judges is based on the model of criminal proceedings, in which the judge appointed for this purpose acts as a prosecutor, and the case is heard by a court that includes other judges of common courts or the Supreme Court. Judges accused in disciplinary proceedings are entitled to procedural guarantees analogous to those enjoyed by defendants in criminal cases, first and foremost, of course, the right to a defence.

On April 3, 2018, the Law of December 8, 2017, on the Supreme Court,[13] which, while amending the Law on the System of Common Courts, fundamentally affected the Polish model of disciplinary responsibility of judges, granting the Minister of Justice the authority to appoint the Disciplinary Spokesman of Common Court Judges and his deputies, as well as assigning the duties of a disciplinary court judge.

The new law on the Supreme Court, however, established the Disciplinary Chamber, to whose jurisdiction was transferred the adjudication of, among other things, disciplinary cases of judges.[14] The structural model established under this law thus involves 11 disciplinary courts attached to appellate courts, which act as first-instance disciplinary courts, as well as the Disciplinary Chamber, replaced on July 15, 2022, by the Professional Responsibility Chamber, which is a second-instance disciplinary court and, in some cases, a first-instance court, and has other powers regarding the status of judges, such as suspending judges or waiving their immunity.[15] Crucially, however, a significant part of the disciplinary judges, including all judges of the Disciplinary Chamber (as of July 15, 2022, the Chamber of

[12] Filipek (2018), pp. 181–189.

[13] Journal of Laws 2018, item 5.

[14] See Venice Commission, Opinion on the draft Act amending the Act on the National Council of the Judiciary, on the draft Act amending the Act on the Supreme Court, and on the Act on the organisation of ordinary courts, Opinion 904/2017, 11 December 2017, CDL-AD(2017)031, see also Pech (2020) and Nelson (2023), pp. 428–429.

[15] Pech et al. (2021), pp. 9–11.

Professional Responsibility),[16] are judges appointed through a procedure in which a constitutionally questionable National Council of the Judiciary presented candidates to the President. However, there are still a significant number of judges in the Supreme Court who were appointed under the "old" procedure and who, despite unsuccessful attempts, have not been retired, hence one can speak of two faces of the Supreme Court.[17]

4 The "Muzzle" Law and the CJEU Ruling

From the point of view of the freedom of expression of judges, the so-called "muzzle law", or de facto Act of December 20, 2019, amending the Law—Law on the System of Common Courts, the Law on the Supreme Court and certain other laws, which entered into force on February 14, 2020, is also extremely important.[18] According to the proposers, the purpose of this legislation was to "put in order the systemic issues related to the status of a judge of the Supreme Court, common courts, military and administrative courts, as well as the organs of judicial self-government and the organs of the courts,"[19] the law, in addition to various systemic changes in the structures of the judiciary,[20] introduced disciplinary liability of judges for actions or omissions that may prevent or significantly impede the functioning of the judiciary, for actions that question the effectiveness of a judge's appointment, and, of particular importance from the point of view of freedom of expression, for public activities that are incompatible with the principles of the independence of courts and judges." Based on this law, an obligation to inform about membership in political parties and associations was introduced,[21] which is important from the point of view of resilient associations of judges (primarily the Association of Polish Judges "Iustitia", the Association of Judges "Themis").[22] In addition, according to the law, the colleges of the courts and also the organs of the judicial self-government may not undertake "political matters." At the same time "in particular, it is prohib-

[16] Currently in the Supreme Court, more than half of the people have been appointed as judges under flawed procedures.

[17] Ziółkowski (2020), pp. 1–16.

[18] See more about this Mazur (2020).

[19] See explanatory notes to the draft. Druk nr 69 Poselski projekt ustawy o zmianie ustawy – Prawo o ustroju sądów powszechnych, ustawy o Sądzie Najwyższym oraz niektórych innych ustaw.

[20] Among other things, the procedure for the election of the First President of the Supreme Court was changed - the right to propose a candidate for this position was given to any judge of the Supreme Court and the quorum necessary to elect the First President of the Supreme Court was lowered.

[21] The prohibition of public activities that are incompatible with the principles of judicial independence and independence of judges, as well as the prohibition of membership of political parties and trade unions, follows from Article 178(3) of the Polish Constitution.

[22] Matthes (2022), pp. 468–487.

ited to adopt resolutions that undermine the principles of the functioning of the authorities of the Republic of Poland and its constitutional bodies."[23]

The law was a reaction to the firm behaviour of many judges, questioning the legality of judicial appointments involving the neo-KRS and openly criticizing changes in judicial power. The law was met with numerous protests from, among others, the United Nations High Commissioner for Human Rights, the Council of Europe's Commissioner for Human Rights, the European Commission, the Venice Commission and the Council of Europe, among others. On April 29, 2020, the European Commission launched an infringement procedure against Poland and then brought an infringement action against Poland before the Court of Justice, aiming to declare that certain changes in the organization of the judiciary in Poland violate Union law.[24] According to the Commission, the changes prohibited any national court from examining the fulfilment of the Union's requirements for the independence and impartiality of the judiciary, and what's more, such an examination under the law can be considered a disciplinary offence. On top of this, the provisions were challenged, according to which it was transferred to the exclusive jurisdiction of the Supreme Court's Extraordinary Control and Public Affairs Chamber to examine issues concerning a judge's lack of independence or judicial independence.

In the course of the proceedings, the Court on July 14, 2021, imposed an interim measure on Poland, ordering it to immediately freeze the activities of the Supreme Court Disciplinary Chamber and suspend the provisions of the muzzle law.[25] This was not complied with, so Poland was ordered by an order of the Court's Vice President on October 27, 2021, to pay a periodic fine of one million euros per day to the Commission. The Polish government did not pay the fine, so the relevant amounts were deducted from time to time from EU funds allocated to Poland. On March 10, 2023, Poland requested the Court to annul or modify the order imposing the aforementioned fine on it. In support of this request, Poland argued that, as a consequence of the changes in the law, it had fully complied with its obligations under the interim measures, including the abolition of the Disciplinary Chamber. In an order dated April 21, 2023, the CJEU Vice President reduced the amount of the interim fine to 500,000 euros per day. According to the CJEU Vice President, Poland had only partially suspended the application of the provisions delegating to the exclusive jurisdiction of the Supreme Court's Extraordinary Control and Public Affairs Chamber the investigation of allegations of a judge's lack of independence or lack of judicial independence. Nevertheless, the vice president considered that the measures introduced by Poland could largely ensure the implementation of the interim measures indicated in the July 14, 2021 order. He pointed out that Poland

---

[23] See more Pech and Scheppele (2017), pp. 3–47.

[24] European Commission, Rule of Law: *European Commission launches infringement procedure to protect judges in Poland from political control*, IP/19/1957, 3 April 2019, Nelson (2023), p. 433.

[25] Pech (2021).

had repealed the provisions granting the Disciplinary Chamber certain powers to rule on the status of judges, and that the Chamber had been abolished.

On June 5, 2023, the Court of Justice of the European Union declared the law inconsistent with EU law, finding it incompatible with the guarantees of access to an independent and impartial court previously established by law.[26] The Court, citing previous case law,[27] confirmed that the Disciplinary Chamber of the Supreme Court does not meet the requirement of independence and impartiality, with the result that the independence of judges may be harmed by the very prospect of exposing judges who are supposed to apply Union law to the risk, that such a body will be able to rule on issues relating to their status and the performance of their office, in particular by authorizing the prosecution of a judge or his or her detention, or by issuing rulings on important aspects of labour law, social security or retirement.

In addition, the Court notes that, given the broad and imprecise nature of the provisions challenged by the Commission and the specific context in which those provisions were enacted, they can be interpreted in such a way as to use the system of disciplinary liability of judges to prevent national courts from assessing whether a court or judge meets the requirements under EU law for effective judicial protection, including, if necessary, using a reference to the Court for a preliminary ruling. The provisions enacted by the Polish legislature in this way are incompatible with the guarantees of access to an independent and impartial court previously established by law, which means that in certain circumstances national courts are obliged to examine whether they or the judges who comprise them, or other judges or courts, meet the requirements under Union law.

The Court also found incompatible with EU law the provision introduced by the muzzle law that it is only the Supreme Court's Chamber for Extraordinary Control and Public Affairs that has exclusive jurisdiction in this regard since respect for the essential requirements for effective judicial protection must be ensured across in all substantive areas of the application of EU law and before all national courts hearing cases in this area. It is also noteworthy from the point of view of the subject matter of this study that the Court found the provisions requiring judges to submit a written declaration of membership in an association or former membership in a political party, and providing for this information to be made available in electronic form, to be in violation of judges' fundamental rights to protection of personal data and respect for private life. Particularly relevant in this regard is the Court's finding that disclosure of data relating to judges' membership in associations or their activities in non-business foundations may reveal judges' political views or religious or philosophical convictions and that making them available in electronic form could allow free access to the said data also to persons who, for reasons unrelated to the declared goal of general interest, seek to obtain information about a judge's personal situation. Due to the specific context of the provisions introduced by the amending law,

[26] Commission v. Poland, C-204/21 R, Judgment Of The Court (Grand Chamber) of 5 June 2023,EU:C:2023:442.

[27] Commission v Poland. Case C-791/19 R, Order of the Court (Grand Chamber) of 8 April 2020, EU:C:2020:277, see more Pech (2021), Mistygacz and Sitek (2020), pp. 7–23.

such electronic access could expose judges to the risk of undeserved stigmatization, unduly affecting their perception both by individuals and the general public. Unfortunately, the CJEU's decision, which of course was neither the only one nor the first one on matters of disciplinary responsibility of judges in Poland,[28] did not cause the withdrawal of these provisions, which are still in force and applied.[29]

5 Cases of Disciplinary Proceedings Against the Freedom of Expression of Judges in Poland

With the reform of the system of disciplinary responsibility of judges in Poland, the phenomenon of initiating disciplinary proceedings against judges active in the public debate has emerged. Since 2018, disciplinary proceedings have been identified as one of the forms of pressure exerted particularly on judges of common courts in Poland.[30] These proceedings are politically motivated, as they are related to the content of rulings issued by judges, their presence at certain public events or their membership in associations and their public statements. According to a report by the Helsinki Foundation for Human Rights, threats of disciplinary proceedings have been formulated against more than half of the judges participating in the survey, they have been summoned to explain themselves before disciplinary spokesmen or disciplinary proceedings are pending against them. Participants in the survey unanimously indicated that the practice of applying disciplinary proceedings has significantly deteriorated over the years since the amended legislation came into force.[31]

Actions aimed at restricting the freedom of expression of judges thus take the form of disciplinary proceedings, which make use of the provisions of the key so-called "muzzle law" mentioned earlier in this regard, but also the provisions contained in the Collection of Principles of Professional Ethics of Judges, which the National Council of the Judiciary adopts. Under Resolution No. 15/17 of the National Council of the Judiciary of January 11, 2017, §23 was added, according to which a judge should exercise restraint in the use of social media. In addition, §16 of this resolution is used in disciplinary proceedings, according to which a judge may not by any of his behaviour create even the appearance of disrespecting the legal order.

As already mentioned, one of the categories of disciplinary proceedings initiated against judges, are proceedings aimed at restricting the freedom of expression of judges. This applies to statements of a public nature, particularly in the press and

---

28 Pech et al. (2021), pp. 27–38.

29 Jałoszewski (2023a).

30 See *inter alia*: Amnesty International, Polska: Wolne sądy, wolni ludzie. Sędziowie bronią swojej niezawisłości; Komitet Obrony Sprawiedliwości, Państwo, które karze; UN Special Rapporteur on the Independence of Judges and Lawyers, Report of Special Rapporteur Diego García-Sayán on his mission to Poland from 23 to 27 Oct. 2017.

31 Kalisz et al. (2019), pp. 36–37.

those published by judges in social media, especially those that express criticism of the introduced or announced reforms in the judiciary, or are related to a negative assessment of the state of the rule of law in Poland, sometimes openly pointing to violations of the law, especially the Constitution of the Republic of Poland.

The peculiarity of disciplinary proceedings in Poland, however, is that an explanatory proceeding is first initiated against judges, where evidence should be gathered to prove the commitment of a disciplinary tort or the judge's innocence. However, very often such proceedings are also initiated to keep judges in the dark and have a freezing effect on them.[32] The very initiation of an investigation for many judges, therefore, is a heavy psychological burden. Some of these proceedings, moreover, are only initiated but not completed, keeping judges in a state of mental uncertainty, which in itself can be a serious annoyance. Most often, however, the disciplinary spokesman follows the investigation by initiating disciplinary proceedings and filing disciplinary charges against the judge. Disciplinary proceedings can also be initiated without initiating an investigation. In the following section, examples of disciplinary cases related precisely to the sphere of judges' freedom of expression will be presented.

One of the judges whose activity in the sphere of public debate has resulted in disciplinary proceedings is Judge Waldemar Zurek, against whom 21 explanatory and disciplinary proceedings were pending at the same time in 2022. Judge of the District Court of Krakow Waldemar Zurek was a member of the National Council of the Judiciary for two terms, and until March 2018 was a spokesman for that Council. The judge is a member of the main board of the Themis Judges Association and has repeatedly spoken in the public debate on the state of the rule of law in Poland, in his statements he has always boldly defended the independence of the courts, the independence of judges and the principles of a democratic state of law, openly criticizing unconstitutional changes introduced in the area of the judiciary. Already in January 2018, Judge Waldemar Zurek was dismissed from his position as spokesman for civil cases of the District Court in Krakow, and in July 2018, was transferred from the Second Civil Appellate Division to the First Civil Division (first instance), which was criticized by the Themis Judges' Association and the Polish Judges' Association "Iustitia," which described the decision as politically motivated harassment against this judge and as an attempt to intimidate judges who speak out against measures aimed at political subordination of the judiciary. Judge Waldemar Zurek continued to participate in meetings with citizens, where current developments in the judiciary, including the independence of the courts and the independence of judges, were discussed. From the point of view of the issue of judges' freedom of speech, among several disciplinary proceedings brought against this judge, it is worth noting the charge brought against him in 2019 of committing a disciplinary offence under Article 107 § 1 of the Act of July 21, 2001—Law on the System of Common Courts, which consists of offending the dignity of the office. Thus, the judge was charged with having made a political manifesto in an interview

[32] Nelson (2023), p. 461.

given and published on the Law.pl website regarding his views and assessments related to the operation of the constitutional organs of the state, including the Constitutional Tribunal and the National Council of the Judiciary, after which he questioned the legality of the appointment of one of the judges of the Supreme Court, which, according to the Deputy Disciplinary Spokesman for Judges of Common Courts, violated the principle arising from Art. 178 (3) of the Constitution, the principle of apolitical conduct of judges, as well as the obligation under Article 82 § 1 of the Law on the System of Common Courts to act in accordance with the oath of office of a judge, i.e. behaviour that brings disrepute to the dignity of a judge and undermines confidence in his independence, impartiality and violates the principles of professional ethics.[33] It should be noted that absurd disciplinary charges were brought against this judge *en masse.* The vast majority (if not all) of these cases have now been dropped.

Another example of disciplinary proceedings against a judge is the case of the judge of the District Court in Gorzow Wielkopolski Olimpia Baranska-Maluszek, who has repeatedly publicly expressed critical opinions about the actions of the legislative and executive authorities in the area of the rule of law, human rights and the administration of justice. In a letter dated 11.10.2018, the Deputy Disciplinary Spokesman for Judges of Common Courts summoned the judge to submit a written statement on disciplinary offences involving the use of insulting terms against other judges and the Minister of Justice during a public appearance at the Pol'and'Rock Festival music festival in August 2018 in Kostrzyn-on-Odra.[34] According to the disciplinary ombudsman, such behaviour of the judge violated the solemnity of his office and undermined the dignity of the judge. In addition, the disciplinary ombudsman summoned the judge to submit a written statement on the untimely preparation in 2016–2017 of a total of 26 written grounds for judgments rendered beyond the statutory deadline. Following these actions, the Deputy Disciplinary Spokesman of Common Courts Judges initiated disciplinary proceedings against the judge and submitted to the judge 10 charges of committing disciplinary violations, consisting in the untimely preparation in 2016–2017 of a total of 10 written grounds for issued judgments. Eventually, the disciplinary spokesman discontinued the disciplinary proceedings initiated against Judge Olimpia Baranska-Maluszek, dropping the

---

[33] *Komunikat Rzecznika Dyscyplinarnego Sędziów Sądów Powszechnych w sprawie wszczęcia postępowań dyscyplinarnego przeciwko sędziom niestosujących się do nakazu powściągliwego korzystania z mediów społecznościowych z dnia 28 sierpnia 2019 r.,* [Announcement by the Disciplinary Ombudsman of the Common Court Judges on the initiation of disciplinary proceedings against judges failing to comply with the social media restraint order, dated 28 August 2019] published on the website of the Disciplinary Spokesman of the Judges of the Common Courts - rzecznik.gov.pl.

[34] Judge Olimpia Barańska-Małuszek, together with other judges from the "Iustitia" SSP, took part in the Pol'and'Rock Festival in Kostrzyn on the Odra River. The judges met with festival participants, conducted simulated hearings and organised numerous debates during which they explained the functioning of the courts to citizens in an accessible manner. The aim of this initiative was to provide legal education to the public and to stimulate the development of legal and civic awareness in society, especially among young people.

charges. However, in August 2019, disciplinary proceedings were initiated against the same judge in connection with the posting on social media of a critical post referring to the filing of a nomination for the Supreme Court Disciplinary Chamber by a prosecutor whose actions in the past led to Poland's recognition of violations of the European Convention on Human Rights, as well as describing the Minister of Justice as a minister who "manufactured the affair" and is "responsible for creating a system of corruption in the courts and prosecutor's office that makes the judiciary dependent on political will." The disciplinary spokesman accused the judge of failing to exercise restraint in his use of social media. As in the previous case, the judge was charged with failing to comply with the dignity of the office and the rules of professional ethics. The Disciplinary Court at the Court of Appeals in Wroclaw discontinued the disciplinary proceedings. It is worth noting at this point that further proceedings have been initiated against the judge, but this time already related to the content of the rulings, such as questioning the legality of the judgment of the Constitutional Tribunal, which included a so-called "double judge.

Another example of a disciplinary proceeding related to a judge's social media post is a case in which a judge is charged with the disciplinary tort of offending the dignity of his office (Article 107.1.5 of the Law on the System of Common Courts). The judge, in an entry published under his name and addressed to the President of Poland, called the President "a bad man, a lousy president, spewing hatred in the name of his immediate and partisan, political goals" and accused him of "harming Poland." The entry was meant as a response to the President's earlier words about the role of the Supreme Court Disciplinary Chamber to "eliminate black sheep" from the judicial community. The Disciplinary Court at the Court of Appeals in Wroclaw discontinued disciplinary proceedings against Judge J.O. (data anonymized), finding that the act did not contain the elements of a prohibited act. In the decision, it unequivocally stated that the entry did not insult the President and that the wording of the tweet was not so much an expression of the defendant's contempt, as a subjective assessment of the President made by him. The court further noted that the entry was a commentary on the political activity of Andrzej Duda and did not intend to insult him, but was only an evaluation of his actions.[35] As the order was appealed by the Minister of Justice, the Disciplinary Spokesman and the National Council of the Judiciary, the case went to the Chamber of Professional Responsibility where it is still awaiting a date to be set.

An exceptionally spectacular manifestation of restrictions on freedom of expression is the series of disciplinary proceedings initiated in August 2020 in response to a letter from 1278 Polish judges (including nearly 1200 judges of common courts, as well as judges of the Supreme Administrative Court and regional administrative courts) to the director of the Office for Democratic Institutions and Human Rights of the Organization for Security and Co-operation in Europe. In the letter, the judges expressed concern about changes in the law governing the elections for the office of the President of the Republic of Poland, ordered for May 10, 2020, and appealed for

[35] Order of 20 June 2022, ASD 1/21.

support, dialogue and careful monitoring of the electoral and legislative process. In addition, the judges noted that the hearing of election protests and the determination of the validity of the elections will take place before the Supreme Court's Extraordinary Control and Public Affairs Chamber, whose members were appointed in a legally flawed process causing its lack of independence.

Following the letter, the Deputy Disciplinary Spokesman for Judges of Common Courts sent a letter to all disciplinary ombudsmen operating at district and appellate courts in Poland, asking whether they had already initiated explanatory proceedings against the signatories of the letter in their districts, demanding that they send copies of the relevant decisions or justify the reasons for not initiating such proceedings. According to the Deputy Spokesman, the judges violated Article 179(3) of the Constitution, which states that "a judge may not belong to a political party, a trade union or engage in public activities that are incompatible with the principles of judicial independence and the independence of judges." In addition, there was a charge of illegally questioning the legitimacy of judges ruling in the Supreme Court's Chamber for Extraordinary Control and Public Affairs.[36] Even before this letter, in May 2020, the Deputy Disciplinary Spokesman at the Piotrkow Trybunalski Regional Court initiated an explanatory proceeding against more than a dozen judges, which resulted in disciplinary charges against 16 judges, relating to, among other things, questioning the legality of the Supreme Court's Chamber of Extraordinary Control and Public Affairs, i.e. a new type of disciplinary offence added by the "muzzle law."

Another quite original manifestation of the mass expression of criticism against the changes in the judiciary was a public demonstration organised by judges' associations together with other NGOs, called the "March of a Thousand Robes", in which judges and representatives of other legal professions took part, walking in silence through the streets of Warsaw in the clothes they usually wear in the courtroom. Although silent, the expression was exceptionally audible in Poland and abroad.[37]

6 Standards of Freedom of Expression for Judges

Explanatory and disciplinary proceedings initiated with the motivation of freezing judges' freedom of expression have no raison d'être by constitutional and international standards. Both in the cases cited above and in the vast majority of other cases, judges, in expressing their opinions on important matters in the field of the judiciary, enjoy the freedom to express their views and opinions guaranteed by Article 54 (1) of the Constitution of the Republic of Poland, Article 10 (1) of the

[36] Jałoszewski (2023b).

[37] Gersdorf and Pilich, (2020), pp. 374–375.

Convention for the Protection of Human Rights and Fundamental Freedoms and Article 11 (1) of the Charter of Fundamental Rights of the European Union.

The right of a judge to criticize the actions of the legislative and executive branches in the judicial field that may threaten the independence of the judiciary was affirmed in Baka v. Hungary, May 27, 2014. (Application No. 20261/12). Also, the European Network of Councils for the Judiciary (ENCJ), in the Sofia Declaration adopted on June 7, 2013, affirmed the duty of judges to oppose government proposals that, among other things, may undermine the independence of judges, or councils of the judiciary. According to point VII of the declaration, the general custom of judges not speaking out on political controversies should not apply when the integrity and independence of the judiciary are threatened. Judges throughout Europe today have a common duty to express unequivocally and convincingly their opposition to government proposals that may undermine the independence of judges or the judicial councils.

Referring to the standards of freedom of expression of judges in the context of Poland, attention should be paid to the ECHR judgment of June 16, 2022, in the case of Żurek v. Poland (Complaint No. 39650/18). The complainant in the case was Judge Waldemar Zurek, already mentioned in the study, who alleged that he was denied his right of access to court to challenge the premature and allegedly arbitrary expiration of his term of office as a judge-member of the National Council of the Judiciary, but, most importantly for the scope of this study, he also raised in his complaint the measures taken by the authorities in connection with the opinions he expressed publicly in his office on legislative reforms affecting the judiciary. First, the judgment is worth noting from the point of view of the ECHR's assessment of the political situation in Poland. Indeed, it maintained the position previously expressed in the case of Grzęda v. Poland (complaint no. 43572/18), in which the Court noted that the entire sequence of events in Poland clearly indicates that successive judicial reforms were aimed at weakening judicial independence, starting with serious failures in the election of Constitutional Tribunal judges in December 2015, through, in particular, the reconstruction of the NCJ and the creation of new chambers in the Supreme Court, to the expansion of the Minister of Justice's control over the courts and his increased role in the disciplinary responsibility of judges. According to the Court, as a result of the successive reforms, the judiciary—an autonomous branch of state power—has been exposed to interference from the executive and legislative branches, and thus significantly weakened.

Secondly, the ECHR recalled the principles established in the Baka case relating to judges' freedom of expression. Thus, the Court recalled that given the prominent place among state organs held by the judiciary in a democratic society, that this approach also applies when judges' freedom of expression is restricted in connection with their function, even though the judiciary is not part of the ordinary civil service. The Court held that public officials serving in the judiciary can be expected to show restraint in the exercise of the right to freedom of expression in all matters in which the seriousness and impartiality of judicial authority may arguably be questioned [...]. Dissemination of even correct information should be done in moderation and in an appropriate manner [...]. The Court has emphasized on many occasions the special social role of the judicial authority, which, as the guarantor of justice, a fundamental value in the rule of law, must enjoy public confidence if it is to successfully carry out its tasks [...]. For this reason, judicial authorities, in the performance of their adjudicatory function, are obliged to exercise maximum discretion with regard to the cases they handle in order to preserve their image as impartial judges [...]. At the same time, the Court stresses that given in particular the growing importance of the tri-partite government and safeguarding the independence of the judiciary, any interference with the freedom of expression of judges in a position such as that of the applicant requires careful consideration by the Court [...]. Moreover, issues concerning the functioning of the judiciary fall within the scope of the public interest, the debate of which is normally subject to a high level of protection under Article 10 [...]. Even if the subject matter being debated has political implications, this is not a sufficient reason to prohibit a judge from speaking on the issue [...]. Issues concerning the tri-partite division of power may involve, in a democratic society, very important matters about which the public has a legitimate right to be informed and which fall within the scope of political debate [...]. In the context of Article 10 of the Convention, the Court must take into account the circumstances and overall context in which the statements in question were made [...]. It must look at the challenged interference in light of the entire case [...], paying particular attention to the position taken by the applicant, his statements and the context in which they were made. It must also not forget the "freezing effect" that the threat of sanctions has on the exercise of the right to freedom of expression, particularly for other judges wishing to participate in the public debate on justice and the judiciary [...].

Importantly, however, the Court in Zurek v. Poland notes that a similar approach would apply to any judge who exercises his or her freedom of expression—in accordance with the above principles—to defend the rule of law, judicial independence or other similar values that are the subject of debate on issues of general interest. If a judge makes such statements not only on his or her personal behalf but also on behalf of a judicial council, judicial association or other body representing the judicial community, the protection afforded to that judge will be strengthened. Of fundamental importance in the context of the subject of this paper, however, is the ECHR's recognition that the general right of judges to freedom of expression on issues concerning the functioning of the judicial system can translate into an analogous duty to speak out in defence of the rule of law and judicial independence when these fundamental values are threatened.

As the ECHR pointed out, this obligation has been recognized by, among others, the CCJE,[38] the UN Special Rapporteur on the Independence of Judges and

[38] Para. 41 CCJE Opinion No. 18 (2015) *The position of the judiciary and its relation with the other powers of state in a modern democracy*.

Lawyers,[39] and the General Assembly of the ENCJ.[40] The Court further reiterated in this regard, citing its previous jurisprudence, that given the prominent place the judiciary occupies among state organs in a democratic society, and the importance attached to the separation of powers and the need to protect independence, the Court must be particularly sensitive to protecting a group of persons performing judicial functions from measures that may jeopardize their judicial independence and autonomy (Ramos Nunes de Carvalho e Sá v. Portugal [WI], no. 55391/13; Bilgen v. Turkey, No. 1571/07, and Grzęda v. Poland, No. 43572/18).

Thus, in relating the cited standards to the case at hand, the Court assessed that, given the accumulation of measures used by the authorities, these measures could be considered a strategy aimed at intimidating (or even silencing) the applicant in connection with the views he expressed in defence of the rule of law and judicial independence. The Court further noted that the applicant is one of the most emblematic representatives of the judicial community in Poland, who has consistently defended the rule of law and the independence of the judiciary. The Court believes that the challenged measures undoubtedly had a "freezing effect," as they must have discouraged not only the complainant but also other judges from future participation in the public debate on legislative reforms affecting the judiciary.

7 Conclusions

The changes which were introduced to the Polish judiciary in a number of areas, particularly those concerning the Constitutional Tribunal and the National Council of the Judiciary, met with a strong reaction from the judicial community, and in particular from judges affiliated with the Themis and Iustitia associations of judges. The judges mainly contested the legal status of the so-called neo-judges appointed by the President on the proposal of the so-called neo-KRS, i.e. the National Council of the Judiciary acting in an unconstitutional composition, but they also expressed criticism of the changes in the judiciary and the state of the rule of law in Poland. This was met with a furious response from the government, which through legislative amendments (so-called muzzle laws) and disciplinary spokesmen appointed by the Minister of Justice, began to initiate disciplinary proceedings against those judges who contested the actions of the government. The purpose of these disciplinary proceedings was to have a chilling effect to deter criticism from judges and to prevent contestation of the status of so-called 'neo-judges'. However, this did not have the desired effect, and judges continue to express their opinions using the freedom of expression guaranteed by the Polish Constitution and international

[39] A/HRC/41/48*: Independence of judges and lawyers - Report of the Special Rapporteur on the independence of judges and lawyers*, para. 101 and 102.

[40] See point VII of Sofia Declaration On Judicial Independence and Accountability of the Justice System, 5th – 7th June, 2013 2013 r.

standards, the scope of which has been determined mostly by ECHR jurisprudence, which was also applied in cases in which Polish judges were the applicants.

References

Bień-Kacała A (2020) Polexit is coming or is it already here? Comments on the Judicial Independence Decisions of the Polish Constitutional Tribunal. Int J Const Law Blog. http://www.iconnectblog.com/2020/04/polexit-is-coming-or-is-it-already-here-comments-on-the-judicial-independence-decisions-of-the-polish-constitutional-tribunal

Filipek P (2018) The new National Council of the Judiciary and its impact on the Supreme Court in the light of the principle of judicial independence, Problemy Współczesnego Prawa Międzynarodowego, Europejskiego i Porównawczego XVI: 177–196. https://doi.org/10.26106/3c60-qv69

Gersdorf M, Pilich M (2020) Judges and representatives of the people: a polish perspective. ECLR 16(3):345–378. https://doi.org/10.1017/S1574019620000206

Grajewski K (2018) Krajowa Rada Sądownictwa w świetle przepisów ustawy z 8 grudnia 2017 r. – zagadnienia podstawowe. Krajowa Rada Sądownictwa 1:17–35

Hoffmann M (2021) [PiS]sing off the courts: the PiS party's effect on judicial Independence in Poland. Vanderbilt Law Rev 51(4):1153–1190

Jabłońska P (2020) Glosa do wyroku Trybunału Konstytucyjnego z 25 marca 2019 r., sygn. akt K 12/18. Przegląd Prawa Konstytucyjnego 53(1):345–351. https://doi.org/10.15804/ppk.2020.01.22

Jałoszewski M (2023a) Pierwsze represje po wyborach za stosowanie prawa UE. Schab uderza w KPO. OKO Press

Jałoszewski M (2023b) Rzecznik dyscyplinarny Ziobry chce ścigania na raz 1278 sędziów. OKO Press

Kalisz M, Szuleka M, Wolny M (2019) Czas próby. Polscy sędziowie wobec zmian w wymiarze sprawiedliwości, Warszawa

Krajowa Rada Sądownictwa (2023) Informacje o działalności KRS z lat 2018–2022. https://krs.pl/pl/dzialalnosc/sprawozdania/2014-informacja-z-dzialalnosci-krs-w-2022r.html

Łukowiak D (2019) Glosa do wyroku Trybunału Konstytucyjnego z 25 marca 2019 r., sygn. akt K 12/18 (wybór sędziów do składu Krajowej Rady Sądownictwa przez Sejm). Przegląd Konstytucyjny 3:101–112

Matczak M (2017) Who's next? On the Future of the Rule of Law in Poland, and why President Duda will not save it, VerfBlog. https://verfassungsblog.de/whos-next-on-the-future-of-the-rule-of-law-in-poland-and-why-president-duda-will-not-save-it/. https://doi.org/10.17176/20170719-182938

Matthes C-Y (2021) Safeguarding democracy and the rule of law by civil society actors? The case of Poland. In: Lorenz A, Anders LH (eds) Illiberal trends and anti-EU politics in East Central Europe, Palgrave studies in European Union politics. Palgrave Macmillan, Cham, pp 263–281. https://doi.org/10.1007/978-3-030-54674-8_11

Matthes C-Y (2022) Judges as activists: how polish judges mobilise to defend the rule of law. EEP 38(3):468–487. https://doi.org/10.1080/21599165.2022.2092843

Mazur D (2020) From bad to worse – the Polish judiciary in the shadow of the 'muzzle act', Annual report for 2020 (second publication), http://themis-sedziowie.eu/materials-in-english/from-bad-to-worse-the-polish-judiciary-in-the-shadow-of-the-muzzle-act-annual-report-for-2020-second-publication

Mazur D, Żurek W (2017) So-called 'Good change' in the Polish system of the administration of justice, https://www.jura.uni-bonn.de/

Mistygacz M, Sitek W (2020) Skutki postanowienia Trybunału Sprawiedliwości Unii Europejskiej z 8.04.2020 r., C-791/19 R, dotyczącego niezależności Izby Dyscyplinarnej Sądu Najwyższego dla postępowań dyscyplinarnych. Przegląd Sądowy 7-8:7–23

Nelson RA (2023) Poland's rule of law snowball: the increasing severity of the rift between Poland and the European union. San Diego Int Law J 24:417–441

Pech L (2020) Dealing with 'fake judges' under EU Law: Poland as a Case Study in light of the Court of Justice's ruling of 26 March 2020 in Simpson and HG, Reconnect Working Paper 8:1–31. https://reconnect-europe.eu/wp-content/uploads/2020/05/RECONNECT-WP8.pdf

Pech L (2021) Protecting Polish Judges from Political Control: A brief analysis of the ECJ's infringement ruling in Case C-791/19 (disciplinary regime for judges) and order in Case C-204/21 R (muzzle law), VerfBlog. https://verfassungsblog.de/protecting-polish-judges-from-political-control. https://doi.org/10.17176/20210720-140052-0

Pech L, Scheppele KL (2017) Illiberalism within: rule of law backsliding in the EU 2017. Camb Yearb Eur Leg Stud 19:3–47. https://doi.org/10.2139/ssrn.3009280

Pech L, Wachowiec P, Mazur D (2021) Poland's rule of law breakdown: a five-year assessment of EU'S (in)action. Hague J Rule Law 13:1–43. https://doi.org/10.1007/s40803-021-00151-9

Sadurski W (2018) Polish constitutional tribunal under PiS: from an activist court, to a paralysed tribunal, to a governmental enabler. Hague J Rule Law 11:63–84. https://doi.org/10.1007/s40803-018-0078-1

Sadurski W (2019) Poland's constitutional breakdown. Oxford University Press, Oxford. https://doi.org/10.1093/oso/9780198840503.001.0001

Śledzińska-Simon A (2018) The rise and fall of judicial self-government in Poland: on judicial reform reversing democratic transition. German Law J 19(7):1839–1870. https://doi.org/10.1017/S2071832200023257

Ziółkowski M (2020) Two faces of the polish supreme court after "reforms" of the judiciary system in Poland: the question of judicial Independence and appointments. Eur Pap 5(1):347–362. https://doi.org/10.15166/2499-8249/362

Freedom of Expression of Judges and Its Limitations in the Context of the Right to an Impartial Court in the Czech and European Context

Pavel Klíma

Abstract In his contribution, the author deals with the complex interconnection between the freedom of expression of judges and the imperative of maintaining an impartial court, both in the Czech legal framework and in the broader European context. The author therefore first of all presents the standards of judicial conduct in general terms and examines how the freedom of expression of judges, limited by the nature of their profession, intersects with the right to an impartial court. At the European level, the author points out the fact that the European Convention on Human Rights forms a key background and reflects on the delicate balance between the right of judges to freedom of expression and the need for an impartial judiciary. In addition, the author refers to the case law of the European Court of Human Rights concerning subjective and objective tests of judicial impartiality. The author also examines the Czech legal context, detailing the constitutional and statutory provisions relating to the conduct of judges, in which context the author presents two practical cases.

1 Introduction

Freedom of expression is one of the oldest guaranteed fundamental rights and freedoms and is one of the basic symbols of a democratic state governed by the rule of law. As a consequence of freedom of expression, every individual can express his or her own views in public without fear, even if they are perceived, or might be perceived, to be minority views. Freedom of expression is one of the main conditions for the progress of a democratic society, as well as for the development of the individual.

However, freedom of expression is not limitless and may be restricted in the event of a conflict with another of the fundamental rights and freedoms, where the

P. Klíma (✉)
Metropolitan University Prague, Prague, Czech Republic

C. Hermida del Llano (ed.), *The Freedom of Expression for Judges in the Sphere of the Judicial Ethics*, Ius Gentium: Comparative Perspectives on Law and Justice 129, https://doi.org/10.1007/978-3-032-06504-9_11

public interest requires that another fundamental principle (other than freedom of expression) be given priority, whose application and protection will be crucial in the light of the particular circumstances.

This issue, i.e. the question of the possibility of limiting freedom of expression, is constantly evolving, also in the light of recent and ongoing dynamic developments in the field of modern (information) technologies. Often the question arises as to how widely the field within which freedom of expression can be exercised without limit is delimited, or where the "demarcation line" stands beyond which the expression in question can no longer enjoy protection.[1]

One of the key prerequisites for the proper administration of justice, as well as for maintaining public confidence in justice, is an emphasis on adherence to the principles of judicial ethics. Judicial ethics can be defined as an applied branch of ethics dealing with the ethical norms and values shared within the judiciary, including the obligations in the professional and personal life of judges, in order to ensure the proper performance of the judicial function, respectively, and to ensure the proper administration of justice.[2]

The rules of judicial ethics imply a whole range of obligations, as a result of which, in terms of compliance with ethical standards, judges are often held to higher standards of conduct in their professional and personal lives than "ordinary" citizens, given the specific nature of their profession.

In this context, the issue of the rules of judicial ethics has long been discussed in connection with the scope of the exercise of one of the fundamental rights, namely the right to freedom of expression, i.e. the extent to which a judge's freedom of expression is limited by his or her judicial function. Even a judge's freedom of expression cannot be unlimited, and—as has already been said—given the specific nature of the judicial function, the scope of its application is narrower than that of "ordinary" citizens, or at least most other professions. The limited scope of applicability of the right to freedom of expression as part of judicial ethics is a conditio sine qua non for the dignified conduct of judicial proceedings, the preservation of the authority and impartiality of the court (the judiciary) in the narrower sense, and the proper administration of justice, including the necessary preservation of public confidence in justice in the broader sense.

However, these "higher principles" are capable of being threatened by improper speech or other conduct by judicial persons, which can generally be understood as culpable conduct or actions by which a judicial person undermines the dignity of the judicial office or undermines confidence in the independent, impartial, professional and fair administration of justice.

According to the Czech disciplinary practice, the prevailing types of inappropriate actions (behaviours) on the part of judges or other judicial persons can be generally traced as follows: lack of restraint in public speeches (civil or political), inappropriate (disrespectful) speeches in relation to participants or parties to court

[1] See Klíma (2023)

[2] See Visinger (2019), Chap. 4.1

proceedings, to other judges and to other court employees, attacks on the independence and impartiality of the court, manipulation of court documents or influence by alcohol or other drugs. Lack of restraint in public speeches may include inappropriate public speeches by a judge interfering with political competition or inappropriate criticism in relation to the functioning of public administration, including the administration of justice. Inappropriate (disrespectful) speeches in relation to participants or parties in court proceedings or court staff may take the form of a variety of expressions consisting of arrogant, contemptuous or other forms of conduct generally regarded as discourteous. Attacks on the independence and impartiality of the court may include a priori cases of impermissible influence on colleagues in their decision-making activities or cases of failure to declare one's own bias despite the existence of legal prerequisites. Manipulation of court documents in practice most often takes place in the form of alteration of court records, which creates a discrepancy between the actual course of the proceedings (recorded in the record) on the one hand and the content of the record which formally proves that actual course on the other hand.[3]

It is obvious that a significant part of possible inappropriate actions (behaviours) on the part of judges, or other judicial persons, which may occur, or actually occur in practice, relates to the issue of freedom of expression and is related to the consequences of restrictions on the right to freedom of expression of judges resulting from their position and in many respects the specific nature of their profession.

2 The Right to Freedom of Expression vs. the Right to an Impartial Tribunal and the Interpretation of the Concept of an Impartial Tribunal Under the Convention

According to Article 10 of the European Convention on Human Rights (below as "the Convention"), everyone has the right to freedom of expression. This guaranteed right, according to the wording of Article 10, includes the freedom to hold opinions and to receive and impart information or ideas without interference by public authorities and regardless of frontiers. The exercise of freedom of expression, is not absolute and may be subject to conditions or limitations which are laid down by law and which are necessary in a democratic society in the interests of national security, territorial integrity or public safety, the preservation of order and the prevention of disorder and crime, the protection of health or morals, the protection of the reputation or rights of others, the prevention of the leakage of confidential information or the preservation of the authority and impartiality of the judiciary.[4]

[3] See Visinger (2019), Chap. 4.2

[4] See for more details Article 10 of the Convention.

This is a list of legitimate objectives for which the exercise of freedom of expression may be restricted.

In this manner, Article 10 of the Convention already foresees as one of the grounds for limiting the scope of the exercise of the right to freedom of expression the postulate of the impartiality of the judiciary, which is one of the fundamental components and conditio sine qua non for the existence and implementation of the right to a fair trial under Article 6 of the Convention, according to which (among other things) everyone has the right to have his or her case heard fairly, publicly and within a reasonable time by an independent and impartial tribunal. Article 6 of the Convention as such thus underlines the right to an impartial tribunal, the preservation of which is a prerequisite for the protection of the confidence that courts must inspire in the public[5] in a democratic society, or, in particular, in criminal proceedings, in the accused.[6]

The requirement of the impartiality of the judiciary as an integral part of the right to a fair trial, as well as the limitation of the right to freedom of expression with regard to the postulate of impartiality is therefore expressed not only in the legal systems of individual countries, but also on the international scale, in particular, at the level of the Council of Europe as well as at the level of the European Union.[7]

As regards impartiality and simply presented: "Impartiality normally denotes the absence of prejudice or bias."[8]

In its case law, the *European Court of Human Rights* (below as "the *ECtHR*") has repeatedly presented the way in which the impartiality of judges is assessed. In order to conclude whether or not the requirement of judicial impartiality under Article 6(1) of the Convention is met, it is necessary to apply the "subjective test"and the "objective test".[9]

The subjective test is used to examine the personal convictions and behaviour of a particular judge (i.e. whether the judge has acted in a biased or prejudiced manner). In contrast, the objective test examines whether the court itself and, inter alia, its composition provided sufficient safeguards to exclude any legitimate doubts about its impartiality. As regards the subjective test, the principle that a judge must be presumed not to be personally biased or prejudiced has long been established in the case law of the ECtHR. A judge's personal impartiality must thus be presumed until the contrary is proved.[10]

[5] See e.g. Piersack v. Belgium, judgment of the ECtHR as of 1 October 1982, no. 8692/79, § 30.

[6] See e.g. De Cubber v. Belgium, judgment of the ECtHR as of 26 October 1984, no. 9186/80, § 26 a Fey v. Austria, judgment of the ECtHR as of 24 May 1993, no. 14396/88, § 30.

[7] See Article 11 in conjunction with Article 52 and Article 47 Charter of Fundamental Rights of the European Union.

[8] See e.g. Sigríður Elín Sigfúsdóttir v. Iceland, judgment of the ECtHR as of 25 February 2020, no. 41382/17, § 45.

[9] See e.g. Kyprianou v. Cyprus [GC], judgment of the ECtHR as of 15 December 2005, no. 73797/01, § 118.

[10] See e.g. Hauschildt v. Denmark, judgment of the ECtHR as of 24 May 1989, no. 10486/83, § 47.

The objective test considers whether, irrespective of the judge's personal conduct, there are ascertainable facts which may raise doubts as to his impartiality. The objective test is crucial in most cases, and in deciding whether there is a legitimate reason to fear that a particular judge or a body sitting on a panel is not impartial in a particular case, the opinion of the person concerned is important but not decisive. What is decisive is whether that concern can be regarded as objectively justified.[11]

In case law, cases of lack of objective impartiality are more common than cases of subjective impartiality. It is obviously not easy to prove cases of lack of subjective impartiality. One of the few cases in which a violation of subjective impartiality has been demonstrated was the case of Kyprianou v. Cyprus, inter alia, with regard to the court's wording in the grounds of the decision sentencing the accused to several days' imprisonment for contempt of court.

First of all, the judges in the decision sentencing the applicant, acknowledged that they had been "deeply insulted" "as persons" by the accused what according to the ECtHR shows that the judges had been personally offended by his words and conduct and indicates personal involvement on their part. Also, the strong language used by the judges in their decision evoked a sense of outrage and shock, contrary to the detached approach expected of judicial pronouncements. In particular, it was stated by the judges that they could not "conceive of another occasion of such a manifest and unacceptable contempt of court by any person, let alone an advocate" and that "if the court's reaction is not immediate and drastic, we feel that justice will have suffered a disastrous blow."[12]

The objective test mostly concerns hierarchical or other links between the judge and other actors in the proceedings.[13] The lack of objective impartiality was found, for example, in the case where there was the dual role of a judge in a single set of proceedings what was reinforced by the involvement of the judge's daughter since the applicant's constitutional complaint had been decided by a panel of judges whose one member and subsequently his daughter had previously represented the applicant's opponents. This situation was capable of raising legitimate doubts as to this judge's impartiality.[14] The lack of objective impartiality was also found in the case where the judge in question judged the applicant while there was a parallel proceeding in which this judge acted as legal representative for one side in question against the applicant.[15]

The objective test of impartiality, which may raise doubts about the judge's impartiality, also applies to situations where a judge who, in the previous stages of a particular criminal proceeding, participated in selected acts of the criminal

---

[11] See e.g. Castillo Algar v. Spain, judgment of the ECtHR as of 28 October 1998, no. 28194/95, § 45 or Micallef v. Malta, judgment of the ECtHR as of 15 October 2009, no. 17056/06, § 96.

[12] See Kyprianou v. Cyprus [GC], judgment of the ECtHR as of 15 December 2005, no. 73797/01, § 118.

[13] See Micallef v. Malta, judgment of the ECtHR as of 15 October 2009, no. 17056/06, § 97.

[14] See Meznaric v. Croatia, judgment of the ECtHR as of 30 November 2005, no. 71615//01, § 24 a 36.

[15] See Wettstein v. Switzerland, judgment of the ECtHR as of 21 December 2000, no. 33958//96, § 47.

proceeding in which he or she did not decide on the merits of the case, e.g. as a detention judge[16]or investigating judge.[17]

Whether such misgivings may be regarded as objectively justified depends on the circumstances of each particular case; the mere fact that a judge has also made pre-trial decisions in the case (including those concerning detention on remand) cannot in itself justify fears as to his impartiality.[18]

However, special circumstances may in a given case can lead to a different conclusion. When for example—according to domestic law—it is required as one of the requirements to decide about detention on remand that there is a "particularly confirmed suspicion"that the accused has committed the crime(s) with which he or she is charged, in other words that the judge has to be convinced that there is "a very high degree of clarity"as to the question of guilt, the difference between a finding of the existence of that degree of suspicion and the applicant's guilt is narrow.[19]

A case of lack of objective impartiality was found also, for example, in a case where the judge had at an earlier stage identified himself as biased in relation to the applicant for a reason which was still ongoing, namely in respect of their working relationship. In spite of the fact that the ECtHR does not consider that the existence of a work relationship between a judge and a lawyer practising in the court concerned necessarily entails a lack of impartiality on the part of the former, the decisive factor in the present case is the fact that judge had previously withdrawn on that very ground, which still pertained when he later participated in the decision to dismiss the applicant's appeal. Therefore, the Court finds that no sufficient guarantees were provided to exclude legitimate doubt as to his impartiality towards the applicant.[20]

Another case of violation of the right to an impartial tribunal in the sense of violation of objective impartiality is, for example, the case when the law did not allow the applicant to be informed of the composition of the court which imposed the penalty, and thus to ascertain the absence of any prejudice on its part or any link between one of its members and the party in question, which might vitiate the proceedings.[21]

In relation to the conflict between freedom of expression and the right to an impartial tribunal, reference may be made to the use of formulation in the course of the proceedings by the judge, including decisions made in the course of the proceedings, from which it is clear that he has already taken a particular position on the question of the applicant's guilt. E.g. the Court found that there has been a violation of the applicant's right under Article 6 § 1 of the Convention to a hearing by an

[16] See Hauschildt v. Denmark, judgment of the ECtHR as of 24 May 1989, no. 10486/83.

[17] See De Cubber v. Belgium, judgment of the ECtHR as of 26 October 1984, no. 9186/80.

[18] See Garrido Guerrero v. Spain, judgment of the ECtHR as of 2 March 2000, no. 43715/98 or Hauschildt v. Denmark, judgment of the ECtHR as of 24 May 1989, no. 10486/83, § 50.

[19] See Hauschildt v. Denmark, judgment of the ECtHR as of 24 May 1989, no. 10486/83, § 52.

[20] See Panyik v. Hungary, judgment of the ECtHR as of 12 July 2011, no. 12748/06, § 31.

[21] See Vernes v. France, judgment of the ECtHR as of 20 January 2011, no. 30183/06, § 42.

impartial tribunal in the situation within the case when a court made statements implying that the applicant had committed the offence in question before the trial was concluded; these statements were made in a decision that had been preceded by deliberations in camera which had been attended by the prosecution service but in which the defence had been unable to take part. According to the ECtHR such statements in the given context can give rise to legitimate and objectively justified misgivings about the impartiality of that tribunal.[22]

There has been also a violation of Article 6 § 1 of the Convention in the situation when a judge remitted the criminal case against the accused for further investigation and expressed the opinion that the accused had committed extortion, which the law-enforcement bodies had failed to investigate. His ruling was couched in terms such as "their actions suggest that they were involved in committing the more serious offence of extortion" that could inspire a grounded fear that the judge in question had already formed an opinion about the applicants' guilt and that it could influence his impartiality when the case file was resent to him for trial. Therefore, the applicants' fears that this judge lacked impartiality can be held to be objectively justified.[23]

3 The Right to Freedom of Expression vs. the Right to an Impartial Court in the Czech Context

The initial legal regulation of the judiciary and the right to an impartial court is contained in the Constitution of the Czech Republic.[24] According to Article 2(1) of the Constitution of the Czech Republic, the people are the source of all state power; they exercise it through the legislative, executive and judicial authorities. Article 4 of the Constitution of the Czech Republic emphasises that fundamental rights and freedoms are protected by the judiciary. According to Article 81 of the Constitution of the Czech Republic, judicial power is exercised by independent courts on behalf of the Republic. Article 36(1) of the Charter of Fundamental Rights and Freedoms explicitly refers to the right to an impartial court,[25] according to which anyone may invoke his or her rights in accordance with the established procedure before an independent and impartial court and, in specified cases, before another body.

[22] See Nešťák v. Slovakia, judgment of the ECtHR as of 27 February 2007, no. 65559/01, § 101.

[23] See Mironenko and Martenko v. Ukrajina, judgment of the ECtHR as of 10 December 2009, no. 4785/02, § 71.

[24] Resp. Constitutional Act No. 1/1993 Coll. as amended by Constitutional Act No. 347/1997 Coll., 300/2000. Coll., 448/2001 Coll., 395/2001 Coll., 515/2002 Coll., 319/2009 Coll., 71/2012 Coll. and 98/2013 Coll.

[25] Resp. Constitutional Act No. 2/1993 Coll. as amended by Constitutional Act No. 162/1998 Coll. The Charter of Fundamental Rights and Freedoms constitutes—in the meaning of Article 112 of the Constitution of the Czech Republic—the constitutional order of the Czech Republic, together with the Constitution of the Czech Republic and constitutional laws.

The basic legislation in relation to this issue at the level of ordinary legislation is the Act on Courts and Judges;[26] this Act regulates the organisation of the Czech courts, including their state administration, and the position of the judge and other judicial persons specified herein. This Act contains a number of obligations that judges are obliged to comply with. First of all, it is stipulated that judges are independent in the exercise of their functions and that they are bound only by the law. They are obliged to interpret it according to their best knowledge and conscience and to decide within a reasonable time without delay, impartially and fairly and on the basis of facts established in accordance with the law.[27]

Judges are obliged to perform their duties conscientiously and to refrain, in the exercise of their functions and in their civil life, from anything that might undermine the dignity of the judicial office or jeopardize confidence in the independent, impartial and fair decision-making of the courts[28] and in order to guarantee the independence and impartiality of the exercise of the judicial office, they are obliged to promote and defend the independence of the judiciary and its reputation and to conduct themselves in such a way as not to cause a loss of confidence in the judiciary and the dignity of the judicial office, refuse any interference, pressure, influence, wish or request which might have the effect of undermining the independence of the judiciary; in the exercise of their functions, they must not be influenced by the interests of political parties, public opinion or the media; they must act impartially and treat parties and participants to court proceedings without economic, social, racial, ethnic, sexual, religious or other prejudice as well as to ensure that their conduct does not call justifiably their impartiality into question.[29] In connection with the performance of his or her duties, a judge shall be obliged to observe due respect for other judges, other persons practising the legal profession and other employees of the court, and for parties and participants to court proceedings. He shall refrain from expressions of sympathy, affection or negative attitudes towards representatives of the participants or representatives of the parties to the proceedings.[30]

However, the performance of the office of a judge involves not only the stricto sensu duties associated with the way in which daily work duties are performed, but the performance of this office also extends into everyday personal life. In this context, it is stipulated, for example, that a judge is obliged, in his or her activities outside the exercise of the judicial office and in the exercise of his or her political rights, to conduct himself or herself in such a way that such activities do not jeopardise or undermine confidence in the independent, impartial and fair decision-making of the court or undermine the dignity of the judicial office or prevent him or her from properly exercising his or her judicial functions. In his or her personal life,

---

[26] Resp. Act No. 6/2002 Coll., on Courts, Judges, Judges and the State Administration of Courts and on Amendments to Other Acts (Act on Courts and Judges).

[27] See Article 79 of the Act on Courts and Judges.

[28] See Article 80(1) of the Act on Courts and Judges.

[29] See Article 80(2) of the Act on Courts and Judges.

[30] See Article 80(6) of the Act on Courts and Judges.

a judge shall ensure that his or her conduct does not undermine the dignity of the judicial office or jeopardise or undermine confidence in the independent, impartial and fair administration of justice.[31,32]

Disciplinary liability of judges is a very important institute serving to prevent possible violations of judges' duties and to punish violations of judges' duties that have already been committed.[33] In the wording of the Act on Courts and Judges, the term disciplinary offence is used for culpable violations of judges' duties, as well as for culpable acts by which judges undermine the dignity of the judicial office or jeopardise confidence in the independent, impartial, professional and fair decision-making of the courts.[34]

Three types of penalties may be imposed for a disciplinary offence, which are known as disciplinary measures in the wording of the Act on Courts and Judges. For a less serious disciplinary offence, the least severe disciplinary measure may be imposed on a judge, namely a reprimand (having the character of a warning). For a more serious disciplinary offence, a judge may be subject to a reduction in his or her salary of up to 30% for a period of 1 year, in the case of repeated disciplinary offence[35] for a period of up to 2 years. The most severe disciplinary measure is removal from the office of judge or removal from the office of president of the chamber. In the case of judicial officials (i.e., in particular presidents and vice-presidents of courts), it is also possible to impose a specific disciplinary measure consisting in the withdrawal of an increased salary coefficient for the performance of this function.[36]

Czech jurisprudence (both judicial and disciplinary) has dealt with various cases in relation to the right of judges to freedom of expression and the aspect of the impartiality of the judges, whereas the expressions of judges reviewed in disciplinary and judicial proceedings on the one hand were made publicly, for example, in the context of a political competition, and on the other hand were were made in the context of judicial activity.

One such case, which was decided by the disciplinary court, relates to an interview given by a judge to a Czech journal, which, as part of a series of its investigative reports, mapped the circumstances surrounding the huge and media-monitored

[31] See and for more details see Article 80(5) of the Act on Courts and Judges.

[32] On the rights and duties of judges, see in particular Articles 79 to 83 of the Act on Courts and Judges.

[33] The disciplinary liability of judges is generally laid down in Article 86 et seq. of the Act on Courts and Judges; the procedural regulation of disciplinary proceedings is laid down in the Act No. 7/2002 Coll., on Proceedings in the cases of Judges, Public Prosecutors and Bailiffs.

[34] See Article 87(1) of the Act on Courts and Judges.

[35] Respectively, if the judge has committed a disciplinary offence again in the period before the previous disciplinary measure was deleted (which generally occurs after 5 years from the legal force of the decision imposing the disciplinary measure, see Article 24 of the Act on Proceeding in the Cases of Judges, Public Prosecutors and Bailiffs..

[36] For more details on disciplinary measures imposed on judges see Article 88 of the Act on Courts and Judges.

amnesty announced by then-President of the Czech Republic Václav Klaus on 1 January 2013. In the interview recorded by the cameras, the judge expressed his belief that the amnesty was prepared for the needs of specific persons and, in response to a question from journalists about the real possibility that the amnesty was actually paid for by specific persons, the judge specifically stated: "It's quite possible, anything is possible in this country." In the subsequent part of the interview, which was no longer recorded by the cameras, the judge, according to the journalist's statement, was to tell her who specifically and in what amount should have paid for the amnesty in the version in which it was announced.[37]

As a result of the interview, a motion to initiate disciplinary proceedings against the judge was filed on the grounds of exceeding the limits of the judge's freedom of expression (or the judge's right to express himself in public), where the judge's actions were supposed to endanger the dignity of the judicial office, trust in the judiciary and judicial decision-making. According to the motion, the judge must have been aware of the fact that the interview would be spread all over the Internet and that the part of the interview he gave outside the recording of the cameras would also be quoted in the interview due to its shocking content. However, according to the motion, not only did the judge jeopardize society's trust in the democratic value of equality before the law, but he was also obliged to report his suspicion that a crime had been committed to the authorities.

In the reasoning of its decision,[38] the disciplinary court first of all recalled, in accordance with its previous decision-making practice, that, on the one hand, a judge cannot be excluded from the possibility of exercising the right to freedom of expression within the meaning of Article 10 of the Convention; on the other hand, the exercise of this right by any person, and even more by a judge, is not unlimited, since, within the meaning of Article 10(2) of the Convention, it includes responsibilities and obligations, and the exercise of the right to freedom of expression may be restricted by law in necessary cases. The disciplinary court divided judge's case it into two acts: (a) the part of the interview with the judge recorded by the cameras, (b) the judge's statements to the journalist outside the camera recording.

As regards the consideration of the act under (a), the disciplinary court concluded that the judge had committed a disciplinary offence. Although the disciplinary court generally recognised the judge's right to express himself in public, the disciplinary court justified its conclusion on the ground that the judge's statements in the interview were his subjective judgments without any real basis, not a general assessment of the situation; the judge himself had not produced any evidence in the proceedings before the disciplinary court to show that the amnesty had been paid. Such subjective statements by the judge could, in the opinion of the disciplinary court, have a significant negative potential for the former President of the Republic and others, who prepared the amnesty, but above all for the public, which may lose

[37] The report with the interview with the judge is available: https://www.seznamzpravy.cz/clanek/klausova-amnestie-za-penize-svedci-promlouvaji-3907

[38] See the judgment of the Supreme Administrative Court of 28 November 2018, no. 13 Kss 6/2017-538.

confidence in the judiciary, its independence and impartiality, and also in the very essence of the democratic rule of law, moreover if the judge is a very experienced criminal judge, i.e. an authority in the eyes of the public.

As regards the consideration of the act under (b), the disciplinary court concluded that the judge had not committed any disciplinary offence. According to the disciplinary court, it was not proven that the judge had disclosed to the journalist the information about who specifically and in what amount was to pay for the amnesty. At the same time, the judge had made it clear to the journalist that he did not want to disclose that information on camera, i.e. that the judge wanted to keep it secret.

Considering the judge's long-successful career performance and the fact that he had become a victim of an investigative journalists who collect unverified informations and use them in their reports, the judge was given the least severe disciplinary measure, i.e. a reprimand.

The second case that can be highlighted relates to the conflict between the right to privacy and the right to a fair trial. However, the case is also closely related to the judge's right to freedom of expression.

During the trial in the criminal case of illegal cigarette production, the court chamber deliberated.[39] The deliberation of the court chamber was secretly recorded by audio device. From the recording of the audio device, which was published on the internet,[40] is apparent the speech of the judge, who compares the defendants to social trash, vulgarly attacks the defendants' family members, vulgarly attacks the defendants' lawyers or celebrates the position of criminal judges before 1989 (i.e. during the period of socialism in the Czech Republic). The judge also complains in general terms about the difficult role of a criminal judge, which she compares to working in a cow shed removing excrements.

In relation to the content of the secret audio recording, the defendants filed a proposal to initiate disciplinary proceedings against the judge, as well as an objection to the judge's bias in this criminal case. The disciplinary proceedings were not initiated, nor was the objection of bias upheld by the courts,[41] due to the inadmissibility of the evidence—the audio recording, which was in the opinion of the courts made in violation of the law, as well as the fact that the judge expressed herself in general terms, not in relation to the defendants or their lawyers, to whom she had no relationship. The judge's statements are according to the courts the result of the psychological strain resulting from the insults from the public and the generally deteriorating attitude of the defendants who do not respect the court's instructions. Moreover, the courts had doubts about the authenticity of the recording, which

[39] According to Article 127(1) of Act No. 141/1961, Code of Criminal Procedure: "In addition to the judges and associate judges who were present at the hearing that immediately preceded the judgment, and the court reporter, no one else may be present at the deliberation and vote. The content of the deliberations must remain confidential."

[40] The judge's speech is available: https://xtv.cz/kauzy-x/krava-kripl-kurva-rika-soudkyne-iveta-sperlichova

[41] The objection of bias is decided by the court against whose judge the objection of bias is directed. The eventual appeal against the decision is decided by the higher court.

lacked the information about the person making the recording, the time and date of the recording.[42]

The defendants were not satisfied with the results of the decisions of the courts and therefore filed a constitutional complaint in relation to the objection of bias of the judge. In its decision,[43] the Constitutional Court expressed its opinion on the admissibility of the secretly recorded recording, stating that it is necessary to balance the right to privacy (during the deliberations of the court chambers) with the defendants' right to a fair trial. The Constitutional Court concluded that the judge's statements were not made in the context of the deliberation of the court chamber itself, as the judge's statements did not constitute a communication of information or an expression of opinion on the content of the decision being prepared, but rather statements or evaluations that were clearly outside the scope of the judges' actions, i.e. they were in no way related to the deliberation of the court chamber. Moreover, the secret recording was the only evidence of the judge's possible bias. The Constitutional Court emphasized the need to protect the defendants' right to a fair trial, i.e. the matter of the judge's potentional bias.

With regard to the content of the recording, the Constitutional Court concluded very briefly that the vulgar statements of the judge justify the conclusion that, at least from an objective perspective (i.e. from the perspective of the objective test), the judge cannot be considered impartial.

4 Conclusion

The relationship between the freedom of expression of judges and the rules of judicial ethics remains a complex and evolving challenge that resonates in the Czech and European context. Although freedom of expression is a fundamental right of everyone and is essential for the development of a democratic society, its exercise is not absolute and can be restricted if necessary. The complex relationship between the right to freedom of expression of judges and judicial ethics is illustrated by the existence of special disciplinary responsibility of judges, which judges bear in order to preserve the dignity of their office, to strengthen public confidence in justice, but also in the context of the right of every person to an impartial court.

Judicial ethics, i.e. the established rules of conduct of judges, place increased demands on judges that reflect the specific nature of their profession. A judge's limited scope of freedom of expression is inherently linked to the dignified conduct of judicial proceedings and ensures the authority and impartiality of the judiciary. However, compliance with these requirements can be jeopardized by inappropriate

[42] See the judgment of the Regional court in Brno as of 24 July 2017, No. 53 T 11/2015-3760, and the judgment of the High court in Olomouc as of 21 September 2017, No. 4 To 59/2017-3962.

[43] See the judgment of the Constitutional Court as of 31 July 2018, Case No. III. ÚS 4071/17.

conduct of judges that forces the legal system to resolve problems that undermines the credibility of the judicial function.

At the European level, the Convention highlights the delicate balance between freedom of expression and the necessity of an impartial judiciary. The ECtHR uses both subjective and objective tests to examine the impartiality of judges and underlines the importance of maintaining public confidence in the judiciary.

Within the Czech legal framework, the Constitution and provisions of the Acts form the basis of an independent and impartial judiciary. Judges are entrusted with the duty to act impartially, above all in their professional duties, but also in their private life, including when exercising their right to freedom of expression. Disciplinary measures, ranging from reprimands to removal from office, serve as a safeguard against possible violations of these duties.

Two illustrative Czech cases concerning judicial expressions are examples of the difficult balance between freedom of expression and the need for an impartial judiciary. In one case, a judge's statements on a controversial amnesty led to disciplinary proceedings resulting in a reprimand. Another case involving disparaging statements made by a judge during a trial raised questions of bias, leading to a constitutional complaint. The Constitutional Court, which gave priority to the right to a fair trial, stressed the need for a differentiated assessment of the judges' statements made within and, on the other hand, outside the framework of the deliberations of the court chambers.

References

Klíma P (2023) Problematika svobody projevy ve světle nenávistných projevů na internetu. Správní právo:1–2

Visinger R (2019) Soudní dohled. Wolters Kluwer ČR, Praha

Harmonizing Rights and Regulations: National Judges and Urban Planning Through the Lens of European Court of Human Rights—Insights from Romania

Chelaru Raluca

Abstract The intersection of property rights and urban planning paints a canvas of ever-evolving dynamics tempered by a certain degree of consistency.

Urban and regional planning isn't just about cityscapes and zoning; it's the arena where the State exerts its control, steering the ship of communal welfare through the sometimes-choppy waters of property control. The European Court of Human Rights (the "Court"), the guardian of our civil liberties, nods in agreement when the State tightens its grip in these settings, acknowledging that the public good often calls for a more flexible hand.

Article 1 of Protocol No. 1 to the Convention on Human Rights (the "Convention") stands guard over property, safeguarding each entity's peaceful enjoyment of their possessions (For a comprehensive analysis, see Bîrsan (European convention for human rights. Rights and liberties, Bucharest, 2005); for a rather humanistic and ideological approach, see Voiculescu and Berna (Universul Juridic, Bucharest, 2023)). However, it's not a "carte blanche" for landowners to build at will. This protection doesn't automatically guarantee construction rights; rather, it allows for diverse building restrictions to ensure the greater good prevails.

1 The State Has a Wide Margin of Discretion in Urban Planning

In numerous cases, the Court emphasized that the State enjoys a broad margin of discretion concerning issues related to urban planning, yet this discretion is not unlimited.

C. Raluca (✉)
Faculty of Law, Bucharest University, , Bucharest, Romania

C. Hermida del Llano (ed.), *The Freedom of Expression for Judges in the Sphere of the Judicial Ethics*, Ius Gentium: Comparative Perspectives on Law and Justice 129, https://doi.org/10.1007/978-3-032-06504-9_12

Article 1 of Protocol No. 1 to the Convention essentially guaranteeing the right to property consists of three separate principles.[1] The first, articulated in the initial sentence of the first paragraph and of a broad nature, establishes the principle of undisturbed property enjoyment. The second principle, found in the subsequent sentence of the same paragraph, addresses property deprivation, and subjects it to specific conditions. The third principle, present in the second paragraph, acknowledges that Contracting States have the authority, among other considerations, to regulate property use in alignment with the public interest. The second and third principles, focusing on particular instances of interference with property enjoyment, should be interpreted in reference to the fundamental principle established in the first rule.[2]

Considering these principles, in The Holy Monasteries v. Greece,[3] the Court determined that a legal provision automatically granting the State the use and possession of specific property resulted in the complete transfer of ownership of the concerned land to the State, constituting a deprivation of "possessions". In 1952, the Greek government expropriated a part of monastery land, offering compensation based on the property's value. By 1987, the monasteries no longer served the same societal roles as before. However, a later law, 1700/1987, didn't provide similar compensation. Instead, it offered a mere five percent compensation to grant land use rights to farmers. This law placed a significant burden on the affected monasteries by depriving them of property without ensuring a fair balance of interests.

But deprivation of "possessions" may also occur in cases where there hasn't been a formal decision to extinguish individual rights. However, the profound impact on the applicant's "possessions" caused by a series of measures implemented by public authorities can be so substantial as to be comparable to expropriation. To establish whether a deprivation of "possessions" has transpired, the Court shouldn't limit itself to assessing mere dispossession or formal expropriation. Instead, it must delve beyond surface details and investigate the actual circumstances in question. Since the Convention aims to secure rights that are "practical and effective", it must be determined whether the situation indeed amounted to *a de facto* expropriation.

For example, in the case of Sporrong and Lönnroth v. Sweden,[4] the applicants in a case involving Stockholm did not contest the legality of expropriation permits and construction restrictions but opposed the extended timeframes for compensation proceedings and the prolonged duration of these measures. They argued that these restrictions hindered property transactions, improvements, and their rights, although they did not claim a formal loss of possessions. The government argued these were standard urban planning measures and didn't violate property rights.

[1] See Guide on Article 1 of Protocol No. 1 to the European Convention on Human Rights, available here: https://rm.coe.int/guide-art-1-protocol-1-eng/1680a20cdc

[2] For an analysis of the public interest as reason justifying the derogatory measures under Protocol 1, see George (2009), p. 273.

[3] See Application No. 13092/87; 13,984/88, available here: https://hudoc.echr.coe.int/eng#{%22itemid%22:[%22001-57906%22]}.

[4] See Application No. 7151/75; 7152/75, available here: https://hudoc.echr.coe.int/eng#{%22itemid%22:[%22001-57580%22]}.

The Court disagreed, noting that while legally the applicants retained property rights, these measures severely restricted their practical exercise, causing uncertainty. The Court found the combined use of these measures significantly interfered with the applicants' property rights over an extended period.

The 1947 Act in Sweden prohibits any construction not complying with the city plan, allowing temporary bans on construction until a municipal-approved plan is adopted. Article 15 permits a ban on new construction in a zone awaiting a master plan decision, extendable up to 3 years by the County Administrative Board. A similar principle applies when adopting or amending city plans. While the Act primarily concerns new constructions, alterations to existing premises may also fall under these rules.

In 1967, the Parliamentary Ombudsman highlighted the effects of long-term construction bans, suggesting potential solutions to protect property owners. They proposed setting time limits on bans, compensating owners for substantial losses caused by prolonged bans, or requiring the municipality to purchase the land after a specified ban duration. The Ombudsman emphasized the need for a comprehensive study to introduce protections for landowners against detrimental effects of extended construction bans.

In the case Vasilescu v. Romania,[5] in her complaints regarding the aftermath of the Supreme Court of Justice's ruling in 1994, Mrs. Vasilescu alleged a breach of Article 1 of Protocol No. 1, stating her inability to reclaim her property following the judgment.

Mrs. Vasilescu argued that the Supreme Court's judgment prevented her from regaining possession of her property, emphasizing that she was acknowledged as the owner of seized items in a previous civil court decision. The government conceded the illegality of the seizure but argued that the Supreme Court's ruling did not substantially impair her property rights and suggested avenues for lawful acquisition of her property.

The Court observed the unlawful seizure of Mrs. Vasilescu's property in 1966, confirming her ownership. Despite Romania's late recognition of the right of individual petition and the Court's jurisdiction, the Supreme Court's judgment in 1994 was after this recognition. The Court concluded that the continued retention of the items couldn't be seen as a deprivation under Article 1 of Protocol No. 1, but the unlawful retention, together with ineffective attempts to resolve the issue domestically, constituted a *de facto* confiscation incompatible with her right to enjoy her possessions peacefully.

Ultimately, the Court ruled a violation of Article 1 of Protocol No. 1 in Mrs. Vasilescu's case.

In the case of Schembri and Others v. Malta,[6] the Court found that although the applicant was still the legal owner of the property, a Presidential Declaration in

[5] See Application No. 53/1997/837/1043, available here: https://hudoc.echr.coe.int/eng#{%22itemid%22:[%22001-58,169%22]}.

[6] See Application No. 42583/06, available here: https://hudoc.echr.coe.int/eng#{%22itemid%22:[%22001-95677%22]}.

1974 indicated that the land was required for a public purpose, essentially rendering the land unusable and impractical for the applicant to enjoy or develop. As a result, the Court determined that there had been a deprivation of possessions as per Article 1 of Protocol No. 1.

Regarding whether the taking was in accordance with the law, the Court reiterated that the Maltese system's form of taking property was lawful, citing previous cases as precedent.

In considering whether the taking served the public interest, the Court acknowledged the broad interpretation of the term "public interest" and the authority of national bodies to assess it. The disagreement between the parties regarding the use of the expropriated land was noted, but the domestic courts confirmed some public interest use. Given the wide discretion afforded to States in such matters, the interference with the applicants' property rights was not deemed devoid of reasonable grounds. Therefore, the proposed transfer of ownership was considered to be in the public interest under Article 1 of Protocol No. 1. The proportionality of this public-interest aim was yet to be assessed by the Court.

The Court emphasized the need for proportionality in property deprivation cases. It stressed the importance of fair balance between public interest and individual rights and the assessment of compensation terms concerning the interference with property rights. Abnormal delays in compensation or prolonged administrative and judicial proceedings were noted to reduce the adequacy of compensation. The Court highlighted that the compensation, calculated decades earlier, wasn't in line with the spirit of the Convention. The compensation awarded was considered inadequate due to the extended delay in payment and the valuation dated back decades. Consequently, this situation upset the balance between property protection and the general interest, leading to a violation of Article 1 of Protocol No. 1.

Moreover, the mere fact that a person owns a piece of land does not *per se* confer a right on the owner to build on that land. It is permissible under Article 1 of Protocol 1 to the Convention to impose and maintain various building restrictions.

In the case Cooperativa La Laurentina v. Italy,[7] the Court found that the passivity of the Rome city council in adopting the general development plan did not represent a violation of Article 1 of Protocol 1 to the Convention, because the applicant had also the possibility to request the State the execution of a development agreement for the purpose of obtaining a building permit. The Court held that there was no evidence that such a move would have stood absolutely no chance of success and the failure of the applications for a building permit was also attributable to the conduct of the applicant. This unfolds the principles of the wide margin of discretion in urban planning and the sanctioning of passivity of the owner.

In other words, in Cooperativa La Laurentina v. Italy, the Court examined the case where the landowner claimed prolonged restriction on property use due to a city's failure to adopt a detailed urban plan. The Court acknowledged State

[7] See Application No. 23529/94, available here: https://hudoc.echr.coe.int/eng#{%22itemid%22:[%22001-64179%22]}.

discretion in urban policy but found no violation, citing the landowner's failure to challenge the municipality's inaction and explore alternatives like lotting (development) agreements. It observed that while the land's purpose changed, essential property rights remained, enabling rental income and potential sale. It dismissed claims that the land became unsellable due to lack of urban planning, concluding that the authorities' actions didn't upset the balance between public interest and private rights, thus not violating Article 1 of Protocol No. 1.

In Gorraiz Lizarraga and Others v Spain,[8] the Court held that building a dam with the consequence of flooding several small villages does not represent *per se* a violation of the Convention. In this case, five applicants and an association of which they were members brought proceedings against plans to build a dam that would result in three nature reserves and a number of small villages being flooded.

The Court stated that urban and regional planning policies are, *par excellence*, spheres in which the State intervenes, particularly through control of property in the general or public interest.

The Allan Jacobsson v. Sweden[9] case concerns a property where construction was prohibited even before the applicant purchased it in 1974. The applicant argued that this prohibition violated Article 1 of Protocol No. 1.

However, the Court decided that restrictions imposed on an owner by the adoption of a development plan restricting the right to carry out other types of construction constitute regulation of the use of property in the general interest and that in striking the fair balance thereby required between the general interest of the community and the requirements of the protection of the individual's fundamental rights, the authorities enjoy a wide margin of appreciation.

The Court decided that a development plan that restricts the possibility to carry out other types of constructions than the ones already existing constitutes regulation of the use of property in the general interest. Moreover, the Court held that it is of great importance the fact that the applicant was aware of the urbanistic regime from the very beginning (from the moment they acquired the property). In Romania, this can be verified by requesting an urban planning certificate from the city hall. This unfolds the principle of the predictability of the limitations in urban planning.

Moreover, the case Frascino v. Italy[10] involves a prolonged dispute over a building permit on a property in Naples. Mrs. M., the original owner, applied for the permit in 1969, but faced repeated refusals and administrative delays, prompting several legal actions. The Council of State ruled in 1991 that the municipality must issue the permit, but this decision was never executed. The applicant, who acquired the property in 1991, claimed a violation of property rights under Article 1 of Protocol No. 1 of the European Convention on Human Rights due to the non-enforcement of the decision. The Court found a violation, ruling that the

[8] See Application No. 62543/00, available here: https://hudoc.echr.coe.int/eng#{%22itemid%22:[%22001-61731%22]}.

[9] See Application No. 10842/84, available here: https://hudoc.echr.coe.int/eng#{%22itemid%22:[%22001-57423%22]}.

[10] See Chiriță (2003), p. 233.

municipality's failure to comply lacked legal basis and constituted an unjustified interference with the applicant's property rights. The applicant was awarded €75,000 for moral damages and €2000 for legal expenses. The Court also set provisions for interest on late payments.

2 The Predictability of the Limitation Matters

In the same case Jacobsson v. Sweden, the Court highligheted that it is also relevant whether the plaintiff could reasonably have been aware of the legal limits of his property to establish whether the plaintiff's rights were protected and whether he was aware of those restrictions when he acquired the property in question.

In several cases, the Court has accepted the total lack of damages where the owner knew, or ought reasonably to have known, of the possibility of future restrictions.

For instance, in Z.A.N.T.E. - Marathonisi A.E. v. Greece,[11] the Court notes initially that the Government relies on the forest character of the relevant area to affirm that its exploitation was in any case impossible. In this regard, the Court observes that the domestic courts did not rule on whether the disputed property was forested or not. Indeed, the subject of the domestic proceedings was the applicant company's right to be compensated for the successive blockage of the exploitation of the island in question. The highest administrative court ruled that the disputed island was located outside the urban area, and lands falling into this category are exclusively intended by their nature for agricultural, poultry, forestry, or public entertainment purposes. Therefore, the Court considers that the forest character of the disputed property is not a matter to be examined in the present case. In any event, it is not for the Court to rule on such a technical point.[12]

In this case, the Court cannot accept the Government's position that there was no interference with the applicant company's right to freely dispose of its property. In this regard, the Court notes that in March 1972, when the applicant company acquired the island in question, the relevant domestic law allowed the construction of buildings on lands located outside the urban area, provided that the land area exceeded 4000 sq.m. and that the building to be constructed did not exceed 10% of the land surface. Subsequently, the exploitation of the island in question was progressively blocked by various administrative acts adopted between 1984 and 1999. In particular, the presidential decree of April 13, 1984, initially limited the right to build on the island to the construction of seven dwellings, each with a maximum area of 60 sq.m., and the presidential decree of December 22, 1999, finally prohibited any construction on the island. Following the consecutive conclusion of

[11] See Application No. 14216/03, available here: https://hudoc.echr.coe.int/eng#{%22itemid%22:[%22001-83871%22]}.

[12] See the case Papastavrou and Others v. Greece, application No. 46372/99, available here: https://hudoc.echr.coe.int/eng#{%22itemid%22:[%22001-67552%22]}.

administrative procedures initiated in 1993 and 1998, which were crucial for assessing the proportionality of the impugned measures, the Court must examine whether the interference with the applicant company's right to the peaceful enjoyment of its possessions was justified under Article 1 of Protocol No. 1.

The Court considers it natural that, in such a complex and challenging field as land planning, the Contracting States enjoy a wide margin of appreciation to conduct their urban policy.[13] It is established that the interference with the applicant company's right to the peaceful enjoyment of its possessions served the requirements of the general interest. However, the Court cannot waive its supervisory power. It is therefore incumbent on the Court to verify that the desired balance has been preserved in a manner compatible with the applicant's right to the peaceful enjoyment of its possessions.[14]

In this case, the Court notes that the legality of the progressively imposed restrictions on the disputed property was examined twice by administrative courts. Both the Council of State and the Athens Administrative Court of Appeal considered, under judgments no. 3135/2002 and 2735/2002 respectively, that the total prohibition of construction on the disputed island did not infringe the right to the protection of property, as the property in question was located outside the urban area. According to the highest administrative court, any site outside the urban area is by its nature intended exclusively for agricultural, poultry, forestry, or public entertainment use. In other words, the domestic courts considered it impossible for the prohibition of construction on the disputed land to affect the right to the protection of property, given that said land was, in any case and by its nature, non-buildable.

The Court considers that the reason given by the domestic courts to reject the applicant company's compensation claims stands out for its particular rigidity: indeed, equating any land located outside the urban area with land intended exclusively for agricultural, poultry, forestry, or public entertainment use introduces an irrebuttable presumption that disregards the specificities of each land not included in the urban area. In particular, the reference to the "destination" of land, a term inherently vague and indefinite, does not allow the domestic court to consider the right that may have governed its actual exploitation before the imposition of the impugned restriction. In cases where the relevant legislation only provides for agricultural exploitation, the "destination" of the land is, indeed, solely agriculture. However, in cases where the relevant law expressly allows the construction on a piece of land, the domestic court cannot disregard this element by simply invoking the "destination" of any land outside the urban area.

In this case, it appears from the case file that the destination of the disputed island was not solely agricultural exploitation. In particular, the gradual prohibition

[13] See the case of Elia S.r.l. v. Italy, application No. 37710/97, available here: https://hudoc.echr.coe.int/eng#{%22itemid%22:[%22001-59625%22]}.

[14] See the case of Saliba v. Malta, application No. 4251/02, available here: https://hudoc.echr.coe.int/eng#{%22itemid%22:[%22001-70875%22]}, and Housing Association of War Disabled and Victims of War of Attica and Others v. Greece application No. 35859/02, available here: https://hudoc.echr.coe.int/eng#{%22itemid%22:[%22001-76315%22]}.

of any construction on the island originated from regulations departing from the ordinary provisions on the conditions for construction on lands located outside the urban area. The Court noted that there is a certain contradiction in the behaviour of the domestic authorities in ensuring the protection of wildlife in this case. Indeed, if the island in question had been *ab initio* non-buildable due to its destination for agricultural exploitation, as suggested by the administrative court judgments, it would not have been necessary for the domestic authorities to impose its non-buildability. However, in this case, the prohibition of construction was the result of a series of restrictions progressively limiting the initially recognized right under domestic law.

Finally, the Court observes that the report dated December 10, 2003, prepared by the Committee on Petitions of the European Parliament, notes the existence of activities on the island that are incompatible with the reasons for which the applicant's property was subject to particularly severe restrictions on its exploitation. The report states that Marathonisi is daily invaded by tourists, its beach is highly polluted, and there are no toilets. The Court notes in this regard that, according to the presidential decree of December 22, 1999, the "National Park of Zakynthos Organization," a private legal entity under the supervision of the Minister of Environment and Planning, is responsible for managing the use of said Park. However, in the Court's view, when the State imposes significant restrictions on the exploitation of private property to ensure effective environmental protection, it must at least refrain from tolerating activities that endanger the achievement of that goal. Otherwise, the purpose of the restriction may become obsolete, and the initially imposed burden on the individual becomes more difficult to tolerate, an element that must be taken into account when assessing its proportionality to the pursued aim.

In this case, it would be unreasonable for the State to demand compliance with severe restrictions on the enjoyment of her property to protect the "caretta-caretta" turtle, while simultaneously failing to take necessary measures against activities that endanger the realization of this goal.

In light of the above, the Court considers that in this specific case, the criterion used by the administrative courts in examining the compensation claims of the applicant company for the complete blockage of its property, along with the subsequent behaviour of the internal authorities, disrupted the fair balance that should prevail in regulating the use of property between the public interest and private interest.

Therefore, the Court found the rigidity flawed as the island's past didn't solely involve agriculture, and restrictions were imposed gradually. Additionally, authorities failed to prevent activities contradicting environmental protection goals. These cumulative factors led the Court to rule that the balance between public interest and property rights wasn't maintained, constituting a violation of Article 1 of Protocol No. 1.

The applicant company seeked substantial compensation for material and moral damages, along with costs and expenses. The Government opposes these claims, labelling them as unfounded and excessive. The Court, however, defers the decision on compensation, leaving it open for further discussion or potential agreement between the parties involved.

In another case, Depalle v. France,[15] the applicant contested the strict enforcement of the Coastal Areas Act, which prohibited his private land use. Despite the property's historical authorization for occupation, the Act's implementation overlooked this, focusing on public-use neighbouring lands. Furthermore, the Act did not contain any clear, binding measure. The applicant argued that, despite the noble cause of environmental conservation, the legislation relied on did not, the applicant argued, have the scope attributed to it by the Government.

The applicant presented various factors—construction of the house in question by other people; lawful acquisition (in good faith); authorisation to build the dyke granted by the authorities; house valued and insured, and liable to taxes and duties; the small area of land involved and therefore only a few dozen metres of shore at issue; other houses in the same area; and lack of compensation—to counter the public interest in demolishing his house.

He considered it contradictory to propose, on the one hand, authorisation to occupy subject to conditions and, on the other hand, should that proposal be refused, to brandish the threat of demolition in the public interest. Demolition would be difficult, moreover, in a landscape that was part of a listed site. He submitted that he was not the only one in this position; other houses in the neighbourhood were also to be demolished, but never had been because such a measure had not been deemed to be dictated by the legitimate aims of environmental conservation and ensuring access to the shore.

Claiming an imbalance between the means used and the intended goal, the applicant felt burdened excessively and disproportionately.

The Court analysed Article 1 of Protocol No. 1, outlining that the interference aimed to protect the coastal area and environment, justifying the control over the property. The Court emphasizes the evolving importance of environmental conservation. It scrutinizes the restoration order in light of the applicant's long-term occupancy but finds no negligence on the authorities' part.

Although demolition after prolonged occupation seems severe, the Court finds it corresponds to stricter enforcement to protect coastal areas. The Court rejects the applicant's plea for exemption and emphasizes the need for better management of private-public use relations and adherence to coastal laws.

Regarding compensation, the lack thereof doesn't alone constitute a violation of Article 1 of Protocol No. 1, considering previous decisions' clear statements about non-compensation. Ultimately, the Court determines that the demolition without compensation wouldn't impose an excessive burden on the applicant, maintaining a balance between community interests and individual rights.

Thus, the Court concludes there has been no violation of Article 1 of Protocol No. 1 in this case.

---

[15] See Application No. 34044/02, available here: https://hudoc.echr.coe.int/eng#{%22itemid%22:[%22001-97978%22]}.

3 The Passivity of the Owner Matters

In the case of J.A. PYE (Oxford) LTD and J.A. PYE (Oxford) Land LTD v. The United Kingdom,[16] the Court analysed whether the loss of the right of ownership through adverse possession represents a violation of Article 1 of Protocol No. 1 and concluded that, essentially, the loss of property was generated by the owner's inaction over a long period of time.

This issue was also analysed by the Court in case Cooperativa La Laurentina v. Italy, where it found that the owner took little to no action against the shortfall of the Rome city council to adopt a general development plan for more than 35 years. The Court noted that the applicant company could have signed a development agreement for the purpose of being able to build a construction on its land, and that there was no evidence that such a move would have stood absolutely no chance of success. The Court considered that this possibility was sufficient to ensure protection of the right to peaceful enjoyment of possessions and noted that the applicant company had not taken any action in that regard.

4 The Wide Discretion of the State Is not Absolute

In Schirmer v. Poland,[17] the Court emphasised that the difficulties in enacting a comprehensive legal framework in the area of urban planning constitute part of the process of transition from a socialist legal order and its property regime to one compatible with the rule of law and the market economy—a process which, by the very nature of things, is fraught with difficulties. However, these difficulties and the enormity of the tasks facing legislators having to deal with all the complex issues involved in such a transition do not exempt the Member States from the obligations stemming from the Convention or its Protocols.[18]

The case centered on a dispute regarding a housing law that required landlords seeking eviction to provide replacement accommodation owned by them. The Government defended the law, stating it protected tenant rights by ensuring the new accommodation was secure. They argued that the applicant's co-operative quasi-proprietorial right didn't meet the ownership requirement but emphasized the law's aim was to prevent the tenant's situation from worsening after relocation.

The applicant countered, highlighting that the offered alternative apartment fulfilled the legal conditions, even though it was based on a quasi-ownership right

---

[16] See Application No. 44302/02, available here: https://hudoc.echr.coe.int/eng#{%22itemid%22:[%22001-82172%22]}.

[17] See Application No. 68880/01, available here: https://hudoc.echr.coe.int/eng#{%22itemid%22:[%22001-66642%22]}.

[18] For a brief analysis of the breaches of human rights during dictatorship in Romania and of the fresh perspectives after December 1989, see Duculescu (2008), p. 32.

rather than full ownership. They stressed the legislative intent to provide secure alternative accommodation for tenants, which, in this case, was met. The applicant also pointed out the co-operative had approved the tenancy transfer to the tenant, meeting the legal requirements of the housing co-operative at the time.

They concluded by arguing that the literal interpretation by the domestic courts disregarded the legislative intent to balance the legitimate interests of both landlords and tenants.

The Court determined that the refusal to evict a tenant because the offered alternative accommodation wasn't owned by the landlord amounted to control of property use, invoking Article 1 of Protocol No. 1.

The Court recognized States' rights to control property use for the general interest, especially in housing, but emphasized the need for a fair balance between public interests and individual rights. The interference with the applicant's rights due to the legislation was acknowledged. The Court noted the difficulty in balancing owners' rights with tenants' acquired rights, which stemmed from historical housing control measures and the transition to a market economy.

It concluded that the legislative emphasis on tenants' rights overlooked the interests of landlords. While the legislation changed later, rectifying some issues, the Court found the applicant bore an excessive burden due to the legislation's application, violating Article 1 of Protocol No. 1.

In Skibińscy v. Poland,[19] in 1979 a plan was adopted for the construction of a hospital, which was never built, but the urban plan was maintained until 2003, when it expired.

Consequently, the Court held that the applicants could not carry out their construction projects and were also threatened with expropriation for an indefinite period and had no effective right to compensation during this period, which led to the conclusion that a fair balance had not been struck between the competing public and individual interests and that the applicants had to bear an excessive individual burden.

In this case, the Court accepts that already in 1994 the measures complained of pursued the legitimate aim of securing land in connection with the implementation of the local land development plan. This corresponds to the general interest of the community.

The applicants faced prolonged obstacles in obtaining building permits due to amendments in the land development plan from 1979. Despite uncertainties about timely implementation, the plan hindered the applicants' construction efforts until its expiration in 2003. The Court highlights the applicants' inability to proceed with construction and the looming threat of expropriation without adequate compensation during this extended period. While legislation intended to improve compensation rights for future expropriations, it excluded plans enacted before 1995, prolonging the applicants' situation for 9 years. Although a 2003 Act introduced

[19] See Application No. 52589/99, available here: https://hudoc.echr.coe.int/eng#{%22itemid%22:[%22001-77993%22]}.

compensation rights for restricted property use, it didn't retroactively address the applicants' plight. The Court finds the lack of a fair balance between public interest and individual rights, resulting in the applicants facing an excessive burden, and rules a violation of Article 1 of Protocol No. 1.

Similarly, in several other cases, the Court concluded that a fair balance was not achieved between competing general and individual interests, as a result of the urban plans adopted in the respective cases which, in essence, prohibited constructions pending works of public interest, which never materialized.

In Rosiński v. Poland,[20] the Court assessed a case involving land development and planning policies where a property was designated for future expropriation in a plan without a clear implementation timeframe. The applicant faced a prolonged threat of expropriation and lacked effective entitlement to compensation for a considerable period from 1993 to 2003. Amendments to the Planning Act extended this situation, excluding compensation entitlements for pre-1995 plans, leaving the applicant without redress until 2003. Despite the 2003 Act introducing compensation rights, it didn't address the applicant's situation retroactively. The Court recognized the challenges in transitioning legal frameworks but found the prolonged uncertainty unjust, failing to balance community interests and individual rights, resulting in an excessive burden on the applicant. Consequently, there was a violation of Article 1 of Protocol No. 1.

In Buczkiewicz v. Poland,[21] over a prolonged period from 1992 to 2003, the applicants faced the prospect of future expropriation without any clear timeline for implementation. The amendments to the Local Planning Act extended this uncertain situation, denying compensation entitlements for plans adopted before 1995 and leaving the applicants without recourse until 2003. Despite provisions allowing compensation claims for future expropriations, they were not retroactive, failing to address the applicants' plight.

The Court notes that the applicants' request for an initial approval of a development project was refused in 2001. In the refusal, the authorities essentially referred to the provisions of the development plan. However, when the applicants requested that approval, there were no sound grounds on which to believe that the land development plan adopted in 1992 would be implemented promptly. As a result, the *de facto* blocking of any construction on the property did not serve any immediate or medium-term purpose in the interests of the community.

The Court acknowledged the complexities in urban planning transitions, but found this prolonged uncertainty unjust, burdening the applicants excessively. As the land development plan lacked clarity on implementation, it failed to strike a fair balance between public and individual interests, resulting in a violation of Article 1 of Protocol No. 1 to the Convention.

---

[20] See Application No. 17373/02, available here: https://hudoc.echr.coe.int/eng#{%22itemid%22:[%22001-81737%22]}.

[21] See Application No. 10446/03, available here: https://hudoc.echr.coe.int/eng#{%22itemid%22:[%22001-85253%22]}.

In Ruxandra Trading v. Romania,[22] the Court concluded that by refusing to enforce a court judgement, the national authorities deprived the plaintiff company of the possibility of using the land in question without providing it with any justification.

In this case, a court order from June 8, 2000, directed the administration to enter into a concession contract and issue a final building permit for the building already constructed on the applicant company's land. The Court has previously established that the right to engage in activities under a concession contract qualifies as "property" under Article 1 of Protocol No. 1. It's evident that the obligations arising from the 2000 court order constituted a financial interest, falling under the protection of Article 1 of Protocol No. 1.

It's undisputed that the authorities failed to execute the 2000 court order, and this failure, solely attributable to the administrative authorities, amounts to an interference with the applicant's property rights.

The Court notes that the court order was final and required no further steps for execution. While the government argued an inability to execute due to an alleged inconsistent and incomplete interpretation, the Court refers to its prior conclusions on this matter.

By refusing to comply with the 2000 court order, the national authorities deprived the applicant company of the ability to utilize the land without justification.

The Court recalled that even though the States enjoy a wide margin of discretion in directing urban development policy, in the case at hand, no change was made to the urban development plans. Even supposing that such a reason could justify non-enforcement, the Court found that the authorities did not propose any compensatory measure to the plaintiff company to ensure that the fair balance required by Article 1 of Protocol No 1 was not disrupted.

In case Fotopoulou v. Greece,[23] the applicant was the owner of a house. Her neighbours built a wall without authorization that exceeded the legally allowed height and obstructed the view from her home. She repeatedly requested the demolition of the wall, but without success. Eventually, the Minister of the Environment requested the local municipality to demolish the wall, but the municipality refused, citing a lack of necessary technical equipment. Over a period of more than 7 years, several administrative authorities intervened, issuing contradictory decisions, some allowing the wall's existence, while others ordered its demolition. The final decision came from the prefect, allowing the wall to remain, despite a previous demolition order that had been confirmed by a court. The applicant challenged the decision in court, but the court deemed itself incompetent to review it.

The Court considered that while the obstruction of the view from the applicant's home did not amount to an outright deprivation of property or a regulation of the use of property, it nevertheless constituted an interference with the applicant's property

[22] See Application No. 28333/02, available here: https://hudoc.echr.coe.int/eng#{%22itemid%22:[%22001-81616%22]}.

[23] See Chiriță (2004), p. 275.

rights, violating the general respect for property. The Court found that the wall's existence was permitted despite a final judicial decision ordering its demolition. Furthermore, the applicant was unable to annul a decision that allowed the wall to remain, which led the Court to conclude that domestic law did not provide sufficient safeguards against arbitrariness. Therefore, Article 1 of Protocol No. 1 was violated. The Court noted that the court's decision ordering the demolition of the wall had not been enforced, and the applicant had no remedy to compel the administration to implement the court's decision. Consequently, Article 13 was also violated.

5 But How Can a National Judge Directly Compensate a Claimant for Losses Suffered as a Result of Urban Planning Measures?

As it results from the practice of the Court, the public authorities benefit from a wide margin of discretion, which is not absolute. This means that, in certain cases, the claimants are entitled at least to compensation, as stated in numerous cases presented before the Court.

In Romania, judges are often called to decide in cases where *de facto* expropriations occur (for example, by including specific plots of land in the so-called green areas, where the private owners are prohibited to carry out any construction works).

To this end, Decision No. 1416/2008 of the Romanian Constitutional[24] seems to be a compelling piece that demands the attention of legal scholars. The subject of the plea of unconstitutionality consists of the provisions of Article 71 paragraphs (1) and (2) of Government Emergency Ordinance No. 195/2005 regarding environmental protection.[25] The legal texts have the following content: "(1) Changing the destination of lands planned as green spaces and/or provided as such in urban planning documents, reducing their areas, or relocating them is prohibited, regardless of their legal status. (2) Administrative or legal acts issued or concluded in violation of the provisions of paragraph (1) are void".

In the opinion of the author of the plea of unconstitutionality, the criticized legal provisions are contrary to the constitutional provisions contained in Article 44 regarding the right to private property.

Examining the plea of unconstitutionality, the Court notes that the constitutionality of the provisions of Article 71 of Government Emergency Ordinance No. 195/2005 on environmental protection has been previously addressed in Decision

[24] Available here: https://legislatie.just.ro/Public/DetaliiDocument/102179

[25] Published in the Official Gazette of Romania, Part I, No. 1196 of December 30, 2005, approved by Law No. 265/2006, provisions amended by Article I point 1 of Government Emergency Ordinance No. 114/2007, published in the Official Gazette of Romania, Part I, No. 713 of October 22, 2007.

No. 824 of July 7, 2008,[26] finding the criticisms unfounded. On that occasion, the Court held that "the protection and guarantee of the right to a healthy environment, provided for in Article 35 of the Constitution, represent the purpose of regulating Article 71 of Government Emergency Ordinance No. 195/2005 on environmental protection".

The Constitutional Court found that the right to property, provided for in Article 44 of the Constitution, is not an absolute right. According to paragraph (1) of this text, "The content and limits of these rights (the right to property and claims against the state) are established by law," allowing the legislator, considering specific interests, to establish rules that harmonize the incidence of other fundamental rights of citizens than that of property, in a systematic interpretation of the Constitution, so that they are not suppressed by the way the right to property is regulated.

Additionally, the limitation on the exercise of the right to property imposed by Article 71 of the criticized ordinance also has a social and moral justification, given that the strict observance of these rules represents a major objective, protecting the environment, and existing green spaces, with a direct connection to public health, constituting a value of national interest.

The circumstance that, in practice, abuses with harmful consequences for the owners of lands subject to the criticized regulations may occur, as indicated by the author of the plea, is exclusively a matter of fact that should be decided by the ordinary courts. The Constitutional Court is not competent to decide on the interpretation and application of the criticized legal provisions.

Moreover, the Court notes that for the lack of use of privately owned lands arranged as green spaces and/or provided as such in urban planning documents, landowners are entitled to compensation. Therefore, nothing prevents the person who has suffered damage caused by the prohibition established by law to request local public administration authorities to repair the damage, according to the provisions of common law.

Therefore, based on the aforementioned Decision No. 1416/2008 of the Romanian Constitutional Court, the claimants that, for instance, would not be entitled to the deletion from the urbanism documents of the so-called green areas would be at least entitled to a fair compensation. But such compensation is not regulated by law, as it is in the case of expropriations.

In such cases, we are of the opinion that the national judges should directly apply the principles held by the Court in similar cases and directly grant a compensation for the claimant, to the expense of the public authority that "affected" the ownership right.

Naturally, the Romanian Constitutional Court's directive on compensating the damage "according to the provisions of common law" still stands, with a nod to the Romanian Civil Code for guidance.

[26] Published in the Official Gazette of Romania, Part I, No. 587 of August 5, 2008.

Last but not least, one should always bear in mind that, as stated in the legal doctrine,[27] the fairness of the process does not guarantee a favorable resolution of the dispute, meaning one that aligns with the claimant's objectives or expectations. It also does not prevent national courts from reaching different conclusions during the process (i.e., interpreting the same legal texts differently or assessing the same evidence differently) unless this indicates arbitrariness. Given the role of the Court, the fairness of the process—as understood in the case law of the European Court of Human Rights—does not involve a "correct" interpretation of domestic law or the identification and sanctioning of factual or legal errors by national courts. The guarantee of a fair trial is 'only' a procedural guarantee, intended to ensure 'procedural justice' rather than 'result-oriented justice,' meaning a decision based on true facts and the correct application of the law.

6 Conclusion

The balance between the State's discretion in urban planning and an individual's property rights is a delicate interplay. While the State does possess a broad margin of discretion, it's not a blank check for limitless action.

Article 1 of Protocol No. 1 to the Convention lays out the principles of property rights, signifying the inviolability of property, the conditions for deprivation, and the allowance for regulation aligned with the public good. But these shouldn't infringe on the fundamental principle of undisturbed property enjoyment.

Predictability and the owner's passivity during measures matter in determining interference. The State's wide discretion isn't absolute; it's bound by principles, including the duty to compensate.

In instances where claimants suffer losses due to planning measures, national judges should consider Court precedents. This should pave the way for direct compensation from the responsible public authority, aligned with the Romanian Constitutional Court's guidance to base compensation on common law principles reflected in the Romanian Civil Code.

After delving into the intricate rulings and nuances of various legal cases, one undeniable truth emerges: the dance between law and individual rights often sways on a tightrope.

From the Romanian Constitutional Court's directives to the complex interplay between property rights and environmental protections, these legal tapestries weave a story of balancing societal interests with individual liberties.

Remember, the law isn't a static entity; it's a living, breathing organism evolving with time, societal needs, and the pursuit of justice. As we dissect these judgments, we unveil not just legal doctrine, but the very essence of our commitment to equitable and harmonious coexistence.

---

[27] See Bogdan (2011), p. 41.

References

Bîrsan C (2005) European convention for human rights, Comment on articles, vol I. Rights and liberties, Bucharest
Bogdan D (2011) Fair civil trial in the jurisprudence of the Court, Bucharest, p 41
Chiriţă R (2003) Collection of rulings. C.H. Beck, Bucharest, p 233
Chiriţă R (2004) Collection of rulings. C.H. Beck, Bucharest, p 275
Duculescu V (2008) Legal protection of human rights. Bucharest, Lumina Lex, p 32
George CO (2009) Universul Juridic, Bucharest, p 273
Voiculescu N, Berna M-B (2023) Universul Juridic, Bucharest

Judges Under Pressure: A Few Remarks About "Ethical Courage" of Judges in Poland

Maciej Serowaniec and Zbigniew Witkowski

Abstract Judges form a special legal corps which, as the bearer of the judiciary's authority, has an exceptionally important systemic and social mission to fulfil. Since 2017, as part of a package of legislative changes to the judiciary, a disciplinary system has been in place in Poland to ensure that judges are subservient to political will. As a result, judges who were against unconstitutional changes to the judiciary were subject to removal at gunpoint. Notably, many judges have shown remarkable "ethical courage" in the fight for respect of constitutional standards. This paper presents examples of this "ethical courage".

1 Introduction

Judges form a special legal corps which, as the bearer of the judiciary's authority, has an exceptionally important systemic and social mission to fulfil.[1] This is because the authority entrusted to them is closely linked to such universal values as justice, freedom or equality. The public interest in maintaining citizens' trust in the institutions of the judiciary therefore obliges the legislator to establish certain ethical requirements for judges.[2] They are intended to ensure that the administration of justice is carried out by persons with adequate knowledge, high ethical standards and an appropriate amount of life experience. At this point, it is also worth mentioning the so-called "ethical courage" of judges, i.e., the ability to cope with the

[1] Serowaniec (2017), pp. 92–95.

[2] Dąbrowski (2010), p. 40.

M. Serowaniec (✉) · Z. Witkowski
Department of Constitutional Law, Nicolaus Copernicus University in Toruń, Toruń, Poland
e-mail: mserowaniec@umk.pl; zbywit@umk.pl

C. Hermida del Llano (ed.), *The Freedom of Expression for Judges in the Sphere of the Judicial Ethics*, Ius Gentium: Comparative Perspectives on Law and Justice 129, https://doi.org/10.1007/978-3-032-06504-9_13

difficulties that legal disputes entangled in conflicts of social values may generate.[3] The notion of "ethical courage" also includes weighing the confronting rationales according to the dictates of reason. As emphasised in the literature, it is an important component of ethical competence.[4] Indeed, it can be inferred that an "ethical courage" judge can be subject to the regime of responsibility for certain professional misconduct and be vetted for knowledge of argumentation in ethical disputes.[5]

The notion of the "ethical courage" of judges took on particular significance in Poland after 2017, when, as part of a package of legislative changes to the judiciary, a disciplinary system was introduced to ensure that judges were subordinated to political will.[6] Particular controversy surrounded the establishment of the Disciplinary Chamber within the structure of the Supreme Court. The introduced solutions were criticised both by the Supreme Court itself in the resolution of the three combined Chambers of 23.01.2020, BSA I-4110-1/20, as well as by the European Commission, which in its position of 3.12.2020 stressed that Poland was in breach of EU law by allowing the Disciplinary Chamber of the Supreme Court—whose independence and impartiality is not guaranteed—to take decisions on matters that directly affect judges and the way they exercise their functions. This includes lifting a judge's immunity to hold him or her criminally liable, followed by suspension from office and a salary reduction. As a result, judges who have opposed unconstitutional changes to the judiciary have come under massive political attack. Their courageous attitude realising the ideals of "ethical courage" deserves special recognition and respect. This article presents examples of Polish judges' attitudes that we can call "ethical courage".[7]

2 Judges Under Pressure: Examples of the "Disciplining of Judges" in Poland

Among the numerous judges of common courts who have defended the rule of law in Poland over the past 8 years and paid a high price for it are Judge Waldemar Zurek and Judge Igor Tuleya.

District Court Judge Waldemar Żurek was a member of the National Council of the Judiciary for two terms and, until March 2018, the council's spokesperson. The judge is a member of the main board of the Themis Judges' Association and has repeatedly spoken in the public debate on the state of the rule of law in Poland. In his statements he has always courageously defended the independence of the courts, the independence of judges and the principles of a democratic state of law, openly

[3] Garlicki (2018), pp. 582–583.

[4] Łętowska (2022), pp. 109–110.

[5] Garlicki (2020), pp. 1040–1056.

[6] Szmyt (2018), p. 59.

[7] Witkowski et al. (2021), pp. 106–143. See also Serowaniec (2019), pp. 135–140.

criticising the unconstitutional changes introduced in the area of the judiciary. As early as November 2016. The Control Proceedings Department of the Central Anti-Corruption Bureau asked the President of the Court of Appeal in Krakow to provide copies of the applicant's asset declarations for 2010–2015 and information on the length of service and positions he held. In January 2018, Judge Waldemar Żurek was dismissed from the position of spokesperson for civil cases of the District Court in Krakow. In July 2018, Judge Waldemar Żurek was transferred from the Second Appellate Civil Division to the First Civil Division (First Instance), which was criticised by the Themis Judges' Association and the Polish Judges' Association "Iustitia", who described this decision as politically motivated harassment against this judge and as an attempt to intimidate judges who speak out against actions aimed at political subordination of the judiciary. On 22.11.2018, the deputy disciplinary ombudsman of the judges of common courts initiated disciplinary proceedings against the judge of the Regional Court Waldemar Żurek. He presented the judge with two charges of disciplinary offences. The first charge concerned failing to file a sales tax return on a John Deere 440 Skider tractor. The second charge, on the other hand, concerned the non-payment of the tax on the sale of this tractor. In addition, on 22.11.2018, the deputy disciplinary ombudsman of the judges of common courts initiated disciplinary proceedings against Judge Waldemar Żurek of the District Court. He presented the judge with a charge of offending the dignity of a judge's office by refusing, from 1.9.2018 to 15.10.2018, to carry out adjudicatory work in the first Civil Division of the District Court in Kraków. Judge Waldemar Żurek was transferred to this department against his will and appealed this decision. Subsequently, on 7.1.2019, the deputy disciplinary ombudsman of common court judges summoned Judge Waldemar Żurek to submit a written statement concerning the judge's possible violation of the dignity of his office by providing false information to the journalists who published this information and to the prosecutor of the District Public Prosecutor's Office in Warsaw. In total as many as five disciplinary proceedings have been brought against Judge Waldemar Żurek.[8]

In turn, Judge of the District Court in Warsaw (Igor Tuleya is a member of the Warsaw Branch of the Polish Judges Assotiation Iustitia). The judge has repeatedly taken the floor in public debates concerning the state of the rule of law in Poland and his statements he has always courageously defended the independence of the courts, the independence of judges and the principles of a democratic state of law, openly criticising unconstitutional changes introduced in the area of the judiciary. The judge regularly meets with citizens in meetings devoted to the rule of law, independence of the courts, independence of judges, principles of a democratic state of law and human rights. During these meetings, Judge Igor Tuleya introduces and explains to citizens the importance of independent courts in a democratic state of law and the role of independent judges in protecting human rights and fundamental freedoms. Judge Igor Tuleya is a model of a steadfast judge, upholding the independence of the courts, the independence of judges and respect for constitutional, convention

[8] Kościerzyński (2019), pp. 46–48.

and EU values. Among other things, the judge issued unfavourable rulings to the ruling camp or concerned politicians from that camp. Judge Igor Tulea's educational and civic activities met with a systemic response from the disciplinary ombudsman. The judge was summoned for questioning several times. Judge Igor Tuleya of the District Court of Warsaw also authorises a preliminary question to the Court of Justice of the European Union. As in the case of Judge Ewa Maciejewska of Łódź, the Deputy Disciplinary Ombudsman of Common Courts Judges summoned Judge Igor Tuleya to submit a written statement regarding possible 'jurisprudential excesses'. In total, as many as five disciplinary proceedings have been initiated against Judge Igor Tuleya. On 10.01.2018, the prosecutor also investigated the possible unauthorised disclosure by Judge Igor Tuleya, as a member of the bench, of information from the criminal proceedings by allowing the media to record the court session of 18.12.2017. The prosecutor then applied to the Disciplinary Chamber of the Supreme Court for a resolution authorising the applicant's prosecution. The public prosecutor intended to charge the applicant with the allegation that, as a public official, he allowed media representatives to record video and audio during a meeting of the Warsaw Regional Court and during the announcement of the order in the case and its oral justification, as a result of which he disclosed to unauthorised persons, without the legally required consent of the authorised person, information from the investigation conducted by the Warsaw Regional Prosecutor's Office, which he had obtained in connection with his official duties, thereby acting to the detriment of the public interest.[9] On 9.06.2020, the Disciplinary Chamber of the Supreme Court, sitting as a court of first instance, decided to dismiss the prosecutor's application, stating that there was no reasonable suspicion that the applicant had committed an offence. After examining the complaint filed against the applicant, the Disciplinary Chamber, sitting with three judges as a court of second instance, partially upheld the prosecutor's complaint and amended the resolution of the court of first instance, waiving the applicant's immunity and allowing him to be held criminally liable. In addition, the Disciplinary Chamber decided to suspend the applicant from judicial duties and reduced the remuneration due to him by 25 per cent for the suspension period. The President of the Warsaw Regional Court immediately implemented the decision to suspend the applicant. This decision was overturned on 29.11.2022 by the Professional Responsibility Chamber, which replaced the abolished Disciplinary Chamber due to the Act of 9.06.2022 amending the Act on the Supreme Court and certain other acts. The Chamber of Professional Responsibility of the Supreme Court found that the applicant's conduct did not fulfil the elements of a criminal act.[10]

[9] Kościerzyński (2019), pp. 17–19.

[10] Laskowski (2023), pp. 7–17.

3 "Ethical Courage" of Judges in the Light of the Jurisprudence of the European Court of Human Rights

The European Court of Human Rights, ruling in Polish cases (Żurek v. Poland, 16.06.2022, para. 222; Tuleya v. Poland, 6.07.2023, para. 544), explicitly stated that "silence in the face of a threat to the rule of law is not a virtue". Here, the Court refers to the principle "recently established in its case law that the general right of judges to speak freely on matters concerning the functioning of the judiciary may be transformed into a corresponding duty to speak out in defence of the rule of law and the independence of the judiciary when these fundamental values are threatened". In turn, in assessing the specific situation, it states that "the applicant expressed his views and criticism on the legislative reforms affecting the judicial system and the effects of those reforms and considers that his statements did not go beyond mere criticism from a strictly professional perspective". Significantly at the same time, the ECtHR's assessment refers to systemic, comprehensive violations of the authority harassing the applicant: "at the same time, the measures taken by the authorities can be characterised as a strategy aimed at intimidating (or even silencing) the applicant in relation to the views he expressed in defence of the rule of law and the independence of the judiciary. The Court considers that the contested measures undoubtedly had a 'chilling effect' in that they must have discouraged the applicant and other judges from participating in the public debate on legislative reforms affecting the judiciary and, more generally, on issues concerning the independence of the judiciary. This emphasised the dual aspect of the judgment—direct, individual, and indirect, systemic. Furthermore, in view of the threats to the judiciary's independence, the duty is not to succumb to suicidal passivity.[11]

In its judgment of 16 June 2022 in the case of Żurek v. Poland (39,650/18), the European Court of Human Rights stressed that the contested interference was a response to views and criticism that the applicant had publicly expressed in the exercise of his right to freedom of expression. In this regard, it must be pointed out that the applicant expressed his views on the legislative reform professionally as a judge delegated to the National Council of the Judiciary (NCJ) and spokesperson of that body. It must be pointed out that the NCJ is a constitutional body whose task is to protect the independence of the courts and judges, so it is clear that the applicant, in his capacity as spokesman for that body, had the right and duty to express his views on the legislative reform affecting the judiciary. The Court attaches particular importance to the office occupied by the applicant, whose functions and duties included expressing his views on legal reforms affecting the judiciary and its independence. It is also necessary to point out the wide range of reforms that, in practice, affected every segment of the judiciary. In the present case, the Court analyses the situation of the applicant, who was a judge, a Judicial Council member, and

[11] Łętowska (2023), pp. 4–11.

its spokesperson. However, it must be pointed out that a similar approach would have to be applied to any judge who exercises his or her freedom of expression (...) in order to protect the principle of the rule of law, judicial independence and other similar values falling within the debate of general interest. When a judge speaks on the subject not only in his or her private capacity but also on behalf of a judicial council, an association of judges or another body representing the judiciary, the protection to which that judge is entitled will be heightened. Moreover, the general right to freedom of expression of judges on matters concerning the functioning of the judiciary may develop into a corresponding duty to speak out in defence of the rule of law and judicial independence when these fundamental values are threatened. The applicant expressed his views and criticism on legal reforms concerning the functioning of the judiciary, the status of the NCJ, the independence and non-removability of judges and the lowering of the retirement age for judges, all in the public interest. His statements did not go beyond criticism expressed from a purely professional perspective. Accordingly, the Court finds that the applicant's situation and his statements, which clearly fell within the scope of a debate on a matter of great public interest, called for a high degree of protection of his freedom of expression and strict scrutiny of any interference, which is consistent with the narrow margin of appreciation afforded to the authorities of the respondent State. Given the key place occupied by the judiciary among the organs of state power in a democratic society, and the importance attached to the separation of powers and the need to safeguard the independence of the judiciary, the Court must have particular regard to the protection of members of the judiciary from measures that may jeopardise their judicial independence and autonomy. Accordingly, the Court must examine the measures taken by the authorities in the applicant's case. Regarding the audit of his asset declarations carried out by the Central Anti-Corruption Bureau (CBA) between November 2016 and April 2018, the Government indicated that the audit was due to doubts about their accuracy and that the checks were routine. However, the Court points out that the audit in question, which was triggered by some unspecified irregularities and lasted quite a long time, that is, 17 months, did not produce any concrete results. According to the Government, it submitted a report to the prosecuting authorities on the irregularities revealed in the applicant's asset declarations. However, the Court was not informed of the nature of these irregularities, which in any event did not lead to further action by the authorities. Furthermore, the Court has some doubts as to the legality of the actions of the CBA officers who entered the premises of the NCJ in order to serve the applicant with an order to inspect his asset declarations, as the Government did not indicate any specific legal provision which required the initiation of the inspection in question through the service of the relevant order on the person concerned by the CBA officers. Concerning the inspection of the applicant's work at the Regional Court ordered by the Ministry of Justice, it must be pointed out that the inspection was initiated only 1 day after the receipt of an anonymous letter, mainly concerning the applicant's critical statements on judicial reform and his presence in the media, as opposed to allegations of irregularities on the part of the applicant or his inability to perform his judicial functions. The Court therefore finds it striking that the Ministry, in these circumstances, resorted to initiating proceedings to dismiss the applicant from his judicial duties. As regards the removal of the applicant from the post of press officer of the Krakow Regional Court, it must be pointed out that, although it was within the competence of the court president to appoint and dismiss the press officer at any time, the decision of the president of the Krakow Regional Court was taken without obtaining the opinion of the collegium of that court, as required by Article 31(1)(1) of the Law on the System of Common Courts. It should be pointed out that the president of the Kraków Regional Court took this decision only 6 days after her appointment to this position by the Minister of Justice. Finally, concerning the applicant's asset declaration, it must be pointed out that the Minister of Justice, without giving any reasons, revoked the earlier decision of the President of the Court of Appeal to make that declaration confidential. In this state of affairs, given the accumulation of measures taken by the authorities, it must be considered that they can be seen as a strategy aimed at intimidating (or even silencing) the applicant concerning the views he expressed in defence of the principle of the rule of law and judicial independence. In view of the evidence presented, the Court finds that no other plausible motive for the measures at issue has been put forward or otherwise indicated. The Court points out that the applicant is one of the most emblematic representatives of the community of judges in Poland, who consistently defends the principle of the rule of law and judicial independence. The Court considers that the measures in question undeniably had a "chilling effect" in the sense that they must have discouraged not only the applicant but also other judges from participating in the future in the public debate on legislative changes to the judiciary and more generally on issues concerning the independence of the judiciary. Given the above arguments, and given the particular importance of the freedom of expression on matters of general interest, the Court concludes that the contested measures taken against the applicant were not "necessary in a democratic society" within the meaning of that article. It must therefore be held that there has been a violation of Article 10 of the Convention.

In turn, on 6 July 2023. European Court of Human Rights judged in cases 21181/19 and 51751/20 Tuleya v. Poland. In this judgment, the Court noted that the applicant (Judge Igor Tuleya) is one of the most emblematic representatives of the judicial community in Poland, who has consistently defended the rule of law and the independence of the judiciary. The Court notes that the applicant expressed his views and criticism of the legislative reforms affecting the judicial system and the effects of those reforms and considers that his statements did not go beyond mere criticism from a strictly professional perspective. The Court further notes that the applicant referred to the principle recently established in its case-law that the general right of judges to speak freely on matters concerning the functioning of the judiciary may be transformed into a corresponding duty to speak out in defence of the rule of law and the independence of the judiciary when these fundamental values are threatened (see Żurek, § 222) on the freedom of expression of judges, paragraph 220 above). Given the circumstances of the present case, it appears that the measures taken by the authorities can be characterised as a strategy aimed at intimidating (or even silencing) the applicant concerning the views he expressed in defence of the rule of law and the independence of the judiciary. The Court emphasised that the contested measures undoubtedly had a "chilling effect" in that they must have discouraged not only the applicant but also other judges from participating in the public debate on legislative reforms affecting the judiciary and more generally on issues concerning the independence of the judiciary (see Baka, § 173; Kövesi, § 209; and Żurek, § 227). The European Court of Human Rights also notes that the resolution of the Disciplinary Chamber of 18 November 2020, one of the constitutive elements of the interference with the applicant's right to freedom of expression, waived his immunity from prosecution and suspended him for an act inextricably linked to the performance of his judicial duties. In this regard, the Court reiterates the importance of protecting judiciary members from measures that may jeopardise their judicial independence and independence, given the prominent place the judiciary occupies among the organs of the State in a democratic society. Considering the general and specific context of the applicant's case, the Court finds that there has been a violation of Article 10 of the Convention.

4 Conclusions

Summing up the considerations presented so far, one must agree with the view presented in the Polish literature that a judge who exercises his office in a time of crisis of the rule of law is obliged to observe one of the basic principles of judges' professional ethics—the principle of integrity, and thus, to put it in the nutshell, to act in accordance with his or her convictions and conscience; in the non-judicial sphere this means the possibility of publicly expressing criticism of specific legal solutions and legal practice.[12] It is necessary here to separate the appearance of judges in two different roles—official and civil. With such a separation of roles, it should be assumed that judges not only can but should be active in the public sphere, especially in conditions of a crisis of the rule of law. Then the defence of independence and its guarantees and the defence of the independence of the judiciary may go beyond the limits accepted when the rule of law, the independence of judges and the independence of the judiciary are not threatened.[13] These statements may, inevitably, contain political content. The injunction to preserve the apolitical nature of judges is weakened under these conditions. It is necessary here to take care of the form of expression and to maintain the restraint expected of judges. Under these conditions, it is also acceptable for judges to participate in peaceful and legal demonstrations and protests. A strong judiciary cannot exist without judges who are strong in personal, intellectual and moral qualifications.[14]

---

[12] Serowaniec and Dorochowicz (2023), pp. 37–39.

[13] Pilich (2020), pp. 411–433; See also Ploszka (2020), pp. 319–340.

[14] Maniewska (2019), pp. 45–46.

References

Dąbrowski S (2010) Kilka uwagi o kondycji sędziów. Kwartalnik Krajowej Rady Sądownictwa 2:20–24

Garlicki L (2018) Sądy – po zmianach. Gdańskie Studia Prawnicze 40:579–591

Garlicki L (2020) "Absorpcja" czy "neutralizacja"? Uwagi o zmianach ustawy o Sądzie Najwyższym w latach 2017-2018. In: Grajewski K (ed) Konstytucjonalizm polski. Wydawnictwo Uniwersytetu Gdańskiego, Gdańsk, pp 1040–1056

Kościerzyński J (2019) Sędziowie pod presją – raport o metodach szykanowania przez władzę niezależnych sędziów. Iustitia, Warszawa

Laskowski M (2023) Granice wolności wypowiedzi sędziego w warunkach kryzysu praworządności. Przegląd Sądowy 3:7–17

Łętowska E (2022) Niezależność sędziowska a trudności zyskiwania społecznego zaufania. Kwartalnik Iustitia 2–3:109–117

Łętowska E (2023) Po pierwszej lekturze wyroku Tuleya przeciw Polsce. Europejski Przegąd Sądowy 10:4–11

Maniewska E (2019) Apolityczność jako wyznacznik granic wolności wypowiedzi sędziego dotyczących ustawowych reform sądownictwa (ich krytyki). Państwo i Prawo 7:45–46.

Pilich M (2020) Nieposłuszeństwo sędziów jako problem filozofii prawa i konstytucjonalizmu porównawczego. Refleksje nad przypadkiem Polski. In: Bodnar A, Ploszka A (eds) Wokół kryzysu praworządności, demokracji i praw człowieka. Księga jubileuszowa Profesora Mirosława Wyrzykowskiego. Wolters Kluwer Poland, Warszawa, pp 411–433

Ploszka A (2020) Granice udziału sędziów sądów powszechnych w debacie publicznej. Standard strasburski a regulacja ustawowa. In: Bodnar A, Ploszka A (eds) Wokół kryzysu praworządności, demokracji i praw człowieka. Księga jubileuszowa Profesora Mirosława Wyrzykowskiego. Wolters Kluwer, Warszawa, pp 319–340

Serowaniec M (2017) Several remarks on the ethics of the profession of a judge in Poland. Toruńskie Studia polsko-włoskie 14:91–102

Serowaniec M (2019) Theoretical and practical aspects of the principle of independence of the judiciary in Poland. Kobe Univ Law Rev 52:135–140

Serowaniec M, Dorochowicz M (2023) Independence of judges and prosecutors in Poland in light of international standards. In: Serowaniec M, Wantoch-Rekowski J, Löhnig M (eds) Poland in good constitution? Contemporary issues of constitutional law in Poland in the European context. Vandenhoeck & Ruprecht Verlag, Wien, pp 37–54

Szmyt A (2018) Trudne czasy "trzeciej władzy" w Polsce lat 2015–2018, Nadanie Profesorowi Andrzejowi Szmytowi tytułu doktora honoris causa Kijowskiego Uniwersytetu Prawa Narodowej Akademii Nauk Ukrainy. Wydawnictwo Uniwersytetu Gdańskiego, Gdańsk

Witkowski Z, Witkowska-Chrzczonowicz K, Serowaniec M (2021) Legislative and executive powers in Poland. Wydawnictwo Uniwersytetu Mikołaja Kopernika w Toruniu, Toruń

Does the Freedom of Expression of Judges Allow Them to Postpone the Trial of Cases, as a Form of Protest Against the Social Policy with Impact on Their Right to a Service Pension?

Carmen Constantina Nenu and Daniela Iancu

Abstract This study aims at analysing the right of judges to make requests and comments on their status, including the social policy regarding service pensions. The analysis takes into account the freedom of expression of judges in the relationship with the Government and the Parliament in matters of interest for the justice system and their obligation to show restraint in their behaviour in order to avoid compromising their independence and impartiality.

The analysis includes the situation created in Romania, when the judges chose as a form of their protest against the social policy of the Government, which changes the conditions for granting the service pensions of the magistrates, the postponement of the judgment of the cases pending before the courts.

1 Introduction

The freedom of expression is a fundamental right of Romanian citizens. As citizens, magistrates enjoy this right established by art. 30 of the Romanian Constitution,[1] as republished in 2003, according to which freedom of expression of thoughts, opinions, or beliefs, and freedom of any creations, by words, in writing, in pictures, by sounds or other means of communication in public, are inviolable.

The Romanian Constitution also states in art. 43 the right to strike of the employees to defend the professional, economic and social interests. The Law establishes the conditions and limitations of the exercise of this right, as well as the guarantees necessary to ensure the essential services for the society.

[1] Published in Romanian Official Journal, Part I no. 767 of 31 October 2003.

C. C. Nenu · D. Iancu (✉)
National University of Science and Technology Politehnica Bucharest, Bucharest, Romania

C. Hermida del Llano (ed.), *The Freedom of Expression for Judges in the Sphere of the Judicial Ethics*, Ius Gentium: Comparative Perspectives on Law and Justice 129, https://doi.org/10.1007/978-3-032-06504-9_14

Art. 1 of Law 367/2022 on social dialogue,[2] defines strike as being—voluntary and collective termination of labour by employees/workers; and the strike against the social and economic policy of the Government—voluntary and collective termination of labour by employees/workers as a result of the consequences of the social or economic policies which lead to diminishing some rights established by the collective labour agreements/arrangements enforceable at the date of adopting such policies. The restrictions of the right to strike are established in art. 170 of the same law. Thus, by law, it was limited the exercise of the right to strike for the following professional categories: prosecutors, judges, military personnel and personnel with special status within the Ministry of National Defence, the Ministry of Internal Affairs, the Ministry of Justice and from the institutions and structures subordinated or coordinated by them, including the National Administration of Penitentiaries, the Romanian Intelligence Service, the Foreign Intelligence Service, the Special Telecommunication Service, the personnel employed by the foreign army forces deployed.

Between the exercise of the two fundamental rights, with their legal limitations, here comes the obvious question, if the magistrates' form of expression to refuse to trial all cases, by granting new terms of judgement, represents a voluntary and collective termination of work, respectively o form of strike, these questions are to be answered in this study.

2 Restraints of the Right to Freedom of Expression of Magistrates

When we analyse the right to freedom of expression, we should have in view, besides the constitutional provisions, also the ones of art. 10 of the European Convention of Human Rights, according to which:

> 1. Everyone has the right to freedom of expression. This right shall include freedom to hold opinions and to receive and import information and ideas without interference by public authority and regardless of frontiers. …
> 2. The exercise of these freedoms, since it carries with it duties and responsibilities, may be subject to such formalities, conditions, restrictions or penalties as are prescribed by law and are necessary in a democratic society, … for the protection of the reputation or rights of others …

The Guide published on 31 December 2020 by the European Court of Human Rights on art. 10 of the European Convention of Human Rights, contains provisions regarding the special status of actors in the field of justice and their freedom of expression in the context of the judicial procedure, states that the general principle enforceable to the freedom of expression of judges are summarized at points

[2] Published in Romanian Official Journal, Part I, no. 1238 of 22 December 2022, with further amends brought by emergency government ordinance OUG 42/2023.

162–167 from Decision Baka v. Hungary (MC). The special mission of the judicial power in the society imposes a duty of discretion to judges [Morice v. France (MC) point 128]. Nonetheless, the latter pursues a certain purpose: the magistrate's word, compared to the lawyer's, is considered the expression of an objective assessment, engaging not only the one expressing it, but also, by its intermediary, the entire institution of justice (ibid, point 16). The Court, exerting its control, has to keep in mind that, when the freedom of expression of public servants is at stake, the "duties and responsibilities" mentioned in art. 10 § 2 play an important part, which justifies granting a certain margin of appreciation to national authorities to decide if the intrusion imputed is proportional to the purpose mentioned [Baka v. Hungary (MC), point 162; Vogt v. Germany, point 53; Guja v. Moldavia, point 70; Albayeak v. Turkey, point 41].

Considering the prominent position of magistracy among the State institutions in a democratic society, this approach also applies to the freedom of expression of judges in the exercise of their function, even if magistrates are not part of administration in a strict sense [Albayeak v. Turkey, point 42; Pitkevich v. Russia (dec.)].

The freedom of expression is one of the essential fundamental rights of a democratic society, one of the basic conditions for its progress and for the development of every person. So, the exceptions to this freedom should be strictly interpreted, and the necessity of any restriction should be established convincingly.

In case of magistrates, their right to freedom of expression has a series of significant restraints. Nevertheless, the Romanian magistrates publicly expressed, even during the court sessions, their opinions regarding the social policy of the Government, in the name of "the independence of justice" and of "protecting the rule of law". The form of expression consisted in a protest of magistrates, materialised in the refuse to judge, by granting new terms of judgement, against the will of the participants to the trial, invoking the principle of independence of justice. Was this protest fair, moral, ethical, legal?

In order to identify a legal qualification of the protest of Romanian magistrates, regarding the project on the law of pensions, it is also necessary to present the analyse of the principle of independence of justice. By the Declaration on judicial ethics, adopted by the General Assembly of the European Network of Judicial Councils, at the London meeting, 2–4 June, 2010, it was emphasized that "independence is the right of every citizen in a democratic society to benefit from a justice which is independent of legislative or executive power and which safeguards the freedom and the rights of the citizens under the rule of law" and "it is up to each judge to respect and to work to maintain the independence of the justice, both in its individual aspects and in its institutional aspects".

The magistrate's right to freedom of expression has a limit, i.e. the citizen's right to an independent, unbiased justice towards political issues, balanced and vertical. Also, the freedom of expression of a judge has as limit the protection of the reputation and rights of the other fellow magistrates.

In "The Bangalore Principles of Judicial Conduct", it is stated that these are meant to establish standards for the ethical conduct of judges, "starting from the prerequisite that judges are accountable for their conduct to appropriate institutions in order to maintain judicial rules, institutions that are independent and impartial themselves".

Also, art. 4 of Law no. 303/2022 on the status of judges and prosecutors[3] states that "Judges and prosecutors, through their whole activity, shall ensure the supremacy of law, respect the rights and freedom of persons, as well as their equality in front of law, and to ensure a non-discriminatory judicial treatment to all participants to judicial procedures, regardless of their quality, respect the Deontological Code of judges and prosecutors, and to attend continuous professional training.

Consequently, magistrates should show morality and enjoy a good reputation. The morality lies mainly into a philosophy of "communication" with the other people. Kant separates the morals from any search of happiness: "So, morality is not properly the doctrine of how we make ourselves happy, but how we make ourselves worthy of happiness" ("Critique of practical reason", 1788). The only moral feeling is respect: "This is the true motive of pure practical reason; it is not something else but pure moral law, to the extent in which it makes us feel the sublimity of our own oversensitive existence and in which, subjectively, at the people who have at the same time the conscience of their sensitive existence and of their dependency resulting from them concerning their nature, pathologically affected, it produces respect for their superior decisions … the respect of moral law dictates the formula of a "categorical imperative": "It acts according to the dictum that can itself pose at the same time in universal law" ("Foundation of the Metaphysics of Morals", 1783). Everyone carries the moral law in himself and therefore has to be object of respect: "Because rational beings are all subjects to the same law, according to which no one should ever treat himself and the others merely as means, but always as some purposes in itself, at the same time".

Therefore, regardless of their opinions, magistrates should carry out their activity with professionalism and balance, and their political beliefs should not be reflected in the decisions taken. Yes, they are free to express their opinions, but this right of magistrates has several limitations and restraints.

The Charter of Fundamental Rights of the European Union regulates at art. 11 the freedom of expression and of information. The first paragraph of this article states: *Everyone has the right to freedom of expression. This right shall include the freedom of opinion and to receive or transmit information and ideas without interference by public authority and regardless of frontiers.*

CCJE Opinion No. 25 (2022) on the freedom of expression of judges,[4] was drafted based on the previous opinions of CCJE, a Magna Carta of Judges CCJE (2010) and of the relevant instruments of the Council of Europe, especially the European Charter on the status of judges (1998) and the recommendation of the Committee of Ministers CM/Rec(2010)12 on judges: Independence, Efficiency and

[3] Published in Romanian Official Journal, Part I no. 1102 of 16 November 2022, as amended by OUG 168/2022. It shall be amended by Law L 282/2023.

[4] http://www.forumuljudecatorilor.ro/wp-content/uploads/Avizul-CCJE-nr.-25-2022-privind-libertatea-de-exprimare-a-judecatorilor.pdf, posted on 20.12.2022.

Responsibilities, the Report of the European Commission for Democracy and law (Venice Commission) on the freedom of expression of judges (CDLAD(2015)018).

The Opinion takes into account the Basic Principles of UN on the independence of the judicial system, the Bangalore Principles of Judicial Conduct and the Report of special Rapporteur of UN on the independence of judges and lawyers, concerning also the exercise of freedom of expression by judges. Also, the opinion is based on the case law of the European Court of Human Rights and takes into account the answers of the members CCJE to the questionnaire on the freedom of expression of judges.

The Opinion addresses the freedom of expression of judges and discusses the main aspects regarding judicial expression. This approaches the legal and ethical obligation of a judge to decide in order to protect the rule of law and the democracy at domestic level, but also at European and international level. It is analysed the judicial expression concerning matters of interest for justice, as well as controversial subject of public interest, and examines the obligation of reserve of judges.

The obligation of reserve is final as a duty of reserve imposed to the judge either by the judicial authority, or by the lawmaker. The judicial reserve includes the notion of judicial discretion, reserve or moderation.

Form the magistrates' point of view, the obligation of reserve imposed to them cannot repress the freedom of thinking and of expression, but it forbids, though, any scandalous critical expressions, that could undermine the trust and respect that their position should inspire to litigants (conclusion of PhD university professor Elena Simina Tănăsescu, member of the Superior Council of Magistracy, expressed during the conference "Freedom of expression of magistrates. Limits ad vulnerabilities").

The magistrates should express their opinions in a prudent and measured way, as their obligation of impartiality should meet the requirements of the public service whose functionality they ensure.

The sanctions applied in case of deviance from these principles should however be weighted in order not to cause a discouraging effort on those who would want to take part in the public meeting regarding the efficiency of judicial institutions.[5]

The principle of separation of powers supports the freedom of expression of judges if a matter of public interest, such as the functioning of the justice system, is concerned. The rule of law ensures the equality of all (citizens or state actors) in front of law. Its efficiency depends partially on the public trust in the independence and authority of justice. The separation of powers supposes both the judicial independence, and the freedom of expression of judges, resulting in a stressful situation between the objective to prevent judges from behaving like politicians and, at the same time, and the objective to support the freedom of expression of judges, as evidence of judicial independence.

CCJE adopts a wide opinion regarding the domain of personal application of the right to freedom of expression of judges as an individual right. Therefore, a judge

---

[5] http://www.forumuljudecatorilor.ro/index.php/archives/608

enjoys the right of freedom of expression like any other citizen. The right to freedom of expression of judges expands to the personal opinions expressed concerning the exercise of their function and gives judges the right to make statements outside the court, but also in the court, both in public and in private, and to be involved in public debates and in social life in general.

In their official function, judges play an important part in the society, as guarantors of the rule of law and of justice. The essence itself of the profession of judge is the capacity to regard subjects of disputes in an objective and impartial manner. It is equally important that judges be seen as having such capacity. This is dur to the fact that they need the public trust in their independence and impartiality in order to be successful in fulfilling the duties and in maintaining the authority of the judicial system to solve the judicial disputes or to establish the guilt or innocence of a person as a result of a criminal charge.

It results that judges should prove such values through their behaviour. Therefore, it is legitimate that the State would impose judges an obligation of reserve that should grant proper consideration to their role in the society.

The limitation of the freedom of expression always requires a fundamental justification. In the case law of the European Court of Human Rights (ECHR), an intrusion is considered necessary in a democratic society when it responds to a "pressing social need" and its "proportional" to the legitimate purpose.

The proportionality of a measure imposes that this be the less restrictive measure. It appears that a balance should be established between the fundamental right of a certain judge concerning his freedom of expression, and the legitimate interest of a democratic society to maintain the public trust in the judicial system. When an intrusion is assessed, the proportionality of the sanction or another measure should also be examined. Sanctions should not have an inhibitory effect for the exercise of the freedom of expression by other judges, that is, it should not prevent other judges from exerting the administration of justice and of the judicial system.

In all declarations of public interest, judges should express themselves with prudence, balance in tone, and respect. They should refrain from discriminatory statements, politics, philosophic or religious proselytism, or militancy.

3 The Protest of the Magistrates in Romania Started in June 2023: Expression of Freedom of Expression or Hidden Strike?

Unhappy with the project concerning special pensions, magistrates from several courts and prosecutors' offices protested, postponing all files for an indefinite period, except the urgent ones. The initiative of the protest actions started from the Superior Council of Magistracy (CSM) which sent a notification urging magistrates to rebel against the provisions of the project of law. Thus, sixteen Courts of Appeal from the country, headed by the one in Bucharest, entered this form of protest. They were joined by more prosecutors' offices and courts of law, including the National Anticorruption Directorate (DNA) and the Directorate for Investigating Organised Crime and Terrorism (DIICOT).

During the protest, only the following categories of cases were judged:

- in civil matter: presidential ordinance, precautionary measures, temporary postponement of execution, international kidnappings of children, foster care, adoptions, public custody, reporting as undesirable status, orders of protection
- in criminal matter: cases when the defendants are under preventive measures, cases of jurisdiction of the judge of rights and freedom, cases in the matter of execution of punishment (first instance and ways of appeal), verification of precautionary measures.

The position expressed by magistrates in the General Meetings regarding the project of law on special pensions, and supported by the Superior Council of Magistracy, was that the situation is very serious and brings fundamental harm to the independence of justice and to the status of magistrates, with direct consequences on the act of justice. They set up as arguments of initiation of protests by postponing the cases, the following:

- the status of judge is not a privilege of his, it is the right of the society to have an independent and impartial justice. The independence of the judge cannot be the object of political negotiation, and a disrespected professional body will no longer offer the society those guarantees of independence that are so necessary.

The pensions of judges, public service pension and not special pension, as stated in the public space, has been consecrated in the national legislation even since 1997, and the lawmaker did not offer any reasonable argument to eliminate it. It was conceived especially to strengthen the status of the judge and the guarantees of independence that it has to offer.

- to eliminate this component of the independence of the judge is not in agreement with the case law of the Constitutional Court which decided that elimination of such pension for judges is contrary to the current requirements, that important international documents express directly regarding the rights of judges, in considering the importance of their role in defending the ruke of law.
- the amendments of the laws of justice adopted in December 2022 represented an accomplished PNRR (The National Recovery and Resilience Plan) milestone, PNRR stating expressly the non-inclusion of the pensions of judges under the category that is to be amended.

The Government and Parliament were accused of "lack of transparency" and of "unfair behaviour" regarding the proposals of amendment of the law on the status of magistrates. It was stated by magistrates that the lawmaker did not consider "the inhuman volume of work among judges, aggravated by the massive departures from the judicial system, in the context of incoherence and lack of transparency of the legislative power, the chronic under-sizing of personnel schemas, not-adapted for years to the huge amount of cases, incompatibilities and interdictions of the profession at the moment of drafting the legislative proposal.

CSM stated that it does not oppose to reforming the system of public service pensions, but that they should find "regulatory solutions to give efficiency to this process, by complying with the independence of justice and with the case law of the Constitutional Court in the matter". The magistrates' requirements aimed "the regulation of a real method of staging the increase of the pension age for a reasonable period of time, so that not to create discriminatory situations between the professionals with a similar seniority in the judicial system, but with a different biological age". Furthermore, it was requested that the legislative solution should prescribe also the possibility of anticipated pension of magistrates, similar to the solution regulated in the public pension system.

The point of view of the government expressed through the voice of the Minister of Justice was that "it respects the right of the magistrates to freedom of expression, but starts from the prerequisite that dialogue is the solution of solving any problem of the judicial system, not protest". They underlined the need to identify some balanced solutions between the imperative of respecting the commitment to reform assumed by the Romanian state, including in the pension system, and to ensure the functionality and efficiency of judicial system, of the quality of the act of justice regarded as public service, the fact that the principle according to which no pension can exceed the salary is a moral one, and also the fact that the project of public service pensions represents a milestone within PNRR.

The declarations regarding worrying subjects for the judicial system as institution are considered by CCJE as being part of the declarations that might have a negative effect on the authority and reputation of the judicial system. In the Opinion of CCJE no. 25 (2022) on the freedom of expression of judges, it is appreciated that "judges have the right to make comments on matters that concern fundamental human rights, the rule of law, matters of judicial appointments or promotion and the proper functioning of the administration of justice, including independence of judiciary and separation of powers. If the matter directly affects the operation of the courts, judges should also be free to comment on politically controversial topics, including legislative proposals or governmental policy. This means that the public has a legitimate interest in being informed about these issues as they involve very important matters in a democratic society. Judges in leadership positions or those holding a position in judges' associations or in the councils for the judiciary, are in a prominent position to speak out on behalf of the judicial system. Judges have the right to make demands and comments concerning their status, their working conditions, as well as all other questions regarding their professional interests. Judges' associations play a prominent role on this issue. Also, judges should exercise restraint to avoid compromising their impartiality or independence. Further, public representations made to the government on matters of concern for the judiciary, must not appear as lobbying the government or as indicating how a judge would rule if particular situations were to come before the court. A high-ranking judge must be particularly cautious in this regard due to his/her prominent position".

4 Conclusions

At the end of the Opinion CCJE no. 25 (2022) on the freedom of expression of judges, they formulate a series of recommendations, from which we mention:

1. A judge enjoys the right to freedom of expression like any other citizen. In addition to a judge's individual entitlement, there is a demand of free participation of judges in debates of public interest, especially regarding matters concerning the judicial system, demand imposed by the principles of democracy, separation of powers and pluralism.
2. In situations where democracy, the separation of powers or the rule of law are under threat, judges must be resilient and have a duty to speak out in defence of judicial independence, of the constitutional order and of the restoration of democracy, both at national and international level. This includes views and opinions on issues that are politically sensitive and extends to both internal and external independence of individual judges and of the judicial system in general. Judges who speak on behalf of a judicial council, judicial association or other representative body of the judiciary, enjoy a wider appreciation in this respect.
3. Aside from associations of judges, councils for the judiciary or any other independent body, individual judges have an ethical duty to explain to the public the justice system, the functioning of the judiciary and its values. By enhancing understanding, transparency and by helping to avoid public misrepresentations, judges may help to promote and preserve public trust in the judicial activity.

In the Guide on case law of European Convention of Human Rights. Mass protests—drafted by the Court Office of the European Convention of Human Rights,[6] it is considered that protests are the expression of opinion in the senser of art. 10.

But analysing the international, European and national regulatory provisions, it results that the protest of magistrates from the summer of 2023 represented a form of strike, not allowed by the law of this professional category, and its consequences were prejudicial, affecting the public trust in the independence of justice, in the power of law and the separation of powers within the state.

[6] www.echr.coe.int/documents/d/echr/Guide_Mass_protests_RON

Does the Wels Declaration of Ethics, Adopted by the Association of Austrian Judges on 8 November 2007, Infringe upon the Freedom of Expression for Judges Within the Framework of Respect for the Principles of Judicial Ethics?

Heribert Franz Koeck

Abstract The Status of Judges and Statutes on the status of judges is an issue that that has been dealt with in various committees and meetings of experts in the framework of the United Nations and of the Council of Europe. The conclusions and recommendations originating from these bodies have never claimed to be of binding force for Member States, but expressed the hope that Member States would take these recommendations into account when working on national statutes for judges or enacting legislation pertinent to the matter.

Austria has not laid down, by specific law, a formal statute on the status of judges, considering the pertinent rules contained in the Constitution or in simple laws as sufficiently covering this issue. In contrast, the Austrian Association of Judges which has no official character and has not been empowered by law to enact rules concerning the status of justice has nevertheless felt compelled to elaborate a Declaration that was adopted in the city of Wels in 2007, and is accordingly referred to as the Wels Declaration. It contains ethical principles which avowedly are guiding the Austrian judges in their work but which in fact spills over also the private conduct of the judges, curtailing, inter alia, their rights to take political positions or to engage in political activities.

The present paper criticizes this stance taken by the Austrian Association of Judges, arguing that judges, being part of the more informed sector of society, are better suited than others to speak up in the political discourse, and that it is not for a private association to interfere with the civic rights and duties of its member. Therefore, political activities of judges in conflict with the rules laid down in the Declaration must not be used against them in procedures concerning their career.

Res publica est res populi.
Cicero, *De Re Publica*, Liber I, Cap. 39.

H. F. Koeck (✉)
Johannes Kepler University Linz, Linz, Austria

C. Hermida del Llano (ed.), *The Freedom of Expression for Judges in the Sphere of the Judicial Ethics*, Ius Gentium: Comparative Perspectives on Law and Justice 129, https://doi.org/10.1007/978-3-032-06504-9_15

My present paper for this Conference will appear unorthodox to many. This is inevitable. In fact, it is my intention to stir complacent minds which are all too content with the present state of affairs originating from so-called Codes of Ethics imposed upon judges. To do so seems fit for the commemoration of Eugene Chelaru, not only a good friend but also a liberal gentleman and an openminded professor of law.[1]

Although the freedom of expression for judges is a general problem not restricted to just one national situation, the title of my paper indicates that I am going to take the Austrian situation under the Wels Declaration as the starting point of my considerations.

1 Legal Restrictions on Political Activities of Judges in Austria

Before doing so I have to say first that Austrian legislation proper does not contain any rules curtailing the freedoms of judges. I may add that the European Convention on Human Rights is part of Austria's constitutional order.[2]

In 2007, the Austrian Association of Judges resolved the so-called Wels Declaration of Ethics, named after the city where the instrument was adopted.[3] Precursor was the Salzburg Resolution of 1982.[4]

2 The Wels Declaration: A Preliminary Overview

The Wels Declaration comprises ten articles containing the ethical principles which avowedly are guiding the Austrian judges in their work. For the purpose of this paper, Article IX, entitled "Private Behavior", contains the essential statement.

[1] I avail myself of this opportunity to express my thanks to Professor Cristina Hermida del Llano for organizing this commemorative event and for inviting old friends of Prof. Eugen Chelaru from the common international network to take part and contribute to this Conference and to the book deriving from it.

[2] Cf. Austrian Law Gazette (BGBl) 59/1964.

[3] The original text of the Wels Declaration together with a quasi-official translation can be found in: https://richtervereinigung.at/ueber-uns/ethikerklaerung/

[4] Cf. the introductory remarks to the Wels Declaration, ibid.

2.1 Art. IX of the Wels Declaration in General

On first glance, its introductory sentence seems to be innocuous, stating that "[w]e [i.e. the Austrian judges] scrutinize carefully and critically whether our actions or statements are suitable to make us dependent on someone, or could even only give the appearance thereof." However, later on in this paper it will appear that formulations like the concluding phrase are open to (what I am going to call) objective as well subjective interpretation; and the latter cannot go undisputed.

As regards the second sentence, careful and critical scrutiny "also applies to our off-duty activities, as far as we can expect that this may compromise our credibility as judges or cause our credibility to be questioned." Here again, the concluding phrase is disputable in as much it lends itself to both objective and subjective interpretation and the latter cannot be relevant.[5]

Whether or not the third sentence can be regarded the core of Article IX, it is certainly that part where (so-to-say) the magician pulls the rabbit out of his hat. It is that part which contains the disputed restrictions on the freedom of expression of judges. This picture with the magician's rabbit holds true, of course, only for the naïve reader; the less so will have expected something like that right from the beginning. The sentence runs: "We are convinced that being a member of a political party or being politically active within such a party can be detrimental to the credibility of independent jurisdiction that is unswayable by political parties and not bound to any interest groups and lobbies."

The last part of the sentence characterizing "independent jurisdiction" as "unswayable by political parties and not bound to any interest groups and lobbies" states a truism; however, in its blind zeal to ban any kind of political activities, the Article fails to see that there are other forms of undue influence, any and all of which should be equally excluded from the ambit of independent jurisdiction. A most important issue is what is called (or rather self-styled) "political correctness", an issue to which to turn back we will have ample opportunity in the course of this paper.[6]

2.2 The Rule Affecting Judges in Particular

The essential part of Article IX is the statement assertion that "being a member of a political party or being politically active within such a party can be detrimental to the credibility of independent jurisdiction." As regards the notion of "credibility", I have already stated that it lends itself to both objective and subjective interpretation, is thus ambiguous, and cannot, therefore, be taken without first being more closely examined.

[5] Cf. infra, Part VII. 8. b. and c.

[6] Cf. infra, especially Parts XI and XIII.

It is interesting to note that the Declaration does not say that membership in, or activity within, a political party "is" detrimental to the credibility of independent jurisdiction but only that it "can have" such an effect. Why this less strict wording was chosen is difficult to tell. It is not unlikely that the drafters of the Declaration have not given any thought at all to the possible difference, in this context, of "is" and "can have" and that the formulation chosen by them could be open to discussion.

A simple answer could be that the drafters of the Declaration did not attribute any different meaning to one or the other of the alternatives; the different wording would thus be a question of linguistics only.

This does not prevent us from looking for some substantive alternatives.

Drafters of the Declaration might have considered the formulation "can have" to be somewhat more accommodating than the harsh "is". believing that even the formulation "can have" should be sufficient to deter judges from even taking the risk of compromising the jurisdiction's independence.

Another reason might have been that in the past participation in partisan politics was not considered in Austria incompatible with the judicial office, that judges have served as members of the national parliament and even as their party's speaker for judicial politics. These judges should not be blamed in retrospect for engaging in political activities.

3 Restrictions on Political Activities of Judges in Other European Countries

A survey of the approaches taken *by law* in the various European countries vis-à-vis the involvement of judges in party politics reveals a mixed picture, from unequivocally banning them over tolerating them to even enhancing them.[7]

However, in the majority of European countries there exist Codes of Ethics (more neutrally also called Codes of Conduct) for judges. These codes are not enacted by law but are imposed upon judges by associations of the latter claiming to speak for (all of) them. If this were correct, one could also regard those Codes as self-imposed. In the majority of these Codes, involvement of Judges in party politics is at least discouraged.

4 The Status of Associations of Judges

The legal status of these bodies, often termed Associations of Judges, varies according to their relationship to the state's institutions.

[7] For more details, see infra, Part X.4.

4.1 Associations as Public Institutions: In General and Regarding Associations of Judges

If they were set up by law they would likely be characterized by mandatory membership including compulsory contribution by all members. In Austria, this is true for the Chamber of Commerce, the Chamber of Labor and the Chamber of Agriculture which are entitled to levy contributions, but not for the Austrian Association of Judges.

4.1.1 Associations of Judges as Private Institutions

In fact, most of the associations of judges in European countries appear to be private institutions set up on the initiative of members of the judiciary. Even if—as in the case of Austria—they may enjoy consultative status[8] with their respective parliaments, they cannot be considered institutions of public law. For their financing, they depend on membership fees that are due only for members; in addition, they may receive private donations and public subsidies.[9]

As regards membership in the Austrian Association, all judges (whether active, retired or still candidates) are eligible; but a personal application is required which may be rejected for certain reasons although this is a most unlikely case.

4.1.2 Excursus. Binding Force of Rules

At this point, two different questions come up. One is for the binding force of rules which are intended to prevent judges from engaging in political activities. Here, we have to distinguish between rules contained in a law—whatever the rules' particular designation—enacted by the competent legal authority, and rules which are not contained in a law but which are based on the decision of a private association. Moreover, we have to distinguish between rules that contain a legal command and those which are a recommendation only.

---

[8] Federal Law of 28.12.2011, Austrian Law Gazette I 136/2011. The consultative status is limited to questions concerning the operation of the judicial service and the judicial working environment. See § 73a of the Law on the organization of courts—Gerichtsorganisationsgesetz (GOG).

[9] However, these subsidies have to remain irregular and restricted to payments for services of public interest; otherwise the private and independent character of the Association might be compromised.

4.1.3 Binding Force of National Law and Its Inherent Limits

In general, the binding force of a law containing a legal command can be limited *ratione materiae*, *ratione personae* and *ratione temporis*. Rules limiting judges' political activities do not, *ratione personae*, apply to persons who are not members of the judiciary. Whether they apply, *ratione temporis*, apart from active judges, to candidate judges and/or retired judges, depends on the provisions of the law.

So far, the limitations are easy to discern. This is different where limitations *ratione materiae* are concerned. First of all, the legal institution from which the law emanates has to be competent for the matter it intends to regulate. And, secondly, the legal institution must be free in the exercise of its legislative power. This freedom can be limited by rules of a higher legal order.

4.1.4 Binding Force of National Law and Its Limits Under Supranational and International Law

In Austria, as in most (though not all) European countries, such rules of a higher legal order are contained in the constitution. In addition, and as regards the Member States of the European Union, the law of the Union takes precedence over national law, even the national constitution.[10] Moreover, those countries which are Members of the Council of Europe are also bound by the European Convention on Human Rights.[11]

In addition to limitations on national legislation by regional legal orders or instruments, there exist also limitations by international law, being the law of the universal community of states. For the purpose of this paper it suffices to state that international law has two sources: customary international law and treaty law.[12] What interests here are the two United Nation Covenants on Human rights, or—more specifically—the UN Covenant on Civil and Political Rights.[13]

---

[10] See Treaty of Lisbon, Declaration 17 concerning primacy: The Conference recalls that, in accordance with well settled case law of the Court of Justice of the European Union, the Treaties and the law adopted by the Union on the basis of the Treaties take precedence over the law of Member States, under the conditions laid down by the said case law. Cf. Apostolovska-Stepanoska and Ognjanoska (2020).

[11] Convention for the protection of human rights and fundamental freedoms, published, inter alia, by the European Court of Human Rights, www.echr.coe.int.—In the present context, the Charter of Human Rights of the European Union, EU Doc. 2000/C 364701, might also be relevant.

[12] Cf., *inter alia,* Mejía-Lemos et al. (2022), pp. 137–160.

[13] Adopted in 1960 by the United Nations General Assembly. See International Covenant on Civil and Political Rights, Resolution 2200 A (XXI) of 16 December 1966.

5 Binding Force of Rules of Private Associations

Restrictions for the political activity of judges contained in rules which are based on the decision of a private association, and, more particularly, of an association of judges, are quite a different matter. First, decisions of private associations are not laws and cannot, therefore, have the same binding force as laws. Nonetheless, decisions of private associations can have binding force inasmuch as it is permitted by the law, on which the foundation of the association is based (in Austria called the Law on Associations[14]). In principle, the regulatory authority of private association comprises the setting of the annual membership fee and decisions necessary for the attainment of the association's object and purpose. In both areas, the decisions may not exceed what is reasonable and normal. All members of the association have the right to have the decisions reviewed by the competent public authority.

As regards membership fees, they are due only for the time of membership. Failing payment, the association has the right to bring an action against the member unwilling to fulfil their financial obligations and to have final judgment in its favor also executed.

In contrast, decisions in other than financial matters cannot be legally enforced, even if they remain within object and purpose of the association. The only sanction left to the association is the expulsion of the recalcitrant member.

6 A *Caveat* Regarding the Wels Declaration on Ethics

As regards the Wels Declaration of Ethics, a caveat has to be registered here. The Austrian Association of Judges may, if it considers it necessary or desirable, expel a judge who ignores the ban, contained in Art. IX of the Declaration, on membership in, or political activities within, a political party by joining a party and/or being politically active within that party. However, it is doubtful whether the Association would do so, because loosing membership in the Association would have little negative impact on the judge if he does not care about a possible negative opinion of him among his fellow judges and is thus not afraid of (equally only possible) negative repercussion on his professional and social environment. Moreover, to open up this case in public might lead to discussions about the legitimacy of the ban in question unwelcome to the Association.

However, the professional career of judges is, to a greater or smaller extent, dependent on the good will he enjoys among those of his pairs who sit in those commissions who have to make a proposal concerning his eventual promotion to a

[14]Austrian Law on Associations (Vereinsgesetz), Austrian Law Gazette (BGBl) I Nr. 66/2002, as amended.

position he has applied for.[15] In this case, his chances will not have been improved by his negative stance towards the ban on judges' party politics. Whether it will help him that the Wels Declaration declares in Art. II that "[i]n selecting and evaluating fellow judges, we are guided according to the criteria of the *Richterdienstgesetz* (Austrian Judicial Services Act) by their professional and social abilities" remains doubtful; whether the formulation "professional and social abilities" will, or will not, be interpreted by some members of the commission as opening a door for regarding the Wels Declaration a relevant standard, may be open to discussion.

Of course, from an objective point of view it is not allowed to take a judge's conforming or not conforming to the Wels Declaration as a criteria in the consideration of his "professional and social abilities", for if the Declaration has no legally binding force it also cannot provide a criterion for a legal decision.[16] The Austria Association of Judges has published in 2017 a statement concerning the tasks of these Personnel Chambers that does not mention the Wels Declaration and only refers to the "professional and personal" suitability of the candidate.[17]

7 Supranational and International Protection of Human Rights, with Special Regard to Judges

I now turn to the question of whether, and to what extent, supranational, regional and universal legal rules protect judges against encroachment upon their human rights, in particular their freedom of expression, to which are closely related their freedom of assembly and their freedom of association. Since I am dealing here with the question of freedom of expression of judges from the point of view of its protection in European countries, and since all of them (with the only exception of Byelorussia) are Member States of the Council of Europe and as such are automatically subject to the European Convention on Human Rights (including all its

[15] The designation of theses commissions as "Independent personnel chambers" *(Unabhängige Personalsenate)* indicates the importance which the legislator attributes to their objectivity. The principle that they must not take orders from outside is relativized, however, by the fact that the proposals of these commission are not binding for the deciding authorities (ministers, the government, the federal president).

[16] 59. For example, the following situation may be considered under the Court's case-law as a form of interference with the right to freedom of expression: [...] a disciplinary penalty imposed on a doctor for breach of professional ethics, for criticizing the medical treatment provided to a patient. See ECHR 2009/6 Case of *Frankowicz v. Poland*, 16 December 2008, no. 53025/99 (Fourth Section).

[17] The Austrian Association of Judges presented in 2017, in a publication entitled *Resources for the rule of law* (Ressourcen für den Rechtsstaat), a Statement dealing with "Democracy and the rule of law" a call for more independence including the request for the binding force of the proposals made by the Independent Personnel Chambers. See https://richtervereinigung.at/wp-content/uploads/delightful-downloads/2019/08/2019_Ressourcen-f%C3%BCr-den-Rechtsstaat-1.pdf, (pages not numbered).

Additional Protocols), I feel justified in dispensing with the other instruments which may also be applicable here, namely the Charter of Human Rights of the European Union[18] and the United Nations Covenant on Civil and Political Rights,[19] which all are in conformity with the principles laid down in the European Convention on Human Rights (ECHR).

7.1 *Freedom of Expression, Freedom of Assembly and Freedom of Association in the* European Convention on Human Rights

In the context of political activities of judges, two articles of the European Convention on Human Rights are decisive.

According to Article 10 ECHR, everyone has the right to freedom of expression and to receive and impart information.[20] This right also covers the freedom of the press. Freedom of expression is one of the essential foundations of a democratic society. Freedom of information, both in its passive and in its active form, is essential for the democratic process of decision shaping and decision making because decisions promoting the common good can be taken only by informed citizens through elections or other forms of direct participation in the democratic process and by informed mandataries in representative democracies.[21]

According to Article 11 ECHR, everyone has the right to freedom of peaceful assembly and to freedom of association.[22] Freedom of assembly and of association also are essential foundations of a democratic society because they not only facilitate the exchange of information but also secure that the voices of participants in an assembly or of members of an association are made stronger by their accumulation and thus will be better heard in the democratic process.[23] The legitimacy of such a joint approach to political matters is confirmed by the fact that Article 11 ECHR expressly states the right to form and to join trade unions for the protection of one's interests to be included in the freedom of association.

[18] Cf. supra, EU Doc. 2000/C 364/01.

[19] Cf. supra, fn. 13.

[20] Cf. Article 10 Paragraph 1, Sentence 1 and 2: "Everyone has the right to freedom of expression. This right shall include freedom to hold opinions and to receive and impart information and ideas without interference by public authority and regardless of frontiers."

[21] For a comprehensive review of article 10, see Guide on Article 10 of the European Convention on Human Rights. Freedom of expression. Prepared by the Registry. Updated on 31 August 2022. European Court of Human Rights Doc. 2/139. Cf. also Bychawska-Siniarska (2017).

[22] See Article 11 Paragraph 1, First half of the sentence. The wording adds to "association" the words "with others", but the value of this addition is questionable because it is difficult to envisage other association than those "with others".

[23] See Guide on Article 11 of the European Convention on Human Rights. Freedom of assembly and association. Updated on 31 August 2022.

7.2 *Limits on, and Restrictions of, the Said Freedoms of Judges*

As in the other instruments for the protection of human rights mentioned above, the provisions stating the various human rights guaranteed by the ECHR allow for their limitation or restriction.[24] These limitations or restrictions center around the standard formulation of being "prescribed by law" and "necessary in a democratic society, in the interests of national security, territorial integrity or public safety, for the prevention of disorder or crime, for the protection of health or morals, and for the protection of the rights of others".[25]

Various Articles of the ECHR provide for additional limitations of restrictions to cope with possible dangers inherent in the respective rights. Thus, Article X allows for States to require the licensing of broadcasting, television or cinema enterprises.[26] Further allowances for limitations or restrictions concern the protection of the reputation and the prevention of the disclosure of information received in confidence.[27]

Both Articles 10 and 11 contain clauses that are, or could be, relevant to the subject of this paper. In this context, Article 10 ECHR provides for "restrictions" necessary "for maintaining the authority and impartiality of the judiciary."[28] Article 11 ECHR states that "[it] shall not prevent the imposition of lawful restrictions on the exercise of these rights by members of the armed forces, of the police or of the administration of the State."[29]

8 Administration of Justice

While applicability of the before-mentioned clause of Article 10 ECHR to judges is indisputable, the contrary seems to be true for the for the just-quoted provision of Article 11 ECHR. The question is: Does the term "administration" open up a loophole for an interpretation that would permit application to judges as well?"

[24] These restrictions and limitations are regularly set out in the paraph that follows the paragraph proclaiming the respective right. The latter is always Paragraph 1, the former usually Paragraph 2.

[25] Cf., in our context, the Second Paragraphs of Articles 10 and 11.

[26] This allowance is already contained in Paragraph 1, Sentence 2 of Article 10. Usually, restrictions are dealt with in paragraph 2 of the various articles.

[27] Article 10 Paragraph 2.

[28] Article 10, Paragraph 2, concluding part.

[29] Article 11, Paragraph 2, Last sentence.

8.1 "Administration" Largo Sensu

In order to better understand the question, it is necessary to compare the Austrian terminology relating to the branches of public power with the conventional terminology as we know it since the early times of American constitutional history. According to the latter, public power is divided between three governmental branches, i.e. the legislative, the executive, and the judicial branch. The first branch is concerned with law-giving, the second with administration, and the third with adjudication. The Austrian terminology distinguishes between "Gesetzgebung", i.e. the making of law, also referred to as law-giving and commonly called legislation, and "Vollziehung", i.e. the execution of law towards the people (consisting of natural and legal persons), also called "administration of law" or administration largo sensu. The execution of law is then divided between "Verwaltung", i.e. the administration of law stricto sensu, and the "Gerichtsbarkeit", i.e. adjudication. The essential difference between administration and adjudication consists in the fact that administration is carried out by officials who are bound by instruction of their superior while adjudication is carried out by officials who are not subject to any instruction by whomsoever.

It follows that, according to Austrian terminology, administration, if understood *largo sensu*, i.e. when given a wide meaning, does also comprise adjudication.

8.2 Administration" Stricte Sensu

If we were to apply Austrian terminology to Article 11 ECHR, and more particularly to the Article's last sentence, then this sentence of Article 11 could be understood as also including the judiciary and thus permitting the curtailment of the right of assembly and association of judges.

There are, however, strong objections to such an understanding of the text of Article 11 Paragraph 2 Last sentence. First of all, it is not permitted to give a meaning to the terms of a treaty that deviates from their ordinary meaning,[30] unless it is established that the parties intended to give a special meaning to a term.[31] According to the ordinary meaning of the term "administration", the term is used, in Article 11, *stricto sensu* and does not cover adjudication. Austria must not even give a larger ODER wider meaning to the term "administration" pro *foro interno*, i.e. for use on the national level, because Austria, as a State party to the ECHR, is bound by the ordinary meaning of the latter's terms with regard to any and all respects of the Convention.

[30] See Vienna Convention on the Law of Treaties, Article 31 (General Rule of Interpretation) Paragraph 1: "A treaty shall be interpreted in good faith in accordance with the ordinary meaning to be given to the terms of the treaty in their context and in the light of its object and purpose."

[31] Cf. Article 31 Paragraph 4.

Secondly, although the ECHR does not contain a general rule of interpretation comparable to that contained in Article 31 Vienna Convention on the Law of Treaties (VCLT) of 1969, and although the VCLT has no retroactive force and does not therefore directly apply to the ECHR of 1950, Article 31 has to be considered as reflecting then existing customary law and is thereby applicable to the ECHR, regardless of the date of its conclusion, due to the latter's character of an international treaty. According to Article 31 Paragraph 1 VCLT, object and purpose of a treaty have to be taken into account when it comes to interpreting it. As appears from Paragraph 6 of the Preamble of the ECHR, object and purpose of the ECHR is "to secure the rights and freedoms defined in this Convention".[32] This is confirmed by Articles 17 and 18 which deal with specific aspects of interpretation.[33]

It follows from these considerations that in a case of doubt the rights and freedoms defined in the ECHR call for their wide, and prohibit their narrow, interpretation. In contrast, any limits and restrictions of these rights and freedoms have to be narrowly construed.

If we apply these conclusions to the question of what can be understood by "administration" in Article 11 Paragraph 2 ECHR, this term has also to be interpreted in a narrow way and therefore does not include "adjudication". Thus, the judiciary cannot be subject to the imposition of restrictions allowed for in the last sentence of this paragraph, not even in Austria.

9 Applicability of the European Convention on Human Rights to Rules Laid Down by National Associations of Judges

I now turn to the question of whether bodies like the Austrian Association of Judges have to respect the rights and freedoms laid down in the ECHR. The question comes up because only States are parties to the Convention and therefore directly bound by it. In contrast, non-State-entities as private bodies—whether national or international non-governmental organizations or private individuals[34]—are not directly bound by an international inter-governmental treaty.

---

[32] According to this paragraph, the rights and freedoms defined in the Additional Protocols to the ECHR are equally to be secured; and therefore, they also form part of the object and purpose of the Convention.

[33] Article 17 prohibits any interpretation of the Convention that could lead to an abuse of the rights defined therein; and Article 18 prohibits any interpretation that would permit restriction on rights "for any purpose other than those for which they [i.e. the restrictions] have been prescribed".

[34] Since individuals are natural and not legal persons, one might be tempted to assume that they are, by their very nature," private". Consequently, the formulation "private individual" seems to be a tautology. However, individuals may be state officials—as, for instance, a Head of State or a Head of Government—and, in this capacity, are "public persons" and cannot be considered any longer to be private individuals.

9.1 Human Rights Protected in International Treaties

Yet, the ECHR claims to create obligations not only for States but also for individuals or groups of individuals. The "prohibition of abuse of rights" as contained in Article 17 of the ECHR[35] protects the rights and freedoms enshrined in the Convention against the attempt to interpret the latter in such a way that it may imply "for any State, group or person any right to engage in any activity or perform any act aimed at the destruction of any of the rights and freedoms set forth herein or at their limitation to a greater extent than is provided for in the Convention."

Where does the Convention derive the right from to enact rules not only for the States parties to it but also for individuals and group of individuals? The most simple answer would be that Article 17 ECHR does only seemingly do so and that the prohibition directed towards individuals or group of individuals constitutes, in fact, an obligation for the States parties to see to it that object and purpose of the Convention are not compromised by individuals and groups.

9.2 Human Rights as Part of the General Principles of Law

However, the better answer should be that human rights do not only form part of the peremptory norms of international law (*ius cogens*) but also are part of the general principle of laws recognized by civilized nation.[36] As such they are applicable to all legal subject, public and private. These principles are derived from the old *ius gentium* for which a separation of norms which would apply, on the one hand, to private persons, and, on the other, to States, was unknown.[37]

[35] So the title of Article 17 ECHR.

[36] As stated in Art. 38 Paragraph 1 Sub-Paraph c of the Statute of the International Court of Justice which forms part of the United Nations Charter.

[37] The artificial separation between the one and the other was the consequence of the emergence of the State as a sovereign entity and the negative consequences drawn from this development by scholars of legal positivism only in the eighteenth and nineteenth century. Positivism reached its peak in the first half of the twentieth century with the works of Hans Kelsen. See his *Pure theory of Law* (*Reine Rechtslehre; Einleitung in die rechtswissenschaftliche Problematik*, published in 1934, Leipzig/Vienna: Deuticke; 2nd ed. Vienna 1960; English edition 1967). But positivism has never recovered after the Second World War with the conclusion of the Charter of the United Nations in 1945 and the adoption of the Universal Declaration on Human Rights in 1948.

9.2.1 Recognition by the UN Charter

That human rights concern individuals and States alike is expressed in Paragraph 2 of the Preamble of the UN Charta that contains the formulation "to reaffirm faith in fundamental human rights, in the dignity and worth of the human person, in the equal rights of men and women and of nations large and small."

9.2.2 Recognition by the Universal Declaration of Human Rights

The principle is also recognized in the first three Paragraphs of the Universal Declaration of Human rights, where "recognition of the inherent dignity and of the equal and inalienable rights of all members of the human family is [considered] the foundation of freedom, justice and peace in [a] world,"[38] "in which human beings shall enjoy freedom of speech and belief and freedom from fear [...] as the highest aspiration of the common people."[39]

Moreover, the Universal Declaration of Human Rights [UDHR] recognizes the right of resistance that is basically founded—as is the body of human rights as a whole—not in any national or international legal instrument but in man's innate rights,[40] which is why "it is essential, if man is not to be compelled to have recourse, as a last resort, to rebellion against tyranny and oppression, that human rights should be protected by the rule of law."[41]

For these reasons, we have to take as a starting point for examining the admissibility of the stance taken by the Austrian Association of Judges towards political activities of judges the conclusion that it is prohibited not only for public institutions but also for private persons or group of persons to engage in any activity or perform any act aimed limiting the rights and freedoms set out in the ECHR[42] to a greater extent than is provided for in the Convention.

---

[38] UDHR, Preamble, Paragraph 1.

[39] UDHR, Preamble, Paragraph 2. This Paragraph also recalls that "disregard and contempt for human rights have resulted in barbarous acts which have outraged the conscience of mankind." This is a likely reference to the Nazi atrocities during World War II (first and foremost the Holocaust) but possibly also a broad hint to the large-scale violation of human rights in the Soviet Union and her emerging satellite States in Eastern Europe.

[40] Article 1 of the UDHR states accordingly: "All human beings are born free and equal in dignity and rights. They are endowed with reason and conscience and should act towards one another in a spirit of brotherhood.

[41] UDHR, Preamble, Paragraph 3.

[42] Cf. again Article 17 ECHR.

10 Application of the European Convention on Human Rights to the Wels Declaration

At this point of our scrutiny of the compatibility of the rules concerning political activities of judges contained in the Wels Declaration of the Austrian Association of Judges with the ECHR, several aspects of the matter have to be specified.

10.1 Binding Force of the Wels Declaration

One aspect is the question of the binding force of the Declaration. Here we have to distinguish between two kind of rules.

10.1.1 Restating Binding Higher Rules

On the one hand, there are rules in the Declaration which are binding because they refer to obligations which are already binding as parts of a legal system to which all persons in Austria are subject. Such obligations may derive from the Constitution and/or the ECHR, other applicable regional and/or universal conventions, and from the general principles of law which also form part of the peremptory rules of international law (*ius cogens*).[43] An example for such rules is offered by Art. I of the Declaration, titled "Fundamental Rights": "Human rights and fundamental freedoms form the basis of our democratic constitutional state. As guarantors of the rule of law, we let our behavior and our decisions be guided by these fundamental rights. We decidedly oppose every attempt to question the democratic and constitutional order of our Republic".

10.1.2 Binding by Own Authority

On the other hand, there are rules which—if they are binding at all—would derive their binding force only from the fact that they are contained in the Declaration. As concerns the political activities of judges, various of those rules have to be taken into consideration; and the central provision is again quoted here in full:

Art. IX. Private Behavior: "We scrutinize carefully and critically whether our actions or statements are suitable to make us dependent on someone, or could even only give the appearance thereof. This also applies to our off-duty activities, as far as we can expect that this may compromise our credibility as judges or cause our credibility to be questioned. We are convinced that being a member of a political party or being politically active within such a party can be detrimental to the

[43] See supra, Part VI.2.

credibility of independent jurisdiction that is unswayable by political parties and not bound to any interest groups and lobbies."

10.2 Political Activities Within Political Parties Versus *Political Activities Outside Political Parties*

It appears from the wording of Art. IX that the disapproval of political activities of judges does not extend to political activities that are exercised outside a political party. Since it cannot be insinuated to the drafters of the Wels Declaration that they considered political activities in themselves to constitute a "party", the text clearly distinguishes between political activities within and outside a party. Why this distinction is made, does not appear from Art. IX; and the distinction cannot be regarded reasonable. Today, given the increasing presence of movements within the civil society, of which the private or non-governmental organizations are only the "official" ones because they are based on the Austrian Law on Associations,[44] there are many political activities which are not exercised within a political party in the meaning of § 1 Paragraph 2[45] of the Austrian Political Parties Act 2012.[46] Yet, all activities which affect the body politic can be qualified as political. Even if they are exercised not within parties but within certain movements of the civil society, these activities are political in character. Why a judge who is a member of a political party supporting climate change should not be suited to be a member of the judiciary, while he may be an activist in the movement claiming to represent the "Last Generation" which tries to exert pressure upon Parliament by organizing road blockades or other disturbances of the public order, I cannot see.

This incomprehensible distinction between "good" and "bad" political activities inherent in Art. IX of the Wels Declaration constitutes a discrimination of judges on the ground of their political opinion and contravenes Article 1 Paragraph 1 of the Twelfth Additional Protocol to the ECHR, which contains a general prohibition of discrimination.[47]

---

[44] *Vereinsgesetz*. See supra, fn. 13.

[45] Unlike in countries with English or American legal terminology, where the sign "§" is often used for "Section", in German legal terminology "§" stands for "Paragraph"; and what is termed "Paragraph" in English, is mostly termed "Absatz" in German. In the present paper, the English terminology is used.

[46] Federal Act on the Financing of Political Parties (Political Parties Act—*Parteiengestz*—2012)

[47] Such is the title of Article 1 of the Twelfth Additional Protocol to the ECHR.

10.3 Political Aspects of the Allegedly Unpolitical Judiciary

Art. IX of the Wels Declaration tries to separate the area of politics from what it evidently considers the unpolitical area of the judiciary. However, other articles of the Wels Declaration stress the interdependence of both areas.

Thus, Art. X of the Wels Declaration entitled "Social Influences" starts by stating: "The judicial office is a fundamental part of our political and social structure." It then expressly recognizes the consequences of this interdependence: "Judicial work can influence this [political and social] structure, but is also influenced thereby." Judges, therefore, have to bear in mind "that judicial decisions can have profound and existential repercussions for the way of life of the affected people."

The principle contained in Article X is corroborated by the assessment, contained in Art. VIII,[48] that "[f]rom time to time, jurisdiction will release a socio-political impulse, or an impulse for legal policy, that goes beyond an individual case."

10.4 Political Parties as Key Elements of the Modern Democratic System

Considered in this context, the ban on membership or activities of judges in political parties, as contained in Art. IX of the Wels Declaration, is incomprehensible. First of all, political parties have always been the main players in the political field. Secondly, they are regarded by the Austrian Constitution "key elements of the Republic of Austria's democratic order".[49] It is strange that judges may not be members of, or active in, these key elements of Austrian democracy.

In addition, we may recall to an old saying, according to which "thoughts are free". This freedom of thought is guaranteed in Article 9 Paragraph 1 ECHR which provides that "[e]veryone has the right to freedom of thought." So, even if a judge is not a member of, or not active in, a political party he can be presumed to have political convictions which might coincide with the principles, and the aims, of a political party. Whether or not the judge is guided, as they should—and as is stated in the German *Grundgesetz*—by "*Gesetz und Recht*", i.e. by written and unwritten law[50] is their personal decision and cannot be corrected as long as the judges remains within

[48] Dealing with "Publicity and Comprehensibility".

[49] § 1 Paragraph 1 of the Political Parties Act which is a "constitutional provision" forms part of the Austrian Constitution. With referenced to Art. 1 of the Federal Constitution Law [B-VG]. Austria does not have an integrity or completeness rule like the German Basic Law (*Grundgesetz).* For this reason (in)numerous "constitutional provisions" exists in "simple" federal laws of which there does not exist an official list.

[50] "Unwritten" law in the meaning of "Recht" is a reference not to customary law but to the general principles of law.

what is sometimes, though quite improperly, called his discretion in the interpretation of legal rules.[51]

11 Political Opinions of Judges

Since judges are citizens of their country, and therefore are affected by the political process in their country, judges are likely to have a political opinion and, therefore, a declared or undeclared political sympathy or affiliation. Now, if a judge has a political opinion—a fact that cannot be prohibited—and if he is suspected to have this opinion unduly influence his decisions, the question comes up if common knowledge of his membership or activity in a particular political party does not put more restraint on an eventual abuse of his judicial power than if his thoughts remain undisclosed. Since transparency as to the judge's political sympathy also facilitates examination of his acts under the aspect of a possible political bias, it is desirable that his political affiliation is disclosed.

12 Political Impulses of Jurisdiction

In the case of Austria, the ban on judges' political activities within a political party deriving from Art. IX of the Wels Declaration is incompatible with the constitutionally enshrined high regard of political parties and flagrantly inconsistent with those parts of the Declaration which recognize the integration of the judiciary in the political and social system of the country. In this regard, reference has to be made, inter alia, to Art. VIII of the Declaration where it is recognized that jurisdiction will release—from time to time—"a socio-political impulse, or an impulse for legal policy".

[51] The fact that not infrequently there is a dispute over the correct interpretation of a rule does not mean that the rule gives the interpreter a choice between two equally correct interpretations; it only means that for some reason or other interpreters differ on what is the (only) correct interpretation. This usually happens if establishing the correct interpretation requires surrounded by longer and therefore more complicated considerations. If they cannot be expected follow these considerations to the end, different interpreters may each claim to have, not the correct but, an arguable interpretation.

13 Inconsistencies in the Wels Declaration

Art. IX is inconsistent with Article VIII and Article X. On the one hand, the Declaration expressly recognizes in Art. X that "[t]he judicial office is a fundamental part of our political and social structure." It then expressly recognizes the consequences of this interdependence: "Judicial work can influence this [political and social] structure, but is also influenced thereby." And in Art. VIII, the Declaration ascribes to the jurisdiction the power to give political impulses.

Since "judicial work" is the work of judges, since the "judicial office" is the office of judges, since judges thereby can influence the political and social structure of the State, since judges are the hub of the interdependence between their work and the State's political and social structure, and since, therefore, judges can be expected to have the best inside into all aspects of the body politic, why should judges be excluded just from that process by which the political and social structure of the State is molded?

Such a postulation is irrational and can only be explained by a prejudice against that process—a process which is inevitably carried on by political parties—and therefore against political parties and party politics. I fail to understand why this irrational postulation has found followers worldwide. But I trust that it will not persist for ever, as today witches are also not burnt at the stake anymore…

14 Judicial Independence

An examination of the different Codes of Ethics (whatever their particular designation) in the various countries reveals that the question of independence is present in almost all of them. In the context of ethics, it is not the question whether the legal framework for the judiciary secures the independent dispensation of justice; rather, it is the question of whether the overall picture of the judiciary is suited to create, for the general public, the impression that justices are independent in their judicial work.

14.1 An Essential Aspect of Jurisdiction

This is indeed an essential aspect of jurisdiction. If justices could not be trusted to be free from undue influence of whatever kind from outside, a cornerstone of the rule of law would be undermined. Therefore, it goes without saying that all necessary precautions for safeguarding the credibility of independence have to be taken. However, the qualification of the precautions as necessary should be borne in mind.

14.2 A Question of Personal Responsibility

It falls to every single judge to comport himself in such a way that the credibility of his independence is not impaired. Of course, this primarily concerns his professional conduct; but it also concerns his private conduct if this conduct may have negative repercussions on the credibility of his independence in the dispensation of justice. The need for taking the necessary precautions is obvious.

While so far there appears to be agreement on the objective—the creation and preservation of the credibility of independence—there are, in the various Codes of Ethics, different approaches as to the means through which this objective could be attained. In this context, a most important issue has so far remained underexposed. This is the issue of the yardstick or standard to be applied.

15 The Subjective Approach

Some of the Codes in question seem to take the—what I call—subjective approach. "Subjective approach" means that that what counts are not facts but opinions. Opinions may or not be based on facts, but if they allege to be based on facts, these facts have not been sufficiently substantiated and verified. Thus, credibility is often not judged by objective criteria, especially the test of reasonableness, but by subjective criteria, taking into account also doubts for which there is no basis in reality. Often, they are based on emotions, e.g. those kindled by populist rhetoric. Sometimes, as in the case of credibility or lack of credibility. Sometimes, opinions are themselves taken as facts. But to deduce legal or quasi-legal consequences is incompatible with justice. Thus, if "lack of credibility" means that people have doubts about the credibility of something (e.g., the judiciary) or of someone (e.g., a particular judge), this is no fact on which a rule can ODER may be based.

16 The Objective Approach

It might be argued that the subjective approach finds its justification in the principle "quidquid recipitur, ad modum recipientis recipitur", meaning that it is not decisive what is said or done (by the speaker or doer) but what (or how) it is understood (by the listener or spectator). Yet, this principle is not applicable here. Here we are not concerned with the opinions entertained by the listeners or spectators. What we are concerned here with is the consequence attached to the opinion by the Wels Declaration. Its drafters cannot invoke the opinion of those who—for whatever reasons—misunderstand or misinterpret the comportment of judges engaged in party politics. What is decisive is the grounds on which the said opinion is based. If it is not based on verified or verifiable facts, it cannot serve as an argument against a judge's membership in, or activity within, a political party. This is—what I call—the objective approach. Unfortunately, the need for taking the objective approach is not recognized in all, or even the majority of Codes, a fact that may lead to an unacceptable ban on the political activities of judges.

The objective approach is all the more called for in the present context, where eventual restrictions on the rights and freedoms of expression, of assembly and of association, as guaranteed in Articles 10 and 11 Ibid, No. 54ECHR, are concerned. Unfounded opinions, often based on unreasonable doubts about the independence of a judge, or the judiciary in general, cannot justify restrictions of, and limitations on, these rights. Provisions in Code of Ethics which convey the impression that they allow for, instead of the objective, the subjective approach, have to be subject to a re-interpretation, and, if this should not render an acceptable result, are to be regarded illegal and therefore inapplicable.

It is deplorable that even the Consultative Council of European Judges (CCJE), in an Opinion of 2022 on freedom of expression of judges[52] seems to adhere to the subjective approach by stating that "[d]irect involvement in partisan party politics can raise doubts as to the separation of powers and the independence or impartiality of a judge which is why many States restrict the political activities of judges."[53] However, the CCJE does not deduce from this assessment an absolute incompatibility of political office with the judicial function. Rather, it invokes the attitude of the European Court of Human Rights which leaves to member states a discretion whether to prohibit or not to prohibit political activities of judges. Still, given this discretion, the Court recognizes as proportionate for countries to exclude judges from political office.[51]

17 *Excursus*: The Code of Conduct of the Court of Justice of the European Union

As regards (what is still traditional called) the European Court of Justice, the Code of conduct for Members and former Members of the Court of Justice of the European Union[54] has been adopted by the Court itself on the basis of the Treaty on the Functioning of the European Union,[55] on the Statute of the Court of Justice of the European Union,[56] on the Rules of Procedure of the Court of Justice[57] and on the Rules of Procedure of the General Court.[58] It therefore is a legal instrument, and the

[52] CCJE Opinion no. 25, Council of Europe, CCJE(2022)4.

[53] Ibid., no. 54.

[54] EU Doc. 2021/C 397/01

[55] Articles 253, 254, 257 and 339.

[56] Articles 2, 4, 6, 8, 18 and 47.

[57] Articles 4 to 6.

[58] Articles 5 to 7 of.

obligations for judges resulting from it have legal force. The Code cannot, therefore, be compared to the Codes of conduct adopted by the various national Associations of Judges which have no legal authority and cannot, therefore, lay down legally binding rules.

It is difficult to decide whether the Code of conduct for active or former "Members of the Court"—a term which (by the way) includes not only judges but also Advocates-General—adheres to the subjective or to the objective approach. The wording of Article 3 Paragraph 4 ("Members shall not act or express themselves, through whatever medium, in a manner which adversely affects the public perception of their independence, their integrity or the dignity of their office") allows for divergent interpretations, depending on whether stress is laid on the manner of Members' action or expression, or whether it is laid on the public perception of their independence, integrity and dignity of their office.

Under the first alternative, only the objective approach makes sense, for the Member can orientate the manner of his action or expression only on the objective criterion of what can reasonably expected to bring about the said negative public perception. Under the second alternative, one might argue that even a negative effect which cannot reasonably be expected, should count, and that, therefore, the subjective approach is fitting. But even here an objective line has to be drawn, because—since the decision on what to do or say can be made only before it is done or said—this decision can but take into account what usually creates a negative effect. And "usually" is again an objective criterion.

18 Closer Scrutiny of the Wels Declaration with Regard to Independence

If one looks for the reason which causes this reservation or even enmity towards political activities of judges within political parties, at first sight it seems to be the concern for judicial independence. According to Art II of the Declaration, "[j]udicial independence serves the protection of people seeking justice."[59] This statement of principle is framed by a number of other statements which appear to be deduced from it, although two of them precede it in the text of Art. II. The preceding ones are a profession and a promise: "We decide exclusively on the basis of statutory law and our free inner conviction. We reject any form of unlawful exertion of influence, invitations and gifts, and disclose all attempts to intervene."

What then follows, is the second part of the sentence proclaiming the principle, but it does not really follow from the latter. That judicial independence "may never be abused as a pretext for arbitrariness" is a matter of course. Equally condemned is a "behavior that is intellectually or socially detached from reality", but what is really meant by this formulation remains unclear. The Wels Declaration deals—in

[59] Article II, Third Sentence.

Articles I to VIII and in Article X—with the professional activity of judges; only Article IX deals with their private conduct. The term "behavior" has an affinity with Article IX, because it would be unusual to speak in the context of a judge's professional activity of "behavior" unless his manners in the contact with parties, colleagues and administrative personnel are meant. But in what way could such "behavior" be socially detached from reality? (I know of a case where the exceptional politeness of a candidate judge was not well received by an elderly lady of the administrative personnel who had never experienced such politeness before and therefore mistook it for a subtle attempt to pull her leg.) And the formulation "intellectually [...] detached from reality" is even stranger. Should this put a break on judges with a higher IQ than the average in order to prevent them from showing their superiority?

Art. V titled "Administration of Justice" deals primarily with the administrative necessities for independent jurisdiction: "We endeavor to provide and maintain the best possible organizational conditions for independent judicial work."[60] This should permit judges to work—"[w]ithin the framework of the duties of judicial administration [...] – for the cause of independent jurisdiction."[61] Still, the Article also recognizes the need for "acquir[ing] all abilities necessary for our organizational and managerial work," even—as one may add here—when this work is not directly concerned with juridical independence.

Art. VI titled "Fairness", Art. VII titled "Decision making", and Art. VIII titled "Publicity and Comprehensibility" do not contain direct or indirect reference to the issue of independence. However, it is noteworthy that Art. VI recognizes (albeit indirectly) that judges might have prejudices by referring to the need to overcome them. Art. VII calls for "full commitment" and "high-quality decision[s]", and Art. VIII for generally "intelligibility in all [...] oral and written statements. The relevance of Art. VIII for the acknowledgment of the political relevance of the work of the judiciary has already been dealt with.[62]

Art. X. which bears the title "Social Influences" stands out in contrast to Art. IX. It starts by stating: "The judicial office is a fundamental part of our political and social structure." Here, reference to Art. I—which otherwise does not appear to be well integrated in the Declaration—is best placed with its statement that "[h]uman rights and fundamental freedoms form the basis of our democratic constitutional state",[63] together with the avowal that "[a]s guarantors of the rule of law, we let our behavior and our decisions be guided by these fundamental rights."

Art. X then continues: "Judicial work can influence this [political and social] structure, but is also influenced thereby. We are aware that judicial decisions can have profound and existential repercussions for the way of life of the affected people." Accordingly, judges are called upon to always consider, in exercising their

[60] Art. V, Second Sentence.

[61] Art. V, First Sentence.

[62] Cf. supra, Part VII.6.

[63] Cf. supra, Part VII.1.

office, "these coherencies and to handle their responsibility conscientiously." Doing so, judges indubitably engage in politics, even if they are not aware of.

19 Does Art. IX of the Wels Declaration Violate Human Rights by Restricting Judges' Freedoms of Expression, Assembly and Association?

Everyone in Austrian enjoys the right to become political active, whether within a political party or within some movement of the civil society. There is a difference, however, if the person is a judge. It can hardly be disputed that Art. IX of the Wels Declaration aims at restricting the freedom of expression of judges as well as their freedom of assembly and their freedom of association by prohibiting them membership in, or political activities within, a political party.

19.1 The Isolated Approach

If Art. IX of the Wels Declaration is considered in an isolated manner, i.e. as it stands and without further considering whether the prohibition contained in Art. IX might be justified by an exception contained in the European Convention on Human Rights itself, then Art. IX clearly violates human rights guaranteed by the European Convention on Human Rights.

Yet, Art. IX of the Wels Declaration must not be considered in an isolated manner. Its lawful or unlawful character can only be determined by looking at it in the framework of a higher order that is applicable to it. This order is again constituted by the European Convention on Human Rights. But what comes into play here are not the various rights guaranteed by the Convention but the limitations and restrictions on these rights allowed for in the Convention itself.

19.2 Criteria for an in Context-Approach

There is a set of criteria for deciding about the lawful or unlawful character of Art. IX of the Wels Declaration, more particularly about the limitations and restrictions it imposes on political activities of judges. The provision of Article 17 ECHR contains several criteria which have to be fulfilled in order to establish a case where the question of the lawfulness of limiting or restricting a right guaranteed by the Convention can arise at all and thus offer the basis for a discussion.

First, there must be an action by a public or private person or group of persons. Since the Austrian Association of Judges is an organized group of persons, this criterion is fulfilled.

Second, there must be an act or activity of this group. In the present context, such act is constituted by the adoption and proclamation of the Wels Declaration of 2007.

Third, the act has to be aimed at limiting rights and freedoms set out in the ECHR. In order to answer the question of whether this is the case, we have to interpret the relevant part of the Declaration. For doing so, we can be guided by the general rule of interpretation laid down in Article 31 of the VCLT which—though not directly applicable here—may be regarded as the expression of common sense and therefore part of the general principles of law.[64]

The incriminated provision of the Wels Declaration has already been quoted in the course of introducing the subject of the present paper and is repeated here. In Article IX of the Declaration, the Austrian Association of Judges declares the following: "We are convinced that being a member of a political party or being politically active within such a party can be detrimental to the credibility of independent jurisdiction that is unswayable by political parties and not bound to any interest groups and lobbies."

At first glance, the provision does not seem contain any direct prohibition of political activities of judges. It only states a conviction of the Association without deducing express consequences for the individual judge. At second thought, however, we must not accept an interpretation which renders part of the Declaration inoperable and therefore meaningless. Rather, the provision has to be interpreted as expressing the expectation of the Association that judges would not engage in political activities. And if this expectation appears to be reasonable, it might be considered a binding rule.[65] Such an interpretation is supported also by object and purpose of the Declaration, in which "[t]he Austrian Judges declare to be guided in their work by the [...] ethical principles" contained therein.

We now turn to what we consider to be the forth criterion. Is Article IX of the Declaration aimed at the limitation of rights and freedoms of provided for in the ECHR? This question has to be answered by Yes. It is evident that the provision negatively affects two rights recognized by the Convention, namely freedom of expression guaranteed by Article 10 ECHR and the freedom of association guaranteed by Article 11 ECHR; and since the right to assembly often accompany freedom of expression because the latter is often exercised in in organized or unorganized groups and also often constitutes the framework within which associations are formed, it is also negatively affected by Article IX of the Declaration.

So far, Article IX of the Declaration of the Austrian Association of Judges which is directed against political activities of judges clearly infringes upon Articles 10 and 11 of the ECHR and violates the judges' human rights. There can be no doubt

---

[64] See supra, Part VI.2 and Part VII.1.a.

[65] This was the idea of the policy-oriented school of international law introduced to Yale Law School by Myres Smith McDougal (1906–1998).

that political activities including membership in a political party are a right that pertains to everyone in Europe. However, this is a judgment passed without regard to a possible justification for curtailing these rights with regard to judges offered by the European Convention on Human Rights itself. Should anything in Article 11 and 12 ECHR permit the imposition of restrictions on judges for the very reason that they are judges, the outcome of the judgment might be different.

20 Can Limitations of Judges' Freedoms of Expression, Assembly and Association be Justified Under the European Convention on Human Rights?

The concluding part of Article 10 Paragraph 2 ECHR seems to lend itself for such a justification. Paragraph 2 first acknowledges that the exercise of the freedom of expression "carries with it duties and responsibilities" and for this reason may be subject to certain restrictions. After reciting the usual grounds for justification which are *mutatis mutandis* applicable to all rights and freedoms provided for in the Convention, Paragraph 2 recognizes restrictions necessary "for maintaining the authority and impartiality of the judiciary."

However, this is not yet the end of the matter. There are two arguments against unconditionally invoking the last part of Article 10 Paragraph in order to justify a ban on the involvement of judges in party politics. One argument insists on an interpretation of the provision that makes such a ban at least questionable. Another argument works with a limitation of principle on justifications for restricting the human rights guaranteed in the European Convention on Human Rights.

First, even after quoting from Article 10 Paragraph 2 ECHR, exhaustive examination of the last criterion is still pending. This requires a closer look into the provision.

Those parts of the European Convention on Human Rights which deal with the possible restrictions and limitations that may be imposed under the Convention, are regularly stated in the Second Paragraph of the various Articles which, in their First Paragraphs, provide for the different rights and freedoms guaranteed in the Convention. While the wordings of these Second Paragraphs may slightly vary, all of them require that the particular restrictions and limitations are "necessary". In determining of what is "necessary", one has to bear in mind the principle of proportionality. Proportionality, also a principle of the law of the European Union,[66] must be considered a general principle of law and, as such, is applicable within the law of the ECHR.

[66] "**Proportionality** is a general principle of EU law. It restricts authorities in the exercise of their powers by requiring them to strike a balance between the means used and the intended aim. In the context of fundamental rights [...], proportionality is key for any limitation on these rights." Necessity and Proportionality, https://edps.europa.eu/data-protection/our-work/subjects/necessity-proportionality_en

Here, proportionality demands that "necessity" for imposing these restrictions and limitations can be regarded as given only when all more lenient means have to be considered as not sufficiently effective. A ban on membership or activities of judges within a political party is therefore permitted only if the purpose of such a ban is legitimate and cannot be realized in any other way. Purpose of the ban is the "credibility of independent jurisdiction". Whether this purpose is legitimate depends on the understanding of credibility.

Credibility means to be credible. It does not mean that credibility is dependent on the subjective impressions derived by others from whatever source. Credibility is an objective fact and thus has to be determined by objective criteria. These criteria are fulfilled if no reasonable doubt can be raised. This exclude unreasonable doubts from being taken into account. Doubts based not upon reason but upon (mere) emotions are not reasonable. It is always possible that the public is induced by populist allegations to believe something that has no base in reality[67] but is spread by populist politicians, tendentious media or self-proclaimed moral authorities who dictate what is, and what is not, political correctness. But this cannot affect (the objective) reality.

Second, all human rights, whether contained in national or international (regional or universal) declarations, bills or treaties, have an essential core[68] which must not be tampered with.[69] If applied to the Freedom of Expression as well as to Freedom of Assembly and Freedom of Association, judges must not be barred from making political statements, from taking part in political assemblies and in political organizations, as long as these statements do not, directly or indirectly, infringe upon human right of others. Even if the prohibition of interfering with the essential core of human rights is not laid down in the Constitution of a particular State, is has to be regarded as a general principle of law and therefore constitutes *ius cogens* which applies not only in international law, but also in national law.

21 Codes of Ethics in General: Terminology and Legal Character

We have already extensively dealt with the Wels Declaration of Ethics. When dealing with such Declarations in general, it is useful to clarify the terminology used in their context and to examined their legal character.

[67] We could speak here, not of fake news but, of fake truths.

[68] In German, *Wesensgehalt*.

[69] In German, *Wesensgehaltsgarantie* and *Wesensgehaltssperre*, respectively.

21.1 *Terminology*

Since declarations purporting to state rules of ethics have different titles in different countries, it seems useful to choose one term when talking about them in general or comparing them among each other. Since some of them are entitled "Code", and since "Code" is briefer than other terms like "Declaration", its use as a general term for a general discussion has a certain appeal. Yet, when doing so we have to bear in mind that the term "Code" often has a legal connotation, as is shown by various definitions given in dictionaries.[70] Such an *a priori* connotation is expressly excluded here. This caveat is all the more imperative since the question of the legal character of these declarations and for the binding character of the rules contained therein is an important issue of this paper. To *a priori* imply legal connotations with the term "Code" would mean to prejudice the answer to this question. This has to be avoided.

21.2 *Ethics/Morals* Versus *Law*

The question of the binding force of rules contained in a "Code of Ethics" depends on the meaning given to the term "Ethics". There seems to be a broad consent that "ethics" has something to do with, or even is tantamount to, morals.[71] The same broad consensus sets morals against law and distinguishes them from each other by the criteria of enforcement: law is enforced by public sanctions carried out by public authorities while the violation of morals may entail (if any) only social sanctions like avoiding further contact with the violator of the moral rule.

21.3 *Legal Character*

It follows that "Codes of Ethics" do not have any legal character unless the law itself attributes such a character to them. This is the case, e.g., when the law calls for, or at least mentions as a possibility, the creation of rules deriving from the ambit of

[70] Cf. the following examples: According to MERRIAM-WEBSTER, "Code" is *a systematic statement of a body of law. DICTIOINARY.COM defines it as a systematically arranged collection or compendium of laws, rules, or regulations. BRITANNICA DICTIONARY gives its foremost meaning as a set of laws or regulations. And* Vocabulary.com *speaks of a set of rules or principles or laws.*

[71] Cf., e.g., the following definitions. According to WIKIPEDIA, "*Ethics* or moral philosophy is a branch of philosophy that "involves systematizing, defending, and recommending concepts of right and wrong behavior". BRITANNICA defines "*Ethics* [as] the philosophical discipline concerned with what is morally good and bad and morally right and wrong." And CANADA.CA states that "*Ethics* examines the rational justification for our moral judgments; it studies what is morally right or wrong, just or unjust."

ethics by authorities, whether the usual ones known in the particular legal system, or specially set up for this purpose by law, or at least recognized by law and endowed with the power to create such rules.

Whether the Code of Ethics adopted by, or for, the Judges of the Court of Justice of the European Union[72] is of this special character need not be discussed here. But the vast majority of the Codes existing in European countries and being discussed here contains, as is implied by their designation, only rules which cannot be considered legal rules.

22 Background of Codes of Ethics

If Codes of Ethics do not—except in special cases which already have been dealt with earlier—contain legal rules, i.e. rules of a binding character: What then is the reason that such Codes have sprung up in most European countries, like mushrooms after rain, in the course of recent decades?[73] I can only venture some explanations.

22.1 Unprecise Legal Rules

The first argument might be that the legal rules in this particular field are not precise enough. Therefore, they would need to be refined. This argument is untenable from the point of legal theory. Either the rule is so incomplete that no obligation for anyone can be deduced from it. In this case, the legislator has failed in his work and has not created any rule at all. Then the issue of an unprecise rule does not come up right from the beginning. Or the legislator has intentionally formulated the rule in such a manner that two or more alternatives have been left open for the user, i.e. the institution or person that has the rule to apply. In this case, the rule is not unprecise. It just empowers the user to choose between the various alternative; and whatever alternative he chooses he keeps within the limits of the discretion granted to him by law. In any other cases, the task of handling the rule falls to the user who has to interpret it in order to find out its intention.

Moreover, it is improbable that lack of precision of the law is a phenomenon that arises or has arisen only where a Code of Ethics is to be, or has been, set up. Rather, it is much more probable that here as there the law is sufficiently precise, and that

---

[72] Nota bene, this term includes not only the judges of the Court and the judges of the Tribunal but also the judges of Special Tribunals if any exists, which is presently not the case. For the judicial system of the European Union, see European Union, Court of Justice of the European Union (CJEU), https://european-union.europa.eu/institutions-law-budget/institutions-and-bodies/search-all-eu-institutions-and-bodies/court-justice-european-union-cjeu_en

[73] This does not only apply to the judiciary but also to other legal (and non-legal professions.

therefore the setting up of the Code of Ethics cannot be justified by a mistake allegedly made, or by a failure allegedly due to, the legislator.

22.2 Complicated Legal Rules

The second argument might be that the Code of Ethics, though not containing anything new in substance, makes it easier to understand the legal rules in question by clarifying aspects which might be otherwise difficult to understand and/or require some demanding brain work. From this point of view, the Code would fulfil a didactive purpose. Even if this argument has some merits and cannot simply be dismissed, the drafters of the Code have to be careful in order not to explain the legal rules in such a way as to have the explanation go beyond what is intended by the rule.

22.3 Backdoor for Doubtful Rules

Moreover, and this is another, a third, explanation for the popularity of Codes. The latter may be used for transporting, in the guise of harmless explanation, contents which are not the subject matter of the law allegedly only explained. A good example for such an abuse of a Code is the ban on membership in, and political activities in the framework of, a political party contained in Art. IX of the Wels Declaration of Ethics adopted by the Austrian Association of Judges.

22.4 Backdoor for "Legislation by Drafters"

A fourth explanation for the popularity of Codes is the fact that it gives, in practice, power to its drafters, who in most cases constitute only a minority of members, to impose rules of their own liking on the majority which remains silent mainly for the fact that most of those constituting the majority are not versant in the niceties of the text, even if niceties might adversely affect them. Rather, "thank and acknowledgment" are usually extended to the drafters who, as a rule, are composed of members of the Association's management delegated to a drafting committee and of the few attentive members who are ready to invest time and energy by joining this committee, if admitted to it.

In fact, most of these Codes pretend that they represent the conviction and/or the will of the body of judges of a particular country as a whole, but for practical reasons their elaboration is left to a group of members of the association of judges who have either been designated for this purpose or have engaged in this exercise. As a rule, these Codes have not been approved by the body of judges as a whole, rather, they have been adopted, at best, by a General Assembly of the association in which participation might be low, and most of those who do participate do not dispose of the necessary information because they have not understood that information is not only an obligation of the management to bring the information to the members but also an obligation of the members to make the necessary efforts to obtain the information from the management.

23 Popularity of Codes

23.1 *The "Elitist" Factor*

I have a fifth and final explanation for what I have come to call the popularity of Codes. Before entering into presenting it, however, I want to make—what I consider—an important remark. It might have been noticed that I have started to use, in connection with the Codes, the word "popularity" only with the third explanation, for the reason that from the third explanation onwards the Codes are not so much concerned with the interests of the individual judge or the body of the judges as a whole but with the interests of those who are able to devise the Code according to their views. These people are those who exercise their influence in the course of the drafting of the Code. This is what I call the "elitist" factor.

These people constitute the management of the respective national association of judges or those persons among them to whom the task of drafting the Code is entrusted by delegating them to the drafting committee, together with those additional busybodies who are admitted to the committee because there is no good ground on which they could be rejected.

23.2 *The "Mission" or "Vision" Factor*

Now I turn to the fifth and final explanation announced earlier. People who are active in professional or extra-professional associations or engage in movements of the civil society in most cases do so because they feel a vocation to fulfill a special mission. This mission is always directed, in one way or the other, to (what we may call) the betterment of the world, either at large (as is the professed mission of the bigger ecological movements) or within a particular section of society (e.g. in labor unions, in cultural associations or religious movements). Behind that mission there is always a particular vision of what a better world should look like and what members of society should do in order to conform to this vision.

It is inherent in the qualification of a vision as "particular" that this vision is not shared by everyone. Disagreement is often caused by the objectives of a movement which is inspired by a particular vision. To give an example: There is probably widespread consensus about the need to slow down and finally stop global warming; but whether the immediate objective of the movement should be primarily the swift elimination of vehicles emitting CO_2 or the increased production of clean energy through the expansion of hydropower plants and wind-power installations or a return to the peaceful use of nuclear energy, is highly controversial. Thus, there is no widespread consensus about any of these specific objectives.

Equally, disagreement can be caused by the means used by the same movement. Here, too, an example from the field of environmental protection can be offered. Democracy is an essential element of European societies. Democracy means that—whenever necessary—decisions are taken by a majority, either of the people or of the representatives of the people in Parliament. It runs counter to the idea of democracy if a minority tries to enforce its ideas by recourse to force, even if this does not mean "brute force" but only "soft force", e.g. by paralyzing certain sectors of social life. To blockade traffic and prevent people from coming in time to their office or workplace is certainly the exercise of "soft force" by which legislative institutions are blackmailed with the intent of making them cede to the demands of a certain group of activists who have not been able to convince the majority of their ideas by democratic process.

24 "Codes of Ethics", "Political Correctness" and the "Cause of the People"

A subtle but widespread form of enforcing visions is what is called "political correctness". What is "politically correct" and, conversely, what is "politically incorrect" is not decided, as the term tries to imply, in the form of a political dialogue between persons or groups with different opinions, a process that finally may lead to a decision made in a democratic process. Rather, it is formulated by people who have a certain moral vision, and is imposed upon society through a net of like-minded people who support each other and form a diffuse group of self-proclaimed moral authorities ("moralizers"). Sometimes, they even have good contacts to, or influence on, the media, a situation that facilitates the spread of their ideas.

24.1 "Political Correctness"

"Political correctness" pretends to fill a lacuna in the legal or even constitutional system of a State. However, it does not attempt to fill this lacuna by way of the legislative process provided for in the constitution. The "creators" of "political correctness" avoid this process because they are well aware of the fact that they might meet with substantial resistance. Moreover, these self-proclaimed moral authorities would have to shed the veil of anonymity they enjoy as members of a diffuse group; and they (or most of them) would shy away from doing so.

24.2 "The People"

The drafters of "Codes of Ethics" are not "the people" as understood since the definition by Cicero in his famous work *De re publica* more than 2000 years ago. According to Cicero, "the people" is not some group which has congregated for whatever reason or purpose but a social body brought together by common benefit and legal consensus. And "the people" behind the opinions concerning, e.g., the "credibility" of the independence of the judiciary as a whole or of a particular judge is even less the people organized in, or as, a State[74] but an elusive phantom to which certain negative positions are imputed[75] in order to justify rules restricting political rights of judges.

24.3 Populist Narratives

Unfortunately, we have to assume that the drafters of "Codes of Ethics" often have fallen themselves victims to their own unfounded opinions. If they feel the temptation to follow populist narratives—and no one can say that he has never been tempted to do so—and if they have not felt the need, or the energy, to look behind the curtain of the populist spectacle, they themselves might believe that it is justified to protect the reputation of jurisdiction from negative imputations. In fact, it is not unlikely that they do not even see through the populist background behind the rules imposed by them on others. This is a widespread phenomenon[76] connected with quite a number of issues, the alleged ecological necessity of some measures—from speed limits on freeways to price regulations favoring meat substitutes over real meat products in the supermarket—being just one example. The suggestive question used there is: If you are for a healthy environment, how can you be against any such measure?

Most unfortunately, sometimes not even legislators seem free from the influence of populist narratives. This explains why the laws of various countries also contain rules which curtail the political activities of judges. Yet, even from this fact of legislative aberration, no justification for enacting such laws or inserting such rules in Codes of Ethics can derive.

[74] In German called the "Staatsvolk".

[75] Typical for this kind of argumentation are formulation like "people might/could think" or "people might/could doubt"; also "might/could be damaging for [the credibility]" or "likely to affect [the, or the trust in, the independence of the courts]".

[76] For the background and the effects of this phenomenon, cf. Sidaneus and Pratto (1999).

25 Cause of the People: Contribution by the People

The final—and probably the most essential—argument against a political correctness that undertakes, by means of a Code of Ethics, to restrict or forbid the engagement of Judges in party politics derives from the following line of reasoning.

25.1 The General Principle

Since the State is the cause of the people, all citizens have to contribute to that cause according to their abilities. This applies to all sectors of social life. It thus also applies to politics, because politics are the way in which issues relating to the common good, namely first, the issue of internal security and external peace, second, the issue of personal freedom, and, third, the issue of social welfare, are dealt with and decided upon.

25.2 Political Engagement: A Civic Duty

The task to engage in politics is incumbent to all citizen according to their ability, and for those who feel able to do so, engaging in politics is a civic duty. Since questions of ability cannot be decided by law, this civic duty remains a moral duty and cannot be transformed into a legal obligation. Moreover, in the beginning of government slowly changing from autocratic to democratic, citizens had to fight hard for the right of political activity until then denied to them. Therefore, what had to be molded into law was this right. Since the spread of constitutional government in the nineteenth century, the various personal rights and freedoms were laid down in specific canons of human rights and fundamental freedoms. When constitutional government changed to parliamentary government in the twentieth century, the principles of the process of democratic decision shaping and decision making were embodied in the various constitutions and the details regulated in laws.

The era of constitutional government was characterized by only limited access to political elections and therefore by the rule of the meritocracy, constituted by well-known representatives from the main sectors of social life including culture and science, therefore also called "notabilities".[77] Only with the introduction of the right to vote for all, political parties became recognized as a means of pooling the strengths of like-minded people in order to be successful in the parliamentary process.

[77] In German, the equivalent is "Honoratioren" or "Notable".

25.3 *Political Parties as Key Elements of Modern Democracies*

Since then, political parties have come to be considered indispensable in the political scenery. In Austria, they have been enshrined in the Constitution which states that "[t]he existence and diversity of political parties are key elements of the Republic of Austria's democratic order.[78] Promising, and therefore meaningful, political activity in Austria can only be exercised within a political party.

A regards judges, it cannot be denied that they are citizens. It also cannot be denied that, at least in general, they possess the abilities required for actively participating in political matters. By doing so, judges fulfill a civic duty. Today, the most promising, and therefore most meaningful political activity can only be exercised within the framework of party politics. Therefore, judges have the duty, and at least the right, to engage in activities within a political party.

The Wels Declaration on Ethics contains, in Art. I, a clear commitment to the Austrian democratic and constitutional order. The Article which deals with "Fundamental Rights" runs as follows: "Human rights and fundamental freedoms form the basis of our democratic constitutional state. As guarantors of the rule of law, we let our behavior and our decisions be guided by these fundamental rights. We decidedly oppose every attempt to question the democratic and constitutional order of our Republic."

26 The Incompatibility of Art. IX of the Wels Declaration with the Modern Democratic Process

This commitment and the fact that political parties are key elements of the Republic of Austria's democratic order,[79] cannot be reconciled with the attempt, undertaken in Art. IX of the Wels Declaration, to ban activities of judges exercised within the framework of political parties. This attempt interferes with three Freedoms guaranteed in the European Convention on Human Rights, namely those of expression, of assembly and of association, and is not justified by the limits on, and restrictions of, contained in the Convention. This has already been substantiated earlier in this paper[80] and need not be repeated here.

[78] § 1 Paragraph 1 of the Political Parties Act 2012—Parteien-Gesetz (PartG), with reference to Art. 1 of the Law on Federal Constitution, cttect abbreviated Federal Constitution Law, Federal Law Gazette No. 1/1930 (Bundes-Verfassungsgesetz – B-VG, BGBl 1/1930).

[79] Cf. supra, Part VII.4.

[80] Cf. supra, Part VIII.3

26.1 Alleged Need for Precedence of Public Over Private Interest

The last and, at the same time, probably the main argument of the drafters of the Wels Declaration will be, that there is a conflict of interest between the said freedoms of judges and the interest of the public in an impartial dispensation of justice, and that the interest of the public has to prevail. This argument is flawed in several respects.

26.2 Involvement in Party Politics Does not Exclude Judges' Impartiality

First, it has not been shown, and indeed cannot be shown that involvement of judges in party politics violates the interest of the public in an impartial dispensation of justice. To show this it would have to be proven that judges involved in party politics inevitably cease to be impartial in their judicial function. So far, however, this obscene allegation has not been made by anyone.

26.3 Unreasonable Doubts in Judge's Impartiality Are not Admissible

Second, it might be possible, and therefore cannot be excluded, that some, or even the majority, of the people would distrust judges who are politically active within political parties. However, since it has been shown that the underlying assumption has no fundament in reality, such a distrust would not be justified and therefore would be unreasonable.[81] Unreasonable opinions must be rejected as unwarranted, and the people holding them should be informed about their error and be taught better. The obligation to do so falls upon the competent public authorities.

[81] The "reasonable" test is supported by the Report of the Special Rapporteur on the independence of judges and lawyers present to the Human Rights Council in 2019, Doc. A/HRC/33/25.

26.4 Precedence of Judge's Fundamental Rights Over Unfounded Opinions

Third, such unfounded opinions must never serve as a ground for limiting or restricting a person's fundamental rights. This principle has to be taken into account when it comes to the interpretation of those rules of the European Convention on Human Rights which contain possible limitations to, or restrictions of, the rights and freedoms contained in the Convention. Positions of those persons who persist in their erroneous and/or nocive opinions cannot serve as justification for such limitations or restriction.

26.5 Public Authorities' Duty to Rectify Unfounded Opinions

Fourth and final, it cannot be argued that it is impossible or too cumbersome for the authorities to rectify unfounded opinions. A State that delivers itself to the reign of unreasonableness or irrationality abdicates as an institution for the common good and loses the right to demand obedience and loyalty of its subjects.

27 The Present Europe-Wide Approach to Judges' Involvement in Party Politics

27.1 The General Negative Attitude

At this point of my exposition, I have to admit that I have not found, neither in international instruments for the protection of human rights nor in the case law of tribunals charged with their interpretation nor in the pertinent writing, the line of reasoning propounded by me in this paper. The idea that the credibility of the judiciary as an independent and impartial institution might be compromised by judges engaging in party politics is so wide-spread and so deeply rooted in public opinion that it seems to be almost ineradicable.

27.2 Early Signs of a Possible Change of Attitude

27.2.1 The Solomonic Position of the European Court of Human Rights

Under these circumstances the position of the European Court of Human rights must already be regarded as a last remainder of open mindedness. The Court refrains from adding its voice to the chorus of those who do not feel any restraint when calling for a ban of judges' involvement in party politics. But even if the Court itself does not come out in favor of such ban, its position is worded in such a way that it cannot be construed as a criticism of those who favor it. Rather, the Court considers legal rules which prohibit such political involvement of judges as compatible with the European Convention on Human Rights on the ground that "it is proportionate for countries to exclude judges from political office."[82]

27.2.2 A Growing Awareness of the Human Rights Character of Judges' Political Freedoms

The European Court of Human Rights must be considered, in this regard, a beacon of soundness at a time when hostility towards the involvement of judges in party politics was on the rise.[83] In the course of recent years, we can observe a development in two different respects. On the one hand, the ban on political activities of judges is confirmed, on the other more considerations are given to the question of how to reconcile such a ban with the political rights of judges. There is a growing awareness that it is difficult to find a just line between the former and the demands resulting from the latter.

27.2.3 The Wels Declaration Revisited in Austria

This finds a remarkable expression in the Statement of the Austrian Association of Judges published in 2018 on "Ten Years of the Wels Declaration—Art. IX. Private Behavior".[84] It sticks to the ban on activities of judges in party politics but devotes the greater part of its consideration to the difficulty of reconciling this ban with the

[82] See Opinion of Consultative Council of European Judges on freedom of expression of judges the CCJE, Opinion No. 25 (2022) on freedom of expression of judges, no. 54.

[83] Yet, this Opinion may be considered ambiguous in this respect. It correctly reproduces the relevant case law but conveys the impression that it favors a restrictive approach regarding the question of how far involvement of judges in party politics should be permitted. It also quotes No. 135 of the Commentary on the Bangalore Principles of Judicial Conduct, adopted in the framework of the United Nations Office on Drugs and Crime, in 2007, which deals with "incompatible activities" and states that "[a] judge's duties are incompatible with certain political activities, such as membership of the national parliament or local council." This quotation, even taken in the isolated manner in which it is made, leads to the conclusion, that, by the use of the word "as", it just gives two examples out of (many) more incompatible activities. And No 136 of the Commentary proper reveals the correctness of this assumption: "The very essence of being a judge is the ability to view the subjects of disputes in an objective and judicial manner. Itis equally important for judges to be seen by the public as exhibiting that detached, unbiased, unprejudiced, impartial, open-minded and even-handed approach which is the hallmark of a judge. If a judge enters the political arena and participates in public debates—either by expressing opinions on controversial subjects, entering into disputes with public figures in the community, or publicly criticizing the Government—he or she will not be seen to be acting judicially when presiding as a judge in court."

[84] Redaktion (2018), pp. 191–192.

freedom of a judge to exercise the political rights pertaining to him as to any person and being protected by national and international law on both the regional and the universal level.

How difficult such reconcilement appears to be is shown by the attempt, made in this Statement, to justify reliance, when imposing the ban in question, on the "effect of [mere] appearances"[85] on a principle stated by the European Court of Human Rights, namely „Justice must not only be done, it must also be seen to be done." I have the gravest doubts about the applicability of this principle in the present context. I would subsume it under the heading of Comprehensibility,[86] but would not restrict it to the strive for general intelligibility in all oral and written statements. I would also include the need to explain to the parties the law on which a decision is based, and the object and purpose of the law. Only by understanding the legal basis of the decision and the background of that basis, the partics it will to see "that justice is done". This is quite different from succumbing to unjustified doubts about judicial credibility.

Unfortunately, the positive tone which might have been be heard from between the lines of the Statement "Ten Years of the Wels Declaration—Art. IX. Private Behavior" is drowned by the negative tone adopted 1 year later (2018) by the Austrian Association's Statement on Image of the judge and independence,[87] which states: "Any appearance of political interference has to be avoided or prevented and judicial independence preserved. Therefore, we regard political activity within a political party as incompatible with the judicial profession."[88] However, a statement that is wrong remains wrong, as often as it might be repeated.

27.2.4 Whose Voice Can Be Heard from the Codes of Ethics?

There is an additional aspect that has to be pointed out here, because it is not restricted to Austria, if not in the wording of related documents then at least in their tenor. The Wels Declaration and other statements of the Austrian Association of Judges tend to use the pronoun "we" in connection with (quasi-) prohibitions, like in the just quoted wording: "[W]e regard political activity within a political party as incompatible with the judicial profession." But it is left open who is meant by the "We". In monarchies including the Catholic Church, the "We" is, or was until recently, used as a *plural maiestatis*[89] by Emperors, Kings, or Popes. But although national associations may have an elitist understanding of themselves, it is unlikely that this would find its expression in the use of the majestical "We". In fact, the use of the "We" is intended to convey the contrary impression. We are reminded of the

[85] In German "Anscheinswirkung".

[86] Dealt with in Art. VIII of the Wels Declaration.

[87] *Richterbild und Unabhängigkeit*, https://richtervereinigung.at/richterbild-und-unabhaengigkeit/

[88] My translation.

[89] Majesty's plural.

phrase “We, the People”, as it is found in solemn instruments, from “We, the People of the United States” in the opening phrase of the Preamble to the United States Constitution to “We, the Peoples of the United Nations” in the opening phrase of the Preamble to the United Nations Charter. “We, the People”, can also be found in the preambles of various countries that become independent after World War II.[90]

Yet, the Austrian Association of Judges cannot—and neither do similar associations—claim to be, or at least to represent, “the people” of their respective countries. Their “people” are their members, i.e. regularly judges, and sometimes also public prosecutors.[91] The “We” in the text of the statement quoted can also only refer to Austrian judges, and not even to all of them but only to those who are members of the Association.[92]

However, the last-mentioned limitation does not appear from the pronouncements of the Austrian Association. Rather, the latter conveys (or does not clearly avoid) the impression that it is speaking for all judges without exception. And it cannot be expected of all people reading these texts to have at hand the Statute of the Association for ascertaining who is, or is not, comprise by the word “We”. In addition, even if the Statute grants to members of an association the right to take part in the internal process of decision shaping and decision making, usually only a small number of members is interested in participation. And even for those who might be interested in one or the other of the issues dealt with in such a pronouncement it is often quite difficult to orientate themselves in the often complex statutory rules pertaining to these proceedings. Thus, the use of the “We” in pronouncements in question, if it is meant to include “the judges”, is but a euphemism.

Of course, disinterest of members in the “ordinary” business, on the one hand, and complexity of the rules regulating participation in cases of “extraordinary” business which is prone to raise interest, on the other, is a problem which all association are confronted with. It becomes delicate, however, when “extraordinary” business means to set up (quasi-) binding rules in contentious matters. This is certainly the case with the ban on party politics for judges.

That the body of judges has not, and still does, not become restive in this context is astonishing, but can be explained by a combination of populism and political correctness. The renewed ban on political involvement in party politics is introduced in two steps. The first step is the formulation of an objective which is probably acceptable to everyone, and hardly anyone will oppose it: “Any appearance of political interference has to be avoided or prevented and judicial independence preserved.” The use of a slogan the essence of which is uncontested is problematic, because he who uses the slogan attempts to monopolize the matter and the issues packaged therein. To do so, is a typical sign of, and an indication for, populism.

---

[90] The give some examples: India, (South) Korea and South Africa.

[91] In Austria, public prosecutors have an association of their own, the Association of Public Prosecutors (*Vereinigung Österreichischer Staatsanwältinnen und Staatsanwälte*).

[92] The Austrian Association of Judges is a free, private Assocation, and consequently membership is not compulsory for judges.

If this approach is successful, then the second step can be made and a demand be tabled which—even if does not follow from what was stated as a first step—has enough nearness to the matter dealt with before that people are led to believe that the demand is but the conclusion from what has been said before. In fact, however, there is nothing to support the conclusion drawn: "Therefore, we regard political activity within a political party as incompatible with the judicial profession."

This can easily be shown by comparing both sentences. Can political activity within a political party *per se* constitute political interference with the judiciary? The answer is clearly "No". Is serving as a judge who is involved in party politics necessarily political interference? Again, the answer is clearly "No". Is it impossible to imagine a judge involved in party politics to fulfil his judicial office in an impartial and unbiased manner? The answer is clearly "No". To allege the contrary seems ridiculous. Yet, the Wels Declaration and the Statement of the Austrian Association of Judges scrutinized here are based on the opposite assumption.

If confronted with our argument, the drafters of the texts in question will first make a disclaimer stating that they had never made such a ridiculous allegation and that, of course, they, too, would be ready to answer the said questions with "No". Then, however, the will withdraw to their next line of defense stating that it is not really important whether involvement in party politics of a judge or judges amounts to political interference or harms the independence of the said judge or judges or of the judiciary as a whole. What counts, they will say, is the appearance. And to the question how it is possible that a judge's conduct appears otherwise than it is carried out, they will answer that it is not even the appearance in its objective form, that counts. What counts is what people believe, what opinions they have; and it cannot be excluded that the people, even if guided by mere prejudices, might doubt that a judge involved in party politics cannot be objective and impartial when handling his cases. Therefore, political correctness would call for his withdrawal from his activities within a political party.

I am convinced that political rights of a person—whether of the judicial or of any other profession—must not be infringed upon because of subjective popular opinions which are based on prejudices and lack any reasonableness. This applies all the more as the prejudices and the lack of reasonableness are the results of conscious or unconscious populist agitation, of which the Wels Declaration and comparable statements of the Austrian Associations of Judges but also all other Codes of Ethics which interfere with the political rights of judges, form a part.

28 *Excursus*: Position of UN Bodies

Sometimes, the issue of curtailing the political rights of judges is left completely outside. Thus, the Report of the Office of the United Nations High Commissioner for Human Rights on the Expert workshop on the right to participate in public affairs, held in 2016,[93] does not contain key words like "judge", judiciary", or "courts".

28.1 Test of "Reasonableness"

An important step forward is the Report of the Special Rapporteur on the independence of judges and lawyers present to the Human Rights Council in 2019.[94] It states that "[i]n defining the appropriate degree of involvement of the judiciary in public debate, two factors need to be taken into account. The first is whether the judge's [...] involvement could reasonably undermine confidence in his or her impartiality." It has already been noted earlier[95] that application of the "reasonableness" test which, in this paper, is considered decisive for a fair equilibrium between the need to enhance the political rights of judges and the need to inspire, in the public, confidence in their independence and impartiality, is indispensable.

28.2 Test of "Necessity"

The second factor, namely avoidance of such involvement in the public debate, which may unnecessarily expose the judge to political attacks or be inconsistent with the dignity of his or her office, deals with two different aspects. As regards the second, it goes without saying that a judge must not act in any way that would harm his dignity. More important is the first aspect which enjoins the judge from incurring unnecessary political attacks. What has been the "reasonableness" test in connection with the issue of confidence, is here the "necessity" test in connection with the issue of political attacks.

Both tests—the "reasonableness" test and the "necessity" test—should suffice to distinguish between acceptable and unacceptable comportment of judges. No further limitations to, or restrictions of, a judge's freedom of expression, freedom of assembly and freedom of association can be regarded as justified.

As if this statement in No. 5 would not already be sufficient, the Report, in No. 6, goes on by stressing that this "does not mean that judges [...] should refrain from expressing their views on any issue that may have political implications." This general empowerment of judges to speak up on political issues goes far beyond the permission, traditionally contained in Codes of Ethics, to defend the judiciary or the judicial system as a whole against possible encroachments from outside, legislature and executive not excluded.

---

[93] Doc. A/HRC/33/25.

[94] Report of the Special Rapporteur on the independence of judges and lawyers, Doc. A/HRC/41/48.

[95] Cf. supra, Part VII.8.c.

28.3 Bleak Outlook on European Situation?

The following Numbers of the Report are less euphoric with regard to the freedom of political activity of judges, probably due to the fact that they are overshadowed by the impressions conveyed by comparative surveys of the various legal and praeter-legal[96] situations in which these freedoms find themselves in the different European countries. For a comparative analysis of these situations in Europe, the 2019 Report of the Special Rapporteur on the independence of judges and lawyers presented to the Human Rights Council strongly relies on the Report on the Freedom of Expression adopted by the Venice Commission[97] in 2015[98] and comes to the following conclusions: "With regard to direct involvement in politics, the Venice Commission expressed the view that judges should not put themselves into a position where their independence or impartiality could be questioned, noting that that was the reason why many States restricted the political activities of judges."

29 The "Mixed" Situation in Europe

29.1 Constitutions and "Simple" Laws[99]

However, this summing up is too pessimistic, and its pessimistic view is not really supported by the survey of the Venice Commission. None of the constitutions of the Council of Europe (CoE) Member States provide for specific restrictions on the freedom of expression of judges. The constitution of only one country restricts the freedom of peaceful and unarmed assembly. The constitutions of only 11 CoE Member States provide for specific restrictions for judges regarding the freedom of association. On the statutory level, only one European country flatly forbids political activities of judges. 23 countries impose restrictions on the freedom of expression and association of judges including their political activities, but the level of these restrictions varies from country to country. A few countries require judges

[96] By *praeter-legal* I refer to the status of Codes of Ethics which is non-legal and therefore have no binding force.

[97] European Commission for Democracy Through Law.

[98] Doc. CDL-AD(2015)018.

[99] The term "simple" law is taken over from the Austrian legal terminology, where the supreme laws are the Constitution properly so called and other "constitutional laws" which have the same rank as the Constitution and supplement the latter, while all other laws are "simple" or "ordinary" ones and therefore must not be unconstitutional. Apart from the different terms used, the difference between the Constitution and "constitutional laws", on the one hand, and "simple" laws, on the other, is the difference in their so-called "guarantee of existence" (in Austrian legal terminology "Bestandsgarantie"). "Simple" laws can be amended or repealed by simple majority, "constitutional laws" only by a majority of two-thirds. "Fundamental" changes in the Constitution also require a referendum.

who want to involve themselves in party politics to lay down their judicial function. Some countries restrict political activities by disregarding the "reasonableness" test while others would apply this test at least in substance. On the other end of the spectrum, very few countries favor political activities of judges; and one country even expects judges to engage themselves actively in politics.

29.2 "Codes of Conduct" or "Codes of Ethics"

In a number of CoE countries "Codes of conduct" or "Codes of Ethics" for judges have been adopted by the national associations of judges[45]. Such codes of conduct for judges do not impose sanctions; and—as shown above[100]—could not have done so because, as a rule, they are no instruments of law, consequently not legally binding and therefore without the possibility of providing for negative legal consequences if judges should disregard them. Whether violations of the rules may result in disciplinary sanctions depends on the respective Laws on the Status of Judges, and whether, in the absence of an express legal basis, the rules contained in the Codes may give guidance to disciplinary authorities for their decisions in disciplinary matters is question.

29.3 "Reasonableness" Test and "Necessity" Test

As regards the application of the "reasonableness" test, we have a picture similar to that which appears in the context of statutory restrictions.[101] When restricting political activities, various Codes, or rather their interpretation, disregard the "reasonableness" test while others would apply this test at least in substance. The same is true for the "necessity" test.

30 *Excursus*: The German Position

30.1 Reservations to, and Rejection of, a Code of Conduct

In some European countries, such Codes of conduct have not been adopted and are even regarded critically. In Germany, it is argued that—even if the *Judiciary* Act[102]in its present form does not provide ready answers for all situation where a conflict

---

[100] Cf. supra, Part IV.1.e.

[101] Cf. supra, Part XII.4.

[102] In German legal terminology *Deutsches Richtergesetz* (DRiG).

between the freedom of judges to engage in political activities and the general interest in an impartial judiciary may arise—such answers cannot be generally applicable or codifiable. Although the lack of specific legal regulations causes legal uncertainty, the attempt to eliminate it by codes of ethics is neither possible nor fitting.

30.2 "Inner" Independence and "Outside" Evaluation

The inner independence of a judge is based by his personal judicial ethos and can be defined—in the context of membership in, and political activity within, a political party—only autonomously, i.e. by the conscience of the judge.[103] This does not exclude an objective evaluation from outside of position taken by the judge in particular case. But the adequate instrument for doing so is the judicial procedure and following decision about his impartiality when challenged by a party.[104] The decisive aspect in the course of this procedure is the examination of all circumstance under the "reasonableness" test; to find a judge unfit to decide in the particular case, reasonable doubts in his impartiality have to established.[105]

30.3 Judge Subject to, and not Aloof from, the Constitutional System

Yet, judges may not only be rejected by a party on the ground of alleged impartiality. Judges may also be suspended, and even removed from their judicial post, if they do not conform to, or even openly reject, the constitutional system of Germany based, in particular, on pluralism, democracy, the rule of law and the respect for, and protection of, human rights. Just recently, the Federal Disciplinary Tribunal, a special Senate of the German Federal Supreme Court[106] for disciplinary offenses of public servants, in a case concerning a judge who was a member of the Action for Germany *(Aktion für Deutschland [AfD]),* a political party considered to be on the extreme right fringe of the political spectrum, confirmed the judge's compulsory retirement by stating that it was not ensured anymore that the judge was still on the ground of the German constitution since he was active within a political grouping which rejected the fundaments of the democratic constitutional state.[107] In addition,

[103] Cf. Burghardt (2010), pp. 351–355.

[104] In German "Ablehung wegen Befangenheit".

[105] Cf. ibid., at p. 354.

[106] *Bundesgerichtshof.*

[107] Cf. Der Fall Jens Maier: BGH definiert Maßstäbe gegen Verfassungsfeinde in der Justiz, *beck-link* 2028571; Kirsch (2023). (Translated and summarized by me.)

the Tribunal stated, that compulsory retirement would also be justified if a judge, by his appearance in the public, would convey the impression that he was henceforth going to decide according to his political conviction and not objectively and with respect for the law.[108]

30.4 The German Approach as a Recommendable Model for European Countries

It should be noted that the Federal Disciplinary Tribunal based its decision on objective criteria which were fulfilled beyond reasonable doubt. The judge was not retired because he was member of, and active in, any old party, he was retired because he was member and active in a political party which rejected the very fundaments of a free and democratic state. For this.

reason, the German approach to judges actively involved in party politics lends itself to generalization and can be regarded a model for distinguishing between acceptable and not acceptable political activities of judges.

31 Condensation of Views

If we sum up the various positions taken vis-à-vis the involvement of judges in party politics in Europe, we may conclude that international instruments are more open-minded in this regard. Drafters of national rules laid down in Codes of Conducts often lack the organ for appreciating the social value of judges who do not sit back on their benches and avoid political responsibility but take an active part in the politics of their countries, both nationally and supra-nationally.

To convince national Associations of Judges of the need to purge their Codes of Conduct from the unwarranted limitations on, and restrictions of, those freedoms which are necessary in order to become, or be, a full-fledged member in the formation of national politics, will be much more difficult than to convince supra-national and international bodies that it is high time for doing so. One—or perhaps the main—reason for the inertia of national bodies is that their members stay in office much longer than the members of international bodies, where a frequent change takes place. And, according to an old saying, “old habits die hard.”

108 Ibid.

32 A Long Way Ahead

I know that the voice of reason is not loud but low.[109] We might therefore still have a long way to go before it is generally recognized that judges, even when active in party politics, do not—as such—compromise the independence and impartiality of jurisdiction, i.e., of the judiciary or of the courts.

33 Codes of Ethics, Elitist Rule, Populism and Political Correctness

33.1 The "Elitist" Factor Revisited

Codes of Ethics are an excellent means for transporting visions of "political correctness" into sensitive areas of the social structure. As we have seen, Codes of Ethics have no democratic legitimacy, because they are not the result of a broad democratic dialogue, and they have no legal legitimacy because they have never been approved by the legislator. Even within the association for which, or for the members of which, these Codes undertake to set up certain "moral" rules the legitimacy of which is questionable because they are, more often than not, formulated in limited circles which are dominated by the management and other "club-freaks",[110] i.e. busy-bodies who feel the same mission as those who formally belong to the management and thus are at the head of the association.

Even if that association has no mandatory membership it arrogates the right to speak and act in the name of the entire target group of actual and possible members and have this tactic appear as an act of care for, and not of overpowering of, most members. (If the association enjoys mandatory membership, the practical aspect would be the same since mandatory membership does not mean that those who are members by law instead of by their free will always approve, or have full understanding, of the decisions taken at the top; rather, in both kinds of associations the same group dynamics, which work at the expense of the "simple" members, exist.)

[109] This statement by Sigmund Freud can also be phrased as "The voice of the intellect is a soft one". It is reproduced on a stele set up in the Sigmund-Freund-Park (previously Votivpark) in Vienna.

[110] In German, there is a special word for this type of member which is "Vereinsmeier".

33.2 *A History of Degradation of Political Parties and Party Politics*

What does in mean, then, if a Code of Ethics contains, as the Wels Declaration of Ethics of the Austrian Association of Judges does in its Art. IX, a rule according to which "being a member of a political party or being politically active within such a party can be detrimental to the credibility of independent jurisdiction".[111] As we have explained above,[112] this rule which comes in the guise of a "conviction" is in fact intended to bar members from the judiciary from membership in, and/or activities within, a political party.

Since we have also shown above that political parties are essential elements of the political process and are even recognized by the Austrian Constitution to be "key elements of the Republic of Austria's democratic order",[113] where does the Austrian Association of Judges take its right from to prohibit membership of judges in, or political activities within, political parties?

There is a long tradition in Austria to discredit politicians and political parties by generalizing and exaggerating the faults and weaknesses which are inevitably connected with all human activities and endeavors. Blame for this has to be laid mainly on the mass media which are known for preferring negative to positive news and which sometimes even run campaigns against certain politicians and/or political parties or against political parties in general.

This development has led wide parts of the public to believe that political parties are centers of wrong-doing and politicians the personification of corruption, and that society would be better off without them. In this climate, a ban on judges' membership in, or activities within a political party corresponds to the wide-spread reservation vis-à-vis the traditional political system and does not meet with much, if any, opposition. I believe that this situation is not confined to Austria but appears to be a general development in European countries. This disrespect runs contrary to the appreciation of the political system in Europe reflected in the European values, which are stated in Article 2 of the Treaty on European Union: "The Union is founded on the values of respect for human dignity, freedom, democracy, equality, the rule of law and respect for human rights, including the rights of persons belonging to minorities. These values are common to the Member States in a society in which pluralism, non-discrimination, tolerance, justice, solidarity and equality between women and men prevail." It also runs contrary to the respect due to all members of society and their political convictions. It puts under general suspicion every judge who feels the duty to take interest in his country's political development and to contribute to this development in that manner he considers the most effective, namely within a political party as a community of common values.

---

[111] Art. IX, Third sentence.

[112] Cf. supra, Part VIII.2.

[113] Cf. supra, Part VII.4.

33.3 *"Codified Distrust" in Party Politics Aids Political Populism*

Why has the political system in Western European countries come under fire not only from outside—the Russian President Putin has repeatedly declared that liberal democracy with the protection of human rights is outdated because it cannot be the basis of a strong country and the political system which it needs—but also from within, and there not only from Hungary, the contemporary trendsetter of illiberal democracy in Europe, but also from likeminded movements of citizens in the rest of European countries? I believe that the basis for this dissatisfaction with our political system is to be found in the populist instigation that the average citizen (the proverbial man in the street) should determine his own fate and the equally populist allegation that he is able to do so, if only he is following his own political instinct.[114] That populist propaganda of this kind has fallen on fertile ground is most probably due to the fact that the average citizen feels unable to do what he is allegedly capable of, namely to decide in person about the course of events that concerns him.[115]

This situation is the basis for present-day right-wing populism, but it lends itself to left-wing populism as well, and both variants differ only slightly in connection with the question of who should pay for the reconstruction of the system and the propagated brave new world of direct democracy.[116]

33.4 *The Strengths of Representative Democracy*

It is the advantage of representative democracy that decisions are taken—if there is no disturbance out of line with the system—in an orderly, i.e. legally ordered, process after lengthy, suspended and resumed discussions and therefor with a high degree of reasonableness. But even if the system is open to certain disturbance by some representatives who do not like representative democracy because they generally fail to convince the rest of their views and therefore refuse to join in a sober discussion, in the end the decision is taken by a vote supported by the majority, the outcome thus being democratically legitimized. Moreover, and though representatives are only bound by their conscience and not by the wishes of those who have elected them, they will be indirectly held responsible by, and will have to answer to,

[114] This situation has recently been summed up Schäfer and Zürn (2021), p. 63 and passim.

[115] Research into populist agitation has been intensified after the experience with populist parties and similar movements during the Corona pandemic where scientific data have been openly questioned and all kinds of conspiracy theories have been spread.

[116] I borrow here the title of Aldous Huxley's novel *Brave New World*, written in 1931 and published in 1932, for its *dystopian character. Together with Brave New World Revisited, it was republished several times, inter alia by HarperCollins Publishers in New York 2005.*

their constituency; because disappointing voters by failing to live up to the stance taken in the course of the electoral campaign will endanger their reelection.

33.5 The Need for Trust in Representative Democracy

Sometimes, the decisions taken in parliament on complex matters are too complicated to be fully understood by the proverbial man in the street. In this case, the issues of trust and of its counterpart, i.e. distrust, arises. Representative democracy requires, and by its essence presupposes, trust in the elected representatives and their ways of decision shaping and decision making as a matter of principle. If, instead, distrust in representative democracy becomes a rule, society is likely to be led astray by populist agitation.

33.6 The Weaknesses of Direct Democracy

In contrast, direct democracy has no regulated process of decision shaping and therefore is not able to come to an orderly exchange of ideas and to no well-considered substantial conclusion at all. This is the point where a populist leader will step in and formulate the "wish of the people". Since direct democracy will never be able to overcome this inherent weakness, the need for a leader will become permanent. When direct democracy has reached this stage, the leader will come to prepare the common decision in good time to have it ready when called for, and direct democracy will thus change to guided democracy,[117] or from liberal to illiberal democracy.

34 Codes of Ethics as Touchpoints of Populism and Political Correctness

So far, it has not been noticed or, if noticed, not addressed that such misgivings regarding, even enmity vis-à-vis, the structures of the modern free and democratic state are the environment in which reservations to the contemporary political system and its key players, the political parties, can even find expression in Codes of Ethics.

Of course, this is not to say that the drafters of the Wels Declaration of Ethics of the Austrian Association of Judges are themselves part of that movement of malcontent citizens who have an aversion in principle against the present political system and would lean towards illiberal democracy with a strong leader. Probably, they

[117] In German called *gelenkte Demokratie*.

have just not been aware of the fact that by imposing a ban on political activities of judges in political parties were they serving the unwarranted prejudices against the present system of Austria's democracy.

Reverting from the specific case of the Wels Declaration of Ethics of the Austrian Association of Judges to the field of the Codes of Ethics for judges in European countries in general, I venture the opinion that comparable clauses in Codes of Ethics are due to a comparable background characterized by a critical position towards the system of modern democracy called for in a pluralistic society.

References

Apostolovska-Stepanoska M, Ognjanoska L (2020) The Doctrine of Supremacy of European Union Law: foundations, scope and future perspectives. Reg Law Rev:21. UDK: 34(EU). https://doi.org/10.18485/iup_rlr.2020.ch2

Burghardt M (2010) Richter und parteipolitisches Engagement – Versuch einer Betrachtung aus ethischer Sicht. Deutsche Richter-Zeitung (DRiZ) 2010:351–355

Bychawska-Siniarska D (2017) Protecting the right to freedom of expression under the European Convention. A handbook for legal practitioners on human rights. Council of Europe Publ, Strasbourg

Consultative Council of European Judges (CCJE) (2022) Opinion No. 25 (2022) on freedom of expression of judges

Guide on Article 10 of the European Convention on Human Rights. Freedom of expression. Prepared by the Registry. Updated on 31 August 2022. European Court of Human Rights Doc. 2/139

Huxley A (1932) Brave new world (published in 1932, republished by HarperCollins Publishers in New York 2005)

Kelsen H (1934) Reine Rechtslehre; Einleitung in die rechtswissenschaftliche Problematik (published in 1934, Leipzig/Vienna: Deuticke; 2nd ed. Vienna 1960; English edition 1967)

Kirsch S (2023) AfD-Politiker muss in Ruhestand: Wie politisch dürfen Richter sein? ZDF heute, 5 October 2023

Mejía-Lemos D, Kammerhofer J, Arajärvi N, Merkouris P (eds) (2022) Custom and the regulation of 'the sources of international law'. The theory, practice, and interpretation of customary international law. Cambridge University Press, Cambridge

Redaktion (2018) 10 Jahre Welser Erklärung. Art. IX, Außerdienstliches Verhalten. Österreichische Richterzeitung 2018:191–192

Report on the independence of judges and lawyers, Doc. A/HRC/41/48

Schäfer A, Zürn M (2021) Die demokratische Regression. Die politischen Ursachen des autoritären Populismus (Democratic regression. The political causes of authoritarian populism [my translation]). Suhrkamp, Berlin

Sidaneus J, Pratto F (1999) Social dominance. An intergroup theory of social hierarchy and oppression. Cambridge University Press, Cambridge

The Judge and Justice: Contradictions of Contemporary Justice

Marius Andreescu and Andra Puran

Abstract This essay represents an attempt to highlight, from a philosophical perspective, the most significant contradictions that can affect the justice throughout a period of social crisis. The object of our analysis consists of the contradictions between: the law and justice; the justice and society and the act to fulfill the justice and what we have just called "the fall in exteriority" of justice. Within this context we refer to some aspects that characterize the person and personality of the judge. This essay is a pleading to refer to the principles, in the work for the law's creation and applying.

Starting with the difference between "given" and "constructed" we propose the distinction between the "metaphysical principles" outside the law, which by their contents have philosophical significances, and the "constructed principles" elaborated inside the law. We emphasize the obligation of the law maker, but also of the expert to refer to the principles in the work of legislation, interpretation and applying of the law. Arguments are brought for the updating, in certain limits, the justice—naturalistic concepts in the law.

1 Judicial Power

The development of modern constitutionalism in relation to the theory of the separation of powers in the state was achieved by affirming and consecrating justice with a distinct function and a distinct system in the state. The constitutionalists emphasized the need to separate the jurisdictions in relation to the governors to allow their control by independent judges.

M. Andreescu
Institute of Legal Research "Academician Andrei Rădulescu" of the Romanian Academy, Bucharest, Romania

A. Puran (✉)
The National University of Science and Technology POLITEHNICA Bucharest, Pitești University Centre, Faculty of Economic Sciences and Law, Bucharest, Romania

C. Hermida del Llano (ed.), *The Freedom of Expression for Judges in the Sphere of the Judicial Ethics*, Ius Gentium: Comparative Perspectives on Law and Justice 129, https://doi.org/10.1007/978-3-032-06504-9_16

Justice, as a state authority and institutional system, expresses judicial power as one of the forms of manifestation of the unique and sovereign power of the state. Thus, justice with judicial power has two meanings:

(a) the system of judicial bodies;
(b) the activity of solving civil, commercial, criminal, administrative processes;

Both meanings know a historical evolution, but the essential element is the guarantee of realization and respect by justice of the principles of legality in the activity of state bodies, legal entities and citizens. This means that the judiciary must be the main guarantor of respect for the Constitution and the law, for fundamental citizen rights and freedoms.

Unlike the other state powers, this activity has numerous points of interference. In achieving the goals, their judicial power must be independent and impartial to any state authority.[1] Therefore, the judge is obliged to resolve the case, pronounce the law and obey only the Constitution and the law. In all forms of state organization, except in dictatorial regimes, the magistrate is an independent[2] and impartial person, vested with the power of the state to resolve disputes brought to court. In the contemporary period, the law recognizes the right of other state bodies to carry out some jurisdictional activities, an example can be the administrative bodies with jurisdictional activity. In this case, the mentioned state bodies do not administer justice and are not part of the judicial power, because they are not absolutely independent, being part of an administratively organized system, a system that resolves disputes between legal entities that are part of it (commercial arbitrations) or whose activity violates the specific rules of the authority in question. Also, the Constitutional Court is not part of the judicial power system due to its dual nature: political and legal. As a result of the dispute settlement activity, judgments are pronounced which, once they have become definitive, are binding and must be respected by all legal subjects.

The specificity of the jurisdictional activity with state power can be concretized in the following aspects:

- the achievement of justice requires the existence of an institutional organization and the application of general principles. The organization of justice is done according to the principle of degrees of jurisdiction;[3]
- in his activity, the judge interprets the law and applies it, but does not create the law. That is why jurisprudence is usually not considered a source of law, except for the Anglo-Saxon system;
- the competence of the courts is established by the Constitution and laws and, consequently, the judicial activity will be carried out in strict compliance with these competences;
- justice is an activity for resolving disputes, the term conferred by the Constitution, law and sometimes by "jurisprudence". The judge, resolving the case, must find

[1] For developments see Mitrofan (2023), pp. 242–249.

[2] For developments regarding the independence of the judge see Mitrofan (2015), pp. 93–102.

[3] For the organization of the judicial system in Romania see Popescu (2013), p. 624.

out the truth in the respective process, apply the law to the factual situation and establish, as the case may be, the legal responsibility, responsibilities, causality of the litigation subject to judgment, in order to pronounce the most equitable solution. Justice is an instrument of repression or social revenge. At the same time, the court cannot refer itself and it is necessary to always be referred by another subject of law, this being a requirement of the principle of impartiality.[4]
- court decisions represent the act by which the judge pronounces the right and the dispute is resolved. They are pronounced in the name of the law and can be enforced by state coercion. In the Constitution of Romania, the seat of the matter is represented by chapter VI art. 124–134.

The Constitution uses the phrase "authority", and not judicial power. However, from the interpretation of the constitutional norms, it follows that the Fundamental Law makes the distinction between the judicial power exercised exclusively by the courts and the judicial authority, an attribute that belongs to the Public Ministry and the Superior Council of Magistracy.

2 Constitutional Justice

The supremacy of the Constitution would remain a mere theoretical matter if there were no adequate guarantees.

In this sense, the term constitutional justice appears in the work of H. Kelsen,[5] meaning the "constitutional guarantee of the Constitution" and in the work of Ch. Eisenmann,[6] who defined it as: "that form of justice or more precisely jurisdiction that concerns the laws constitutional, without which the constitution is only a political program, binding only morally". Constitutional justice designates the set of institutions and procedures through which the supremacy of the Constitution is achieved.

The components of constitutional justice are:

(a) a state body competent to carry it out with the attributions provided by the Constitution and the law;
(b) a set of technical means and forms of performance that present specific and exclusive elements;
(c) the purpose of constitutional justice is to ensure the supremacy of the Constitution.

In the specialized literature[7] the attributions of constitutional justice have been emphasized:

(a) ensuring the authenticity of the manifestations of will of the sovereign people;

[4] Tabacu (2019), p. 45.

[5] Kelsen (1928), pp. 197 and next.

[6] Eisenmann (1984), p. 50.

[7] Deleanu (2006), pp. 810–817.

(b) vertical and horizontal respect of the competences conferred by the Constitution on the various public authorities;
(c) protection of the fundamental rights and freedoms of citizens;
(d) the resolution of some of the contentious issues given by the Constitution in the competence of the constitutional justice.

There is no identity between the concepts of constitutional justice and, respectively, constitutional control of laws. The latter is only a component part of the former.

In the sense of the definition proposed above, the general features of constitutional justice can be identified:

- it is a genuine jurisdiction, but having some particularities compared to other forms of jurisdiction considering its purpose;
- can use common procedural rules but also its own procedural rules inscribed in the Constitution, laws and regulations determined by the nature of the constitutional litigation;
- it can be carried out by a specialized state body (political, jurisdictional, or with a dual nature), or by common law courts;
- it is an exclusive justice because it has a monopoly on constitutional disputes.

It is not always focused because common law courts can have perspectives in the field of constitutional litigation:

- the independence of the constitutional justice consists in the existence of a "constitutional statute" of the body that exercises this type of jurisdiction, consisting in the statutory and administrative autonomy independent of any public authority; the verification of one's own competence, the preeminence of abuses of constitutional justice over any other jurisdictional decisions: the independence and immovability of judges and, in some cases, their designation using criteria other than those regarding the recruitment, appointment and promotion of career magistrates;
- the constitutional control of laws represents only one part of constitutional justice, the other component refers to attributions regarding the assurance of the authenticity of the manifestations of will of the sovereign people and the jurisdictional guarantee of respect for the Constitution. Therefore, not all the attributions belonging to the constitutional judge are carried out within jurisdictional procedures.

George Alexianu believed that legality is an attribute of the modern state. The idea of legality in the author's conception is formulated as follows: all state organs operate on the basis of a legal order established by the legislator and which must be respected.

Referring to the supremacy of the Constitution, George Alexianu affirms with full reason and in relation to today's realities: "When the modern state organizes its new appearance, the first idea that concerns him is that of curbing administrative abuse, hence the invention of constitutions and the judicial establishment of a control of legality. Once this abuse is established, a new one appears, much more serious, that of the Parliament. The supremacy of the Constitution and different systems to guarantee it are then invented. The idea of legality thus acquires a powerful lever of strengthening".[8]

The constitutionality control of laws is the main form of constitutional justice and constitutes a basis of democracy, guaranteeing the realization of a democratic government, which respects the supremacy of the law and the Constitution.

The first problem is to define the notion of control of the constitutionality of laws. In legal doctrine, it was emphasized that the issue of this attribution must be included in the principle of legality.

Legality is a fundamental principle of organization and functioning of the social and political system.

This principle has several coordinates: the existence of a hierarchical legal system at the top of which is the Constitution. Therefore, the ordinary law must be in accordance with the Constitution in order to fulfill the condition of legality; state bodies must carry out their duties in strict compliance with the competence established by law; the development of normative acts to be done by competent bodies, following a pre-established procedure with compliance with the provisions of higher normative acts with legal force and compliance with the law and the Constitution by all state bodies.

In essence, the control of the constitutionality of the laws involves the verification of the conformity of the law as a legal act of the Parliament, but also of other categories of normative acts with the norms included in the Constitution. Conformity must exist both from a formal point of view (the competence of the issuing body and the drafting procedure), and from a material point of view (the content of the norm in the ordinary law must be in accordance with the constitutional norm).

In the doctrine, the constitutionality control of laws was defined as: "the organized activity of verifying the conformity of the law with the constitution, and from the point of view of constitutional law, it includes rules regarding the competent authorities to make this verification, the procedure to be followed and the measures that can be taken after the completion of this procedure".[9]

The analysis of the definition reveals the complex significance of the constitutionality control of laws. This is an institution of constitutional law, respectively the set of legal rules relating to the organization and functioning of the authority competent to exercise control, as well as the set of procedural and regulatory legal rules that can be ordered by a constitutional court.

At the same time, it is also an organized activity through which the supremacy of the Constitution is guaranteed by verifying the compliance of the norms contained in laws and other normative acts with the constitutional regulations.

---

[8] Alexianu (1930), p. 7.

[9] Andreescu and Puran (2023), p. 58.

3 The Ailing Contradictions of the Justice

Justice should be a harmonious system in order to be in its truth and reality. "The truth is real only as a system"[10] said Hegel and by confirming this statement, justice is in its truth only if it satisfies this condition. The system means coherent order, functionality, suitability to the real and its purpose, but mainly unity in its diversion, a concrete universal in which each part to express the whole and this one to legitimize through the created order, the component parts. The system, including the justice one manifests itself dialectically, transforms itself, become a historical being, without losing the harmony and coherence. The thinker of Jena pointed out that "Truth is the whole. The whole is only the essence that fully accomplishes itself through its development".[11] Like any other system, justice has its components or subsystems: ideal, value, normative, jurisprudential subsystem (the act of justice), institutional and perhaps the most important component, man as a producer, but also as a beneficiary of the act of justice. The truth of the judiciary system involves the making in its wholeness but also by each component of own existential purpose, which is at the same time its being, namely the *righteousness* as a value ideal but transposed into reality's concrete.

To the extent that the functions, we may say, the mission of justice, fulfill and express at the same time the functional harmony of a system, which at any time attempts the adequacy to its purpose as a value, the fulfilling of justice, justice finds itself in its truth, otherwise said, it gives its own legitimacy without waiting for it to be given, in forms sometimes inadequate, from outside.

The contradictions and in general any malfunction in the coherence of the system or inadequacy to the purpose are maladies, deficiencies of the justice, that departs it from its role and truth. When the maladies of the justice become chronical but with manifestations which lead towards aggravation, one may speak about a crisis of the system of justice. Our justice is obviously in such a chronical crisis with tendencies towards aggravation. The main cause is the ailing contradictions of the system. In contrast to the beneficial contradictions that give the becoming, the unhealthy ones tend to depart more and more the justice from its reality and truth. In the followings we try to emphasize the sickly contradictions of the justice system specific to the crisis in which this is located:

1. The fundamental contradiction of the justice, expression of the profound crisis in which this is between law and justice, and on the other side the constructive order of the norms and jurisprudence. The *law,* the justice don't represent the purposes and truth of justice, substituting these values, the law, norms and jurisprudence, that will find legitimacy in itself, in the abstract forms, the ephemeral realities, interests and precarious purposes but not in the ideal and reality of justice. Ofcourse even when a judicial system is harmonious functional and does not have this malady, there isn't always a formal overlapping between law and

[10] Hegel (1965), p. 18.

[11] Hegel (1965), p. 18.

justice. In the healthy justice system, between the justice and law there is a unilateral contradiction in the meaning that the law may contradict the justice, but this one does not contradict the law. The crisis of the judiciary system expresses sometimes in aggravated forms the inadequacy in absolute terms between the justice and law.

The abovementioned contradiction unleashed the "will of power" of the governors to impose their own order and legitimacy to justice by norming and legislating in the meaningless and illusory attempt to create an "order of the norms" that will replace the being and truth of justice: *the righteousness*. Reality shows that this false order proves itself inconsistent, contradictory and mostly inadequate to the realities it is destined for. The mere accumulation of rules, laws even codified, does not lead to the settlement into their being and purpose of the man, the "social" and justice if the norms do not express as a phenomenon the essence: the superior order of the values of justice, equity, truth, proportionality, tolerance. Jurisprudence is manifested the same in the exclusive concern to correspond to itself or to the norms, to be sufficient in itself and not be related to the higher order of the values named above. The act of justice accomplished by the magistrate obstinately seeks for exclusive legitimation only by the rules of law and not through the value order that should be its own.

This ailing contradiction is confirmed, but not made aware by the judicial technique and formalism. A judgement is not pronounced in the name of the justice but in the "name of the law". That is in the name of an order constructed by a temporary political will for the fulfilling of some temporary interests steeped into their particularity and often contrary to the common good and not, as it should naturally be done, in the name of the order *given* and not *constructed* of the values outside the justice but which represent its truth and purpose.

The doctrine asserts that the judge pronouncing a decision "is saying the law". It would be good to be so. In fact, most of times, the magistrate by the judgment pronounced "is saying the law"—when he is not doing it—trying to include his sentence in the order of law, which is not necessarily the order of justice, the judge if having the conscience of achieving an act of justice, respecting his moral and professional statute, does not contradict the law, yet there are situations when he should and could do so in the name of a superior order formed out of the values subsumed to the justice concept. For such an act, that is not only an act of justice but also an act of righteousness, courage is needed. The magistrate must assume the risk to exceed the constructed imperfect order of the law in order to legitimate the act of justice achieved in the superior values reality of the metaphysical principles of law. Such an exiting from the normality of the inadequate forms of the concrete reality is risky for the judge, because the order constructed of the law can impose its coercive force.

The contemporary justice is dominated by the order of normativity, of forms that are not abstracted from reality but ignores it.

The sickly rupture between the law and justice (the law as expression of the will of the legislator, of the temporary power, the only one seeking such a separation) should be reflected in the legal education plan. For a correct suitability to the crisis of justice emphasized by this contradiction, but also in order to reflect the order of law and not of righteousness, taught to the students, the faculties in speciality shouldn't be called "Law" Faculties but "Faculties of Laws", as it once was.

2. The contradiction between the justice and "world', throughout "world" we understand both the human in his individuality as the society as a whole. It seems it is increasingly present in the actuality of justice and placed in a place of honour the dictum "Fiat justiţia et pereat mundus." It is not a simple dictum but a tragic reality, a disease of the justice consisting in the inauthentic legitimizing of the separation of justice from the world and man. Justice cannot live, triumph, *be* if the world dies. Bteween justice and the world there is a unilateral contradiction: justice can contradict the world, but the world cannot contradict the justice, because the world is the medium, the element that justifies the manifestations of justice. The righteousness through justice involves he man, both as a performer of the act of justice and as a beneficiary.

In its contemporary manifestations, the justice in crisis is increasingly making the dictum "Fiat justiţia et pereat mundus", tring to become a closed system, existing for itself and in some cases, even worse, directed against human, the only beneficiary of the act of justice, denying its own reason for being. The crisis of justice, by this disease, is also found in the meaningless rethoric of proclamation of the "abstract man" through rights equally abstract with the intention to give teleological form to its manifestations. But the true existential meaning of justice and its finality at the same time is the man considered in his human dignity. The rhetoric specific to the separation between the justice and world in favour of the abstract man, impersonal has obvious manifestations. Before the court, in a judgment, man is no longer in the concrete of his dignity as a person, but he becomes the "named" at most identified through a locus standing equally impersonal.

The existential rupture between the justice and world, further more the attempt of justice to deny its own medium that justifies its own reason to be, cannot confirm the natural dialectical order that should characterize a good placing of justice in its truth, but may have at the end of the road the nothingness, justice as an empty form, void of the fullness which only the "just" is offering when existing in relation to human's dignity.

3. The contradiction between the justice understood and even in the acception of the normative order of law, and on the other side, the act of justice and the magistrate performing it. In philosophy one speaks about an autonomous world of the values existing per se and for itself independent even to man. As stated, justice is undeniable a reality and a normative institutional system but also a system of values. Unlike other systems of moral, religious values and in general cultural ones, the essence of justice consists also in its achieving and fulfilling through the act of justice of the magistrate without which the justice system does not close. One can speak at most about the autonomy of the right understood as an order of values, but not about the autonomy of justice outside the act by which it

gets concretized. Unlike other systems of values or by other nature, justice is a clear example of a universal concrete fulfilled through the act of justice whose expression is firstly the decision of the judge.

Therefor the act of justice may confirm or refute the normative order of justice and equally as much the right as a system of values. It is a situation similar with the relation between the experiment and the scientific theory "the first being able to confirm or refuge the theory, according to the case. Only that in the sphere of scientific theories an experiment may invalidate a theory legitimizing a new, superior order, that will include the old one such as it once happened with Einstein's relativity theory. In contrast, the act of justice, if contrary to the normative order or the value order of law is only but a mere judiciary error, willfully, unintentionally or accidental of the magistrate which denies even the justice itself and implicitly the right abolishing thus the order of juridical and the lawful order having as finality not another order but the disorder, the chaos. How many judicial errors are now known or unknown.

One needs to emphasize the fact that the act of justice cannot dissociate the person of the one performing it from the magistrate. A judgment even anonymized is not anonymous: the act of justice contains in itself the person but also the personality of the magistrate. We can say that not only the magistrate is the author of the act of justice, but also the act of justice "makes" the magistrate. When the judiciary errors become obvious—the cause being the abandonment by the magistrate of the moral, social, professional statute, he being at peace with the disorder that is specific to the existential non-values—it is customary to say that these are isolated cases that do not characterize the justice system and lawful order. This is not true. Justice as a system of values needs to be confirmed in its own being, coming to truth by each act of justice, by each court judgment. A single judiciary error, a single corrupted or immoral magistrate "denies it by sending the judiciary and lawful order into nothingness, into non-existence. The contemporary reality still provides too many examples for such situations so that you wonder if there's anything left into the value being of justice. Here is an acute manifestation and not only a chronical one of crisis of justice.

Justice located into its being and truth imposes the magistrate, as a fact of conscience, the object of judgment: the deeds of the man and not the man, meaning the phenomenal that is specific to the humanity of man. Being aware at the principles of law and implicitly the justice as a value specific to an order higher than the normative one, the judge, by fulfilling the act of justice, must although to teleologically relate to the concrete man even if he will rule only over the deeds (actions and omissions) thereof. Unlike this, in case of a sickly justice, the judge imagines that he has the power to judge the man.

4. The falling in exteriority. Of course, the justice made by man and for man is profane, to the "measures of man", but the sacred values are part of his being.

Being a component of the human temporary reality, the justice understood in its value dimension involves the relationship between transcendent and transcendental to which Kant[12] and Heidegger referred to. As a reality of man and society, justice should not be transcendent, meaning "beyond" the man and the world and neither beyond his own reason for being. If this happens, we are in the presence of a sickly manifestation specific to the crisis of justice, firstly by its separation from the "world" as mentioned above. Justice must be and remain in its *transcendental* being respectively "on this side" of the existential precariousnesses of this world and outside the conflicts and political interests of all kinds, without implications in the struggle for power or power games. The transcendental of justice is this one's being in its values dimension, is the right as justice manifested phenomenally through the act of justice.

The contemporary crisis of justice means falling from the immutability of the own existential and values transcendental into the social and political exteriority with the consequence of diminishing or even losing the very being of the "right as value". Unfortunately the examples are too numerous: conflicts and contradictions inside the institutional system of justice; transformation of justice into a tool for the political actors or of another kind; involving into the struggle for temporary power or into the power games both of the whole justice system and of the magistrates; shifting from the publicizing of the acts of justice, to the media justice, done by the prime mass media; magistrates' abandonment of the moral and professional statute for the illusory gain conferred by the involvement into the precariousnesses, sometimes miseries of the world; arrogarnt and aggressive rhetoric without substance by random using, and mainly for the satisfaction of some selfish interests many times immoral, in the sacred name of justice and law: "in the name of law", "in the name of the right" which become simple formulas for legitimizing of what is lacking legitimacy. The falling into exteriority is a painfull manifestation of the crisis of justice which is sensed not so much by the judiciary system itself but mainly by the system's beneficiaries: the man, people and society.

We discussed about the crisis of justice. There is a justice of the crisis consisting in the illusion of the system to exist through the sickly contradictions presented above in a world which is not in the realization of the "progress in the conscience of liberty" such as Hegel believed, but mainly in a process of abolition, abandonment of the values cultural being and its replacing through civilization elements, excessive technicization, in a single word through the domination of the forms of civilization over the culture and not vice versa like normal. In social and political plane, the world's *dissolution* process is manifested through *mass democracy* and the *democratic individualism* with the consequence of ignoring the man as person and personality, man becoming an individual in a political and economical normative, social order in which he does not confirm his *self* as he has become a mere number taken over by the rhetoric of forms and void ideals.

The crisis of justice cannot have a being as it is outside truth and its purpose like the society of crisis to which is trying to adapt itself. There can be no proper relation between the justice that is in serious sickly contradictions and a society that is in crisis with the purpose to legitimize the existence of a justice of crisis. The justice

[12] Kant (1928), p. 50.

of crisis can however be a reality but devoid of truth, of being, because not all that exists it really *is*.

4 The JUDGE and the Justice

It is spoken, somehow with bewilderment about the lonliness and intransigence of the judge. The judge, the magistrate in general, cannot be lonely, he cannot isolate himself, cannot alienate himself. But he can be *a secluded one*. Living in community he must be in communion with the others and at the same time he can take in his being and mainly in his conscience as much of the feelings, values, aspirations of others, of course if all these bear the mark of the being, they are beneficial and not ailing. The common good, but only as a Christian value, must become the own good. The seclusion, the withdrawal in oneself does not imply abandoning the social environment on the contrary it implies its regaining and evaluation by one's own self: "is something deeper in us than ourselves", said Holly Augustin. Only by seclusion in own self, the judge may understand man, he can assimilate him, he may understand a few about the world's self. Seclusion but not loneliness: to be with you in deeper own self, but in communion with yours' another one.

The judge must relate to the concrete man, not to the abstract one, the latter as Goethe understood the sum of all people. He must bring closer to his being Eminescu's words" "in every man a world starts its existence", discovering and understanding this world in every man that comes before the judgment seat. In his solitude the joy of the judge must be that to which Kant is referring to: "two things fill the soul with ever newer and growing admiration and veneration: the starry sky above me and the moral law inside me".

Of course, the judge is looking down the ground or (at the earth), such as Aristotel's hand is pointing to in Rafael's painting. Only thus can he take the real, the concrete, the existing, so that together with Plato, to rise up to the idea. The judge is looking down the earth naturally in order to feel, to know not only the rational in the real, but also the real as a rational and to be aware of piety's meanings." Taller is the man kneeling than standing"—pointed our priest Arsenie Boca.

Intransigence can not be in the nature of a judge's being, because it implies the impersonal authority, manifested in the name of the law and justice, but in fact without man and without justice. Intransigence means being placed in the exclusive plan of the formal logic with its categoric distinction between the true and false, between "yes' and "no". Yet, how many senses, how much richness of meanings life is offering between these extreme values to which judicial needs be identified.

Not the intransigence, but piety, mercy should characterize the judge because only thus can he see and understand something of every person's humanity. Noica said: "one needs to have mercy for the insignificant ones to see their meaningness".[13] The piety of the judge is the piety of justice. How well the being and meaning of

[13] Noica (1998), p. 257.

justice was described on 1919 by the great legal expert Matei Cantacuzino, and how far we depart today from the truth of justice to immerse ourselves into the unauthentic of the "other justice", of the crisis: "In a small church in Rome I saw the painting with a woman holding the black earth into her hands. She warmly embraced it; her expression showed she was a mother, with her eyes turned up to the sky she seemed she was trying to pull the light out of the sky's blue. I was expecting to be written underneath: Charity or Justice or Philanthropy. It was not. It was *Justice*! A justice unblindfolded and understaning all pains, and not the other justice, blind with the sword in one hand and holding a scale with the other hand, so little, that it couldn't contain any of our miseries".

5 Justice and the Principles of Law

In the above we supported the higher order, in the sphere of values, which the concept of justice should confer on justice and the act of justice so that they do not remain only in the formal order of the normative. Justice as a value is legally expressed primarily through the principles of law that must be found in the rules of law.

An argument for which the philosophy of law must be a present reality not only in the theoretical sphere but also for the practical activity of drafting normative acts or the administration of justice, is represented by the existence of general and branch principles of law, some of which are enshrined in the Constitution.

The principles of law, by their nature, generality and depth, are topics of reflection primarily for the philosophy of law, only after their construction in the sphere of the metaphysics of law, these principles can be transposed into the general theory of law, can be normatively enshrined and applied in jurisprudence. Moreover, there is a dialectical circle because the "meanings" of the principles of law, after the normative consecration and jurisprudential elaboration, are to be elucidated also in the sphere of the philosophy of law. Such a finding nevertheless imposes the distinction between what we could call: constructed principles of law, and on the other hand metaphysical principles of law. The distinction we propose has as its philosophical basis the distinction shown above between "constructed" and "given" in law.

The constructed principles of law are, by their very nature, legal rules of maximum generality, elaborated by legal doctrine or by the legislator, in all situations explicitly established by the rules of law. These principles can constitute the internal structure of a group of legal relations, of a branch or even of the unitary system of law. The following features can be identified: (1) they are elaborated within the law, being, as a rule, the expression of the will of the legislator, enshrined in legal norms; (2) are always expressed explicitly by legal norms; (3) the work of interpretation and application of the law is able to discover the meanings and determinations of the constructed principles of the law which, obviously, cannot exceed their conceptual limits established by the legal norm. In this category we find principles such as: publicity of the court session, the principle of adversariality, of the supremacy of the law and the Constitution, the principle of non-retroactivity of the law, etc.

Therefore, the constructed principles of law have, by their nature, first of all a legal connotation and only in the subsidiary a metaphysical one. Being the result of an elaboration within the law, the possible metaphysical meanings and meanings are to be after their consecration established by the metaphysics of law. At the same time, being rules of law, they are binding and produce legal effects just like any other normative regulation. It is necessary to mention that the legal norms that enshrine such principles are superior in legal force to the usual regulations of the law, because they usually target social relations considered to be essential in the first place for the respect of the fundamental rights and legitimate interests recognized by the subjects by law, but also for the stability and fair, predictable, transparent conduct of judicial procedures.

In the situation of this category of principles, the dialectic circle mentioned above has the following appearance: (1) the constructed principles are elaborated and normatively consecrated by the legislator; (2) their interpretation is carried out in the law enforcement work; (3) the value meanings of these principles are later expressed in the sphere of metaphysics of law; (4) metaphysical "meanings" can constitute the theoretical basis necessary for broadening the connotation and denotation of principles or for the normative elaboration of such new principles.

The number of constructed principles of law can be determined at a certain moment of legal reality, but there is no pre-constituted limit of them. The evolution of law is also manifested through the normative elaboration of such new principles. As an example, we mention the "principle of subsidiarity",[14] a construction in European Union law, adopted in the legislation of many European states, including Romania.

The metaphysical principles of law can be considered as a "given" in relation to legal reality and by their nature are external to law. At their origin, they do not have a legal, normative or jurisprudential elaboration. They are a transcendental and non-transcendent "given" of law, therefore, they are not "beyond" the sphere of law, but they are "something else" in the legal system. In other words, it represents the value essence of law, without which this constructed reality could not have an ontological dimension.

Since they are not constructed, but represent a transcendental, metaphysical "given" of law, it is not necessary to express them explicitly through legal norms. Metaphysical principles can also have an implicit existence, discovered or exploited in the work of interpreting the law. As an implicit given and at the same time as the transcendental essence of the law, these principles must be found, after all, in the content of any legal norm and in any act or manifestation that represents, as the case may be, the interpretation or application of the legal norm. It must be emphasized that the existence of metaphysical principles also underpins the teleological nature of law, because any manifestation in the legal sphere, in order to be legitimate, must be appropriate to such principles.

[14] For development see Vâlcu (2022), pp. 368–374.

In the specialized legal literature, such principles, without being called metaphysical, are identified by their generality and that is why they were called "general principles of law".

We prefer to emphasize their metaphysical, valuable and transcendental dimension, which is why we consider them metaphysical principles of legal reality. As a transcendental "given" and not constructed by law, the principles in question are permanent, limited, but with determinations and meanings that can be diversified in the dialectical circle that encompasses them.

In our opinion, the metaphysical principles of law are: the principle of justice; the principle of truth; the principle of equity and justice; the principle of proportionality; the principle of freedom. In a future study, we will elaborate on the considerations that entitle us to identify the principles mentioned above as having a metaphysical and transcendental value in relation to legal realities.

The metaphysical dimension of these principles is indisputable, but the normative dimension remains under discussion. A broader analysis of this problem exceeds the object of this study, which was intended to be a broad excursion on the philosophical dimension of the principles of law. However, some considerations are necessary. Contemporary ontology no longer considers reality by referring to the classic concepts of substance or matter. In his work,[15] "Substamzbegriff und Funktionsbegriff", Ernest Cassirer opposes the modern concept of function to the ancient concept of substance. Not what the "thing" is or the concrete reality, but their way of being, their inner fabric, their structure interests the moderns. Concrete objects no longer exist in front of knowledge, but only "relations" and "functions". In a way, for scientific knowledge, but not for ontology, things disappear and give way to relationships and functions. Such an approach is cognitively operational for material reality, not for ideal reality, that "world of Ideas" that Plato spoke of.

The normative dimension of legal reality seems to correspond very well to the findings formulated by Ernest Cassirer. What else is the legal reality than an ensemble of social relations and functions that are transposed into the new ontosogical dimension of "legal relations" through the application of the rules of law. The principles built applying to a sphere of social relations by means of the legal norm transform them into legal relations, so these principles correspond to a legal reality, understood as a relational and functional structure.

But there is a deeper order of reality than relationships and functions. Constantin Noica said that we must call "element" this order of reality, in which things are fulfilled and which makes them be. Between the concept of substance and that of function or relationship, a new concept is imposed, which preserves a substantiality and, without dissolving in function, manifests functionality.

---

[15] Cassirer (1910), p. 54.

6 Conclusions

It is spoken, somehow with bewilderment about the lonliness and intransigence of the judge. The judge, the magistrate in general, cannot be lonely, he cannot isolate himself, cannot alienate himself. But he can be *a secluded one*. Living in community he must be in communion with the others and at the same time he can take in his being and mainly in his conscience as much of the feelings, values, aspirations of others, of course if all these bear the mark of the being, they are beneficial and not ailing. The common good, but only as a Christian value, must become the own good. The seclusion, the withdrawal in oneself does not imply abandoning the social environment on the contrary it implies its regaining and evaluation by one's own self: "is something deeper in us than ourselves", said Holly Augustin. Only by seclusion in own self, the judge may understand man, he can assimilate him, he may understand a few about the world's self. Seclusion but not loneliness: to be with you in deeper own self, but in communion with yours' another one.

The judge must relate to the concrete man, not to the abstract one, the latter as Goethe understood the sum of all people. He must bring closer to his being Eminescu's words" "in every man a world starts its existence", discovering and understanding this world in every man that comes before the judgment seat. In his solitude the joy of the judge must be that to which Kant is referring to: "two things fill the soul with ever newer and growing admiration and veneration: the starry sky above me and the moral law inside me".

Of course, the judge is looking down the ground or (at the earth), such as Aristotel's hand is pointing to in Rafael's painting. Only thus can he take the real, the concrete, the existing, so that together with Plato, to rise up to the idea. The judge is looking down the earth naturally in order to feel, to know not only the rational in the real, but also the real as a rational and to be aware of piety's meanings." Taller is the man kneeling than standing"—pointed our priest Arsenie Boca.

Intransigence can not be in the nature of a judge's being, because it implies the impersonal authority, manifested in the name of the law and justice, but in fact without man and without justice. Intransigence means being placed in the exclusive plan of the formal logic with its categoric distinction between the true and false, between "yes' and "no". Yet, how many senses, how much richness of meanings life is offering between these extreme values to which judicial needs be identified.

Not the intransigence, but piety, mercy should characterize the judge because only thus can he see and understand something of every person's humanity. Noica said: "one needs to have mercy for the insignificant ones to see their meaningness".[16] The piety of the judge is the piety of justice. How well the being and meaning of justice was described on 1919 by the great legal expert Matei Cantacuzino, and how far we depart today from the truth of justice to immerse ourselves into the unauthentic of the "other justice", of the crisis: "In a small church in Rome I saw the painting with a woman holding the black earth into her hands. She warmly embraced it; her expression showed she was a mother, with her eyes turned up to the sky she seemed

[16] Noica (1998), p. 257.

she was trying to pull the light out of the sky's blue. I was expecting to be written underneath: Charity or Justice or Philanthropy. It was not. It was *Justice*! A justice unblindfolded and understaning all pains, and not the other justice, blind with the sword in one hand and holding a scale with the other hand, so little, that it couldn't contain any of our miseries".

References

Alexianu G (1930) Drept constitutional (Constitutional law). Casa Şcoalelor, Bucharest

Andreescu M, Puran A (2023) Drept constitutional. Justiţia constituţională-garant al supremaţiei Constituţiei. Doctrină şi jurisprudenţă (Constitutional law. Constitutional justice-guarantor of the supremacy of the Constitution. Doctrine and jurisprudence). C.H. Beck, Bucharest

Cassirer E (1910) Substamzbegriff und Funktionsbegriff (Concept of substance and concept of function). Verlag Von Bruno Cassirer, Berlin

Deleanu I (2006) Instituţii şi proceduri constituţionale (Institutions and constitutional procedures). C.H. Beck, Bucharest

Eisenmann C (1984) L'espirit des lois et la separation des pouvoirs (The spirit of law and the separation of the powers). Cahiers de philosophie politique 2-3. Ousia, Bruxelles

Hegel GWF (1965) Fenomenologia spiritului (Phenomenology of the spirit). Academy Publishing House, Bucharest

Kant I (1928) Foundations of the metaphysics of morals. Antaios, Bucharest

Kelsen H (1928) La garantie jurisdictionnelle de la Constitution (The jurisdictional guarantee of the constitution). Revue de Droit publique, Paris

Mitrofan F (2015) The Independence of Judge – a guarantee of the rule-of-law state. J Law Adm Sci., Special Issue:93

Mitrofan F (2023) Reflecting the principles of judicial independence and impartiality in doctrine and jurisprudence. In: Proceedings of the international scientific conference history, culture, citizenship in the European Union. In memoriam Prof. Eugen Chelaru, 15th edn. C.H. Beck, Bucharest

Noica C (1998) Devenirea întru fiinţă (Becoming within being). Humanitas, Bucharest

Popescu V (2013) The analysis of the human resources management in the Romanian legal system from the perspective of the cooperation and verification mechanism. In: Proceedings of the international conference challenges of the knowledge society, 17th edn. ProUniversitaria, Bucharest

Tabacu A (2019) Drept procesual civil, Legislaţie internă şi internaţională. Doctrină şi jurisprudenţă (Civil procedural law. National and international legislation. Doctrine and jurisprudence). Universul Juridic, Bucureşti

Vâlcu E (2022) Brief considerations regarding the supremacy of the Union regulation in relation to national acts. Int J Leg Soc Order 1:368–374

The Right to Freedom of Expression of a Judge and Its Limits in the Polish Legal System

Agnieszka Malicka

Abstract In Polish law, freedom of expression is one of the fundamental rights of an individual guaranteed in the Constitution and in the norms of international law binding on Poland. However, this is not an unlimited right. In the case of judges, the Polish legislator has provided certain limits. They result primarily from the special position of judges in the system of authorities and their specific public function. This study attempts to find answers to the questions: Can a judge participate in public debate, express his opinions on current reforms of the judicial system, or comment on political events?

1 Introduction

In recent years, there has been much public discussion in Poland about the legal position of judges and their extrajudicial activities. The main reason and starting point for these discussions have been the far-reaching reforms of the judicial system that have been implemented at all levels of the judiciary in Poland since 2015, i.e. since the populist and right-wing Law and Justice party (*Prawo i Sprawiedliwość*) came to power.[1] These reforms caused numerous protests by judges, which were also actively supported by the population and opposition parties. Despite these protests, the government changed the organisation and functioning of the Constitutional Tribunal and the Supreme Court. However, the judicial reform also affected the system of courts of general jurisdiction.[2] The consequences of the

[1] This Article is updated as of November 2023.

[2] Judicial reform is not the subject of this article and will not be discussed or analysed in detail here. The so-called constitutional crisis, which affects, among other things, the organisation and opera-

A. Malicka (✉)
Faculty of Law, Administration and Economics, University of Wroclaw, Wroclaw, Poland
e-mail: agnieszka.malicka@uwr.edu.pl

C. Hermida del Llano (ed.), *The Freedom of Expression for Judges in the Sphere of the Judicial Ethics*, Ius Gentium: Comparative Perspectives on Law and Justice 129, https://doi.org/10.1007/978-3-032-06504-9_17

judicial reform were thus felt by judges in all courts in Poland. Since the independence of the judiciary and a properly and constitutionally functioning judiciary are one of the guarantees of a democratic state of law, and the Republic of Poland is defined as such in Article 2 of the 1997 Constitution,[3] it is particularly important that the current regulations on the judiciary actually guarantee the independence of judges.

2 Guarantee of Freedom of Expression

In connection with these reforms and numerous comments on them by representatives of the judiciary, there has been a public debate about the right of judges to express their opinions freely. In particular, the question of whether a judge has the right to speak publicly and critically about the organs of state power is being discussed. Is he or she allowed to participate in the public sphere, comment on the current political situation in the state in the media, belong to social organisations or take part in demonstrations?[4] In the case of judges in particular, we are dealing with people whose opinions are highly sought after due to their professional knowledge and legal expertise. The right to freedom of expression is one of the fundamental rights of the individual, which is guaranteed to everyone both in the Polish Constitution[5] and in the regulations of international law[6] that are binding on Poland.

tion of the judiciary, has been ongoing in Poland since 2015. In the years 2015–2016, numerous changes were made to the regulations relating to the organisation and operation of the Constitutional Tribunal in Poland. The controversial reforms began with the amendment to the Act on the Constitutional Tribunal of 25 June 2015 and the subsequent amendments to this Act. More on the amendments to the provisions on the Constitutional Tribunal and their negative consequences for the rule of law and the principle of separation of powers in: Szuleka et al. (2016), p. 4. In the following years, other laws were also amended, including the Act on the Supreme Court and on the National Council of the Judiciary. The reform of the judiciary, which began in 2015, continues to this day.

[3] Konstytucja Rzeczypospolitej Polskiej, Dz.U. z 1997 r. nr 78, poz. 483/The Constitution of the Republic of Poland, Journal of Laws of the Republic of Poland of 1997, No. 78, item 483. The Republic of Poland shall be a democratic state ruled by law and implementing the principles of social justice. Article 2 states the following: "The Republic of Poland is a democratic state governed by the rule of law, which realises the principles of social justice." English translation of the Constitution: https://www.sejm.gov.pl/prawo/konst/angielski/kon1.htm

[4] Barcik (2017), pp. 35 f.

[5] The fundamental right to freedom of expression is guaranteed in Art. 54 of the RP Constitution. Art. 54 para. 1 states the following: "The freedom to express opinions and to obtain or disseminate information shall be guaranteed to everyone English translation of the Constitution: https://www.sejm.gov.pl/prawo/konst/angielski/kon1.htm

[6] Freedom of expression and freedom of information are guaranteed in the most important human rights catalogues of the United Nations, the Council of Europe and the European Union, see: Art. 19 of the Universal Declaration of Human Rights of 10 December 1948: "Everyone has the right to freedom of opinion and expression; this right includes freedom to hold opinions without interference and to seek, receive and impart information and ideas through any media and regardless of

Those in favour of freedom of expression by judges hold the view that a judge is also a citizen and can freely exercise all the rights granted to citizens.[7] In fact, however, in the case of the expression of opinion we are dealing with a right that is not unlimited. Particularly in the case of judges, there is a conflict between the freedom of expression and the special rules of conduct in public sphere incumbent on judges. The Polish legislator has provided for certain restrictions in such cases.[8] These result primarily from the special position of judges in the system of state power and their specific public function in society.

In this article I will try to present the most important regulations on the legal position of judges in Poland, with particular emphasis on the right to freedom of expression, and to find an answer to the question of whether under Polish law judges are allowed to participate in public debate and express their opinions on current reforms in the judiciary and on political events.

3 The Legal Position of Polish Judges

The legal position of judges is regulated in the Polish legal system at both the constitutional[9] and statutory level.[10] In addition, there are special regulations, the so-called fundamental rules of professional ethics for judges.[11] In this article, the legal position of judges is discussed only to the extent that the relevant regulations relate directly or indirectly to the expression of opinions by judges.

---

frontiers.", Art. 19 para. 1 and 2 of the International Covenant on Civil and Political Rights: "1. Everyone shall have the right to hold opinions without interference. 2. Everyone shall have the right to freedom of expression; this right shall include freedom to seek, receive and impart information and ideas of all kinds, regardless of frontiers, either orally, in writing or in print, in the form of art, or through any other media of his choice." Art. 10 para. 1 of the European Convention on Human Rights: "Everyone has the right to freedom of expression. This right shall include freedom to hold opinions and to receive and impart information and ideas without interference by public authority and regardless of frontiers." Or Art. 11 para. 1 of the Charter of Fundamental Rights of the European Union: "Everyone has the right to freedom of expression. This right shall include freedom to hold opinions and to receive and impart information and ideas without interference by public authority and regardless of frontiers."

[7] According to the Polish constitution, freedom of expression is a human right, not only for Polish citizens, but for everyone.

[8] See Jabłoński et al. (2023), p. 53 f. and Kaczmarek (2022), p. 90

[9] The Constitution of the Republic of Poland contains provisions on courts and tribunals in a separate chapter. It is Chapter VIII Courts and Tribunals (Art. 173 to Art. 201).

[10] Applicable laws regulate the organisation and functioning of the courts and tribunals, as well as the legal position of the judges at these courts and tribunals. I will refer to these provisions later in the article.

[11] Resolution of the National Council of the Judiciary of 19 February 2003, adopted on the basis of Art. 2 para. 1 no. 8 of the Act of 27 July 2001 on the National Council of the Judiciary, Journal of Laws No. 100, item 1082; this is a set of the so-called moral standards that are addressed to judges and regulate their conduct both on and off duty.

3.1 *Constitutional Regulations of the Legal Position of Judges*

The relevant constitutional provisions regulating the legal position of judges can be found in the chapter of the Constitution[12] on fundamental rights and freedoms,[13] as well as in a separate chapter regulating the organisation of the judiciary in general.[14] Article 45(1) of the Constitution of the Republic of Poland guarantees everyone the right to be heard in court.[15] The legislator emphasised that the court should be independent[16] and impartial. This provision directly concerns the rights of the individual, but indirectly refers to the important principle of the independence and impartiality of judges. Other provisions concerning the legal status of judges are contained in Chapter VIII of the Polish Constitution. Of particular importance are the provisions of Article 173, which guarantees the independence of the courts, and Article 178 (1), according to which judges are independent in the exercise of their office and subject only to the Constitution and the law. Section 3 imposes certain restrictions on the public activities of judges, which also affect their right to freedom of expression. According to Article 178 (3), judges may neither belong to a political party or a trade union nor engage in public activities that are incompatible with the principles of the independence of the courts and judges.

The freedom of expression by judges is therefore not explicitly guaranteed in the constitution for the representatives of this professional group. It is only a general provision of this freedom, which applies to all people, regardless of their profession. It is therefore a general fundamental right guaranteed by the Constitution of the Republic of Poland.

---

[12] Konstytucja Rzeczypospolitej Polskiej Dz.U. z 1997 r. nr 78, poz. 483./ The Constitution of the Republic of Poland, Journal of Laws of 1997, No. 78, item 483.

[13] Chapter II Freedoms, rights and duties of the individual and of the citizen, general principles (Art. 30 to Art. 86).

[14] Chapter VIII Courts and tribunals.

[15] Article 45 states the following: Everyone shall have the right to a fair and public hearing of his case, without undue delay, before a competent, impartial and independent court. English translation of the Constitution: https://www.sejm.gov.pl/prawo/konst/angielski/kon1.htm

[16] In the Polish legal system, one speaks of both the independence of the courts and the independence of judges. The Polish legislator uses two terms: "niezależność sądów" and "niezawisłość sędziów". The first term, "niezależność sądów", is translated as the independence or autonomy of the courts and also refers directly to the principle of the tripartite division of powers. According to this principle, the judicial power is a separate and independent power in the state from the other two powers, the legislative and executive powers. The term "niezawisłość sędziów" is translated as the independence of judges and means that judges are only bound by the constitution and the law in their work and should therefore remain free from instructions or other unauthorised influence from other persons, including their superiors.

3.2 Statutory Regulations of the Legal Position of Judges

When it comes to statutory regulations, these are laws that regulate the organisation and functioning of courts in Poland and thus also the legal position of all Polish judges. The most important and comprehensive law in this area is the Act on the Organisation of Courts of General Jurisdiction.[17] The provisions of this Act supplement and develop the general rules contained in Articles 173 and 178 of the Constitution, which emphasise the principle of the independence of judges. Reference should be made in particular to Article 66 (1) of the Act on the Organisation of Courts of General Jurisdiction, which states that when appointed by the President of the Republic of Poland, judges shall take the following oath before him: "I solemnly swear to serve the Republic of Poland faithfully as a judge of a court of general jurisdiction, to uphold the law, to fulfil my judicial duties conscientiously, to administer justice in accordance with the law and impartially according to my conscience, to maintain the confidentiality protected by law and to be guided in my proceedings by the principles of dignity and honesty".[18] The content of the judicial oath contains the essence of judicial professional ethics and a model of judicial behaviour. Maintaining confidentiality also relates, among other things, to freedom of expression and represents a legal restriction on this freedom. This provision is supplemented by Article 82 of the Act on the Organisation of Courts of General Jurisdiction. Article 82 directly imposes on judges the duty to act in accordance with the oath they have taken and to uphold the authority and dignity of the judicial office. This rule must be observed both on and off duty. Furthermore, judges are obliged to avoid anything that could bring the dignity of the judge into disrepute or weaken confidence in his or her impartiality. A judge can be prosecuted in disciplinary proceedings for violating these principles pursuant to Article 107 of the Act on the Organisation of Courts of General Jurisdiction. Public activities that are incompatible with the principles of the independence of the courts and the independence of judges and misconduct that violates the dignity of the office are expressly specified by the legislator as grounds for disciplinary proceedings against a judge.

The Act on the Organisation of Courts of General Jurisdiction therefore does not expressly guarantee freedom of expression by judges, but neither does it prohibit it. This freedom can be derived from the regulations governing the behaviour of judges, but special restrictions must also be observed.

According to the views of legal scholars and commentators (doctrine), the principle of the impartiality of judges and the preservation of the dignity of the judicial office applies not only in court proceedings, but also in public. This means that

[17] Act of 27 July 2001 on the Organisation of Courts of General Jurisdiction, Journal of Laws, 2001, No. 98, item 1070. Relevant provisions on the legal status of judges are also contained in the laws relating to special courts, namely the Act on the Organisation of Military Courts, Journal of Laws of the Republic of Poland, No. 117, item 753. 1997 No. 117 item 753, the Act on the Organisation of the Administrative Courts, Journal of Laws, 2002, No. 153 item 1269 and the Act on the Supreme Court, Journal of Laws, 2018 item 5.

[18] The person taking the oath can add the sentence: "So help me God" at the end.

judges are obliged to behave accordingly, even outside of their office, and to take into account the restrictions resulting from the legal regulations when expressing their opinions. Judges should therefore refrain from expressing their religious views, political opinions or opinions about persons holding public office. These restrictions are directly related to the exercise of the office of judge and at the same time constitute a restriction of the freedom of expression guaranteed to everyone in Article 54(1) of the Polish Constitution.[19]

3.3 *Regulations in the Area of Professional Ethics*

The Code of Ethics for Judges constitutes a special regulation relating to the legal position and conduct of judges. This regulation is not a source of generally applicable law within the meaning of the Polish Constitution but remains binding on judges as an internal regulation.[20] The uniqueness of this regulation lies in the fact that its legal basis is contained directly in the statute.[21] Moreover, it was also adopted by a special constitutional body that has been responsible for monitoring the independence of courts and judges since 1989, namely the National Council of the Judiciary.[22] This also guarantees that this set of professional ethical principles for

[19] See, among others, Wróblewski (2017), p. 30.

[20] Mikosz (2015), p. 61.

[21] The obligation to adopt a set of principles of professional ethics for judges stems from Article 3(1)(3) of the Act on the National Council of the Judiciary, Journal of Laws of the Republic of Poland, 2011, No. 126, item 714. 2011, No. 126, item 714; it should be noted that Poland is the only country in Europe where the adoption of such a code of professional ethics for judges is required by law. See the commentary by Romer and Najda (2007), p. 177.

[22] The organisation and tasks of the National Council of the Judiciary are governed by Articles 186 and 187 of the Constitution of the Republic of Poland and the details are set out in the Act on the National Council of the Judiciary, Journal of Laws of the Republic of Poland, 2011, No. 126, item 714. 2011, No. 126, item 714. Since the reforms of the judicial system in Poland, the position of the National Council of the Judiciary has also been called into question. The reason for this is the amendment to the Act of 8 December 2017, Journal of Laws of the Republic of Poland, item 3. According to the new regulations, the method of appointing the National Council of the Judiciary was changed so that the Sejm took over the election of judges as members of the National Council of the Judiciary. In addition, the amendment to the Act prematurely interrupted the current term of office of the members of the National Council of the Judiciary, which is contrary to the provisions of Art. 187(3) of the Constitution of the RP. The term of office in the National Council of the Judiciary was equated with the legislative term of the Sejm, which, with the new method of electing members, significantly jeopardises the principle of the independence of the National Council of the Judiciary from the legislative and executive power. This contradicts the provisions of Art. 173 and Art. 10 of the Polish Constitution (principle of the separation of powers and the independence of the judiciary). Until the controversial amendment to the law was introduced, representatives of judges to the National Council of the Judiciary were elected by judges and not by the legislature. The change in the law was widely criticised by constitutional lawyers, representatives of the judiciary and lawyers' organisations. As the National Council of the Judiciary proposes candidates for judicial office to the President of the Republic of Poland, the entire appointment

judges was drawn up by those who know the judiciary best and for whom it is of particular importance that the constitutionally guaranteed right to a fair hearing is actually guaranteed to everyone at the highest level and with a guarantee of independence.[23] The Code of Ethics for Judges contains certain restrictions relating to both the professional sphere and the private sphere of judges. It was first adopted on 19 February 2003[24] and has since been amended several times, most recently in 2017.[25]

4 Professional Ethical Restrictions on the Expression of Opinions by Judges

This set of ethical principles for judges consists of three basic parts. The first part contains general principles on the rules of conduct for judges; the regulations in the second part concern the exercise of the office and the third part contains regulations on the principles that a judge must observe outside the office.

In this article, I will focus only on the provisions relating to freedom of expression by judges. The remaining provisions are not discussed here.

Section (§) 1 of the Code of Ethics for Judges is the most significant for the entire professional ethics regulation discussed here. It states that the exercise of the office of judge is associated with special obligations and personal restrictions. This provision is then supplemented and developed in §2 and §4 of the Code. According to §2, a judge should always be guided by the principles of decency, dignity, honour and a sense of duty and observe good morals. Section (§) 4 states the following: A judge should have regard to the authority of his office, the welfare of the court in which he serves, and the good of the administration of justice and the constitutional position of the judiciary. According to Section (§) 6, these general principles also apply to retired judges and assessors (associate judges). A judge is therefore bound by the

procedure for judges appointed under the amendment (at all levels of the judiciary in Poland) is being called into question.

[23] The decision of the National Council of the Judiciary on the professional ethical principles for judges was a reaction to the increasing criticism of the judicial system.

[24] Resolution of the National Council of the Judiciary No. 16/2003, Uchwała Krajowej Rady Sądownictwa nr 16/2003, https://krs.pl/pl/o-radzie/zbior-zasad-etyki-zawodowej-sedziow.html

[25] Resolutions of the National Council of the Judiciary No. 741/2009, No. 1295/2015, No. 14/17, No. 15/17, No. 25/2017, Uchwały Krajowej Rady Sądownictwa nr 741/2009, nr 1295/2015, nr 14/17, nr 15/17, nr 25/2017, https://www.krs.pl/pl/o-radzie/zbior-zasad-etyki-zawodowej-sedziow/591-uchwala-nr-25-2017-krajowej-rady-sadownictwa-z-dnia-13-stycznia-2017-r.html; The need to adopt professional ethical principles for judges was not addressed in the Polish legal system until the turn of the twentieth and twenty-first centuries. However, the first discussions on this topic took place at the end of the nineteenth century. For more on the history of professional ethical principles for judges, see, among others, Korzeniewska-Lasota (2017), pp. 265 ff. and the literature cited there.

principles of professional ethics both in the exercise of his or her office and outside of it, as well as after retirement.

Among the individual provisions, Section (§) 13 contains a direct prohibition on making public statements about court proceedings conducted or to be conducted by the judge. This prohibition appears to be clear and in principle does not give rise to any doubts.[26] As in the case of other professions of public trust, judges are also obliged to maintain the confidentiality of the information entrusted to them.[27]

The third part contains the regulations on the conduct of judges outside of their official duties. Here, judges are prohibited from belonging to any organisations operating outside the legal system and from supporting them in any way.[28] This section also contains specific prohibitions relating to the financial affairs of judges.[29] The last provision, which relates directly to the use of social media and thus also to freedom of expression, is a new addition to the set of professional ethics principles for judges. This provision was added in 2017. Pursuant to Section 23, judges must use social media with restraint. Before this provision was added to the set of professional ethics principles, the National Council of the Judiciary published its opinion and interpretation on public statements by judges.[30] This opinion emphasised that the office of judge is associated with special duties and personal restrictions and that a judge must uphold good morals, ensure the authority of his or her office, the welfare of the court in which he or she serves, the welfare of the administration of justice and the constitutional status of the judiciary. These restrictions concern, among other things, participation in public life. The National Council of the Judiciary referred to the provisions of the Constitution and the Act on the Organisation of Courts of General Jurisdiction, which prohibit judges from participating in public activities that are incompatible with the principles of the independence of the judiciary and the independence of judges.[31] The fundamental provisions of the Code of Ethics for Judges on the protection of morality, the authority of the office of judge and the court in which he works and the constitutional status of the judiciary were also mentioned.[32] This opinion was a direct reaction of the National Council of the Judiciary to the increasingly frequent activities of judges on social media, where

[26] Since this case concerns confidentiality obligations, which are also common in the exercise of other professions, I will not deal with this aspect of the judges' freedom of expression in detail.

[27] See, among others, Mikosz (2015), p. 68.

[28] § 22 of the Set of Principles of Professional Ethics (the Code of Ethics for Judges).

[29] According to § 17–19 of the Code of Ethics for Judges, the acceptance of financial benefits or economic contacts that could in any way compromise the impartiality and impartiality of judges is prohibited.

[30] The opinion of the National Council of the Judiciary of 13 October 2016 on public Statements made by Judges, Stanowisko Krajowej Rady Sądownictwa z dnia 13 października 2016 r. w sprawie publicznych wypowiedzi sędziów, https://sip.lex.pl/akty-prawne/akty-korporacyjne/publiczne-wypowiedzi-sedziow-286864843

[31] This is Article 178(3) of the Constitution of the Republic of Poland and Article 82(2) of the Act on the Organisation of the Courts of General Jurisdiction.

[32] §2 and §4 of the Code of Ethics for Judges.

they have criticised the judicial reform.[33] In principle, according to these opinions, a judge should uphold the dignity of his office both on and off duty and avoid anything that could discredit the judge's dignity or weaken confidence in his impartiality.

In its opinion, the National Council of the Judiciary emphasised that a judge, as a citizen, can enjoy the right to participate in public debate if this concerns, for example, legal issues, the independence of the courts and the independence of judges, the organisation of the judiciary or the position of judges. However, a judge should carefully consider the content and form of any public statement he or she makes. This also applies to statements made in online forums, on social media (e.g. Facebook, Twitter—currently "X"), blogs published on the internet and any other activity in electronic media. When using these forms of participation in public life, a judge should exercise restraint and ensure in every situation that the content of his or her statements does not give rise to accusations of lack of impartiality, political engagement or a breach of public decency. A judge should also consider whether there is actually a need to actively use these forms of expression in the particular case. The National Council of the Judiciary concludes its opinion with a reference to the fact that a violation of the rule contained in the Code of Judicial Ethics may result in disciplinary proceedings being initiated against the judge.[34]

Disciplinary proceedings were indeed initiated against a number of judges on the grounds that they had violated the dignity of a judge by expressing their opinion in public. Many were suspended from office and their salaries were reduced. The purpose of these disciplinary proceedings and penalties was above all to prevent judges from engaging in any public activities; the aim was to achieve a so-called deterrent effect.

In 2021, the National Council of the Judiciary once again published an opinion. This time it was about the so-called certain statements made by judges on social media.[35] The National Council of the Judiciary justified this opinion with great concern and disappointment that statements made by some representatives of the judiciary, in its view, disregard the statutory bodies of the courts and call for their statutory powers not to be recognised. The National Council of the Judiciary therefore emphasised once again that such statements can weaken public confidence in the courts and impair the fulfilment of duties by these bodies. In its view, such behaviour may constitute a breach of the judge's duty to look after the welfare of the

[33] These critical statements were of course not to the liking of those in power and the National Council of the Judiciary, which has since been reappointed by those in power, in an attempt to restrict the activities of the judges in this way. This description refers to the situation prior to the October 2023 elections.

[34] A special chamber of the Supreme Court is responsible for initiating and conducting disciplinary proceedings against a judge, namely the Disciplinary Chamber established in 2017 as part of a reform of the Supreme Court; in 2022 it was replaced by the Professional Responsibility Chamber.

[35] The opinion of the National Council of the Judiciary of 29 October 2021 on certain statements made by judges on social media, Stanowisko Krajowej Rady Sądownictwa z dnia 29 października 2021 w sprawie niektórych wypowiedzi sędziów w mediach społecznościowych, https://sip.lex.pl/akty-prawne/akty-korporacyjne/niektore-wypowiedzi-sedziow-w-mediach-spolecznosciowych-287626369

court in which he or she is working, as well as the welfare of the judiciary and the constitutional status of the judiciary, and may violate the duty to act conscientiously in accordance with common decency. With this opinion, the National Council of the Judiciary has once again appealed to judges to exercise restraint and courtesy when publicly expressing their opinions, so that they always take into account the legal order of the Republic of Poland and the welfare of the administration of justice.

5 Ethical Code of a Judge at the Constitutional Court

It is noteworthy at this point that the judges of the Constitutional Court have adopted a separate code of ethics. The legal basis for this was Article 6 para. 2 point 10 of the Act of 30 November 2016 on the Organisation and Procedure before the Constitutional Court.[36] The manner in which the resolution was passed was peculiar. The Code of Ethics was adopted during the General Assembly of Judges of the Constitutional Court on 31 August 2017, but the resolution was never published, neither in an official journal nor on the website of the Constitutional Court.[37] The provisions of Chapter 4 regulate the participation of Constitutional Court judges in public life, and Section 16 sets out the principles of their participation in public debates and the expression of their own opinions. According to these provisions, a judge at the Constitutional Court may enjoy freedom of expression in a manner that is compatible with the dignity of the office and has no influence on the independence or impartiality of the judge. A judge at the Constitutional Court may also participate in public debate on legal issues, but may not comment on matters pending before the Constitutional Court. The participation of judges in public political debate is completely prohibited. A judge at the Constitutional Court should avoid statements that could jeopardise the status, authority and integrity of the Constitutional Court.[38]

These provisions actually deviate from the aforementioned general principles that apply to all judges. As this code has never been the subject of debate and there has been no official information on its application by the Constitutional Court, it is

[36] The Act of 30 November 2016 on the Organisation and Procedure before the Constitutional Court, Journal of Laws of 2016 item 2072.

[37] In the middle of the holiday period, the judges were informed of the date of the meeting by means of a note left on their desks on 30 August 2017, i.e. the day before; they were neither sent an email with the invitation to the meeting nor informed by telephone. See Sitnicka (2019) and Kodeks Etyczny Sędziego Trybunału Konstytucyjnego. Czy K. Pawłowicz i S. Piotrowicz spełniają jego surowe wymogi? A Julia Przyłębska, czy Kodeksu przestrzega?, https://monitorkonstytucyjny.eu/archiwa/11259

[38] See e.g. Laskowski (2023a), p. 11.

not possible to judge what impact it actually has on the judges at the Constitutional Court.[39]

6 Conclusions

So if we ask ourselves the question of whether a judge who publicly expresses his usually critical opinion on the current state of the judiciary is actually violating judicial dignity and weakening the reputation of the courts, we can hear different answers.

From the point of view of those still in power (Prawo i Sprawiedliwość),[40] this is of course an obvious and gross violation of the special ethical standards that apply to judges. However, those for whom the principle of the rule of law and the principle of the independence of courts and judges are particularly important will even praise such judges for their public activities.[41]

Judges are people who, thanks to their knowledge of the law and often many years of professional experience, as well as the exercise of this particularly highly regarded profession in society, are also considered an authority. And such authorities are also expected not to remain silent, especially in a situation in which the rule of law, as a special democratic value guaranteed in the constitution, is jeopardised by the activities of other public authorities.[42] At a time when many citizens actually only obtain their information from the internet and social media, the participation of experienced judges in the debates conducted there is even desirable.

To summarise, then, I would say that every judge is also a citizen who may enjoy certain rights and freedoms granted to him and who can and definitely has certain political views. However, the right to freedom of expression should be regarded by judges as a restricted right because of the nature of the profession they exercise. Therefore, as long as the activity of judges in public and the opinions expressed there by judges do not have a negative influence on the exercise of their profession and the administration of justice in specific cases, and as long as judges act in accordance with constitutional, legal and ethical principles, i.e. in particular with regard to the dignity of the judicial office and the principle of the independence of the courts, their right to freedom of expression should not be further restricted, let alone completely withdrawn. In view of their special position in society, judges are obliged to maintain higher standards of behaviour in public than the average citizen. This also results in responsibility for public statements. Restrictions in the area of

[39] Unfortunately, there are judges at the Constitutional Court who frequently violate these provisions and compromise the dignity of the office of judge on their social media or in public statements. However, these violations have not yet led to disciplinary proceedings.

[40] This statement refers to the situation prior to the October 2023 elections. A change of government occurred on 13 December 2023.

[41] See among others, Laskowski (2023a), p. 8.

[42] See also a commentary by Laskowski (2023b); Wróblewski (2017), p. 32.

freedom of expression are therefore justified in principle, particularly if the independence and impartiality of judges and the authority of the judiciary are called into question by public statements.[43] The problem of whether and to what extent the right to freedom of expression may be restricted in the case of judges lies more in the vagueness of the restrictive provisions and their interpretation.[44] This causes these regulations to be understood and interpreted differently and also leads to a shift in the limits of freedom of expression in individual cases and in special circumstances.

References

Journal Article

Barcik J (2017) Standardy udziału sędziów w sferze publicznej w dokumentach międzynarodowych. Krajowa Rada Sądownictwa 1

Jabłoński P, Kaczmarek P, Wojtanowski M (2023) Wolność ekspresji sędziego. Próba konceptualizacji, Państwo i Prawo 1:53–79

Kaczmarek P (2022) Wolność wypowiedzi sędziego w perspektywie pełnionych obowiązków. Krytyka Prawa 14(4):90–104

Korzeniewska-Lasota A (2017) Z polskich prac nad kodyfikacją zasad etyki sędziowskiej. Studia Warmińskie 54:265–275. https://doi.org/10.31648/sw.71

Laskowski M (2023a) Granice wolności wypowiedzi sędziego w warunkach kryzysu praworządności. Przegląd Sądowy 3:7–17

Laskowski M (2023b) Jakie są granice wypowiedzi sędziego. https://www.rp.pl/sady-i-trybunaly/art2377431-jakie-sa-granice-wypowiedzi-sedziego

Sitnicka D (2019) Tajny Kodeks Etyczny Sędziów TK dyskwalifikujący dla Pawłowicz i Piotrowicza. Publikujemy dokument. https://archiwumosiatynskiego.pl/wpis-w-debacie/tajny-kodeks-etyczny-sedziow-tk-dyskwalifikujacy-dla-pawlowicz-i-piotrowicza-publikujemy-dokument/

Szuleka M, Wolny M, Szwed M (2016) Kryzys konstytucyjny w Polsce 2015–2016, Warszawa. https://archiwumosiatynskiego.pl/images/2017/10/HFPC-Kryzys-konstytucyjny-w-Polsce-2015-2016.pdf

Wróblewski M (2017) Granice ekspresji i wypowiedzi sędziego - zarys problemu. Krajowa Rada Sądownictwa 1

Books

Romer T, Najda M (2007) Etyka dla sędziów. Rozważania, Warszawa

---

[43] See, among others, Laskowski (2023a), p. 10.

[44] Op.cit. p. 15.

Book Chapters

Mikosz R (2015) Granice wolności wypowiedzi sędziego. In: Biłgorajski R (ed) Granice wolności wypowiedzi przedstawicieli zawodów prawniczych. Wolters Kluver, Warszawa, pp 56–83

Online Document

Kodeks Etyczny Sędziego Trybunału Konstytucyjnego. Czy K. Pawłowicz i S. Piotrowicz spełniają jego surowe wymogi? A Julia Przyłębska, czy Kodeksu przestrzega?, https://monitorkonstytucyjny.eu/archiwa/11259

Stanowisko Krajowej Rady Sądownictwa z dnia 13 października 2016 r. w sprawie publicznych wypowiedzi sędziów, https://sip.lex.pl/akty-prawne/akty-korporacyjne/publiczne-wypowiedzi-sedziow-286864843

Stanowisko Krajowej Rady Sądownictwa z dnia 29 października 2021 w sprawie niektórych wypowiedzi sędziów w mediach społecznościowych, https://sip.lex.pl/akty-prawne/akty-korporacyjne/niektore-wypowiedzi-sedziow-w-mediach-spolecznosciowych-287626369,

Uchwała Krajowej Rady Sądownictwa nr 16/2003, https://krs.pl/pl/o-radzie/zbior-zasad-etyki-zawodowej-sedziow.html, https://krs.pl/pl/o-radzie/zbior-zasad-etyki-zawodowej-sedziow.html

Uchwały Krajowej Rady Sądownictwa nr 741/2009, nr 1295/2015, nr 14/17, nr 15/17, nr 25/2017. https://www.krs.pl/pl/o-radzie/zbior-zasad-etyki-zawodowej-sedziow/591-uchwala-nr-25-2017-krajowej-rady-sadownictwa-z-dnia-13-stycznia-2017-r.html

An Ethical Vision of Judicial Secrecy and Judicial Discretion in an Environment of Transparency

Cristina Hermida del Llano

Abstract This contribution reviews the three main principles enshrined in judicial ethics (independence, impartiality and integrity) and shows how ethics have become pillars for the Rule of Law (legality, separation of powers, and protection of fundamental rights and freedoms). Within the professional ethics of judicial power, a distinction is made between the ethic virtues of an impartial, independent and upright judge or magistrate, which are related to the principles of judicial ethics, and the professional skills exercised by the judge or magistrate in his or her specific professional activity (diligence, listening skills, empathy, circumspection, caution, etc.). The task of judging is proper to a "craftsman of the law". The author reflects on the ethical duty of judicial secrecy, and how judicial secrecy and judicial discretion in an environment of transparency implies that every judgment must be "pronounced according to the right reason of prudence".

This article is part of the research project, which I am the main researcher of, entitled "La libertad de expresión del juez en el marco del respeto a los principios de ética judicial en España" (PID2021-127122NB-I00). Ministry of Science and Innovation—E05071301. This contribution was translated by Verónica Guillén Melo for the *Newsletter of the Academy of Yuste*, nº 20, October, 2022, and published in the *Anuario de la Fundación Yuste*, 2023.

C. H. del Llano (✉)
Department of Public Law, Universidad Rey Juan Carlos, Madrid, Spain
e-mail: cristina.hermida@urjc.es

C. Hermida del Llano (ed.), *The Freedom of Expression for Judges in the Sphere of the Judicial Ethics*, Ius Gentium: Comparative Perspectives on Law and Justice 129, https://doi.org/10.1007/978-3-032-06504-9_18

1 Introduction

Ethics as "speculatively practical science",[1] performs an important task, which s to reflect on and substantiate the actions, conduct or behaviors of people in ociety. It could be said that while morality as a structure reveals the radically moral and inalienable structure of human behaviors, that is, the adjustment of the act to the situation, on the other hand, morality as a content, following the terminology of Zubiri and Aranguren,[2] would indicate that the act must be adjusted not to the given situation or reality, but to the ethical norm. As Aranguren emphasised, "ethical perfection must be made in time and over time. Our projects are forged in time, perfection is qualitatively different over the years, «life experience» is the experience of the life one lives".[3] The latter indicates that it is also up to ethics to deal with what is moral in its specificity, without limiting itself to a particular morality, which is precisely what concerns us here: judicial secrecy and discretion in an environment of transparency.[4]

Indeed, this issue obliges us to enter the world of the legitimacy of law, which crosses the borders of mere systems of legality, always assuming that legality and legitimacy are two different things[5] that are worth keeping differentiated, even if we know that any system of legality responds to a certain system of legitimacy.[6] In fact, the ethical vision of judicial secrecy and judicial discretion invites us to note that behind every system of legality a certain conception of justice emerges that tries to break through to impose itself socially through adherence or social legitimation. We must not forget that social coexistence must be subject to a rationality that is shared by all subjects, while aware that it is us citizens who must worry about guaranteeing a minimum of ethics in order for the rule of law to function properly.[7] This mainly indicates two things: firstly, that appealing to non-negotiable ethical principles is not a form of intolerance that disqualifies for democracy or the proper functioning of the

[1] As Aranguren (1958) explains: "The moral work of man seems to consist in the thread of the Greek etymology, in the acquisition of a way of being. But this way of being is achieved and affirmed gradually, so that there are different levels of appropriation, so to speak. The lowest would be that of pathos, that of feelings, which are certainly mine, but perhaps temporary and, in any case, scarcely dependent on my will. Customs already imply a higher degree of possession. Above them, character constitutes an impression of traits in the person him/herself: character is the personality we have conquered through life, what we have made of ourselves, when living", p. 23.

[2] See J. L. L. Aranguren: Chap. 7 "Moral como contenido" of his book Ética, ibidem, pp. 176–187.

[3] Ibidem, p. 147.

[4] Let us bear in mind, following Cortina, that "civic ethics is reinforced when the organisation of democratic life encourages the development of virtues such as the passion for justice and freedom, the embodiment of solidarity, active respect for positions other than one's own, recourse to a fair dialogue to resolve conflicts, provided the conditions are in place". See Cortina (2007), p. 17.

[5] Ferrajoli (2011, 2016), p. 803.

[6] Díaz (1996).

[7] Nieto Blanco (2020)

rule of law;[8] secondly, that the lifeblood of the rule of law is precisely the civic ethics of citizens. As we must not forget, as Cortina points out, that "ethics is intended to contribute to the formation of the character of individuals, institutions and peoples".[9]

This defense of individual freedom to embrace an ethical code is very important when dealing with the subject tackled here. It should be made clear that what is reasonable for political institutions not to be those which shape the personal and moral convictions of citizens—since paternalistic positions are not supported here[10]—but that citizens themselves be the ones who, making use of their individual freedom, shape political institutions, acting in them according to their own personal and moral convictions, that is, according to their conscience.[11] As Laporta rightly pointed out: "For Kant, the paternal government that treats subjects as children is the greatest conceivable despotism, and anything but a legislation that guarantees the coexistence of individual freedoms is the expression of a political constitution.

The State that seeks the happiness of citizens over their freedom is an illegitimate State".[12] However, when developing a dialogically shaped public reason, ways must be created in the democratic society to increase the moral responsibility of its citizens because, as Rawls himself states, "deliberative democracy also recognises that without a broad education of all citizens in the basic aspects of democratic constitutionalism, and without an informed public on priority issues, crucial political and social decisions cannot be made".[13] This is so to the point that this dialogically shaped public reason is nourished by ethics, understood as a "moral compass" that will not function in a defective way. In short, we have to be aware that a better or worse use of our moral compass leads us to change the world in a positive or negative sense. Let us not forget that ethics serves to change and try to enhance attitudes that make a different world possible,[14] ultimately turning out to be a launch pad for social change, as happens with law. That is why it is worth opting for a civic ethics that, as Cortina stresses, "encourages the ethics of religious and secular leaders to present their offers of life in full, provided they do not violate the values of freedom, equality, solidarity, active respect and dialogue".[15]

[8] On the material conception of the rule of law, vid. Waldron (2020). Also vid. Bingham (2010). In like manner, I recommend Reading Ferrajoli, Luigi's book. (2020).

[9] Cortina (2013), p. 34. As specified by Aranguren, J. L. L. in his book Ética, op. cit.: "It is through the actions that we carry put through life that we become good or evil", p. 180.

[10] On the juridical-political meaning of paternalism, vid. Laporta (1995).

[11] Orientaciones morales ante la situación actual de España, Madrid, 23 November 2006. Instrucción Pastoral. Available at: https://mercaba.org/CEE/orientaciones_morales_ante_la_si.htm

[12] Laporta F. Entre la moral y el derecho, op. cit., p. 54.

[13] Rawls (2001), pp. 163–164.

[14] Cortina A. ¿Para qué sirve realmente la ética?, op. cit., p. 17. I recommend reading the thesis that led to Rodríguez Medina's master's degree (2015).

[15] See Cortina A. Ética de la razón cordial. Educar entre la ciudadanía, op. cit., p. 17.

2 From Ethics to the Principles of Judicial Ethics in the Rule of Law

The transference of ethics to the rule of law necessarily involves professional ethics. I would like to stress here that respect for the principles of professional ethics is crucial for the proper functioning of the Rule of Law. Let us bear in mind that the rule of law is not an immutable legal structure, but rather depends on continuous citizen action for its development. In short, the rule of law is a field for dialogue, debate and rational confrontation of social projects aimed at reforming existing institutions, where ethics cannot be relegated to the background. We must, therefore, flee from the position that professional ethics is detached from general ethics. Every trade serves a social purpose or, what is the same, serves an end in society. I would like to insist on this. Regardless of the profession held by each, care should be taken consciously to forge the êthos, the character of the professional activity that each one carries out, which is formed with values, principles and virtues, not with the mere observance of legal norms. In fact, the idea of complementing deontological codes, that are based on legal norms with threats of punishment, with others of an ethical nature, are based on this desire on the premise that when the exercise of professional activity requires excellence, then legal compliance alone is insufficient. As Bonete pointed out: "the problem of what is the «unconditional good» constitutes (…) the primary objective of professional ethics that seeks to minimally guide the moral life of a profession through norms, values and virtues".[16]

It is important to stress that the disciplinary regime has nothing to do with general ethics. The latter is conceivable only in terms of strict voluntariness and absence of legal responsibility, unlike the disciplinary one that refers to a set of mandatory rules whose violation carries legal consequences of greater or lesser importance. General ethics operates as a positive stimulus to excellence, while the disciplinary regime operates on the basis of negative stimulus, that is, through penalising norms.

It is worthwhile to remember the rationalist ius naturale philosopher Thomasius (1655–1728), among others, who, in his classification of the three spheres of human behaviour in honestum, iustum and decorum, could not see it clearer.[17] Indeed, the differentiation made by Thomasius reveals that if ethics is to be differentiated from deontology it is because in the ethical sphere there is no state coercion as it is part of a circle of intangible individual subjectivity, which understands the world of ideas, beliefs and what has to do with oneself, which is protected by the protective mantle of freedom and where no one can enter.[18]

The principles of professional ethics are very versatile to the extent that they are adapted and modulated according to each specific professional activity. Here, as an example, we will take the functioning of ethical principles within the judicial sphere, assuming that the judiciary is endowed with state dignity as an important part of the

[16] Bonete Perales (1995), p. 27.

[17] Laporta F. Entre la moral y el derecho, op. cit., p. 46.

[18] A preliminar study of thework by Locke (1999), pp. XXXIII-XXXVI.

rule of law. It could be said that a "Good Judge", following the terminology of Sancho Gargallo, does not lose sight of the fact that, rather than holding an office with honors, he/she serves society and citizens in a democratic system, which is compatible with being aware of the dignity of his/her mission.[19] It was the General Council of the Judiciary in Spain that initiated the process of drafting *Principios de Ética Judicial (Principles of Judicial Ethics)*, which were drafted by a commission composed of representatives of judicial associations, non-associated members of the judiciary and some experts, with the valuable participation of delegates from each High Court of Justice appointed by the respective Governing Chambers, always with the aim that the plurality of opinions in the judicial career would be reflected.

The *Principles of Judicial Ethics* in Spain were adopted at the session held on 16 December 2016 by the Working Group for the elaboration of a Code of Ethics for the Judicial Career. As stated in the Preamble, the *Principles of Judicial Ethics* aim to reflect the values and rules of conduct shared by the Spanish judiciary. They intend to serve as a guide in the performance of jurisdiction and to promote collective dialogue and personal reflection on the challenges faced by those who exercise it, in a legal and social framework that is as complex as changing. The *Principles of Judicial Ethics* also aim to strengthen the confidence of citizens in the justice system by making the models of behaviour under which judges commit themselves to carrying out their duties explicit».[20] This is so since the authority of the judge, in the end, is linked to the public confidence that he/she needs precisely to be able to exercise his/her imperium.[21]

The adoption of a text on judicial ethics originated within a favourable international framework initiated with the adoption of the *Bangalore Principles of Judicial Conduct* (2001)[22] within the framework of the United Nations, which would be followed by the *Opinion of the Consultative Council of European Judges of the Council of Europe on the Ethics and Responsibility of Judges* (2002), the *Ibero-American Model Code of Judicial Ethics* (2006)[23] adopted by the Ibero-American Judicial Summit, which was endorsed by the General Council of the Judiciary by the Plenary of 25 February 2016, and the *London Declaration on Judicial Ethics* (2010), promoted by the European Network of Councils for the Judiciary. Finally, *Recommendation No. R (2010) of 17 November of the Committee of Ministers of the Council of Europe* urges the Member States to adopt a *Code of Judicial Ethics*.[24]

This approach to judicial ethics has been welcomed at European Union level, which in recent years has shown that a large number of Member States have been

---

[19] Sancho Gargallo (2007), p. 121.

[20] Principios de Ética Judicial (2018), p. 11.

[21] Varios (2005), p. 279.

[22] The Bangalore Principles of Judicial Conduct. Adopted by the Judicial Group on Strengthening Judicial Integrity, as revised at the Round Table of Presidents of High Courts held at the Peace Palace in the Hague, the Netherlands, on 25 and 26 November 2002.

[23] Código Iberoamericano de Ética Judicial comentado (2019).

[24] See Principios de Ética Judicial, op. cit., pp. 11–12.

encouraged to subscribe to texts of judicial ethics (codes, guides, compilation of principles) with different origins (Higher Councils of the Judiciary, judicial associations, conferences of judges, presidents of courts, etc.),[25] which has highlighted the importance of respecting not only legal duties but also ethical duties in the professional sphere.

Because they are placed in normative terms on the ethical plane, in reality, the degree of effectiveness of the Principios de Ética Judicial may be greater or lesser depending on how far each judge assumes them as his/her own, internally, and manages to translate them into models of conduct.[26] In other words, effectiveness will depend, finally, on the degree of commitment of judges to the principles of professional ethics in their field of activity. As the preamble to the Principios de Ética Judicial states, «judicial ethics pursues the promise of good justice insofar as it incorporates the qualities necessary to achieve the goal assigned to it by the Constitution: the protection of the rights of citizenship».[27]

The Spanish normative text contemplates three main general principles which the judiciary is familiar with: firstly, independence, which defines a space for judicial decision free from undue influence.[28] This means that judicial independence will necessarily be based on the principle of subjecting the judge to the rule of law,[29] which requires him/her to rule solely and exclusively in accordance with the just rule drawn from the law in the light of the facts prosecuted. It is a prerequisite of the principle of legality and a fundamental guarantee of a fair trial.[30] Apart from the necessary independence of the judiciary as an organ of government, the independence of each individual judge in the exercise of his or her judicial function must be preserved.

Secondly, impartiality, which highlights the role of the judge as a third party alien to the interests at stake.[31] As Andrzej Rzeplinski warned in the opening speech of the judicial year of the European Court of Human Rights on 26 January 2016, judges must approach their work without prejudice and being open-minded, willing to pay attention to all parties and bear in mind that the person affected by their prosecution is a human being and not a mere subjective element of the case.[32] Ultimately, this feature of judges' character encompasses the ability to apply the law to the facts and to understand how a court decision will affect persons appearing in court.

---

[25] Ibidem, p. 12.

[26] Ibidem, p. 12.

[27] Ibidem, p. 13.

[28] Ibidem, p. 13. As well as Waldron (2013), pp. 433–468.

[29] On this matter, vid. Dworkin (1985), pp. 9–32. As well as, vid. Sánchez Hidalgo (2020).

[30] The reference to judicial independence in the Bangalore Code begins with this mention, approved in 2002, by the Judicial Group on Strengthening Judicial Integrity, with the assistance and support of the United Nations.

[31] Principios de Ética Judicial, op. cit., p. 13. I recommend the reading of the book written by Barry (1997).

[32] Rzeplinski (2016).

However, judges must not only be impartial, but must also be impartial in all their activities, especially when they work in community justice. The appearance of impartiality does not mean hypocrisy, but being careful not to give an image of lack of impartiality that does not correspond to reality and that harms confidence in justice.[33] The impartiality of the judge presupposes his independence.

Lastly, integrity as a principle requires those exercising jurisdiction to be consistent with the above principles and with respect for human dignity, including in their social life, in all circumstances where public confidence in justice may be in question.[34]

The Preamble to the *Principios de Ética Judicial* in Spain also contains models of conduct relating to justice as a service, such as courtesy, diligence and transparency. As stated there, their degree of compliance is directly perceived by those who go to court, thus contributing decisively to the formation of public opinion on justice and, due to that very reason, they cannot be underestimated as "minor" issues.[35]

3 From the Right to Intimacy to Judicial Secrecy

One of the characteristics that define us people is intimacy, understood as an opening inward, which corresponds to any human being simply on account of being one. It is something that one cannot renounce to. One could speak of an area that is actively and passively unavailable to individual subjects. Intimacy, as Yepes Stork pointed out, "... is not just a place where things are kept for oneself... but it is also, so to speak, an interior that grows, from which unprecedented realities spring... That is why the person is an intimacy from which novelties spring, a creative intimacy, that is able to grow".[36] Consequently, "it is not only a question of protecting something internal from strange looks, but of ensuring that what's 'internal' guides the full development of each person according to his or her dignity without illegitimate interference".[37]

In human relations, it is common to entrust matters concerning intimacy to friends, relatives, professionals, etc. If the receiver of the secret is not able to keep it and divulges it, he/she is violating the agreement which, implicitly or explicitly, he/she had settled with the speaker. With this, a part of the subject's intimacy is exposed. Hence, secrecy has its basis and raison d'être, both in the professional

[33] See Sancho Gargallo (2020), p. 449.

[34] Principios de Ética Judicial, op. cit., p. 13.

[35] Ibidem, p. 13. The system includes a Judicial Ethics Commission whose composition, functioning and procedure guarantee the confidentiality of consultations and the purely indicative nature of the opinions it issues. Duly anonymized, the Commission's opinions, recommendations and reports will be a very useful body of doctrine.

[36] See Yepes Stork (1996), pp. 76–77.

[37] Megías Quirós (2002). Quoted by Aparisi (2006), p. 253.

sphere and in a more general context, in the protection of intimacy and, ultimately, of personal dignity.

The right to intimacy is reflected in numerous declarations and constitutions. Specifically in Spain in art. 18.1 of the *Spanish Constitution* which states: "The right to honour, to personal and family intimacy and one's own image is guaranteed". One should take the fact that the concepts of intimacy and privacy are closely related into account, although they cannot be considered identical. As Espín points out, personal intimacy should be considered "the most private redoubt of the individual's life", including "the most personal extremes of his/her own life and family environment".[38] Privacy, in turn, will include broader aspects such as honour, image, the secrecy of communications, the inviolability of the home, etc. In this manner, professional secrecy would protect not only intimate data, but also public facts known by reason of professional practice.

As in the case of the health professions, in the legal field the provision of the professional service may require that, previously, intimate or private data of persons be revealed. Therefore, a strict duty of reserve and discretion arises in relation to the information obtained. As Aparisi points out: "The requirement implies not only not externalising the gathered data through this path. The reservation required by ethical virtue also includes the habit of discretion, prudence, moderation, care of oral and written language…".[39] Thus, in the case of judges, as well as for prosecutors, lawyers, court clerks or any other official in the administration of justice, there is a requirement of caution, discretion, judiciousness—professional virtues—that has numerous consequences in the field of professional ethics.

It is true that it is a requirement of professional ethics for judges to have the necessary data to be able to knowingly deliberate. In other words, judges must have in-depth knowledge of the facts and conduct of the litigants in those aspects that are related to the subject matter of the proceedings. However, this obligation is circumscribed to certain limits.

The judge must not reveal or disclose data and information known through the exercise of his office outside the scope of his professional practice. Therefore, the most appropriate thing is to extreme the virtue of discretion and prudence within an area of transparency, as referred to in number 35 of the *Principios de la Ética Judicial* in Spain: «Judges must adopt a positive attitude towards transparency as a normal mode of operation of the Administration of Justice, and to this end, they can count on the institutional communication bodies to be at their disposal». Well then, even if the individual had no objection to depriving the judge of his or her ethical duty to maintain professional secrecy, he or she must maintain an attitude of restraint and moderation. In short, it is a question of safeguarding an adequate separation between what is the particular life of the professional and "procedural life". The requirements of professional secrecy of judges and prosecutors are also clearly reflected in the legal sphere. Consider Article 24.2 and 120.1 of the Spanish

[38] Espín Templado (2003), p. 181.

[39] Aparisi A, *Ética y deontología para juristas*, op. cit., p. 256.

Constitution or the provisions regulating this issue in the Organic Law of the Judiciary, the Law of Criminal Procedure or even the Criminal Code.

The principle of professional secrecy always applies, except in case of conflict with a higher requirement of justice or with irreparable damage to democracy, the rule of law and fundamental freedoms, as contemplated in principle 21 of judicial ethics in Spain: «When democracy, the rule of law and fundamental freedoms are in danger, the obligation of reservation gives way to the duty of denunciation». In this manner, judges cannot ignore: (1) the requirement of proportionality, understood as the weighting of the goods at stake,[40] assessing the extent to which the possible damage to a third party is sufficient reason to disclose the information covered by professional secrecy; (2) the suitability of the information disclosed for the intended purpose; (3) the requirement to disclose only strictly necessary information.

In addition, judicial secrecy and discretion in an area of transparency oblige judges to behave prudently. Prudence is not only an intellectual virtue—with wisdom, intelligence, art and science, as Aristotle wrote in *Nicomachean Ethics*—but it is also a moral virtue, which applies the principles of practical reason (from *phronesis* or practical wisdom, as Plato said in *The Republic*). The practical truth is what the prudent man finds in the internal dynamics of human praxis; therefore, "Prudence constitutes true practical knowledge; the virtuous not only knows the true principles of action, but he/she acts correctly and knows how to explain and defend his/her action", in the words of Yarza.[41] Thus, following Massini, prudence, acting on intelligence, "empowers reason to know what is good in every circumstance and which is the evil to be avoided".[42] And this, like all virtue, also has an effect on the individual who acts prudently since "«the prudent not only does the work well, but does well to «him/herself», perfects him/herself in his/her more specific dimension», which has a consequence of future of great importance, because carrying out prudent acts, strengthens the prudence of those who make such decisions, making him/her acquire a practical experience, increasingly valuable and worthy of recognition".[43]

Let us bear in mind that prudence as a Dianoetic virtue is in charge of the directive function of action; as Aristotle himself says "an individual is prudent not only by knowing (what must be done), but also by being able to practice it".[44] Well, here I would like to emphasise that the prudence for the approach of a correct public reason becomes determinant for the good functioning of the rule of law.[45]

Accordingly, in my view, the judge's judgment must be a combination of two virtues: justice and prudence, since every judgment must be "pronounced according to the right reason of prudence", as Saint Thomas Aquinas observed. Safeguarding both judicial secrecy and judicial discretion in an area of transparency therefore

[40] On this topic, see Alexy (2008).

[41] Yarza (2001), p. 28.

[42] Massini Correas (1982), p. 40.

[43] *Ética del juez y garantías procesales*, Manuales de Formación Continuada 24, op. cit., p. 433.

[44] Aristóteles (1999), p. 1152.

[45] Ferrer Santos (1990), pp. 111–129. Vid. Also, Sancho Gargallo (2020), pp. 446–461.

implies acting in the interests of that "right reason of prudence" which we refer to here.

4 The Ethical Duty of Judicial Secrecy

In normative terms, the duty of professional secrecy is reflected within the principle of impartiality in chap. II of the *Principios de la Ética Judicial* in Spain, however, it also connects with the principle of the integrity of chapter III, because this as a principle reminds us that the judge represents (for many it is his image) an institution of the State: the Judiciary. The judge must put a lot of effort, as Sancho Gargallo says, into the fact that his conduct, to the extent possible, does not detract from the dignity proper to a judge, avoiding personal discredit and especially from the institution he represents.[46]

Number 22 of the *Principios de la Ética Judicial* in Spain, after noting that integrity requires the judge to observe «a conduct that reaffirms the confidence of citizens in the Administration of Justice», states that «not only in the exercise of jurisdiction, but in all those facets in which he/she is recognisable as a judge or invokes his/her status as such». Indeed, the standard of conduct required of the judge is very high, higher than that which can be demanded of any citizen. This is highlighted by all international texts. In fact, assuming the thesis that not only "being" but also "appearance" matters, the *Bangalore Principles* emphasise that the judge «shall ensure that his or her conduct is above reproach in the view of a reasonable observer» (3.1), adding that «The behaviour and conduct of a judge must reaffirm the people's faith in the integrity of the judiciary. Justice must not merely be done but must also be seen to be done» (3.2).

For its part, the *London Declaration* states that «The judge fulfils his role with integrity, in the interests of justice and society. He has the same duty of integrity in his public life and in his personal life» and adds that «Two duties can result from this principle of integrity: the duty of probity and the duty of dignity or honour». The latter, honour, «requires to a judge to ensure, through his professional practice and person, that he does not jeopardise the public image of the judge, the court and the justice system».[47] Well then, demands derived from these duties are precisely other duties included in chapter II of the *Principios de la Ética Judicial* in Spain dedicated to impartiality: the duty of professional secrecy and discretion.

Regarding the duty of professional secrecy, it should be noted that the judge is aware of many things about persons and institutions that he or she should not disclose, not only because of legal imperative relating to data protection, but also to safeguard the right to good repute of the persons involved and to avoid providing inside information.

[46] Sancho Gargallo (2022).

[47] Ibidem, pp. 58–59.

The basis for this professional secrecy lies, on the one hand, in the safeguarding of «the rights of the parties and those related against the misuse of information gathered by judges in the exercise of their duties» (art. 62 *Ibero-American Model*). *Code* This means that judges must keep absolute secret in relation to pending cases and to the facts or data known in the exercise of their functions or in connection with them, which are subject to the exceptions provided for in the legal system (art. 63 of the *Ibero-American Model Code*).

The *Bangalore Principles* (4.10) focus primarily on the requirement not to disclose inside information: «Confidential information obtained by a judge in the exercise of his judicial powers shall not be used or disclosed by the judge for any other purpose unrelated to the exercise of his judicial powers». For its part, number 19 of the *Principios de la Ética Judicial* in Spain, referring to the social life of judges and their relationship with the media, apostille at the end that «they must, in any case, show diiscretion with respect to the data that may harm the parties or the development of the process». The latter has led the Commission on many occasions to reiterate this requirement to be particularly careful not to disclose information on specific cases known, which he or she has a duty of reserve on. Not only while the trial is pending, but also in the aftermath.

For example, the opinion of the Judicial Ethics Commission in Spain of 25 February 2019 (reference 10/18) on the intervention of the judge in social networks when reflecting on the content of such participation, or the opinion of 23 October 2019 (reference 17/19) on the relationship of judges with the media in relation to pending cases. As stated in principle 20 of Judicial Ethics in Spain: «In their relations with the media, judges can play a valuable pedagogical role in explaining the law and the way fundamental rights operate within the process».

As regards confidential information, the opinion of 3 December 2020 (reference 5/20) maintains that it is forbidden to disclose data reserved for not only ethical but also legal imperatives.[48] However, this secret must be kept not only in relation to social networks, the media and public opinion, but also in the private sphere (art. 67 of the *Ibero-American Model Code*), since this information is easily expanded. Sancho Gargallo sharply points out: "The persons involved in a trial, especially when they are accused or arrested, have the right to good repute and intimacy, which breaks when these events are disclosed in the form of gossip".[49] The duty of secrecy also extends to deliberations in the case of a collegiate body (art. 64 *Ibero-American Model Code*). In this manner, the meaning of the decision and aspects of the deliberation that are not reflected in a dissenting vote should not come to light before due time.

It is quite common for texts of Judicial Ethics to refer to the duty of integrity in judicial activity. This is rightly justified by Aparisi: "In reality, the entire judicial system in a State governed by the rule of law is based on the confidence of citizens that those who are going to make fundamental decisions about their lives and their

---

[48] Ibidem, p. 65.

[49] Ibidem, p. 66.

rights deserve such respect".[50] In the same sense, the *Principios de la Ética Judicial* in Spain proclaim it through a positive formulation, noting that integrity requires that judges «observe conduct that reaffirms the confidence of citizens in the Administration of Justice not only in the exercise of jurisdiction, but in all those facets in which they are recognisable as judges (…) or where their status is invoked as such». As article 54 of *the Ibero-American Model Code* also recalls: «the integrity of the conduct of the judge outside the strict scope of jurisdictional activity contributes to a well-founded confidence of citizens in the judiciary». This idea in the *Bangalore Principles* (6.7) translates into the following practical application: «a judge shall not engage in conduct incompatible with the diligent discharge of judicial duties».

Actually, this consideration should not determine the judge's private life, nor his or her hobbies or amusements, but it should be taken into account, at least, to avoid possible scandals. As Aparisi pointed out: "in the field of professional ethics it is very difficult to defend the existence of a sharp separation between public and private life (public ethics and private ethics). (…) Thus, for example, it seems evident that for the judge who lacks the virtue of discretion in the private sphere, and does not strive to acquire it, it can be difficult to maintain professional secrecy in other fields".[51]

The *London Declaration* understands that the judge's obligation to reserve does not prevent him or her from leading a normal social life: he or she should merely take certain precautions with discernment in order to avoid undermining the dignity of his profession or his or her ability to perform his or her duties. In the words of Sancho Gargallo: "It is a question of having some common sense in order to act with freedom, but at the same time being aware of the dignity of the position we hold and of the need for people to appreciate an integrity of life in us. And to be aware of the fact that «the exercise of the jurisdictional function entails requirements that do not apply to the rest of the citizens and whose failure to do so affects confidence in the judiciary» (art. 56 *Ibero-American Model Code*)".[52]

At this point, we cannot fail to address the vivid and complex debate about the link that the morality of private life has in the judge's public life. Laporta referred to this issue in his book *Entre el derecho y la moral* (1993) calling it "the Mill problem".[53]This is because it was precisely John Stuart Mill who stated in his essay *On Liberty* that "The only part of the conduct of any one, for which he is amenable to society, is that which concerns others. In the part which merely concerns himself, his independence is, of right, absolute. Over himself, over his own body and mind,

[50] Aparisi Á. *Ética y deontología para juristas*, op. cit., p. 232.

[51] Ibidem, p. 234.

[52] Sancho Gargallo I. *El paradigma del buen juez*, op. cit., p. 67.

[53] Laporta F. *Entre el derecho y la moral*, op. cit.

the individual is sovereign".[54] Thus, in Mill's opinion, society should not interfere in the private actions of human beings that do not harm others.[55]

Now, if we think about it carefully, this leads us to ask ourselves: can one be a good judge in the public sphere and a bad person in the private sphere? According to Laporta, there would be no ethical basis for coercively impose any moral model of private life.[56] Moreover, "perfectionism", that is, the position that defends that it is possible to force citizens to practice private "virtue" through political measures, is the first step—Laporta continues—towards intolerance or paternalism, anyone who resists "virtue" will be stigmatised or punished to "save" his morality. In literal words: "Private life does not serve as an indication of the quality of political action. Both must be configured as two different spheres of action that do not have to conflict or mix stupidly. Neither do the ethical criteria that govern private life serve to morally judge public action, nor does the morality of political action teach anything about the private ethics of those who practice it".[57]

The question here is not that referred specifically to the political sphere but to the judicial sphere, that is, if there are private actions of judges that can be considered to cause harm to third parties, let us say to society, we would be entitled to judge them in moral terms if we follow what the *Bangalore Principles*, for instance, indicate. I think this question could be answered affirmatively. However, I would like to underline that this is not, in my opinion, a question of defending a closed or poorly illustrated morality, or of giving excessive prominence to public morality, which could enclose a fundamentalist stance in moral terms, but to use the questioning of justice or the loss of trust in the judiciary by society as a criterion or yardstick. Whether they like it or not, judges, like politicians, have a public image that makes their private lives subject to moral scrutiny.[58] In my view, thanks to the *Principios de la Ética Judicial*, it is precisely possible to prevent moral scrutiny from depending on mere changing social environmental prejudices. I would thus agree with Sancho Gargallo when he claims that: "Regardless of what the judge's private life is like, at the very least he or she should be required to perform his or her judicial duties in the most correct way possible, although experience shows that when some vices or addictions become pathological, they easily transcend the boundaries of the private sphere and affect the exercise of public office".[59] With the stance that is defended here, in fact, the unity of the individual subject is being preserved, trying to avoid schizophrenic pathologies, aware that the individual cannot be broken into two different beings or identities depending on whether he or she is acting as a subject in the public or private sphere. In the words of Aparisi, which cannot be blunter: "The person is a unit and is inclined to integration, so it becomes difficult (and

[54] Mill (2001).

[55] Laporta F. *Entre el derecho y la moral*, op. cit., pp. 47–48.

[56] Ibidem, pp. 48 y 125.

[57] Ibidem, p. 129.

[58] Ibidem, pp. 125–127.

[59] Sancho Gargallo I. *El paradigma del buen juez*, op. cit., p. 67.

dangerous) to maintain contradictory or opposite behaviours in the different areas of life".[60]

5 Conclusion

The Rule of Law is not an immutable legal structure, since it depends on the continuous citizen action for its development as *social êthos*.[61] When judges use the instrument of law, they must do so in an appropriate way, always relying on ethical values and principles, a morality and a culture that, in the end, is forged by the *êthos*, a moral character or personality that each of us builds as citizens and moral subjects throughout our existence.[62] It has rightly been stated that the antidote or control system that is most effective against any form of corruption in the sphere of public life is not found in mechanisms that are external to the individual but within the latter, through «educational values, ethical virtues» rather than rules or laws[63].

Taking what the proper abilities of judges represent into account, we must distinguish between those that have to do with the virtues of an impartial, independent and integral judge, which are related to the *Principios de la Ética Judicial* and others that constitute the professional skills that he or she exercises in his or her specific professional activity (diligence, listening ability, empathetic attitude, caution, etc.).

I believe that García Paz is right when he points out that in law, the human condition itself is reflected: "a material body, the legal norms, and something else that is essential, which we can call its soul or reason, and which is the one that guides the movements of those who apply the norm and the norm itself, so that they may seek to make effective the realisation of Justice in the world or pursue the opposite. A type of Law without Ethics is a body without soul or reason: that is, a monster. True Law must unite under the same concept positive norm and moral norm: law and honesty"[64] As was recalled by Seneca, philosopher, politician, excellent orator and Roman writer, known for his works of moral character, who was also the maximum exponent of stoicism together with Epictetus and Marcus Aurelius, *honesty may prohibit what laws don't*, but he furthermore highlighted, with absolute ingenuity, what differentiated us humans from the gods: the fact that we were given a finite amount of time to build our *êthos*. As Aranguren recalled: "There is a moral task for each of our hours and the moral task, the *êthos*, also has its determined time, its «numbered days»".[65] Recently, Barraca acutely recalled how when we discover a

[60] Aparisi A. *Ética y deontología para juristas*, op. cit., p. 234.

[61] World Justice Project. *World Justice Challenge 2021: Advancing the Rule of Law in a time of Crisis*. Outcome Report. World Justice Project | Advancing the rule of law worldwide. https://worldjusticeproject.org/sites/default/files/documents/WJCOutcomesReport_F_3.pdf

[62] Aranguren, JLL. *Ética*, op. cit.

[63] Laporta and Álvarez (1997), p. 28.

[64] García Paz (2022).

[65] Vid. Aranguren JLL. *Ética*, op. cit., p. 147.

fruitful sense in a duty and professional responsibility, these are integrated with what our vocation represents—which we must be faithful to—contributing to our personal fulfilment as a way of aspiring to excellence.[66]

References

Alexy R (2008) Teoría de la argumentación jurídica, 2nd edn Translation by Atienza M, Espejo I. Centro de Estudios Políticos y Constitucionales, Madrid
Aparisi A (2006) Ética y deontología para juristas. EUNSA, Pamplona. 1st ed. 2006 and 2nd ed. 2008
Aranguren JLL (1958) Ética. Revista de Occidente, Madrid. Quoted after its fifth reprint in Alianza Universidad Textos, Madrid, 1990
Aristóteles (1999) Ética a Nicómaco. Centro de Estudios Constitucionales, Madrid
Barraca J (2022) Formar para un cumplimiento organizativo fecundo, on 30 March 2022. Available at: https://diarioresponsable.com/actualidad/5097
Barry B (1997) La justicia como imparcialidad. Paidós, Barcelona. Original title: Justice as impartiality. Oxford University Press Inc., New York
Bingham T (2010) The rule of law. Allen Lane, London
Bonete Perales E (1995) Introduction: De la ética filosófica a la deontología periodística. In: Éticas de la información y deontologías del periodismo. Bonete Perales E (Coordinator). Tecnos, Madrid
Código Iberoamericano de Ética Judicial comentado (2019) Directed by Fernando Alberto Castro Caballero. CIEJ, Bogotá
Cortina A (2007) Ética de la razón cordial. Educar entre la ciudadanía, 2nd edn. Ediciones Nobel, Oviedo. 1st reprint 2009
Cortina A (2013) ¿Para qué sirve realmente la ética? Paidós, Barcelona
Díaz E (1996) Estado de derecho y sociedad democrática. Cuadernos para el Diálogo, Madrid
Dworkin R (1985) Political judges and the rule of law. In: A matter of principle. Harvard University Press, Cambridge, pp 9–32
Espín Templado E (2003) Los derechos de la esfera personal. In: López Guerra L et al (eds) Derecho Constitucional, vol I. Tirant lo Blanch, Valencia
Ferrajoli L (2011, 2016) Principia iuris. Teoría del derecho y de la democracia. 1. Teoría del derecho. Trotta, Madrid. Original title: Principia Iuris. Teoria del diritto e della democrazia. 1. Teoria del diritto. Spanish translation by Andrés Ibáñez P, Bayón JC, Gascón M, Prieto Sanchís L, Ruiz Miguel A
Ferrajoli L (2020) Iura Paria. Los fundamentos de la democracia constitucional. Trotta, Madrid
Ferrer Santos U (1990) Perspectivas de la acción humana. PPU, Barcelona
García Paz D (2022) Entre la ley y la honestidad. Literatura Abierta (Grupo Torre de Lis), Madrid
Laporta F (1995) Entre la moral y el derecho. Fontamara, Mexico. 1st ed. 1993 and 2nd ed. 1995
Laporta F, Álvarez S (eds) (1997) La corrupción política. Alianza Editorial, Madrid
Locke J (1999) In: Prieto Sanchís L, Betegón Carrillo J (eds) Escritos sobre la tolerancia. Centro de Estudios Políticos y Constitucionales, Madrid
Massini Correas C (1982) La prudencia jurídica. Abeledo-Perrot, Buenos Aires
Megías Quirós JJ (2002) Privacidad y nuevas tecnologías: intimidad, comunicaciones y datos personales. Anuario de Derechos Humanos 3
Mill JS (2001) On Liberty. Sobre la libertad. Alianza Editorial, Madrid
Nieto Blanco C (2020) Discurso sobre la democracia. Ediciones Universidad Cantabria, Santander

[66] Barraca (2022).

Principios de Ética Judicial (2018) Consejo General del Poder Judicial, Madrid
Rodríguez Medina, FA (2015) Master's degree in philosophy at the University of Concepción and which was directed by Rodrigo Pulgar Castro, entitled Rumbo a una ética intercultural y mundial: una prioridad en Adela Cortina. Available at: http://repositorio.udec.cl/bitstream/11594/1868/1/Tesis_Rumbo_a_una_etica_intercultural_y_mundial.pdf
Rzeplinski A (2016) To be a judge. In Solemn hearing for the opening of the Judicial Year of the European Court of Human Rights, 26 January 2016
Sánchez Hidalgo AJ (2020) Tradicionalismo político y Filosofía del Derecho Privado en Juan Berchmans Vallet de Goytisolo. Atelier, Barcelona
Sancho Gargallo I (2007) Ética Judicial: el paradigma del buen Juez. ICADE. Revista Cuatrimestral de las Facultades de Derecho y Ciencias Económicas y Empresariales, no. 72, Madrid, September–December 2007
Sancho Gargallo I (2020) Judge Craft: El oficio o arte de juzgar. InDret 4:446–461
Sancho Gargallo I (2022) El paradigma del buen juez. Tirant lo Blanch, Valencia
Varios (2005) Ética del juez y garantías procesales. In: Manuales de Formación Continuada 24. Consejo General del Poder Judicial, Madrid
Waldron J (2013) Separation of powers in thought and practice. Boston Coll Law Rev 54:433–468
Waldron J (2020) The rule of law. In: Zalta EN (ed) The Stanford encyclopedia of philosophy (Summer 2020 edn.). https://plato.stanford.edu/archives/sum2020/entries/rule-of-law/
Yarza I (2001) La racionalidad de la ética de Aristóteles. Eunsa, Pamplona
Yepes Stork R (1996) Fundamentos de Antropología. EUNSA, Pamplona

The Rule of Law, Civil Law and the Judges' Freedom of Expression

Rainer Arnold

Abstract The rule of law is the basis and essential element of a constitutional order. Law is not only the formal instrument of order, but also conveys the fundamental values of the state community. This is not only important for the vertical relationship between the state and the individual, but also has a manifold effect on the horizontal relationship between private individuals, i.e. in the area of civil law. An independent, functioning judiciary is essential for the rule of law. This is also linked to the specific question of the extent to which a judge may express his opinion and the extent to which he must exercise restraint.

Today's conference is dedicated to the memory of Eugen Chelaru, a great scholar of international renown, an excellent academic teacher, Dean of the Faculty of Law and Administration of the University of Pitesti for many years, a very responsible, helpful and friendly person, highly appreciated and loved by all. He left us far too early and we remember him with great sadness and the highest respect. I, too, have lost a friend in him whom I greatly admired and revered. He was a frequent participant in my international congresses and made important contributions. As the recipient of an honorary doctorate from his university, I will always remember him with gratitude.

This also prompts me to mourn the recent death of another world-renowned scientist who belonged to Eugen Chelaru's inner circle, Professor Herbert Schambeck, former President of the Federal Council of the Republic of Austria. A friend and confidant of both personalities, Professor Heribert Köck, Dean of the Faculty of Law at the University of Linz for many years, is here today to chair this workshop. It is a great honor for me to be able to speak here with him and Professor Cristina Hermida del Llano, both of whom are very good friends of mine.

Civil law and public law are separate areas according to Roman legal tradition, but they are nevertheless linked in many ways. Both areas are overarched by the constitution, often also by international and especially supranational law. The

R. Arnold (✉)
University of Regensburg, Regensburg, Germany
e-mail: cristina.hermida@urjc.es

C. Hermida del Llano (ed.), *The Freedom of Expression for Judges in the Sphere of the Judicial Ethics*, Ius Gentium: Comparative Perspectives on Law and Justice 129, https://doi.org/10.1007/978-3-032-06504-9_19

primacy of the constitution in domestic law is an essential element of the modern concept of the rule of law and means the common validity of the basic principles and values relating to human beings in their core function in all areas of law. The constitution has a harmonizing, unifying effect. The constantly growing complexity of matters, not least under the influence of globalization, also means that the boundaries between the two areas of civil law and public law are being shifted, particularly in important areas such as environmental protection, consumer protection, artificial intelligence law and technology law in general. It can also be observed that extra-state standardization processes, especially those of the European Union and international organizations, are dissolving these boundaries even more than is visible in internal state law.

Eugen Chelaru has expressed his views on public law issues in a variety of works, which were also published in the congress proceedings I edited, such as on constitutional interpretation, on the relationship between the Romanian Constitutional Court and ordinary jurisdiction, on the political dimension of constitutional jurisdiction, especially in Romania, together with Ramona Duminica on the right to property and environmental protection in the case law of the Romanian Constitutional Court[1] and on the consultative referendum in Romania.

I also remember the conferences in Alba Julia, where he spoke impressively about the development of the right of personality in Romanian civil law.

1 On the Rule of Law

This inclusion of public law in civil law in Eugen Chelaru's contributions prompted me to reflect on whether the rule of law is limited to the vertical relationship between the state and the individual or whether the rule of law also applies to a certain extent in relations between individuals under coordination law, i.e. in private law.

The rule of law is an essential characteristic of an authentic, human-centred constitution.[2] The state as a social community is founded on the law, is bound by the law and has to observe the law as the only rule of behaviour. Law binds the state on the internal, national level as well as on the external, supra- and international level.

People in the state of nature, who are born free and find themselves in this freedom in a society, must unite and form a community in order to survive and have their needs met. To this end, they conclude a contract, a contrat social, as Jean-Jacques Rousseau[3] calls it, with which they establish institutions and their freedom for communities, insofar as this is necessary for the fulfilment of their tasks. This contrat *social* is the constitution. The means of community building is the *law as an*

---

[1] Chelaru and Duminica (2022), pp. 53–63. See also Chelaru (2021), pp. 31–39. See further Chelaru and Duminica (2020), pp. 119–136.

[2] See Arnold (2025).

[3] Rousseau (1762, re-ed. 1966).

instrument of order, which alone brings with it the necessary prerequisites and objectives. The law creates order by establishing rational rules and securing them due to their binding nature. Law is therefore an instrument for the rationalisation of security and thus stabilisation. This stabilising function inherent in law is necessary for the permanence of the community and creates trust in the existence of this community. This necessarily combines the objective element of stability and the emotional-subjective element of trust, the basis for the identification of the members of the community with the body as a whole.

At this point, we can already identify the following as essential individual elements of law and thus of the state based on law: stability, i.e. the security that law creates, thus legal certainty, which necessarily presupposes clarity and precision, i.e. the certainty of the law. The more important goods are encroached upon, such as personal freedom in the area of criminal law, the more precisely the law must define everything that is necessary for understanding the legal norm in question and the resulting consequences for behaviour. The necessary consequence of legal certainty is trust in the law, which is ultimately trust in the community. Positions acquired in accordance with the law must not be devalued, retroactive legislation is highly dubious from a legal point of view and is clearly excluded, for example in the area of criminal law. The fact that this is generally recognised and is based on a long tradition is shown by geographical and historical comparative law.

Stability of the law also requires judicial protection of the law. Effective legal protection means that the law is upheld, that deviations from the law are corrected and that this is done by independent institutions, i.e. courts, that are only committed to the law and not to politics. Thus, effective and fundamentally comprehensive legal protection is one of the essential elements of the law. Its enforcement and the judicial control of its application is therefore a necessary part of its regulatory function. This applies to all areas of jurisdiction, civil, criminal and administrative justice as well as to constitutional jurisdiction.

Judicial enforcement of the law also includes ensuring that it is comprehensive. However, there are historical imperfections here, which have been increasingly reduced in modern times in favour of full legal protection. This is particularly evident in the area of judicial review of state acts, which is so important for the rule of law. It was a characteristic of pre-democratic state systems that claims against the monarch and thus the executive in his hands could not be asserted in principle, or only to a very limited extent. *The* phrase "The King can do no wrong" was a defining feature for a long time.[4] This was clearly relevant in common law systems, in which, however, the law was then opened up in favour of greater judicial review. Occasionally, it was case law itself that initiated such developments. One need only think of the French system of state liability, which was only made possible in the first place by the famous *Arret Blanco* in 1873 and then as a separate, administrative court claim.

[4] See for this in England de Smith (1971), p. 123–124.

However, law is only an instrument of order with a specific objective: namely to serve *justice*. The second important function of law, which is inextricably linked to the first function of order mentioned above, is that of *determining values.*[5]

When people join together to form a community, they want to retain the basic attribute they have acquired through birth, their freedom. They delegate their fundamental freedom to community institutions only to the extent that this is absolutely necessary for the fulfilment of community tasks. Every person is entitled to this freedom on the basis of their human dignity: this results in the triad of the fundamental values of human dignity, freedom as a principle and equality. Freedom, inseparably linked to human dignity, encompasses individual and political freedom, the latter also known as democracy. Individual freedom is specified by fundamental rights, in open form. The written fundamental rights are supplemented by unwritten fundamental rights, based on the fundamental right to safeguard freedom against all existing and future dangers. Only this comprehensive claim to freedom does justice to human dignity. While human dignity is an absolute, non-restrictable fundamental value that cannot be weighed against other values, freedom always exists in principle, but it can inevitably be restricted in favour of the community and other members of the community, to the extent that it is necessary to restrict the freedom of the individual for the legitimate common good.[6]

The principle of proportionality indicates the correct boundary between freedom as a principle and the restrictions necessary in favour of the freedom of the community. This principle has gained universal significance and also overrides the idea of *rationability* that prevails in quite a few systems.

The rule of law is therefore necessarily *value-orientated and* is not only a formal rule of law, but also a rule of law. This rule of law is characterised by its commitment to the constitution, which is given priority; it is a *constitutional state.* The values explicitly or implicitly standardised in the constitution are the primary binding guidelines for all state authority, including the legislature. The constitution as a basic order manifests itself in these values. If, according to Rousseau and the French Revolution, the law, as an expression of the majority will of politics, is the expression of the will of the people of the volonté générale, today's idea, which corresponds to the material constitutional state, is that which the French Constitutional Council, the Conseil constitutinnel, formulated in classical form in its Nouvell Calédonie decision in 1985: *La loi n'exprime la volonté générale que dans le respect de la Constitution.*[7] The decisive factor today is the constitutional conformity of the

[5] T. confl., 8 févr. 1873. This decision has opened the way for claiming damages against agents of the State in a public law dimension.

[6] See also Arnold (2022), pp. 41–56.

[7] Décision n° 85–197 DC du 23 août 1985. « 27. Considérant donc que la procédure législative utilisée pour mettre en conformité avec la Constitution la disposition déclarée non conforme à celle-ci par le Conseil constitutionnel a fait de l'article 23 de l'ordonnance du 7 novembre 1958 portant loi organique une application ne méconnaissant en rien les règles de l'article 10 de la Constitution et a répondu aux exigences du contrôle de constitutionnalité dont l'un des buts est de

law, which is thus also in conformity with the anthropocentric fundamental values of the constitutional order.

We can therefore see that the material rule of law protects freedom—this is the value dimension inherent in law and in constitutional law in particular. For this reason, the individual elements of the constitutional state that protect freedom include fundamental rights, the principle of proportionality as a yardstick for demarcating freedom and restriction, judicial review that protects freedom (as a supplement to the above-mentioned judicial review that realises rights) and, in particular, the separation of powers that prevents the abuse of power.

The separation of powers is the deconcentration of the exercise of power, as opposed to the accumulation of powers. The power of the state, which emanates in its entirety from the people, is distributed among various institutions, which, according to their essential function, are the legislative, executive and judicial branches. This is a functionally appropriate division, which means a substantial balance of functions.

There is also no universal fixed principle of the separation of powers, but rather systems of institutional division defined by the various constitutions. And we do, however, see the idea of the distribution of functions, which must be done in such a way that an abuse of power is ruled out or at least made significantly more difficult. The principle that there must be checks and balances in a constitutional order is inherent in a liberal, i.e. liberal-democratic constitutional order.

Constitutional practice shows that a certain relativisation of the strict division of functions is a given and is also necessary for the functioning of a state. As is traditionally said, however, an overlapping of functions must not lead to interference with the core of the other functions. Co-operation and thus the distribution of functions beyond the boundaries of one functional area are common and also appropriate. For example, the creation of a law is linked to the action of the legislative branch, which, however, as in Germany, must co-operate with the executive branch, i.e. with the Bundesrat, which is made up of government representatives from the federal states. This is deliberately designed by the constitution so that the federalist principle can also be realised through the Bundesrat. Furthermore, the law must be signed by the members of the government, i.e. by the gubernative, which in a broader sense belongs to the executive, and signed, i.e. executed, by the Federal President, also an institution belonging to the executive. We see cooperation across functional boundaries, as it is entirely appropriate and definitely represents a functional balance. However, control mechanisms also exist, e.g. in various states the head of state (for different reasons depending on the constitutional system) can intervene to limit the power of parliament. However, parliament can overrule, often with a qualified majority, so that a functional inhibition is built into this in the sense of the separation of powers. Separation of powers also means that the legislature is

permettre à la loi votée, qui n'exprime la volonté générale que dans le respect de la Constitution, d'être sans retard amendée à cette fi;»

scrutinised by a constitutional court. One could go even further and understand the constitutional process before the legislature as a material limitation of powers.

We can therefore recognise the special freedom-securing effect of the separation of functions and balance of powers. Let us return to our narrower topic, which is certainly related to the substantive rule of law. Two constitutional values compete with each other here: the fundamental right of freedom of expression on the one hand and the institution of the court, characterised by the independence and impartiality of the judges appointed to make decisions.

2 Rule of Law and its Impact on Civil Law

The rule of law is not only an obligation of the state (or supranational authority), but also of society, which is part of the state as a whole. The value orientation of law also finds its way into social relations, into civil law, through legislation that is bound to and implements the constitution. In many legal systems, such as the German one, the constitutional norms, in particular the fundamental rights, are understood as protective norms that contain the obligation to adequately realize these values. In fulfilling this task, the legislator realizes the central function of the constitutional state through civil law. The judge, as an organ of the state, must interpret and apply the law in its entirety, in particular the civil laws in the light of constitutional values. However, if the legal system allows it, the judge may also apply the constitution directly in civil law.

The special nature of civil law, its largely coordination law structure, makes it necessary to pay particular attention to the individual's freedom under civil law, his or her private autonomy, and to adequately weigh it up against other constitutional rights.

The focus is on the functional protection of the individual, be it as the addressee of public authority, as a partner under private law in contractual relationships or in other areas of civil law. Where there is a need for protection, the state must act through legislation or through the protection-oriented interpretation of existing norms. This functional approach exists regardless of whether the state acts in a sovereign capacity, whether it chooses private law forms for its actions or whether this situation arises in the midst of purely private law relationships. The individual's need for protection is particularly pronounced in relation to powerful private partners such as social media. It seems obvious that fundamental rights protection obligations must be implemented here to a particular extent.

We can see that the influences of constitutional law are visible in many areas of civil law. The right of personality and its numerous aspects or property law are particularly striking areas in this respect. Both areas were shaped by civil law a long time ago, then became areas of particular relevance for constitutional law, and today constitutional law in turn shapes the current civil law forms of these areas. As already mentioned, these influences are also and especially visible in contract law, which appears to be largely free from the principle of equality and from the protection of fundamental rights in general due to the constitutionally protected private autonomy of the individual. However, this is broken in many ways in order to adequately protect the individual.

As a result, we can say that the rule of law is by no means limited to the exercise of state power, but also has manifold effects on individual civil law.

3 Judicial Independence as a Core Element of the Rule of Law

Let me now draw a line, albeit a wide one, to the core topic of the conference: the ethics of the judge, specifically the question: is the judge free or restricted in his freedom of expression? This question is also related to my chosen topic of the rule of law, as the function of the independent and impartial judge is central to this.

I can only touch on this very briefly in this context: freedom of opinion is a fundamental right to which all people, including judges, are entitled. However, restrictions can arise from his position, from his status.

This leads to the question: are there such restrictions in ethical rules or in the law? First of all, it should be noted that fundamental rights cannot be restricted by guidelines, orientations or soft law. This requires formal laws that provide for such restrictions or allow them to be concretized through guidelines.

With regard to ethical rules, they do not yet exist for the judiciary in general, although their necessity is being discussed. Only the judges of the Federal Constitutional Court have given themselves guidelines for conduct, which are assumed to be observed voluntarily; however, they have not been cast in legal form. They contain numerous variants of conduct and also include the right to make statements. However, the rules require restraint and, in general terms, appropriateness with regard to the dignity of their office during and after their term of office.

For other judges, the DRiG (Deutsches Richtergesetz), the German Judges Act, is relevant, paragraph 39 of which reads as follows:

> The judge must conduct himself within and outside his office, including in political activities, in such a way that confidence in his independence is not jeopardized.

It is derived from this that he must also behave moderately in his expression of opinion. It is therefore up to the disciplinary jurisdiction to concretize this provision.

The Federal Constitutional Court (FCC) itself has only commented slightly on this. It also referred to the traditional principles of the civil service, which are part of the constitution in accordance with Article 33 (5) of the Basic Law. They also apply to the judiciary in general and permit a restriction of their fundamental rights based on the historical development of the institution of the civil servant and the judge, if this is established by a formal law.

Let us have a look at the FCC guidelines of conduct[8] as far as freedom of opinion is concerned.

How is the judge's freedom of expression restricted under German law? There are two dimensions relevant to the judge's freedom of expression: firstly, the judge's assessment of the case to be decided, i.e. the internal debate during the deliberations. Secondly, expressions of opinion that take place independently of the decision-making process, be it about the specific case or the legal issues related to it, be it about topics that are not directly connected to the case or also behaviour that reveals the judge's inner attitudes and, in a broader sense, documents the judge's opinion.

Firstly, a few statements on the first dimension of our topic: It seems evident that the secrecy of counselling must be preserved. The Rules of Conduct of the Federal Constitutional Court also emphasise this: Rule of Conduct 8 reads: "The judges of the court shall maintain discretion with regard to the work of the Federal Constitutional Court, without prejudice to the confidentiality of deliberations." This rule of conduct supplements Section 43 of the German Judges Act, which stipulates the confidentiality of counselling for judges in general and extends it beyond the end of their term of service. This provision reads: "The judge must remain silent about the course of deliberations and voting even after the termination of his or her employment.". This is also taken up by the Federal Constitutional Court Act and Section 30 (1) expressly describes the deliberations as "secret". The obligation to maintain the secrecy of deliberations is a restriction, covered by Article 5 (1) and (2) of the Basic Law, on providing information about the deliberations and also on commenting on these proceedings. The Act on the Federal Constitutional Court itself provides for certain, narrowly defined exceptions, in which it is possible for the ratio of votes achieved in the vote on the content of the decision to be published or for the dissenting opinion of a judge in the deliberations to be set out in a special vote.

The behavioural guidelines of the Federal Constitutional Court focus on statements made by judges which—beyond a specific case in which a judge is active—concern the court's jurisdiction in the present and past and which are directed at the court as an institution. This applies not only to the time in which the judicial office is actively exercised but also to the time after the end of this activity. In general, as the first sentence of the Code of Conduct states, judges are expected to behave as follows: "Judges of the Federal Constitutional Court shall conduct themselves within and outside their office in such a way that the reputation of the court, the dignity of the office and confidence in their independence, impartiality, neutrality and integrity are not jeopardised." This basic rule is then specified:

Firstly, it is required that the judges actively contribute to conveying a functionally appropriate image of the Federal Constitutional Court and its case law to the legal and non-legal public at home and abroad: "Due to the position of the Federal Constitutional Court as a constitutional body and the social and political

[8] https://www.bundesverfassungsgericht.de/DE/Richter/Verhaltensleitlinie/Verhaltensleitlinien_node.html

significance of its decisions, the members of the Court contribute beyond the primary fulfilment of their judicial mandate to the presentation and communication of its position, functioning and case law at national and international level. "This is a form of mandatory expression of opinion and evaluation and serves the public's need for information and the court's self-presentation.

On the other hand, judges are expected to show restraint when assessing the case law of their own court and also other courts at home and abroad and at international level and also to respect the opinions of others and, if they appear to the judge to be worthy of criticism, to criticise them with restraint. For this reason, the sixth statement of the Code of Conduct reads as follows: "The judges of the Federal Constitutional Court shall express criticism of other opinions and legal positions with the restraint appropriate to their office. This applies in particular to decisions of their own court, but also to other national, foreign or international courts". This obligation to exercise restraint applies in particular if the expression of opinion is made in a communication medium: "When dealing with the media, the judges of the Federal Constitutional Court shall ensure that the nature of their statements and the respective format are compatible with their duties, the reputation of the court and the dignity of the office" (Code of Conduct 12).

Written expressions of opinion in the form of expert opinions on constitutional issues are not permitted, so that they are not interpreted as a general and a priori commitment by a judge to a particular point of view, which would preclude open-ended internal deliberation in the proceedings. Similarly, judges may not make predictions about the probable outcome of ongoing proceedings and, in particular, not of proceedings that are to be decided in the foreseeable future. Code of Conduct 11 expresses this clearly: "Judges shall not give expert opinions on constitutional issues, nor shall they make predictions about the outcome of proceedings pending before the court or proceedings that are likely to be decided in the foreseeable future." This obligation to exercise restraint continues after the end of the term of office, but is then limited. The principle of proportionality, which is relevant for restrictions on fundamental rights, applies here.

The duty of discretion also applies after the end of the term of office. Conduct Guideline 13 states: "The judges of the Federal Constitutional Court shall maintain restraint and discretion in their statements and behaviour in court matters even after the end of their term of office." This is specified in more detail, also with reference to professional statements, in Code of Conduct 14: "After the end of their term of office, judges of the Federal Constitutional Court shall not act in cases that were pending before the Federal Constitutional Court during their term of office or that are directly related to such cases. In these cases, they do not provide expert opinions, do not assume any legal or counselling obligations and do not appear in court." This limitation to specific cases that were pending during the judge's term of office or are directly related to such cases. In more general terms, abstention from commenting is required 1 year after leaving office if legal issues from the former department, i.e. the judge's area of responsibility during the term of office, are in question. Accordingly, Code of Conduct 15 reads: "During the first year after leaving office, judges of the Federal Constitutional Court shall not provide advice, give expert opinions or appear in court in the subject areas of their department. Nor do they represent before the Federal Constitutional Court thereafter. They avoid the impression of inappropriate utilisation of internal knowledge." The requirement not to appear at all in a case before the Federal Constitutional Court after the end of their term of office, i.e. not to make statements to the court, applies in general, as otherwise at least the strong suspicion could arise that the former judge is utilising insider knowledge acquired during their term of office.

Expressions of opinion in a broader sense can also consist of participating in an event organised by a particular group or party and thereby expressing that one agrees with the aims of this group. Here, too, the Rules of Conduct rightly stipulate a duty of restraint Rule 10 therefore provides: "When participating in any form of event, the judges of the Federal Constitutional Court shall ensure that the nature of the event is compatible with the dignity of the office and the general principles of its exercise as well as the reputation of the court." It should be added that the appointment to the office of a constitutional court judge does not end their possible party affiliation or membership of a particular social group and does not have to be interrupted. However, restraint must be exercised. This leads to the often vehement debate as to whether judges who have held a parliamentary mandate or a certain state office due to their party affiliation must be considered biased. In this case, which occurs quite frequently, there is again a reason for exclusion and a reason for bias. The grounds for disqualification are set out in special legislation in section 13 of the Act on the Federal Constitutional Court. According to this, anyone who "is or was involved in the case" or has already been involved in the same case ex officio or by profession is disqualified. As this is often a contentious issue, paragraph 2 of section 18 of the Act states that anyone who is "interested in the outcome of the proceedings by virtue of his or her profession or affiliation to a political party" or "from a similarly general point of view" is not a party. Subsection 3 of the same provision then clarifies that a contributory activity that leads to the judge's exclusion from the proceedings does not include participation in the legislative process or "the expression of an academic opinion on a point of law that may be relevant to the proceedings".

It should be noted that a ground for disqualification is automatic; no decision by the court is required. The court only determines that a particular judge is excluded by law. The situation is different in the case of recusal pursuant to section 19 of the Act on the Federal Constitutional Court. Any party to a case can challenge a judge if there is a reason for recusal. It is also possible for a judge to recuse himself. A reason for recusal is concern about a judge's partiality, i.e. there must be a reason that casts doubt on the judge's impartiality. Objectively, it depends on whether a party has reason to doubt the impartiality of the judge based on a reasonable assessment of the specific circumstances.[9] This is the case, for example, if a judge has previously issued a supportive opinion on the matter in dispute[10] close personal

[9] FCC vol. 73, 330, 335 (established case law); see also Lechner and Zuck (2015), §19 para 4.

[10] See FCC vol. 88, 1, 4.

friendship or intense enmity.[11] However, a judge's refusal is only successful in rare cases. A violation of the behavioural guidelines as such is not sufficient to justify a refusal. There must be special circumstances that objectively and clearly suggest that the judge is biased. If the judge expresses an opinion, an application for recusal is only likely to be successful in difficult circumstances.

If we consider the restrictions on the judge's freedom of expression in terms of constitutional law, Article 5(1) of the Basic Law is relevant. However, we already encounter a first difficulty here: fundamental rights apply to the individual in a situation that jeopardises his or her freedom. This situation of danger is not relevant if the state or a state functionary acts itself. According to the traditional view, the state itself could not invoke fundamental rights as a defence against itself. Exceptions are only permitted if autonomous functional areas exist to which the functionary can refer. This is the case for universities, which can invoke the academic freedom of Article 5(3) of the Basic Law against state interference in their autonomous academic and teaching areas, for public broadcasting organisations, which can invoke the freedom of broadcasting of Article 5(1), and for religious communities organised as public corporations, which can invoke the protection of freedom of belief in accordance with Article 4 (1) and (2) of the Basic Law and also for the municipalities, which can rely on their right to self-government (Article 28 (2) of the Basic Law), albeit not as a fundamental right but as an institutional guarantee. It is by no means impossible to transfer this idea to the judge, who possesses the judicial independence required and protected by the Basic Law and whose protection cannot be diminished by the fact that the judge is a functionary. Judicial independence is specifically enshrined in Article 97 of the Basic Law, which prohibits external influence on the judge and the court, while the concept of the court, which is referred to in Article 92 of the Basic Law, implies the impartiality of the judge. This is also implicitly expressed in Article 97 of the Basic Law, which states that the judge is subject only to the law and must therefore apply its objective will as the exclusive guiding principle. Certainly, neither Article 97 nor Article 92 of the Basic Law are fundamental rights, but the concept of the judge with its essential characteristics of independence and impartiality is taken as a basis in the judicial rights of Articles 101 to 104, which are conceived in the Basic Law as being equal to fundamental rights. The ECHR also has an impact on fundamental judicial rights and reinforces their meaning through interpretation.

It has just been established that it is problematic in German constitutional law to recognise a public functionary, such as a judge, as a holder of fundamental rights. However, this cannot be doubtful if the judge speaks as a private individual. He is then not exercising his function as a judge, but is acting as a private individual. Article 5(1) of the Basic Law should offer him protection from this point of view. However, one could again doubt whether the judge gives up or interrupts his status in his private time or whether he is to be regarded as a public functionary through his continuing status. The same considerations apply to the period after the end of

[11] FCC vol. 73, 330, 339; Lechner/Zuck, ibidem, para 5.

the term of office. It is recognised that official duties also apply during the private time of a public official and that he/she must also exercise the necessary restraint during this time. Is he/she protected by fundamental rights during this time? One will probably have to answer in the affirmative in order not to undermine the potential protection of fundamental rights intended by the constitution.

Let us therefore assume that the judge can invoke Article 5 (1) of the Basic Law both in his/her function and in his/her private life. However, this fundamental right, which is organised as a human right in the German constitution, is not guaranteed without restrictions. So-called general laws can restrict freedom of opinion, in accordance with Article 5 Paragraph 2 of the Basic Law. These restrictions arise from the legal provisions relating to the judiciary and judges, which have already been mentioned, but the Basic Law's guarantee of independence is also a direct barrier to freedom of expression. The concept of general laws, which dates back to the Weimar period, means that these laws are not intended to exclude a particular opinion, but to guarantee other legitimate protected interests, such as honour, the protection of minors and also judicial independence. This is undoubtedly the case with our topic.

If freedom of expression is restricted by a general law, the traditional, albeit not undisputed, theory of reciprocal effects applies. This means that the law restricting freedom of expression is interpreted in the light of freedom of expression, i.e. this particularly important fundamental right, just as freedom of expression as such is opened up to restrictions to an appropriate extent. However, this doctrine of interaction does not appear to be suitable for the specific constellation. The independence and impartiality of the courts is a constitutional requirement that cannot be restricted and plays a fundamental role in a constitutional state and democratic system. It cannot be restricted by weighing up the facts. It is an attribute of the court that can only ever be fully present and never reduced in order to fulfil constitutional requirements. Therefore, freedom of opinion is fully restricted by the requirement of independence and impartiality of the judge.

It is certainly a question of judgement as to which statements or behaviour are likely to call into question the impartiality and independence of judges. It should also be noted that it is not only the objective circumstances that are important, but also the possibility that external persons could have the impression that these basic principles have been violated. In doing so, the judgement of a reasonably thinking person must be taken into account. Not only the actual violation of these principles is protected under constitutional law, but also any questioning of trust in these principles, so that even the objective impression of a violation must be avoided. Nevertheless, the importance of freedom of expression as a central value of the constitutional order must also be taken into account in the assessment.

Finally, a look must be taken at Article 33 (5) of the Basic Law. It concerns the so-called traditional principles of the civil service, a provision that also includes the judiciary. It reads: "The law of the civil service shall be regulated and developed with due regard to the traditional principles of the civil service." This provision is not a fundamental right, but it is possible to challenge its violation by means of a constitutional complaint. In historically important periods of time, principles have emerged that are associated with the image of the civil service and professional judges. They have become part of their essence. These should be upheld and adapted in the present. These include the duty of loyalty of civil servants and judges to the state, but also, and of particular importance, the independence of the courts. Both are therefore part of traditional constitutional law: the independence that is part of the nature of the judiciary and also the restraint in behaviour and, in particular, in statements that grows out of this and also out of the idea of obligation to the state for which the judicial function is exercised. The relevant laws have concretised this.

4 A Look at the Case Law

There is relatively little case law on this topic. It should be emphasized that a recent decision by the Federal Court of Justice is significant.[12] In this decision, a judge who had made right-wing extremist statements was temporarily retired in accordance with Section 31 of the German Judges Act.

This reads: Section 31 Transfer in the interest of the administration of justice.

A judge for life or a temporary judge may be transferred (1) to another judicial office with the same final basic salary, (2) to temporary retirement, or (3) retirement if facts outside of his judicial activity make such a measure imperative in order to avert a serious impairment of the administration of justice.

The Federal Court of Justice confirmed this, citing the fact that the employment of judges requires, among other things, that they accept the free democratic basic order and stand up for it. Section 9 of the German Judges Act stipulated this as a prerequisite for appointment as a judge.

The Federal Constitutional Court (FCC) itself dealt with the issue of an unrestrained expression of opinion by a judge in the Preliminary Examination Committee (a three-judge panel that examines whether a constitutional complaint is accepted for decision).[13]

The judge had co-signed an appeal in the *Hannoversche Allgemeine Zeitung*, stating his office as a judge, to lift the so-called professional ban on a person who was a candidate for the German Communist Party (which rejects the Basic Law) and was therefore unable to exercise his teaching profession.

The FC, with reference to the decision of the Service Court for Lower Saxony, argued as follows:

> Like every citizen, judges also enjoy the protection of freedom of expression. In particular, they may engage in political activities and express and defend their views in speech and writing. However, the fundamental right of freedom of expression is only guaranteed for civil servants and judges to the extent that it is not incompatible with the duties enshrined in Article 33 (5) of the Basic Law, which are indispensable for the maintenance of a func-

[12] Judgement of October 5, 2023 - RiZ(R) 1/23.

[13] BVerfG (FCC) (Vorprüfungsausschuß) (Preliminary Examination Committee), Beschluß vom 30-08-1983 - 2 BvR 1334/82, NJW 1983, 2691.

> tioning civil service and the intact administration of justice (see FCC vol.39, 334, 367...). These duties include, above all, that the judge must perform his office in a politically neutral manner as a servant of the law. For it is part of the nature of judicial activity that it is exercised by a non-participating third party in factual and personal independence (FCC vol.26, 186, 198) ...; established case-law). The position of the judge within the democratic community therefore requires that he or she performs the tasks assigned to him or her independently of extraneous influences and without prejudice. This significance of his office has the consequence for the judge personally that he must conduct himself within and outside the office, including in political activities, in such a way that the confidence in his independence guaranteed by Article 97 (1)I of the Basic Law is not jeopardized. This applies all the more as the judge is often called upon to judge and decide disputes that are the subject of political controversy in public. Accordingly, expressions of opinion by a judge in public are only constitutionally protected by Article 5 (1) of the Basic Law if they are not incompatible with this duty of restraint arising from the special position of the judge and required by Article 33 V of the Basic Law, as expressed in section 39 DRiG (Deutsches Richtergesetz). In each specific case, the compatibility or incompatibility of a judge's statement with his official duties must be determined in accordance with the principle that legally justified limits of Article 5 GG are to be interpreted in the light of the fundamental right limited by them. In this sense, the provisions of civil service and disciplinary law that are consistent with Article 33 V of the Basic Law are general laws under Article 5 (2) of the Basic Law (see FCC vol.39, 334, 366 et seq.)

The Federal Constitutional Court in the preliminary review committee confirmed for these reasons the decision of the Service Court for Lower Saxony with the following words:

> Measured against this standard, the decision of the Service Court is not objectionable under constitutional law. The court recognized the interdependence between the special official duties of a judge and the general fundamental right to freedom of expression and considered and weighed them in accordance with the constitutional requirements. It correctly assumed that the confidence of the general public in the independence and objectivity of the judiciary is of considerable importance, and in this regard it found in a constitutionally unobjectionable manner that the complainant's attitude expressed in the complaint lacked the degree of openness and distance that is generally required of the judiciary in all legal matters in order to maintain and strengthen the confidence of the general public in an independent, unprejudiced administration of justice that is free of personal evaluations and based solely on the respective factual and legal situation. In addition, the court also considered that it is quite plausible that publicly propagated wishful thinking on the part of social forces can pose a risk to independent judicial decision-making, particularly in cases where lay judges are predominantly active and where, due to their lack of experience in dealing with legal cases, such influence is more likely to have an effect than with professional judges. In this respect, it was possible here without violating Article 5 (1) Basic Law that the complainant had not fulfilled his judicial duty to exercise restraint (section 39 DRiG) by participating in a public statement on a pending case, which in its striking presentation contained a completely one-sided claim made with an absolute claim to validity and through which the judges of the LAG were to be influenced and their decision influenced in the sense of the "complaint". This was all the more so as the complainant's statement was accompanied by an express reference to his judicial office. The fact that the complainant considered his conduct to be lawful was taken into account by the service court (see also Schmidt=Räntsch, DRiG, 2nd ed., § 39 para. 4).

We can recognise in this decision the basic structure of the FCC's line of reasoning.

5 Conclusion

In conclusion, we can say that judges also enjoy freedom of expression, but that this is necessarily limited in order not to jeopardise the independence and impartiality of judges, central values of the judiciary and the rule of law. The restrictions are appropriate under German law. When assessing which expression of opinion violates the principle of judicial independence, the principle of proportionality, in particular the necessity of the restriction, must be observed.

References

Arnold R (2022) Struttura ed interpretazione della Costituzone – Alcune riflessioni. In: Caravale G, Cecanti S, Frosina L, Picciacchia P, Zei A (eds) Scritti in onore die Fulco Lanchester, vol I. Jovene, Napoli, pp 41–56

Arnold R (2025) Rule of law. In: Babeck W, Weber A (eds) Writing constitutions, Vol. III. Constitutional principles. Springer. (in press)

Chelaru E (2021) La cour constitutionnelle et l'interprétation des normes constitutionnelles. In: Tudorascu M (ed) Constitutionalism and civil law. Some reflections on recent developments, Comparative law studies, vol 13, Regensburg, pp 31–39. ISBN: 978-3-88246-451-139

Chelaru E, Duminica R (2020) Jurisprudence de la Cour constitutionnelle de Roumanie en matière de référendum consultatif national. In: Arnold R, Daneliene I (eds) The concept of democracy as developed by the constitutional justice. The Constitutional Court of the Republic of Lithuania, Vilnius, pp 119–136

Chelaru E, Duminica R (2022) The right to property and the environmental protection in the jurisprudence of the Romanian Constitutional Court. In: Arnold R (ed) The protection of the environment and constitutional law, Comparative law studies, vol 15. Regensburg, pp 53–63. ISBN: 978-3-88246 9

de Smith SA (1971) Constitutional and administrative law. Longman, London, pp 123–124

Lechner H, Zuck R (2015) BVerfGG Kommentar, 7th edn. CH Beck, München. §19 para 4

Rousseau J-J (1762, re-ed. 1966) Du Contrat Social ou Principes Du Droit Politique, Livre premier, Chap. I et Chap. VI. Re-edited by Flammarion, Paris

MIX
Papier aus verantwortungsvollen Quellen
Paper from responsible sources
FSC® C105338

If you have any concerns about our products,
you can contact us on
ProductSafety@springernature.com

In case Publisher is established outside the EU,
the EU authorized representative is:
Springer Nature Customer Service Center GmbH
Europaplatz 3, 69115 Heidelberg, Germany

Printed by Libri Plureos GmbH
in Hamburg, Germany